LARRIKINS IN KHAKI

LARRIKINS IN KHAKI

Tales of irreverence and courage
from World War II Diggers

TIM BOWDEN

ALLEN&UNWIN
SYDNEY • MELBOURNE • AUCKLAND • LONDON

Allen & Unwin
83 Alexander Street
Crows Nest NSW 2065
Australia
Phone: (61 2) 8425 0100
Email: info@allenandunwin.com
Web: www.allenandunwin.com

NATIONAL LIBRARY OF AUSTRALIA

A catalogue record for this book is available from the National Library of Australia

ISBN 978 1 76052 854 6

Set in 11.5/17 pt Minion by Midland Typesetters, Australia
Printed and bound in Australia by Griffin Press, part of Ovato

10 9 8 7 6 5 4 3

MIX
Paper from responsible sources
FSC www.fsc.org FSC® C009448

The paper in this book is FSC® certified. FSC® promotes environmentally responsible, socially beneficial and economically viable management of the world's forests.

For Hank Nelson and Peter Stanley

CONTENTS

INTRODUCTION

There is a possibly apocryphal story told of two Aussie Diggers' experience in the trenches of World War I. General William Birdwood, an Englishman, commanded the ANZAC Corps, and by mid 1916 the Anzacs were in action on the Somme. You can imagine the trenches, churned mud, duckboards and shell-holed no-man's land. Two Diggers are leaning against the side of a trench, smoking and holding their .303 rifles in one hand. They watch a senior British officer followed by a gaggle of attendant junior officers pick their way briskly along a front-line trench. The Diggers don't take their eyes off the officers, but they don't shift to allow a wider passage and they don't salute. After the senior officer has passed, a junior officer spins around and comes back. He says, 'Don't you know who that was?' The Diggers consider the question. One answers: 'Nope. You ever met him Barney?' 'Nah, not me.' Junior officer: 'That was General Birdwood!' The first Digger says, 'Well he didn't have feathers on his arse like any other bird would.'

General Birdwood was one of the better English generals. At least he was in the trenches seeing for himself what was going on.

While the Diggers' fighting abilities were respected, the British found the Australian soldiers hard to take. Their relaxed attitude to military discipline and niceties like saluting officers was not appreciated. It has been ever thus, continuing on to World War II.

My late friend, historian Professor Hank Nelson, who collaborated with me in a major oral history radio series, *Prisoners of War: Australians Under Nippon* first broadcast on the ABC in 1984, delighted in collecting self-published books by Australian Diggers. These often larrikin accounts contained vivid descriptions of the fighting they shared in the Middle East, South-east Asia, New Guinea and the Pacific Islands, but also equally colourful descriptions of the rackets, skulduggery, drunken escapades in brothels, hatred and loathing of military police as well as less than flattering portraits of the officers they did not respect in and out of combat.

I shared this interest and also started a modest collection of similar frank and forthright narratives. We had discussed the possibility of collaborating on a book based on these accounts. Shortly before Hank's untimely death in February 2012, I was in Canberra for what we both realised was almost certainly our last meeting. He made a point of handing over to me the self-published books he had in his library. I have now had to fly solo.

This is not in any sense a military history of the Australian army's involvement in World War II. While many of the major theatres are featured—Palestine, North Africa, Greece and Crete, Malaya, Java, Thailand and Burma, Borneo, Papua New Guinea and the Pacific Islands occupied by the Japanese, there is no mention of Australian involvement in Timor, Ambon, Hainan or the infamous Death Marches in Borneo, for example. This is because the Australian Diggers who feature in this book control the narrative, depending on where they were and what happened to them. Here are their highly individual stories—warts and all.

Tim Bowden

MILITARY UNITS

Section	(about 10 men)
Platoon	(about 30)
Company	(150–200)
Battalion	(up to 1000)
Brigade	(3 battalions)
Division	(3 brigades)

Chapter 1

JOINING UP

Australia's longest-serving prime minister Robert Menzies once famously opined that Australians were 'British to the boot-straps'. How many Australians wore boot-straps or even knew what they were is unclear, but it was a graphic illustration of Australia's dependence on the 'Mother Country' particularly when the British Empire's interests were threatened by war. Until well into the twentieth century, it was the only foreign policy Australia had. However, the Commonwealth government had strongly supported the British government's policy of appeasing Hitler when, in September 1938, he incorporated the Sudetenland province of western Czechoslovakia into the Reich. But Australia was equally ready to reverse that policy when Britain changed tack, and in March and April 1939 guaranteed support for Poland, Greece and Romania in the event of German or Italian aggression.

Australia's loyalty became strongly affirmed on 3 September 1939 when Prime Minister Menzies' sonorous tones were heard on the radio, saying: 'It is my melancholy duty to inform you officially that, in consequence of a persistence by Germany in her invasion of Poland, Great Britain has declared war upon her and that, as a result, Australia is also at war.'

Clearly an expanded army would have to be recruited—and quickly. One problem flowed from the so-called 'two-army' system. There was the Australian Imperial Force (AIF), an elite expeditionary force composed entirely of men who had volunteered to fight anywhere in the world. Then there was the Australian Militia, whose service was limited to Australia and its territories. In October 1939 Cabinet decided to reintroduce conscription, last in existence in 1929. It was hoped to have a part-volunteer, part-conscript Militia of some 75,000, calling up those with trades or skills that were needed. This dual system had some unhappy consequences as the war went on, with the derogatory term 'Chocos' (Chocolate Soldiers) for those in the Militia, or conscripts. Many officers in the regular army would have preferred one army which could have been used wherever the national interest dictated. But opposition to the conscription of men to fight overseas, because of the divisive referenda in the Great War, was too deeply entrenched for this to be politically possible.

This rivalry manifested itself very early, even in the training period. Ingleburn camp was still being constructed in Sydney, as AIF recruit Bob 'Hooker' Holt later wrote:

> On returning by train to Liverpool from Sydney we AIF men always went in a body into Liverpool to catch the bus back to camp. At this time the Militia men who had signed up for home defence duties were paid eight shillings a day, while the men of the AIF who had volunteered for active service abroad were paid the princely sum of five shillings a day. This created quite a deal of ill feeling and there were regular brawls in Liverpool between the two groups. Small numbers of single men were often viciously attacked by gangs of twenty or

more, spoiling for a fight. Liverpool was a good place to keep away from in those days.

Whenever a group of AIF men outnumbered the Chocos, you could bet money on someone chanting a parody on the song 'The Legion of the Lost' and shortly afterwards the skin and hair would start to fly.

The second AIF they call us, the second AIF we are:
Bread and jam for breakfast and greasy stew for tea.
Marching all the day in the sun drilling,
While the mug Militia is up at the pub swilling.
We do most of the work and do all the killing.
Scum, scum, the Militia can kiss my bum.
The life and the canteen is as dry as hell –
The second AIF are we.

Young men flocked to join the services, as they had in the Great War. The age limits for joining the AIF were 20 to 35—the upper limit to discourage World War I veterans from signing up again. But this did not work. Young men inflated their ages, and older men dropped theirs. Medical examinations were conducted in noisy halls by overworked doctors, and many keen recruits were able to conceal disabilities that should have failed them. The situation of young Clarrie Thornton, a farm boy from Berrigan in the Riverina who had joined the Light Horse a few years before the outbreak of war, is a classic case.

Thornton caught the train to the recruitment centre and sailed through the preliminaries of his medical, coughed, peed in a bottle, touched his toes and breathed in and out deeply as ordered. Then came the eye test. He was told to cover his right eye and read the test chart, which he did with no problems. 'Now, right hand over left eye.' Clarrie slapped his other hand over his right eye again and read the letters in descending size equally well. He was accepted into the army A1 and fit for overseas service by the end of that day. But he actually had no sight in his right eye. The teenager had been chopping firewood for his mum when a splinter flew up and blinded him in that eye!

As it happened the army was blessed with a very good soldier. Sergeant Clarrie Thornton of the 4th Anti-Tank Regiment was a key member of a gun crew that destroyed eight Japanese tanks near Muar in Malaya during the Japanese advance on 18 January 1942—even though he had been wounded earlier that day. To sight a gun, you only need one eye.

'Hooker' Holt was only fifteen, but said he was 21 when he fronted the Marrickville drill hall, Sydney, for his medical:

> The doctor's inspection was an eye-opener in more ways than one. The potential recruits lined up in the altogether and filed past the Medical Officer. They came in all states of sobriety and in all sorts of shapes and sizes. All eyes were on 'Bud' Buderous, as he swaggered to front the doctor, his muscular arms and chest black with tattoos that covered him from waist to neck. But the man next to him stole the show. It was the white-skinned, pigeon-chested 'Boxer' Dominey, who had an over-sized whistle slung on his heron-gutted body with 'FOR A GOOD GIRL' tattooed along the length of his enormous tool.

Ken Clift and his fellow recruits were amused to be told in an official letter from the army to report to Victoria Barracks in Sydney with a 'cunt lunch'. When it came to the urine test, one of Ken's school mates, 'Horrible' Horrie Wilson, had spent several hours quenching his thirst at the Olympic Hotel just over the road. Then came the medical:

> We all stripped while the Medical Officer, a very dapper English captain complete with a silk khaki shirt, tie and jodhpurs, did the unpleasant task of examining us for piles, tonsillitis, heart, teeth and

> took a sample of our water. Some of the fellows had difficulty supplying such a sample, but not Horrie who obligingly filled the pint beaker to its brim with foaming suds, handed it back to the Medical Officer with the remark, 'Empty her, sport, and I'll fill her up again!' This he very nearly did after our dignified doctor had to reluctantly trot to the basin and get rid of the first generous issue.

Joe Dawson was under-age, and his parents had expressly forbidden him to enlist. An evening or so later, he found himself drawn to the Footscray drill hall—the headquarters of the 32nd Militia Battalion. Outside Joe met a young fellow and told him the sorry tale about his parents not letting him join up. The fellow said, 'Look, what you do is join the Militia, get to know a bit about the army, and then transfer to the Australian Imperial Force. They won't worry about your age then. You can join the Militia at eighteen without your parents' signature.' Joe recalled:

> That sounded alright to me, so I went in and spoke to a warrant officer, telling him I wanted to join up. When he asked me my date of birth I answered 3 January 1921, which made me eighteen, a year older than I actually was. He took more personal details and then gave me a form to take to a doctor in Barkly Street. There I was given a thorough medical examination, which was a little embarrassing for me at that age, particularly when it came to the 'cough, cough' bit. [It was standard practice for the doctors to grasp a recruit's testicles in their hands firmly to check for a hernia, revealed by a bulge into the scrotum during coughing.] However I passed the medical without any problems.

Dawson joined the Militia on 12 September 1939. The warrant officer told him to report back to the drill hall on the following Saturday, when he would be issued with his kit—which included a service jacket, breeches, long puttees, tan boots, felt hat, .303 rifle, bayonet, water bottle, ammunition pouches and pack.

At first Joe didn't mention his enlistment to his parents, but decided to wait until Saturday, when he would arrive home with all his gear. As expected, all hell broke loose.

> Dad said something like, 'We'll see about this!' Auntie Nell, who was married to my father's brother, poked her head over the fence to see what the commotion was about. Her response was, 'Good on you, it's good to see someone with a bit of guts around here!' Surprisingly my father did not say any more on the matter.

By 1941, when concern was growing whether Japan would enter the war and things were not going well for the Allies in Europe and North Africa, recruitment standards—including the age limit—were eased significantly. Bill Young and his mate John Lecardio were both fifteen years old and stony broke when they fronted up to a recruiting office in Melbourne to enlist in the AIF on 27 July 1941. They were both big lads and looked more mature than their age. Both were orphans, so parental permission could be bypassed. The recruiting officer asked if they had any aunts, and they said they had. Taking the forms away, they made up names of mythical aunts and each forged a signature on the other's form. The recruiting officer could see their forms were shonky, but didn't care. The war was going badly. Germany had invaded Russia, London was being bombed, Greece and Crete had fallen in the Middle East, and the Japanese were also showing signs of belligerence.

The medical examination was high farce. Bill Young later wrote in his self-published book, *Return to a Dark Age*:

> A tall thin fellow dressed in a long white coat peered across at me through glasses so thick they must've been the last resort before

a seeing-eye dog, and asked me to read the top line of a chart big enough to lead a May Day procession. Then, counting my eyes, and finding I had two, he passed me as having all the prerequisites for shooting anyone legally suitable.

I can still remember the smell of whisky coming at me as he belched. 'Right lad, strip and hop on the scales. Good, turn around and bend over, good. Now turn around and face me. Breathe in, breathe out, mouth wide open. Say ah-ah-ah. Very good.' Then he grabbed me balls and, weighing one against the other, told me to cough. 'Now sit down and cross your legs', and he whacked my knee and almost took a bow for the reaction it achieved. With a final, 'Good, good, excellent, excellent', I was allowed to get dressed and that was that. I was passed with flying colours and declared medically A1, fit to be a soldier in the King's army.

Chapter 2

VERY BASIC TRAINING

Only months before the first AIF troops were sent away overseas, training had to be sandwiched into a short time, with little resources available both in experienced instructors and basics like rifles, machine guns, artillery and ammunition. Gunner Colin Finkemeyer was one of many young recruits who had to do what they could in the face of Australia's utter lack of preparedness for a war of any kind.

All they had was youthful enthusiasm and energy, and they surely needed that because their so-called training could be described as high farce.

In November 1940, when the 4th Anti-Tank Regiment was formed at Puckapunyal, the idea of defending against attacks from enemy tanks was far ahead of the AIF's ability to provide the guns and everything else needed to get them into action. Undaunted, the gunners resorted to make-believe and soldiered on without their guns, as Finkemeyer described:

So we went through the drills in the Little Red Military Handbook with the impressive Australian coat of arms embossed in gold and marked confidential—Armed Services only. This hallowed little red handbook contained in minute detail all the steps necessary for a gun crew to get a 2-pound anti-tank gun into action and fire it. We trained under the spreading red gums of Artillery Hill at Puckapunyal, using a couple of knotted and gnarled old tree trunks, one propped up over the other to serve as a gun barrel. The boys, eager to serve the country as best they could, took it all in good spirits. With the innocence of youth as yet unblemished by their army experience, they had blind virginal faith in their army's top brass.

On these exercises the gunners would take up their imaginary places on the make-believe gun and stand awaiting their next order. On the command 'Load', the gun loader would push an imaginary 2-pound shell into the imaginary breech, moving the palm of his hand upwards with sufficient vigour to ensure that the imaginary gun was correctly loaded and the imaginary breechblock closed firmly. On the command 'Take aim', the gun-layer would wind the imaginary traverse handle and set the imaginary trajectory, then make the finer adjustments through the imaginary grid on his imaginary sights until he was 'dead on' his imaginary target.

With a tap on the shoulder from the gun sergeant as he commanded 'Fire', the gunner would dutifully depress his left foot on the imaginary firing pedal and away would go the imaginary 2-pound shell on its way to demolish an imaginary enemy tank. After the first exercise, the gun crew would then reform behind their imaginary gun and the sergeant would give the order 'Change round', and each member would take two steps to the right and the whole process would begin again, each one having a different task. In this way their versatility and confidence were assured. Well, almost! Colin Finkemeyer recalled their commanding officer came out to inspect the gun crews in operation: 'He was most impressed with their zeal and expressed his confidence in the ability to handle the real McCoy when our genuine two-pounders arrived.'

Fortunately, before they embarked for overseas, two Anti-tank Guns Mark I did arrive at Puckapunyal and the gunners drilled feverishly on them preparing for their first 'live' shoot. Drivers hauled a target in the rough shape of a tank well back in the hills, on a very long lead—safely, it was hoped—behind their trucks. The gunners opened up on the tank shapes with great enthusiasm and a surprising degree of accuracy. This was followed by the appearance of silhouettes of tanks, which popped up at various spots in the scrub beside the hill about 1000 yards away, which the guns promptly annihilated.

Finkemeyer was confident. 'The shoot was a good indicator of our promise. Having once fired our guns with live ammunition we were ready to leave Australia confident that wherever we were going, when we received our guns, there would be no holding us back. We were ready to tackle any enemy tanks that came our way.'

In February 1941, the 13th Anti-Tank Battery boarded the passenger liner *Queen Mary* for a destination unknown, believing their complement of anti-tank guns was on board. The troops were full of enthusiasm to be finally on their way to do their bit for their country. On disembarking they discovered that their mystery destination turned out to be Singapore, where they were put on a train to Seremban on the Malay Peninsula.

Their accommodation was a disused school, its large playing field ideal for parades and pack drills for the battery gunners now far from home. But their guns were not on the *Queen Mary*. However, loyal and conscientious as ever, they marked the outlines of the guns on the school's playing field—there being no old red gum logs to be found—and dutifully carried on their make-believe training with phantom guns.

After three months, word came that their guns had arrived and were actually waiting on the wharves of Singapore. Drivers were quickly sent to collect them. It was thought it would only take a couple of days at the most to bring them up from Singapore and the gunners' excitement was palpable.

But a week went by, then ten days, and still no sign of the guns. What on earth could have gone wrong? The gunners clung desperately to their faith in the army that all would be well. Just as they were beginning to lose hope, out of the blue came the message: 'The guns will arrive at 1500 hours tomorrow'. Anticipation by this time was at fever pitch. At 2 pm, well ahead of the estimated time of arrival, the gunners were lined up on both sides of the driveway to form a guard of honour to receive the guns.

To their great joy, they heard the rumble of approaching vehicles. It had to be the guns! In rolled the vehicles towing World War I, 18-pound Royal Artillery pieces, clad with iron wheels. The iron wheels had accounted for the delay in their arrival as their towing speed was restricted to 5 miles per hour. Then, to everyone's astonishment, they noticed the words prominently displayed on the shield of each gun in large white letters, 'FOR SALUTING PURPOSES ONLY'.

Finkemeyer said the guns had reportedly been taken from the palace grounds of an Indian rajah and sent post-haste to Singapore so that they could play their role in defending their 'illustrious, impregnable isle'.

Clarry McCulloch was a Tasmanian boy from Ulverstone, in the north of the island. He was one of a number of north-west coast boys who had been in the 22nd Light Horse Regiment before joining the AIF. They had, on arrival at Brighton camp, just north of Hobart, been drafted into the 2/40th Infantry Battalion which was just forming—much to their chagrin, having previously been indoctrinated in the Light Horse with a healthy contempt for the lowly 'footsloggers', as infantrymen were called by those on horseback. 'However, all was not lost,' McCulloch wrote, 'as it soon became known that a new unit was being formed which, in addition to being a machine gun unit had the advantage of being fully mechanised.' This they thought meant no marching! They were not to know that at a later stage of training their battalion would set a new army record by marching 200 miles carrying full kit.

As the boys who had been in the Ulverstone troop had been trained in the use of the Vickers machine gun, they headed straight for the headquarters of C Company, 2/3rd Machine Gun Battalion. There they were welcomed with open arms and the necessary transfers arranged immediately.

Here it was that McCulloch met a most remarkable fellow-recruit. He was tall and angular with bright red hair and a prominent chin and his name was Lorimer Anzac von Stieglitz.

> Naturally he became known as 'Blue', like all other redheads in the army, and in a short time we became good mates. Blue came into 11 Platoon on the same day as myself and was allotted the bed space next to me—well actually floor space. Instead of beds we had long hessian bags, called paillasses, filled with wheat or barley straw. These were folded in three and stacked against the wall during the day and rolled out on the bare boards at night with three feet between each paillasse. In this way each hut could accommodate a full platoon of approximately 40 men.

C Company, 2/3rd Machine Gun Battalion, like most AIF units, was made up of men from all walks of life. There were lawyers, rabbit-trappers, miners, bank tellers, farmers' sons, schoolteachers, wharf labourers, sailors (including one who had sailed around Cape Horn in a windjammer) and sawmillers. Also included in their ranks were several members of Tasmania's leading grazier families who, incidentally, went on the records as farm labourers. This was to avoid being hauled out of the army as essential members of a protected industry.

Their commanding officer was a Victorian, Captain 'Speed' Gordon, quickly nicknamed after the cartoon character. He had a rather pedantic manner but McCulloch and his mates soon discovered that he knew what soldiering was all about, having been an officer in a Melbourne Militia battalion for several years.

Their training began with a series of parades where they were issued with all the gear necessary for a fighting soldier. First came the rifle and bayonet, with the old admonition that it was a soldier's best friend so it should be cared for above all else. Then came the steel helmet, or tin hat. Although this was heavy to wear, the recruits could see the sense of it and did not complain.

The next major item was shown on the records as 'respirator, gas troops for the use of', and loathed by all. The gas mask consisted of a close-fitting face mask with glass eyepieces and an exhaust valve which was attached by a short corrugated rubber hose to a canister containing a filter. These were carried, when not in use, in a haversack which was to be strapped to the chest of the novice gunners at all times during training hours. They were then given endless lectures on the correct use of the mask and the types of gas they could expect to encounter—and field tests. They soon found that phosgene was colourless and smelt like musty hay or rotten apples. Chloropicrin was sweet smelling and induced vomiting.

A special sealed hut had been prepared where the various gases could be generated and each man in turn would have to pass through this area. During this exercise the mask had to be removed from the face temporarily so the gas could be identified later. Then during normal gun training it was common practice for the sergeant or platoon commander to suddenly shout, 'Gas alert!'—usually at very inconvenient times.

'A lot of the boys found the gas haversacks were a very useful place to store cigarettes, tobacco or lollies, and if one of these gas alerts came while we were marching along the road, it sometimes caused some confusion, with small items going in all directions and lots of bad language,' McCulloch recalled. 'Thank goodness we didn't have occasion to use them in action, as they were vile things to wear.'

The aspiring machine-gunners soon settled into a steady routine of rifle drill, route marches and lectures on tactics. Brighton camp was bitterly cold in a Tasmanian winter, and the issue of woollen scarves and balaclava caps was warmly welcomed.

It was frustrating at first not having any machine guns, but as soon as they arrived (twelve of them—Tasmania's total supply) enthusiasm picked up. There were some rocky hills quite close to the camp and day after day the recruits would scramble up the slopes, carrying or dragging the guns into various attacking positions, then dismantling them, and racing down the hill ready to start all over again. This was no easy task as the gun and tripod each weighed about 50 pounds and, for realism, the ammunition boxes were filled with stones.

Overall, the troops were in good spirits, according to McCulloch:

> Sometimes as a break from training, the commanding officer would decree that the company would march to Bridgewater or Bagdad [a quaintly named local village far from the Middle East] and return. This was quite enjoyable as, apart from leaving and entering the camp, we were permitted to march 'at ease', which meant talking was allowed. After the evening meal we were free to amuse ourselves until lights out at 10 pm when everyone was expected to be in bed in the hut. Some would choose to stroll a half mile to the Pontville pub, where the landlord was always happy to greet us. That is, until some of the troops—not machine gunners—decided to liberate a full keg of beer which they'd found in the backyard.

Others would spend the time in the hut reading, or wander down to the Red Cross or Salvation Army huts where there was always warmth, a plentiful supply of writing paper for letters to family or friends, and a hot cup of tea or coffee at 9 pm. The 'Sallies' always offered a short homily before the drinks were served, always cheerfully endured.

From time to time, leave would be granted from 5 pm until midnight and it was possible to catch a train from Brighton to Hobart—about 18 miles—for a few hours recreation. It was about half a mile from Brighton Station to the main camp, and frequently well-lubricated gunners would have difficulty negotiating the track from train to camp if the evening had been a particularly convivial one.

One night two soldiers were seen staggering towards the gate, supporting a mate between them. Upon reaching the gate and surrendering their leave passes, the two dumped their mate on the ground and began stumbling towards their billets. Immediately there was a plaintive cry from the prostrate soldier: 'Hey, come on Blue, give me a hand mate.' From the darkness a voice replied, 'Die you bastard, die!' Clarry McCulloch was glad to report that Blue did come back for him eventually. 'Mates are like that!'

On Sunday morning all troops not on leave or guard duty were expected to attend a church parade. The Roman Catholic members had their own service while the Protestants were lumped together for the other one. As this meant sitting on hard seats for an hour or more, listening to predictably boring sermons, an alternative seemed attractive.

Clarry and Blue discovered that declared agnostics could be excused from attendance, so one Sunday before the service they approached the sergeant major and explained they were now agnostics. Without a smile he agreed that this was so, and excused them from church parade. Immediately, however, he wiped the grins from their faces by telling them that there were three bags of spuds to be peeled in the cookhouse so they'd better get down there and get started. After peeling spuds for two hours,

Clarry and Blue decided that they had ceased to be agnostics—for army purposes anyway.

There were training excursions outside the camp. On one occasion the company went on a three-day bivouac on the south-east coast near the town of Sorell. There, much time was spent digging and sandbagging gun positions among the coastal dunes at Seven Mile Beach followed by live ammunition firing out to sea.

On the last night a campfire concert was held and many interesting items were performed by various members of the group. The variety and vigour of many of these items was enhanced by one of the local farmers who had donated a 5-gallon keg of locally brewed cider for the occasion. After a very explicit recitation by one bloke, Captain 'Speed' Gordon was heard to remark, 'Don't you think that your language was a trifle expressive, private?' To which the soldier replied quite nonchalantly, 'I'm fucked if I know, Sir!'

This cider was a fairly dynamic brew and as most of the recruits were beer drinkers and not used to cider, this led to some unfortunate results. One involved Clarry's mate, Lorimer Anzac von Stieglitz—Blue. He had been raised in an apple-growing area in the Tamar Valley and when many of the blokes were reluctant to drink their allotted pints of cider, Blue was only too pleased to help them out, saying, 'I can drink the stuff all night.'

> When the concert ended we all made our way to the area where we had previously made our beds under some boobialla trees. Blue, by this time in a rather happy frame of mind, decided that it would be a good idea to go down and pull our Commanding Officer Colonel A.S. Blackburn out of his bunk, just for a joke. All arguments were in vain, so to forestall a possible court-martial and discharges from the army, I decided that drastic action was called for.
>
> Distracting his attention for a moment, I delivered a hard uppercut to his jaw. This put him down for the count, so we all dragged him

> over to his bed and covered him with a blanket. In a few seconds he was snoring soundly. Next morning when we were getting ready for breakfast, Blue complained that his jaw felt rather sore and couldn't understand why everyone in the platoon thought this was so hilarious. Sometime later he was told the truth, and after much strong language agreed that the joke was really on him.

Ivan 'Ivo' Blazely was a knockabout young man from northern Tasmania who had left school at the age of twelve, and whose first job was an apple packer at an orchard, then wood cutting, sawmilling, fruit picking and underground mining. At seventeen he bumped his age up to 21 and managed to join the AIF at the Melbourne Town Hall. After a week's leave, it was time to 'get down to the serious business of soldiering', Ivan said.

> One of the first things I remember was dental parade. At the initial medical our teeth were examined and whoever had crook teeth were paraded to the next dental tent, where we formed a queue and at the next call we went in and sat down. Those who had to have extractions received the appropriate injection, then went outside and got on the end of the queue waiting your turn to go in again and get your teeth pulled. Bad luck if the effect of the needle was wearing off when your turn came.

Early in the piece Blazely was put on picket duty, posted on the side gate into the camp and told to stop anyone who did not have a leave pass from entering. It was late afternoon and there were plenty of customers, but Blazely got over this by pointing out to those who lacked the necessary document that there was a hole under the fence about 30 yards away. 'This system went well until a sergeant approached and I gave him the same message. It turned out that he was one of the camp Provosts [military police]. He gave me my first army dressing-down—but to give him his credit the matter ended there. After this episode I trusted no one in camp with three stripes and very few with two.'

For a week or two Blazely and his fellow recruits were kept busy getting injections against tetanus and typhoid, plus the occasional mess orderly duty and learning that you never just 'went' anywhere in the army, you 'marched', and you did not just 'gather together', you went 'on parade'. One day an order was given for all recruits to fall in for a selection parade. All rookies paraded while teams of officers interviewed each of them about their civilian occupations and previous army experience if any. Quite a few had served in the Militia. When Blazely's turn came he told them 'timber worker' and was told to fall in near the peg marked Pioneers. He wanted to join the artillery, but had been told they only wanted personnel with previous experience. He asked a more experienced soldier what the Pioneers were about, and was told, 'It's just a fancy term for the infantry.' Blazely recalled, 'I thought I'm out of this at the first opportunity.'

Shortly after, an officer came along asking for volunteers for the postal unit. Blazely thought that would at least give him a little time to work things out, and was accepted with no questions asked.

There were about 30 postal recruits and their daily routine, after the morning roll call and breakfast, was to be marched along Flemington Road towards the city for about half a mile to a largish building, where they sorted army mail until about 3.30 pm, after which they were marched back to camp. Blazely stuck this for two weeks, but it did not coincide with his idea of soldiering, nor did he particularly like his coworkers.

He had himself paraded to the commanding officer and told him he had changed his mind about being a postman. The CO was not happy and asked the reasons for the change of mind, wasting all that valuable training. Blazely replied, 'I joined the AIF to do a bit of fighting, not to sort letters all day.' So he became eligible for another selection parade. This time he chose a different method. As soon as soldiers started breaking off the main column and falling in on the various pegs labelled infantry, artillery, engineers and so on, Blazely took matters into his own hands and just walked over and put himself in the artillery, and that was that.

> From living in tents at Royal Park, we came to the standard 'air-conditioned' accommodation of the permanent army camps like Puckapunyal. This consisted of galvanised iron huts. The air-conditioning was basically stinking hot in the summer and freezing in the winter. The fixings, table, chairs, beds and so on were all combined in one item—the floor, on which you slept, sat or walked about as your fancy took you. The authorities kindly provided us with a bag of straw for a mattress, which when folded up made quite a good seat. Hardly gracious living really.

Training at Puckapunyal was the usual routine of route marches, squad drilling and lectures, with a few kitchen fatigues and guard and picket duty thrown in. Blazely remembered one lecture on the composition of an artillery battery given by a lieutenant who was later to become a senator in the Australian parliament and, later still, knighted. In his account of his army experiences, Blazely nicknamed him 'Lieutenant Senator'. One Saturday afternoon Lieutenant Senator had the bright idea that some gun drill would be in order. At that stage the Japanese hadn't yet come into the war and training camps were conducted more or less on union rules—that Saturday afternoon was occupied in washing, spine-bashing (lying on their bunks) or better still heading into Seymour for a few beers. Lieutenant Senator dispatched a sergeant major, Mac, a big Irishman and an old soldier, to round up the necessary bodies to make up four gun crews totalling 24 men.

All Mac, the Sergeant Major, could find, was half a dozen blokes doing their washing. Somehow all the other gunners left in the battery got wind of it and made themselves scarce. Mac had just got the drill organised when Senator appeared on the scene.

'What's this Sergeant Major?' exclaimed Lieutenant Senator. 'When I said I wanted four gun crews, I meant four gun crews.'

Mac drew himself up to his rather impressive height and replied, 'I may be a troop sergeant major, Sir, but I am not Jesus Christ.'

The whole time Ivan Blazely was at Puckapunyal, he recalled, he did not do one session of gun drill—there were simply not enough guns to go round. But one afternoon there was a short route march, when one of the instructors laid a dead tree branch on the ground representing the barrel of a gun and another lying across it for the wheels, on which they drilled for a while. 'But you could hardly call it gun drill,' Blazely remarked.

Bob 'Hooker' Holt trained at Ingleburn camp, which was still being built when he enlisted in the AIF.

While the majority of us were issued with boots and an army hat, we trained in our own clothes and you could tell how anyone was going financially by the state of the gear he was wearing. We must've had an awful lot of swagmen with us. We were given army fatigue clothes a few weeks later. These were immediately named 'Giggle Suits' as we looked as if we'd come straight out of an asylum. I knew we were supposed to salute someone, but for the first few days I wasn't sure whether it was the fellows with the pips on their shoulders or the superior beings with stripes on their arms—and there were many recruits in the same boat as myself.

The vast majority of new soldiers had no military experience whatsoever and some rough diamonds weren't amenable to any sort of discipline, with many of them recently not long 'off the track'. The officers were most understanding and made allowances for this ignorance of military etiquette. Early on the commanding officer had occasion to speak sharply to a private of several weeks, Jackie White, of West Wyalong. After a belly full of beer at the Crossroads Hotel, Jackie returned to camp later in the evening and performed outside his CO's sleeping quarters.

'Come out and act the man and fight me, you undersized, black-whiskered little bastard.'

Next day Jackie was fined 5 shillings. Three months later the same offence landed him in the Jerusalem Detention Barracks for 28 days.

Holt was fifteen years of age, but big for his years—his good mate 'Snowy' Parkinson was small, boyish, blond and eighteen. They had enlisted together and on receiving their slouch hats and boots, proudly took off to Sydney to celebrate. They lined up at the bar of the Great Southern Hotel and called to the barmaid for two beers. She looked at the two of them and said to Bob, 'You're all right and you can have one, but your young mate had better piss off and come back when he turns eighteen.'

Back in camp the lads were introduced to the delights of the game of two-up which was run by very battered ex-boxer, Bob Delaney. There were never any prolonged arguments over bets after the famous ex-lightweight champion of Australia had given his decision. Bobby was still a very capable pug and even the look of him would frighten most players into agreeing with any ruling he gave.

In those early days there were no wet canteens for the troops. Two shops which were run by a private contractor sold soap, toothpaste, lollies, ice cream and soft drinks at highly inflated prices. It was not long before there was an undercurrent of bitterness among the troops at the rip-offs by the get-rich-quick operator.

One evening Holt was talking to Sid Elliott—with whom he had boxed at the Leichhardt Police Boys Club—when a soldier protested at the price of a bottle of soft drink. The owner of the canteen told him if he didn't like it he could take his business somewhere else. The soldier threw the bottle, which splintered against the wall. Somebody else did the same, and then everyone got into the act. 'Let's burn it down!' was the cry and inside of two minutes the canvas structure was up in flames. 'Let's burn the other one down too!' and with that the mob ran to the second so-called canteen and that also went up in flames in short order.

It was a drastic action to take. As Holt said at the time: 'But the smart businessman had been warned about rorting the soldiery and he could only blame himself and his profiteering for his misfortune.' Later the army took over the canteens and prices dropped dramatically.

Roy Sibson was born in Bowen, Queensland, and, like Ivo Blazely, was a tough bush kid who left school early—in his case at fourteen. He was actually only fifteen when he joined the Australian Militia, but said he was sixteen. His military training began immediately.

Sibson went to drill every Tuesday night, then went to a camp in Townsville at Kissing Point for two weeks a year. He got no pay until he turned eighteen, although the other soldiers used to take the hat around to collect a few bob for the young recruits.

> When I was eighteen we got eight shillings and sixpence a day. We got our shirts and uniforms issued free, and sometimes wore them as work clothes. The army let us take our rifles home, one Sunday in four. They took us to the rifle range. When we were shooting with the Lewis guns they had a target about six feet long and three feet high and we had to shoot at this. Any holes in the target told the men in the

butts—the trench behind the target—how straight we'd shot. Some of us used to aim along the top of the mound so the stones would fly up and poke hundreds of holes through the target. The men on the butts would get hit with the stones also. The phones would ring hot to 'Tell the silly buggers to raise their sights'.

One day Sibson had a young cadet on the range. He was shooting with the .303 rifle which was dirty and the recoil was kicking hell out of his shoulder. After lunch they changed to Lewis guns, which fired about 600 rounds a minute. However, when the lad's turn came to fire the Lewis gun, he could not be found. When he was located he said that 'If the rifle hurt his shoulders one shot at a time, what would 600 a minute do?' Sibson told him that Lewis guns didn't kick back. 'They actually walked away from you and had to be pressed back against your shoulder. That lad took some convincing.'

Up to then life had been fun and games. But then things started to get serious. When Sibson's unit landed in Townsville on 6 September 1939, a lot of young men joined up straight away with them. Some had civilian clothes, wore sandshoes and 'looked a raggedy lot'. When they got off the train and formed up outside the Townsville railway station, they were marched down the main street to Kissing Point. They could be only described as 'a ragtime army'. When they marched back down the street a couple of months later, 'You would never know it was the same mob.'

Their first job was to guard the aerodromes, fuel supplies, wireless stations and other essential installations in Townsville. Sibson's first assignment was to guard the aerodrome on Ross River. The louts in Townsville used to think it was all a joke and would crawl up in the dark and throw stones. There were a few shots fired, but no results. The commanding officer told Sibson the stones could just as easily have been a hand grenade and 'If there were any more shots to be fired, he wanted to see the body.' Sibson obliged:

> The hangars where the aeroplanes were, were all floodlit. While I was on guard, I saw the grass moving where the light met the dark. I thought it was somebody crawling up closer. I eased my safety catch on the rifle forward and waited until he broke cover. It was the biggest black cat I'd ever seen. The commanding officer never said what sort of a body, so I shot it. Next morning the CO congratulated me for being the first man to hit something. The rest of the guards were sleeping and did not wake up or turn out. So he made them dig a hole six feet deep and bury the cat. I wasn't too popular that day.

At the aerodrome gate where Sibson was on guard duty, visitors had to present a pass to get in. One of the commercial airline executives in Townsville wanted to catch a plane which was ready to take off, and as he was running late the car was speeding down the road, with the driver leaning out the window and waving a piece of paper, thinking he would be let straight through. 'I lifted my rifle, eased the safety catch off and aimed at the driver. That car must've had six anchors. He threw them all out at once. I never saw anything stop so fast. Then I waved him on and he came, very slowly. I read his pass, and I let him through. I really would have shot him, too.'

On another occasion Sibson took part in an exercise at Duck Creek. There was intense competition between local Militia units, so one company from Ingham was dug in along the creek and was supposed to be defending it. Sibson's job was to infiltrate their lines. They were issued with dummy hand grenades that only made a loud bang and were not supposed to be thrown closer than 25 yards from anyone. As he was sneaking through the outposts and foot patrols, Sibson heard one patrol coming his way and lay down in a plough furrow while seven men walked past him so near, 'I could have undone their bootlaces.'

He eventually got through their lines and found the command post, then crawled up to about 20 yards from them. They were all bent over looking at their maps using a tiny torch. Sibson lit his Bakelite grenade and threw it among them. 'Just as well it wasn't a true grenade as they would never have known what hit them.' He reckoned they got such a fright, 'they must've had a smell about them when they got back to camp'.

There were still some laughs to be had in camp, though, as Sibson recalled:

> Two of my mates got weekend leave and went to Proserpine. They must've had a good time because they arrived back the worst for wear. One took out a big girl because he arrived back at camp with her voluminous bloomers. I don't know if he did any good. When he got back on Sunday night he hoisted her bloomers up to the top of the flagpole and in the morning when we were all on parade, they had to pull the bloomers down to hoist up the Aussie flag. When the bloomers were coming down, the lads on parade started singing The Old Red Flannel Drawers That Maggie Wore.

Sibson's unit had three and a half months at Miowera in 1942 then were sent home for a few days leave before they were moved back to Townsville. The Americans had started to arrive, and the Militia's job was to unload their ships. They worked all week including Sundays as they sensed the war was starting to get serious.

At this stage of the war they were getting 8 shillings and sixpence a day, and the wharfies were getting 10 shillings an hour, and used to call Sibson's mob 'scabs'. They were Communists and tried to pick arguments. Looking back with hindsight Sibson didn't know why they took any notice of their officers and didn't throw the wharfies into the sea. The soldiers were doing twice as much work as they were, and when Russia came into the war on the Allied side, they gave no more trouble. 'But later on when I went to New Guinea, some of our cases of beer had as many as six bottles missing and a few stones put in their place. I hope it made them feel proud.'

Joe Dawson, also a Militia recruit, attended the Footscray drill hall in Melbourne for three nights a week and at weekends, and was eventually accepted. They were intensively drilled with rifles and other weapons. Gradually the rifle that seemed extremely heavy when he first got it 'began to feel lighter'.

The recruits were also taught army regulations and other necessities such as how to use a gas mask. War games were set up on a type of elevated sandpit with small artificial trees and miniature soldiers. Scenarios were provided for them to solve. For example, they were told how an attack would be started and they would have to follow through while covering fire from light and heavy machine guns and mortars were simulated around them. Then the ground features were altered and situations changed for the next exercise.

Dawson's battalion went into camp at Mount Martha on the Mornington Peninsula, near Frankston, south of Melbourne. The camp was just being established so they lived there under primitive conditions with hardly any facilities. It was a tented camp, with eight men to each tent. Meals were cooked on open fires at the end of each company line of tents and food eaten inside the tents. The showers were galvanised iron sheds with a rudimentary system of cold water shower heads. The ablutions block was simply rough-hewn timber covered with galvanised iron. There was no hot water. Eventually a cookhouse was built and cold showers and ablution benches were installed.

> I remember on one occasion seeing a fellow busily scrubbing his rifle with a brush, soap and water. He had obviously been told 'clean'

his rifle. I'm not sure whether he decided he didn't like the army or whether he really was a nutter. Once when I was shaving, my toothpaste and toothbrush were sitting on a bench nearby. The same fellow pointed to the toothbrush and said, 'What's that?' It became apparent he was a real bushie and I don't think he had too many friends! He was not in my unit so I don't know what happened to him.

However, despite the rough facilities and make-believe scenarios, most of the troops considered themselves well-trained soldiers, ready for whatever the army had planned for them.

Chapter 3

SAILING TO WAR

In 1940, few Australians had travelled abroad. Many of the troops about to head for the Middle East had not left their own states in their young lives. The Australian government, short of shipping for essential cargo work, had no capacity for sending troops abroad, and with the agreement of Britain, co-opted luxury passenger liners for the task. Some of the liners, but not all, were stripped of most of their luxury fittings before becoming troop carriers but were still an exotic experience for Australian soldiers.

On 4 May 1940, the liner *Queen Mary* sailed from Australia in convoy with the *Aquitania*, *Mauretania*, *Empress of Britain*, *Empress of Canada* and the unfortunately named *Empress of Japan*. Other smaller foreign-flagged ships were also pressed into service. Leaving Australia on some of these behemoths was a never-to-be forgotten experience.

This was an exhilarating part of army life, leaving Sydney on a fine morning. It was supposed to be a secret, but the ships' presence disclosed that something big was happening and every privately owned boat in Sydney Harbour was out as the *Queen Mary* led the convoy down towards the Heads. There were bands on the forepeak playing 'Now is the Hour' (the haunting Maori farewell), people were cheering, and the boats were tooting their sirens as they headed out to sea. Every craft that could float turned out to see the troops off, from canoes to packed ferry steamers—whistles blowing—and the soldiers were all cheering.

Gunner Bob 'Hooker' Holt was also looking forward to getting away. Early on the morning of 9 January, Holt's battalion moved out and boarded the liner *Orcades*. All embarking troops had been issued with full uniforms and the 16th Brigade put on quite a show as the smartly dressed men marched through Sydney on 4 January 1940. But Holt was not among them. He was unfortunate enough to be in hospital with a poisoned arm. By the time he was discharged, he found himself dropped from the embarkation rolls. 'I believe I would have been the most despondent AIF man in Australia,' he wrote.

After a few weeks in Melbourne, Holt was transferred to Puckapunyal camp in Victoria and told he was now a member of the 2nd Australian General Hospital. He quickly discovered that the soldiers in the hospital unit were different from those in the battalions.

> Our training consisted mainly of erecting and dismantling tents and I (together with most Sydneysiders from the other battalions in the 16th Brigade who were with us) made up my mind to re-join my battalion at the first opportunity. None of us were sorry to see the last of Puckapunyal and we were more than pleased to board the *Strathaird* on 15 April 1940. We were seen off by a team of high-ranking

> officers including our Commander in Chief General Thomas Blamey, while the band played 'Wish Me Luck as You Wave Me Goodbye' and the unforgettable Maori farewell. We lived the life of Riley aboard the *Strathaird*, sleeping in two and four berth cabins without any duties to speak of. There were physical jerks twice a day. The two-up school was booming on deck, as was the dice game in the ship's canteen of an evening.

Signalman Ken Clift's ship was *Otranto* and on board there were reinforcements for the 2/1st and 2/2nd Battalions, many of whom had embarked without even being issued with a uniform. One of these was Frank Sandow, a World War I Digger—a likeable but irascible character who quickly clashed with the officers of his battalion. He was so intransigent he was confined to the ship's brig during the whole voyage from Perth to Colombo. At this time Ken and some of his mates had been detailed as ship's lookouts for submarines and part of their duties included acting as guards to check on the welfare of the miscreants in the brig.

Grog was a very scarce commodity on *Otranto*. Each afternoon the troops were rationed a beer or two which they could purchase after parade in the 'wet' canteen for about an hour. Ken and his comrades were somewhat surprised to find Frank Sandow more than a little intoxicated every time they had occasion to talk with him in the brig, and their envy and curiosity were greatly aroused.

> We found out that Frank, fossicking around in the lockup, had discovered some loose boards which, after lifting, led down into the hold where part of the cargo consisted of quantities of Australian bottled beer packed in straw. Frank had a right royal old time on the voyage, packing his empties back into the crates as he drank them and went so

far as to shout abuse at any officer attempting to organise his release. They would go off in high dudgeon, saying, 'Let the cranky old bastard stay there.' Frank was very generous to any of us lookouts he felt he could trust and so the whole arrangement was very amicable to all concerned—except the canteen people—when we eventually reached our destination.

The accommodation on *Otranto* was in the tourist class, as time had not permitted the removal of bulkheads to convert any of the convoy properly into a troopship. Food was not only poor, but inadequate. So much so there was almost a riot aboard. The cooks were pelted with food scraps from all quarters of the mess one evening and their commanding officer Lieutenant Colonel Ivan Dougherty threatened to charge the whole lot of them with mutiny unless they quietened down.

The sights and sounds of the first Asian countries ever experienced by young Australian soldiers were exotic—particularly for those who avoided just getting drunk on their leave and explored these new experiences. Gunner Clarry McCulloch on the *Isle de France*, in company with the liner *Mauretania*, sighted Colombo, the capital of Ceylon (now Sri Lanka), on 26 April 1941, while the *Queen Mary* went on to the naval base of Trincomalee in the north of the island. The *Queen Elizabeth* went on alone, because its speed enabled it to outrun any submarine.

The *Isle de France*'s stay in port was extended to ten days in an attempt to repair accidental fire damage. Clarry and his mates didn't object at all, as it was their first encounter with a foreign culture.

On their first trip ashore they were all lined up on Galle Face Green, a large grassed area facing the Galle Face Hotel, where they were given a lecture by a British captain on local customs and what was expected of them while on leave. Apparently some of the Sixth Division troops who had passed through Colombo earlier had created quite a bad impression because of their wild behaviour, and the authorities did not want a repeat performance. McCulloch recalled:

> During the course of this lecture we were absolutely fascinated by the accent of our first experience of an upper-class, really pukka Englishman. When he finished off his speech by pointing at the two hotels on site and declaring in ringing tones, 'I think you will find that the beeah ovah hayah is much better than the beear over thayah,' we all gave him a big round of applause before moving off.

Clarry and two of his friends set off into the bazaar. There were rickshaws for hire everywhere, so selecting the three least villainous-looking rickshaw men, they climbed aboard and set off. Starting at a modest pace, it wasn't long before they were urging on their rickshaw pullers to make a race of it. With loud shouts of encouragement and Blue pretending to belabour his man with his felt hat, they arrived.

The first thing that they noticed was the filthy condition of the footpaths and roadways, which were covered by thousands of large red blobs that looked like fresh blood. These turned out to be the residue spat out by the betel nut chewers and that meant practically everyone. The locals' teeth were stained almost black and were not a pretty sight. In a letter home Clarry reported his first impressions: 'Going through the markets was great fun, with hundreds of bargains being offered to all sides, but the smell was horrific. The thing which amazed me most was the friendly manner of the natives. The ones that could speak English would gather round and start off by abusing Hitler, but I suspect that this may have been done to get our custom.'

Conditions in the meat market section did not impress the Australians. The carcasses were all hanging up in the open air, covered by millions of flies, mauled by dirty children, and every now and then a raven would fly down and pick off a juicy morsel. Clarry did not eat much meat during his time ashore.

Strolling through the better parts of town later, they would often be stopped by groups of smiling kids begging them to have a game of cricket on the street. They were very enthusiastic and, when batting, would thump their chest and say, 'Me Don Bradman!', much to the amusement of the Australians.

On their third day ashore the three Australians decided to explore the countryside on the outskirts of Colombo and spent a very pleasant few hours strolling through coconut and banana plantations. During their trek back to the main road, they were passing a very neat bungalow when an elderly English lady came out and invited them for afternoon tea.

> Would you believe it? Cucumber sandwiches! She and her daughter lived there on their own most of the time as the old lady's son was an inspector of police and was rarely at home. They were extremely nice people and loaded us with cigarettes and fruit when we left. They explained a lot about native customs in the island's industries, but we were amazed at their ignorance of living conditions in Australia. We had a hard job convincing them that our native population was not in the majority and that there were no bullock teams on the streets of Melbourne and Sydney.

For a ship of 45,000 tons the *Isle de France* had a very deep draft and at low tide it was not uncommon for the keel to rest in the mud and the ship would list gradually to one side. Clarry found that rather disturbing at first but was reassured by the crew that it was perfectly safe. 'Still, that's what they said about the *Titanic*. We were never completely convinced.' Also in the harbour were ships of every shape and size, including a large merchant cruiser with a huge hole blown in her bows just on the waterline.

Seeing this did not do much to allay their fears about submarines, as they still had a long way to go.

On 6 May tugs began manoeuvring their ship out of the harbour and they set off, once again bound for Egypt—surprisingly without an escort this time. The *Isle de France* ploughed on at a steady 21 knots. The *Mauretania* and *Aquitania* being faster ships had gone on ahead. By the time they passed Aden on the evening of 10 May and entered the Red Sea, they were on their own. It had been expected that conditions in the Red Sea would be hotter than ever, but it was just more of the same—very uncomfortable. The Australians spent a lot of time under the saltwater showers on deck, which kept them reasonably cool.

On *Otranto* Signaller Ken Clift did not have happy memories after leaving Colombo. Training on the ship was almost entirely disrupted by an outbreak of dysentery and vomiting. They had not taken rations on in Colombo but had taken on local fresh water and this was probably to blame. Whether the water was foul or intentionally polluted they could never know, but during the course of the war he received treatment for amoebic dysentery and believed that the Colombo water was the cause of it.

Gunner Ivan 'Ivo' Blazely from Tasmania and his unit embarked on the majestic Cunard Line's *Queen Mary.* He shared a cabin on a deck with about a dozen others. The cabin was designed for two in peacetime, but the twelve had their own bath and at least they were above the waterline and had a porthole.

The morning after they boarded was spent having a look around the ship, which was still being loaded, and informing newcomers that they 'would be sorry'. In the afternoon some of the ships were inspected by the governor-general, Lord Gowrie VC. All Blazely can remember of him was an old gentleman wearing a funny-looking hat, 'like Lord Nelson's'.

A little after dawn next morning, someone in the cabin said, 'She's moving.'

After a brief stop in Fremantle, without shore leave, the *Queen Mary* and the rest of the convoy headed across the Indian Ocean. For Blazely, life on the *Queen Mary* was like nothing he'd known:

> The *Mary* was a mighty ship. One could imagine what it would have been like travelling on her in peacetime. She was a veritable floating hotel. On board and undercover between decks she was fitted out with two large swimming pools, a cinema every bit as big as the newsreel theatrettes that used to abound in Melbourne and Sydney. At different deck levels there were little shopping squares, each containing stairways and a lift to make access to other decks easy. The shops had been beauty salons, gift shops and so on, but of course these and the lifts were closed for the duration.

Blazely thought that with a few thousand Australian troops on board, you could almost call the ship a floating casino. 'After the evening meal there was always a couple of swy games [two-up] going on the after deck as well as Crown and Anchor, Under and Over and other dice games. After dark the action moved below decks. Heads and Tails dice took over from the pennies and Housie Housie [bingo] also started up.'

After a fairly pleasant and uneventful voyage across the Indian Ocean, the *Queen Mary* pulled into Trincomalee, Ceylon. There the convoy refuelled and took on water and supplies. The first night in the harbour, they were anchored about a quarter of a mile offshore. The beckoning lights of the port got too much for five of the likely lads and Ivo and his mates decided they would go and have 'a bit of a shufti ashore'. After being fortified with a few pots of canteen beer, they threw a life raft overboard, dived after it, clambered on board and made their way to land. Ivo thought they lasted about half an hour before being nobbled by British military police and escorted back to the ship, where they spent the remainder of the voyage in the brig.

Disembarking at Tewfik, in Egypt, Gunner Blazely and his mates got the 'first sight and smell of the mystic East'. The staging camp had a good canteen provided, and most headed there after the evening meal. Blazely and his friend George settled for the canteen and beer, but some of his mates went in search of Tewfik's other pleasures without success. After they banged at the door of a house of ill fame, an old lady appeared at the door and said, 'No fish . . . no fish.' They informed her that they didn't exactly have fish in mind. Blazely later realised that what she was actually saying was '*Ma feesh*', Arabic for 'finish', meaning the brothel had closed for the night.

The next morning Ivo and his unit entrained for the journey up through Egypt to Palestine. There were quite a few Australian troops in the area, men who had been wounded or for various other reasons were going back to Australia. Just as the train was pulling out, Blazely remembers, one of them sang out, 'Don't worry boys, we'll take care of your wives and sheilas when we get home.' Quick as a flash came the reply, 'That's all right mate, we've been looking after yours.'

The train line ran past a series of German and Italian prisoners of war camps. The Italians didn't take much notice, but a lot of the Germans ran to the wire and made obscene gestures and shouted insults, and the Australians responded in kind.

The railway line to Kantara ran parallel to the Suez Canal for about 80 miles—a monotonous journey broken only by a few stops at sidings where hordes of Arab hawkers descended on them, selling lukewarm 'ice cold' lemonade and Scotch whisky in sealed bottles. These contained weak tea—or worse, strong urine. This was done by boring a small hole in the bottom of the bottle, draining the contents and refilling it with whatever was most handy. The locals also sold the ever reliable 'eggs a bread', 'egg a cook' and filthy pictures as a sideline. 'At the first stop, I wondered where all the Wogs came from,' Blazely said, but he soon found out. As the train started moving again, they all clambered up on top of the carriages and hitched a ride to the next station. 'I suppose you'd call them commercial travellers.'

The unit detrained at Kantara, went across the canal on pontoons, and after a hearty army meal—hard-boiled eggs being the main course—entrained again and 'like Moses and his mob' headed out across the Sinai Desert, bound for the 'Promised Land', Palestine.

At about 4 am the soldiers were jolted awake by the train pulling up. Looking out the carriage window, Blazely saw they were in the middle of a plain, with a couple of lights shining in the distance. The order came to detrain. As they started to get their gear on and scramble down the railway embankment in the dark, 'the shit hit the fan'.

> The head of our welcoming committee was none other than 'The Turk', short for 'Turkey Arse'—a sergeant-major so-called because on parade he didn't walk, he strutted. The Turk was shouting like a demented boy scoutmaster, 'Over here Eight Troop, silence, stop that talking, hurry up!', not necessarily in that order. Someone behind me said, 'Geez we'll have to watch this bloke, the bastard sounds like he's mad.'

In the confusion of troop movements, a batman (an officer's servant) named 'Wingy' finished up as a reinforcement to the 2/8th Infantry Battalion. How he got into the army must be one of the greatest mysteries of the war—as he only had one hand; the other was missing at the wrist, hence his nickname. Up till then he'd had at least six months service as an officer's batman. 'Anyway, it buggered The Turk as he couldn't get him to stand to attention with both his thumbs in line with the seams of his trousers. He was sent home on the first draft out.'

When they reached Nusarat, they stumbled across about a mile of rough going; Turkey Arse had thoughtfully provided himself with a torch and led the way at something between a fast walk and a dog trot. They were allotted tents and got their heads down and 'after what seemed like ten minutes' shuteye', it was, 'Fall out Eight Troop at the double.'

> At roll call we were told what the routine and timetable would be after breakfast when we would present ourselves, shaved, boots shining, slouch hats at the ready and all the other army spit and polish. The cookhouse itself was that far away you just about needed a cut lunch to get back to base. One of the lads queried the timetable saying, 'It doesn't give us much time, Sarge.'
>
> 'No,' said The Turk, 'and if you've only got time for a shit or a shave, you'll have the shave.'

Bob Holt also started his experience of the mysterious East in Suez, still suffering from his slow-to-heal poisoned arm. He was given leave ashore in Port Said, and as a fresh-faced young man in hospital blue, he was fair game for the first tout to come along. He'd hardly stepped off the gangway when he'd acquired a guide in tow. He showed Holt the town, where he was shocked to find two middle-aged French women of easy virtue selling their charms for the princely sum of 1 shilling. 'I eventually paid off my guide and he left, taking my wallet and fountain pen with him. The stench of the Arab Quarter nearly knocked me down.

I don't really know whether the place was so stinking or whether my nose became acclimatised. But then, it seemed no city in the world smelt so foul and fearful as did Port Said in 1940.'

Holt travelled by train from Egypt and finished up in the 2/2nd Australian General Hospital outside Gaza in Palestine. Gaza had been the scene of several ferocious battles of the Great War in which the Australian Light Horse was involved. Nothing could be seen from Gaza itself but from several miles away the imprint of the old entrenchments could be made out quite clearly.

> I went to have a look at Gaza town and was immediately surrounded by hordes of Arab children yelling and screaming for me to give them 'Bucksheesh'. I was on my own, up an alley, and when they became nasty and dived their grubby little hands into my pockets, I coo-eed and whistled, kicked arses and thumped heads until I got out of the alley. It would have been a blot on the Diggers' escutcheon to be rolled by a team of ten to twelve-year-olds but, by gee, it was a close thing.

After a few days Holt hitch-hiked to Julis camp and sought out Colonel Viv England, the commanding officer of the 2/3rd Australian Battalion, who told him he would be pleased to accept Holt if the hospital unit would release him. On his return to the unit Holt applied for a transfer back to the battalion but this was refused. He had an altercation with a sergeant and was fined. He 'gave himself leave in Tel Aviv' and pottered around the city in the flesh pots of Jaffa until his money ran out. When he returned to the hospital unit, he was awarded fourteen days detention.

> I'll never forget Jerusalem Gaol, for it was my first association with strict discipline under the Military Police and I can truthfully say that I did not enjoy the experience.

> I was met at the gate by a Pommy staff-sergeant who in no time at all was frothing at the mouth and screaming obscenities. He doubled [ran] me to the Commandant's office who laid the law down in no uncertain terms and then had me doubled to a cell. Any place I went in the following 14 days was done at the gallop. The whole of the prison staff made a practice of ranting, raving and bellowing all the time, and I sincerely hope this gave them throat trouble for the rest of their miserable lives.

Equipment had to be stacked just so, at the head of the bed boards, and woe betide any prisoner whose gear was not laid out perfectly. Spare boots had to 'shine like a shilling on a black gin's wither', the soles had to be polished and the eyelets had to be brassoed. Work consisted of sitting in the sun and, at attention, banging two rocks together to make powder of them. Inmates had to look straight ahead and no talking was allowed. After being locked in the cell each evening, prisoners had a task to perform—usually rubbing a malodorous black 4-gallon food container with brick dust until it sparkled like a new billy can. The food was light on, and Holt was perpetually hungry. Cigarettes and tobacco were practically non-existent.

He recalled 'Plonky' Staben lining up in front of him one day asking for a Craven A, 'because they don't hurt my throat'. Holt laughed, and was immediately 'doubled to the commandant's office'.

> I was then doubled to the isolation cells where I was stuck for three days on bread and water. These cells were tiled and below ground level and were as cold as charity. At reveille the blankets were taken out of the cells and a lump of bread and a bucket of water were left on the floor. There was nothing to do but to count the tiles and walk up and down the cell as it was too cold to sit on the floor. An Arab cemetery backed onto the jail (which was Kaiser Wilhelm's Palace

> before 1914). The first couple of days I leapt and pulled myself up to a small barred window and swapped the bread for cigarettes and matches with an Arab working among the gravestones. I was always a good tooth man and on the third day I decided against smoking and munched on stale bread—besides I didn't think I could have reached the window anyway. What cannot be cured has to be endured and the fourteen days eventually passed. I was one happy chappy when I was discharged.

Returning to the hospital unit, Holt again applied for a transfer. The commanding officer gave him a dressing-down and told him that his attitude left a lot to be desired, and if he thought that his behaviour would get him a transfer he had another thing coming. What Holt needed was discipline and the CO had just the man to instil this military virtue into him.

> The sergeant was all set to do just that, till I gave him a whack in the eye. The CO must've given up on me, for my services as a hospital 'pisspot juggler' were terminated forthwith and my transfer back to the 2/3rd Battalion was arranged for the following day. The 2/2nd Australian General Hospital was as pleased to get rid of yours truly as I was to leave them.

Back at the battalion at Julis camp, Holt was returned to his original section in B Company. They trained hard and he became familiar with the new weapons such as Bren guns and Boys anti-tank rifles among other artillery.

> Our section became notorious in the battalion and we were known as the 'Bing Boys'. An ex-sailor, Peter White, put three needles on a stick and tattooed a star on the arm of everyone in the section. 'Plonky'

Dean was away somewhere and missed out on the tattoo. He worried Peter for a week, till one night he set to work. Peter had his needles in one hand and a bottle of beer in the other, while Plonky hung on grimly to a bottle of Stella. The light was bad and neither could see very well anyhow, but the tattoo was done eventually to their mutual satisfaction. When Plonky saw his arm the following morning his squeals of anguish were piteous. Peter endeavoured to repair his work of art but Plonky had to wear it until he was killed in action against Germans in Greece.

An Arab known to all as 'Jimmy the Shit' looked after the toilets. The Diggers spent a good deal of time chiacking and having fun with him until a visit from the Palestine police. It turned out that Jimmy the Shit was one of the most notorious terrorists in the country during the Arab Jewish troubles, which were held in abeyance during the war. 'At this time there was a policy of friendly relations with the Arabs. A platoon of us would go to an Arab village. The officer and two or three men would go and drink Turkish coffee while squatting on the floor of a mud hut with the Muktar [village leader], while the rest of the platoon in full equipment were on guard.'

It was widely believed that an Australian soldier named Spinney had taken his discharge in the Middle East after the First World War. He must have finished up a very wealthy man for nearly every camp in Palestine was eating Spinneys' sausages. According to Holt:

> Roman Catholics could eat them with impunity on Fridays, as I'm positive they didn't contain any meat. There was no beef in the Middle East and it wasn't until years afterwards I realised that the tasty steaks we consumed with relish in the cafes while on leave were camel meat.
>
> We had our fill of bully beef and McConachee's Meat and Vegetable and there was a surfeit of tinned herrings in tomato sauce. We had the

herrings so often for so long that eventually the smell of the newly opened tin would turn even my stomach. At breakfast we usually had bread and then an argument with the cooks as every fellow and his brother crowded round the cookhouse fire to make toast.

Some character wrote some doggerel and it had an element of truth:

The Australian soldiers' weakness, in spite of what you hear,
Isn't cigarettes or women or even Aussie beer;
It isn't baked potatoes or a brown and gravy roast;
It isn't scrambled hen fruit; it's a lump of buttered toast.
When the bugle sounds for breakfast or for dinner or for tea,
He's not content to stand in line, to get his 'mungaree',
He's around the cookhouse fire like a dog around a post,
With some rounds of bread he's lifted and is busy making toast.
And when he's fighting battles and the shells are falling around,
And bombs from Fritz's aeroplanes are tearing up the ground;
Quite cheerfully he'll run the risk of giving up the ghost,
To reach a fire if he can – and make himself some toast.

But they were in the Middle East to fight a war, and in 1941 that became a reality.

Chapter 4

DESERT DIGGERS PREPARE FOR WAR

Australian soldiers, sailors and airmen fought in North Africa and the Mediterranean for nearly five years following Italy's entry into the war in June 1940. Italy's dictator, Benito Mussolini, aimed to expand Italy's colonies in North Africa at the expense of British and French colonies. Always the self-serving optimist, Mussolini remarked to his army's chief of staff, Marshal Pietro Badoglio, 'I only need a few thousand dead so that I can sit at the peace conference as a man who has fought.'

Although Australia had sent its naval ships and aircraft to the Mediterranean, pressure began to mount from the British to send the Sixth Division to Egypt or Palestine to finish its training, believing a second Australian division would soon follow. Prime Minister Robert Menzies obliged, despite the fact that the Sixth Division was not even fully trained at that stage. That would have to be finished on foreign soil.

The Sixth Division troops who had arrived in Palestine would not see combat until the Australians took part in Operation Compass, the successful Commonwealth offensive in Egypt which began in December 1940. Before that there was an urgent need to finish training before the troops faced up to combat, although they were still not fully equipped.

For Gunner Ivan 'Ivo' Blazely, this meant continuing under the ministrations of Sergeant Major 'Turkey Arse', and he was about to meet his new troop leader Lieutenant 'Slit Trench' George—so-called because of his propensity for heading for cover even if it was only rumoured that hostile aircraft were heading his way. His main job seemed to be standing about trying to look like a soldier. Blazely observed: 'Actually he looked like a slightly larger version of The Turk, immaculately turned out, a little moustache, cap at a jaunty angle, wearing a Sam Browne belt and carrying a swagger stick. It was none other than Slit Trench George.'

After a few days some of the draft went to signals school, others to driving school and to learn cooking. The rest furthered their training as gunners and were pleased to find that 'at least there were real 25 pounder guns to fire'.

Training went pretty smoothly and Blazely fell foul of the system only once. The residents of his tent decided on one Sunday morning to give Church Parade a miss. They were charged and the presiding officer asked Ivo if he was a conscientious objector. He said, 'No I'm in the Army, ain't I?' The officer patiently explained he meant Blazely's religious beliefs and told him he had to attend the parade whether he went to church or not—then awarded him seven days confined to barracks. 'If you didn't go to church, you were given a fatigue which kept you occupied until after the parade was over, so from then on I was a regular believer.'

After a few weeks the strutting and fretting Sergeant 'Turkey Arse' and Lieutenant 'Slit Trench' left the unit and were replaced by another lieutenant and warrant officer. By comparison, the new troop leader turned out to be 'not at all like old Slit Trench'. Ivo thought 'Lieutenant Brian was a true officer and gentleman by Act of Parliament.'

Christmas came and went, the first of several Blazely was to spend in the Holy Land. On New Year's Eve his gun troop went to the artillery range at Beersheba to test their training on a shoot with live ammunition. By then it was thought they ought to be proficient enough to handle things without blowing themselves up. 'Each gun crew had an instructor standing by to make sure there were no really bad stuff ups' and under the overall fatherly eye of Lieutenant Brian things went off pretty smoothly.

Shortly after the new year began, a draft of gunners was sent to join the regiment at Qastina. Blazely thought he was lucky to be included—anything was better than Nusarat. They arrived about mid-morning and were allotted different troops in the 15th Battery. Some went as ammunition lumpers to battery headquarters and others to their gun troops. Ivo just had time to settle in a tent with what seemed to him to be 'a group of pretty good jokers'. After lunch an afternoon parade was called. Then he heard the command, 'Fall out Gunner Blazely', and was told to report to battery headquarters. When he arrived there, his reception committee of Captain 'Swivelneck' and Sergeant Major Roysie were waiting.

> Captain Swivelneck immediately started to lecture me on my deportment—at that stage of the game I didn't even know what that meant. Another humungus crime I'd committed was wearing a blue jumper. Hardly my fault as I'd been issued with it. Sergeant-Major Roysie was very dapper with a little Errol Flynn moustache and somehow seemed out of place in a mob of mostly rough soldiers. However he wasn't a bad sort of bloke and kept a pretty fair duty roster. Swivelneck, also known as 'Gertie', was so-called because as he walked or marched his head used to bob around like a puppet. After these minor matters were sorted, Roysie took me to meet my gun-sergeant and crew.
>
> The sergeant who rejoiced in the nickname 'Fish Eyes' didn't impress me at first sight and things deteriorated from then on. His second-in-command Bombardier 'Silver Tongue' wasn't much better.

In my opinion then if you'd booted either of them in the arse you would have kicked their teeth in.

Before Blazely's unit left for Syria, General Sir Thomas Blamey briefly addressed a divisional parade and praised the Ninth Division as a whole. Ivo recalled, 'After his speech, as the convoy of staff cars moved off, one of a group of soldiers near some trucks close by the gate out of the parade ground, called out loudly, "Goodbye Tom—you old cunt!" I reckon if I could hear it from where I was, the general surely did.'

After Italy entered the war B Company was ordered to strike their tents and dig them into the ground. Route marches and manoeuvres were the order of the day. One of Bob 'Hooker' Holt's officers earned his nickname during this period, in the Hebron Hills. One night he sneaked up on a sentry, Joe Gray, who let him get quite close before roaring out, 'Stand up on your hind feet. What are you doing crawling round on your belly like a bloody lizard?' From that moment Lieutenant Fulton became 'Lenny the Lizard'.

The Australians, sharing the casual racism of the times, shamelessly exploited the local tradesmen. Jewish jewellers came around the camp selling their wares from a tray full of watches and rings, and all the troops were on the lookout for a bargain. A technique was developed where a soldier would pass a watch around one way and a ring the other. Someone else would select a ring and then pass it on to another who would inspect it. Another would pick up a watch—and then one of them would take off and run like a deer. The jeweller would catch up with the absconder at the toilet, where the Australian would explain he had been taken short. By the time the jeweller had got back to the tent, his clientele would be missing and so were the rest of his wares.

At a Jewish barbershop, soldiers could get a haircut and pay for it the following payday if they put their names in the book. This happy state of affairs didn't last for long, however, for there were far too many Ned Kellys, Ben Halls, Sydney Ferries, Sydney Bridges and Sydney Domains sprinkled through the book and these credit privileges were quickly stopped.

Holt's platoon commander was Lieutenant 'Slops' Calman, who was highly regarded by his men. According to Holt:

> Slops spoke with a lisp and didn't look like a military man, but he was a soldier and a gentleman to boot. He tried to keep us on the straight and narrow with his man-to-man talks. He never did have a great deal of success, but he never stopped trying and he had the respect and affection of every man in the platoon. We would have crawled over glass for him.

(Unhappily Lieutenant Calman was later transferred to Headquarters Company and was killed in action against the Italians in Badia in January 1941.)

Commanding Officer Colonel 'The Black Panther' England also featured in Holt's recollections:

> About this time there was a great deal of bad language being used by the men and it caused our commanding officer Colonel Viv England some heart burning. 'The Black Panther' was never one to hide his light under a bushel and he certainly believed in calling a spade a spade. On a battalion parade he told us he wanted the swearing to cease forthwith. 'Only the other day I heard an English soldier talking to his mate who was exhausted. He said, "The fookin' fooker's fooked." You don't want to finish up like that, so stop the bloody swearing as of now.'

Two characters from B Company, Frankie Richardson and Harold Gobert, used to take 'French Leave' occasionally and would dress up as

Arabs or Jews. They were able to make themselves understood in both languages. They enjoyed themselves around Arab coffee houses, sucking on 'hubble bubble' pipes and gossiping. On other occasions they would don shorts and Panama hats and take off to the Jewish settlements. To the uninitiated they really looked and acted the part. But on their last escapade in mufti, a Jewish informant had a word to the military police. They were travelling by bus when it stopped near the provosts' post and everyone had to step down from the vehicle. The MPs didn't seem particularly interested in the identity of the travellers, but were very interested in their footwear. 'Shalom,' said Frankie as he raised his Panama hat to the military police. 'I'll shalom you, you Australian bastard,' roared a big beefy MP as he belted Frankie on the head with his baton. He had sighted Frankie's tan Australian military boots under his Arab robe.

Like Hooker Holt, Gunner Clarry McCulloch was camped with his unit near Gaza while their training continued before going into action.

Some of the route marches took them through Arab villages which looked as though they had not changed much since Biblical times. Wheat and barley was harvested by hand and the grain was threshed by driving donkey teams round and round on the straw. The practice which caused the most amusement to the newly arrived Australians was the use of any kind of animal droppings, which were dried in the sun, as cooking fuel. Firewood was almost non-existent, as McCulloch learned:

> One day when marching through a village we met a man riding a donkey. When quite near us the donkey lifted his tail and began to defecate. A young Arab girl, probably about eleven, immediately rushed out from a nearby mudbrick house, caught the dung as it fell

into her bare hands, formed it into a neat circular pancake and stuck it on the wall of the family house to dry.

Route marches in the surrounding area was the army's way to keep the gunners occupied while they waited for their Vickers guns to arrive. On some of these outings it was not uncommon to meet well-dressed Arabs mounted on very smart Arab stallions. The ex–Light Horsemen in the group would cast envious looks at them as they slogged on foot across the sand. It was high summer and one day the temperature climbed to nearly 50°C so the route marches were cancelled and the gunners spent most of the day sitting through lectures in one of the large demonstration tents.

So far no enemy aircraft had come anywhere near their camp and complacency had set in. That was shattered rather rudely one day. While resting in their tents after lunch, there was a tremendous roar and three planes thundered up along the gully, about twenty feet above the tents. Then they suddenly zoomed up at an acute angle and the resulting slipstream stirred up a short, blinding sandstorm. 'Fortunately, they were British Tomahawk fighters on a low-flying exercise and, despite all the bad language which ensued, we realised just how vulnerable we could be.'

They never did find out whether the exercise had been set up by the authorities to alert them to the danger, or whether it was just sheer bloody-mindedness on the part of the pilots. Plenty of threats were made of dire consequences to the pilots if caught skylarking while on leave. In McCulloch's view, the Royal Air Force redeemed itself later in Syria by destroying a lot of the enemy aircraft in that area.

By this time everyone was anxiously waiting for the first leave to be granted. In the first draw Dick Clark and I were the lucky winners from No 11 platoon so, with our boots shined and passed as satisfactory by the Sergeant-Major, we joined the other happy winners from the battalion and boarded a bus bound for Jerusalem for the day.

The first part of the trip was uneventful but I still remember quite vividly how the bus hurtled down the very steep last couple of miles into the city. Swooping down around the seven hairpin bends at breakneck speed, the Arab driver obviously had complete faith that Allah would see us safely to the bottom—and He did! This, to us, was our first miracle in the Holy Land.

The lucky Diggers raced around, absorbing all the sights, smells and sounds of this fascinating city. A first port of call was the Australian Services Club for a soothing ale to celebrate their safe arrival. This was served in what were known as 'Lady Blameys'. Because of the war, drinking glasses were scarce and the rate of attrition was high, so someone came up with a brilliant idea. Large beer bottles, when empty, were cut off neatly just below the shoulder, the edge of the bottom section sanded smooth, creating a very serviceable and generous drinking vessel.

Early in June there was great rejoicing in the camp when the trusty Vickers guns and associated equipment arrived so they could now function properly as a fighting unit. Then a second miracle occurred. 'Each seven-man gun crew received a brand-new Ford V8 one-ton utility truck. For us this meant one thing only—no more marching! Next day, the icing on the cake—we were issued with shiny new British mess dixies plus new modern webbing equipment and were able to get rid of the old World War I stuff which we had used for so long.'

After getting all the guns back in good working order, they had to learn how to use the new Mark VIII ammunition which had also arrived. These new streamlined bullets had much greater range than the old Mark VII used in Australia. Their gun sights were still calibrated for the Mark VII and, as the new ammunition had an effective range of 3500 yards, against 2500 for the older bullets, this needed many calculations by section commanders to work out new settings for the gun sights. Rumours started to circulate that they might soon be seeing some action at last. Most of the crew started to stockpile tins of sausages, vegetables, fruit, condensed milk and chocolate bought from the canteen and stored in their new trucks for emergency use later.

The French forces in Syria and Lebanon had remained loyal to the Vichy government in France after the collapse in that country, and had been ordered to allow the German and Italian air forces full use of all the aerodromes there. This presented a serious threat to the Allied forces in Egypt and Palestine and, of course, the Suez Canal.

Clarry McCulloch recalled that, 'After discussions with General de Gaulle, Winston Churchill ordered the invasion of Syria and Lebanon, and we would be part of this campaign. We were told that it was to be peaceful penetration, but someone neglected to tell the Vichy French about this, so when we did move in, we received quite a lively reception.'

Ken Clift, with Sixth Division Signals, was sent to Qastina near Gaza. He eventually scored two days leave, and took off to the fleshpots of Jerusalem—such as they were—with his mates Harry, Tiny and Frank Inman, an Englishman with one of the other infantry sections. In Jerusalem, they were billeted in the King David Hotel, which had been converted to house troops on leave. The first day passed without incident. They saw the sights, visited numerous cafes, got a little drunk and retreated to their bunks.

> On the second morning, however, the room we occupied was raided by the Australian Military Police and we were packed off to the Jerusalem Gaol, much to our bewilderment. I, for one, didn't have a clue whom or what we had offended but during the lengthy interrogation it appeared that in a less sober moment with cash running out, Frank had offered to barter or sell his respirator to some Arab bigwig who promptly reported to the gendarmes who, in turn, decided as we all

> came on leave together they'd put us all in the boob and then find out just what was going on. We were eventually escorted back to camp, charges were dropped against all but the unfortunate Frank, who received a penalty, but mercifully not a severe one.

Ken's experience in the Jerusalem Gaol reinforced his opinion that the military police 'was run by a bunch of vicious malingering non-soldiers who would go to any lengths to avoid contact with the front line. Needless to say, their social activities were confined strictly to their own units or messes. They were not welcomed anywhere else except under duress.'

Eventually the Sixth Division Signals formed their own camp at Kilo 89, for eight weeks. To relieve the monotony, Blue, Tiny, Harry and Ken decided to take a risk and borrow Captain 'Rusty' Reeve's utility and have an evening in Tel Aviv, absent without leave.

> We had our evening all right, but a report must have been signalled to the Tel Aviv military police. We all experienced a hectic trip back to camp with Tiny at the wheel driving like a maniac and myself in the centre with Harry sitting on Blue's lap, and his long legs hanging out of the window—Tiny crashing through a Provosts' roadblock en route. Luck was with us and we avoided the Provosts, but were bailed up by Lieutenant Rusty Reeve in his pyjamas, dressing gown, webbing, pistol and boots with his pickets who—after we had been verbally reprimanded by him—promptly bundled us into the Guard Tent dragging poor unfortunate Archie out of his bunk and detailing him to get his rifle and guard us during the night. Poor Arch copped a lot of abuse and remarks such as 'Provo bastard', when he didn't seem to want to do anything but go to sleep.

Next morning they were paraded to Colonel Ken Eather by peppery Captain Arch Molloy, who shouted at Blue, 'Get back into line, you bloody lout!' Whereupon Blue put up his fists and challenged Molloy to a fight. After a lot of argument they fronted their sour old commanding officer (who they thought looked as if he had consumed too much whisky the evening before). Eather listened to the charges, fined them a hefty 5 pounds each, and gave them 30 days confined to barracks for good measure.

To get away from parade ground drill and the eternal exercises on the Hebron Hills, Clift wangled a dispatch rider's duty for a week between Kilo 89 camp and Gaza. He found it quite pleasant running between the orange and grapefruit groves with the countryside not unlike his native Australia. 'There were even a lot of gum trees which had been planted years ago. On the last day of my duty, I collided with a Jewish car which had come out on the wrong side of a convoy which I was passing. The kick-start on my BSA motorcycle hamstrung me and so off to the field hospital I went with a gaping wound in my calf.'

Clift was sent to a general hospital consisting of large tents, dirt floors, hospital beds, male orderlies—whom the patients called 'pisspot jugglers'—severe-looking nursing sisters and medical officers who seemed to spend most of their time threatening to discipline all and sundry under their care.

Ken recalled that the routine of the Australian General Hospital was very established:

- About 4 am, the nurses came around to rouse the patients and insist they washed their face and hands.
- The 'pisspot jugglers' reluctantly provided the patients with a cup of milky tea and maybe a biscuit, at the same time breathing over them 'the remains of last night's alicante, arrack, or any other vile brew they'd managed to drink'. Hospital orderlies and army cooks were notorious tipplers—which Ken and his companions soon discovered and used to full advantage.

- The nurses then left for their breakfast. At 8.30 am they returned and 'harassed the guts out of everyone, patients and "jugglers" alike'. The dusty tents then had to be made ship-shape and agreeable for the appearance of their commanding officer Colonel Stygrad.
- The medical officers would inspect each patient (not too intimately) and prescribe aspirin for pain, or Number 9—a huge pill that would send the recipient racing to the toilet in a matter of minutes. After these episodes the patients would spend the rest of the day 'telling lies, relating anecdotes, reading the *Palestine Post* or just waiting for the next meal'—but envying their mates who, still training hard, would be lining up for a few beers at the wet canteen after parade.

Blue and 'Snapper' Smith came to see Ken—and put the hard word on him for money. The patients had just received their specialists' pay and with the philosophy and logic of all soldiers, they could not see what possible use money was to anyone in hospital.

While in hospital, Ken met a couple of very interesting characters indeed: 'Pissy' Wilson from the 2/3rd Battalion, and a giant of a man by the name of Rupe Heiptmann from the 2/1st Field Ambulance.

'Pissy Wilson was in the cot to my left, Rupe in the cot to my right, and as anyone who has spent any time in hospital can tell you, life can be boring in the extreme, especially when you're young, you're mindful of adventure, your loins full of lust and the world your oyster.'

Wilson had an injured leg and his face was cut to ribbons due to his efforts as a dispatch rider for the 2/3rd Battalion while drunk. He confided to Ken that his main source of revenue for the war was counterfeiting—but not in a big way. Two-bob coins were his only transgression on the Australian Mint, and he had fallen foul of the Commonwealth police on a few occasions and had seen the inside of His Majesty's prisons more than once. Pissy explained that the head and tail of the two-bob piece presented very little problem, but the milling of the edges did.

Just before enlisting, he'd adjusted the technicalities of that side of his counterfeiting with a small machine which he had thoughtfully included in his haversack before embarking. After looking over the local coinage, he felt confident that he could do a much better job, and proceeded to do so as soon as he was discharged from hospital. His raw materials came from disused toothpaste tubes, pieces of solder from army workshops and any other non-ferrous material he could lay his hands on.

This coinage passed fairly freely without question on his leaves to Jerusalem, Haifa and Tel Aviv, but he made a faux pas by letting his thirst get the better of him and spending some of his homemade currency in the 2/3rd Battalion canteen. This was far too close to home and he was hauled up before Colonel Viv England, a very imposing soldier, and penalised. Pissy had to make amends from his pay book and he never passed any more dud money in the 2/3rd canteen, but it didn't deter his further dealings with civilians and the whole Middle East, which he considered fair game.

In the hospital cot on Ken's other side was an equally dubious fellow:

> Rupe Heiptmann's mode of making a crust was horse, cattle or sheep duffing in the Wyalong district. Rupe informed me of these facts quite airily and then dismissed them to discuss more important urgent requirements such as getting some amenities whilst in hospital. He disclosed that he was quite well cashed up having been the 'boxer' at the swy game at the 2/1st Field Ambulance for some weeks before being hospitalised. Furthermore he was very friendly with the English NAAFI canteen sergeant only a mile or so away from the General Hospital. Although the canteen wasn't officially open until after parade, he felt we may be able to manage to get a beer if we limped along there, unbeknown to our militant nursing sisters. We both made off in our dressing gowns and after a few rests, arrived at the canteen where we were received with open arms.

It was a long day as they sampled Whitbreads and Barclays beer (all tinned) and finally Rupe purchased several bottles of more potent brews such as cherry brandy for their comrades in the hospital ward.

They wended their way back at a time when they knew the nursing staff would be at the mess and they would only have to contend with their mates and the pisspot jugglers—who, along with the patients, promptly demolished the firewater they had brought back in quick time. Remarkably even 'Darkie' White, who had just had a goitre removed from his throat and had to take his cherry brandy through a tube dangling from his larynx.

All hell broke loose when the sisters arrived back, much to Rupe's amazement. They summoned the colonel and most of the medical officers but as everyone in the ward smelt of grog, nothing much could be done individually. From then on, discipline in the ward was very severe and the patients were all greatly relieved to get their discharges some weeks later, and get back to their units. According to Ken, Rupe was not cut out for the military life:

> Rupe invariably paid no deference to rank. All attempts to awe him with threats from colonels, regimental sergeant-majors, sergeants and their ilk were of no avail. He was the despair of the Field Ambulance, and even on parade would address his commanding officer Colonel Cunningham by his nickname 'Nugget'. Rupe was eventually sent back to Australia as incorrigible and was discharged.
>
> The last we heard of him was that he was on a manslaughter charge, due to a broken neck sustained by one of our American allies who had an altercation with Rupe in a Kings Cross dive not long before the war ended.

On arriving back at Sixth Division, Clift found his feisty officer Captain Arch Molloy had again 'hit the headlines'. On his rounds as adjutant the previous evening, he'd visited the other ranks' wet canteens to find Signaller

Henry 'Mac' MacIntosh in a truculent mood. Mac was a rough knockabout sort of character with a penchant for bar room and street brawling. 'His scarred countenance gave mute testimony to this habit and it seemed that after being chipped by Captain Molloy, Mac indicated that the good captain would not be so overbearing if he had the guts to remove his officers "pips", put up his fists and meet Mac man-to-man out on the parade ground.'

No sooner had the challenge been issued than it was accepted and so captain and signaller—much to the delight of all Digger onlookers—stepped out to do battle royale with their fists. It was a massacre, Mac getting a scientific hiding that he wouldn't forget in a hurry. It was discovered later that Molloy was not only Middleweight Champion of Military College Duntroon, but also the Indian Army.

> Captain Molloy was a fine soldier even if we disliked him at first. He was promoted, and sent to Air-Ground Liaison Group and was captured by the Germans in the desert, only to escape and find his way back by sheer guts and ingenuity, to his own lines. 'Tubby' Bruce's theory was that the Huns didn't like him any more than we did so they let Captain Arch go to get rid of him.

The weather had changed from bitterly cold to extremely warm so it was necessary to issue the troops with lighter clothing and later with shorts. The first batch of shorts they were given, while ordnance waited for supplies from Australia, came from the British and were known as 'Bombay bloomers'. The Australians were less than enchanted with these. Well named, they looked and felt like bloomers with great billowing legs and 'our skinny shanks poking out of them like sticks. The flies, as always in the Middle East, were with us in their thousands and unless you were ever alert, would take a Cook's Tour up one bloomer leg, trot around your vital zones and exit from the other leg.'

Like Signaller Ken Clift, Private Bob 'Hooker' Holt's unit, the 16th Brigade of the 2/3rd Infantry Battalion, was also sent to Helman camp in Egypt as the prospect of combat loomed ever closer. Bob, too, experienced the indignities of wearing Bombay bloomers when the surprisingly cold Middle East winters turned to a desert summer. When leave was granted, he had planned to hire transport and see the pyramids, but never made it past the Egyptiana Café, where the beer was cold and the salted peanuts were 'on the house'.

A district called the Berka was the mecca of the drunken and licentious soldiery of a dozen nations and it catered to the depraved tastes of all. The Berka, otherwise known as the Wazza, had been familiar to the 1st AIF. The whole area resembled an overturned ant heap as hordes of servicemen wandered from one establishment to another at all hours of the day or night. About a mile long, it was lined with three- or four-storey brick buildings: brothels on one side, and cafes, drinking shops and more brothels on the other. The girls were a polyglot mix of races and unfortunately for them not well paid. The going rate was 20 ackers (about 4 shillings). However, if money was short, Bob heard of some men sneaking in to patronise the houses of ill fame that catered to the carnal appetites of the Indian soldiers. The charge there was only 10 ackers. The notorious 'Bull Ring' was an alley off the main street and it resembled a rabbit warren, with girls hanging out of the windows importuning the soldiers in a dozen different languages. Bob recalled:

> The whole area had a distinctive smell all of its own. It wasn't too bad in the mornings—but of an evening—phew! Drunken soldiers would urinate from the top of the stairs of some of the establishments and this would collect on the worn portions of the marble steps. Late-night soldiers wishing to visit ladies on the top floors would have to paddle and splash through pools of piss. It definitely wasn't the scene for anyone with a weak stomach.

> After a visit to one of the brothels it was customary for the soldier to go to a Blue Light Clinic for a washout. This involved some sort of ointment that left a greasy salve on the end of the penis, which was then covered with a piece of tissue paper. Most of us had to wear the wide-legged Bombay Bloomers. It was quite a usual sight, and it never failed to tickle my sense of humour, to see a team of soldiers wandering along the street with tissue paper falling from the front of their shorts like confetti!

Jack Humphreys, Peter White and Bob Holt took 'French Leave' from camp and were meandering along the main street on the day of what became known as the 'Battle of the Berka'. No one was ever sure what it was all about, but a roar and a scuffling starting at one end of the crowded street gradually worked down to the other end of the Berka. It would die out only to start up again an hour or so later. A form of mass hysteria, perhaps? The Australians and New Zealanders 'thumped the tar' out of anyone who happened to be near.

> At one stage of the game we were drinking with an Egyptian policeman and some Sudanese soldiers. We brawled with provosts from New Zealand as well as the Australian variety. During the course of the evening Peter and I had a difference of opinion with several English Military Policemen. I was thumping one gentleman and on the only place I could reach, his stomach. Someone leaned across me and punched the provost to the ground, whereupon the Red Cap got up and took himself off at the gallop. I thanked my mate Peter, but he denied any knowledge of it, as he was more than busy with his own opponent. It appears that a soldier with a big punch and a dislike for Military Police had seen I had my work cut out, and let go with a right hand punch over my shoulder as he was passing. I take this opportunity to thank the unknown soldier!

We were eventually escorted to the train by the Australian Picket. At Helman Railway Station the Egyptian police had a picnic working us over with their belt buckles. We arrived back at camp, sick, sore and sorry for ourselves. We were even more sorry for ourselves later when we lost 28 days pay and Jack Humphreys went to the English Detention Barracks at Abbasia for 28 days.

Chapter 5

HIGH JINKS IN EGYPT

The desert war was starting to hot up and in October Bob Holt's infantry unit was moved to Amiriya, a dry and dusty camp outside Alexandria.

The Italians bombed Alexandria regularly and it was a picturesque sight when the searchlights caught one of the high-flying Italian aircraft in their web. The Egyptian anti-aircraft gunners were enthusiastic but not very successful at bringing any of the Italians down. An Australian battalion provided anti-aircraft protection on the supply trains which travelled regularly from Alexandria to the British base at Mersa Matruh and all stations in between. The ack-ack guard consisted of two men with a Bren gun on a special compartment built on a carriage in the middle of the train. The return journey would take two to three days. Holt said the gunners would be issued with bully beef and biscuits and some tea and sugar and were then on their own.

At lunch-time the troops could pour the bully beef out of the tin and the water would be nearly hot enough to brew tea. With rations like that it was an incentive to scrounge edible food and drink whenever possible.

On one occasion I managed to have a look through some crates in a British NAAFI canteen at Mersa Matruh and we won some tins of Australian pineapple to supplement our ration of warm bully beef. As a bonus we liberated a case marked 'whisky' but didn't open it as we intended to host a party when we returned to our section. We sat on the case on the return journey to Amiriya. Dirty, tired and weary we dragged our gear, equipment and the whisky case over the desert to our section's tent and told them of our luck. Everyone got out their dixies and we opened the case—to find it contained bottles of ink! The air was as blue as the ink and the language awful. It was quite a while before we were allowed to forget that incident.

In December 1940, the British and Indians routed the Italians at Sidi Barrani. The Sixth Division had moved up and were occupying the Mateen Bagush defences. Holt's 2/3rd Battalion was occupying a World War I–type trench system. They then moved again, and finished up below the escarpment at Solum on 19 December. B Company had been taken by bus alongside an old cemetery. The Italian bombers appeared and gave them 'a pretty decent sort of going over'.

We were pleased to hug the deck in and amongst the sunken and dilapidated graves. Some ghoulish chappies decorated their foxholes with a collection of old skulls and bones which were lying around the ground in great profusion. We didn't believe there had been any casualties, but a call to stretcher bearers went up. One of our platoon, 'Troubles' Black, had suddenly discovered he had developed flat feet and couldn't walk another step! (To say the stretcher bearers were sour would be an understatement.)

That night the battalion marched over Halfya Pass to its positions outside the enemy-held coastal town of Bardia, when they were startled to hear two rifle shots from another company. It turned out that a soldier named Galway had shot his brother then himself in the foot. 'We didn't hear what happened to the cowardly creature as a result of the self-inflicted wounds, but the next thing we heard was that Galway had joined the Military Police, and was a provost at Central Railway Station in Sydney. He made quite a name for himself, even among these creatures, for his viciousness and this would really take some doing.'

Holt believed that the vast majority of the military police had neither the heart nor the stomach for joining a combat unit. This damning judgement was from a man who encountered the wrong end of a copper's truncheon. But an army, like any society, needed policemen—especially with larrikins like 'Hooker' Holt and his mates.

With the so-called 'Phoney War' over in Europe, and Italy joining the war in June 1940, the impending reality of action was uppermost in the minds of Australian troops in the Middle East. Signaller Ken Clift was attached to the Sixth Division's 16th Brigade, which quickly moved to Egypt where it was camped outside Cairo at Helwan, but not for very long.

> We were quickly packed off to the edge of the Western Desert to a camp called Amiriya some miles out of Alexandria and on the edge of a salt marsh. This proved to be a wonderful interlude. We still trained hard on the fringe of what was later to be a battleground, and got leave to Alexandria. Tiny, Harry, Blue and I gate-crashed a theatre

in Alexandria. It was exclusively for officers and warrant officers—a flashback to the Victorian era, a setup which must've had many setbacks whenever the AIF arrived. We saw an Australian girl under a spotlight singing softly and waltzing to 'Wonderful One'. She was dressed in blue and we were completely entranced! At this moment we felt very homesick. I think the only reason we weren't thrown out was that we looked rather formidable and perhaps the management felt that compromise in this case was the better part of valour.

The Fleet Club in Alexandria was well established, a comfortable place in which to eat and drink, and gifts to send home were good value. Ken sent some filigree home to a girlfriend and to his sister. Unfortunately, some scrapping between Anzac groups saw them banned from the club and they had to resort to local dives.

The signs of war, however, were never far away now. Most nights they could sit in their slit trenches and enjoy displays of 'fireworks' while drinking their quota of Aussie beer. Practically every evening at about 9 pm, high-level Italian and German bombers would fly down the coast to bomb shipping thronging Alexandria harbour, including, of course, its naval installations. Searchlights would probe the sky until they caught one or more of these intruders. Bombs would be crumping in patterns from time to time, and pom-pom tracers would rise up in a continuous stream to mingle with the ack-ack bursts. Clift and his mates called the pom-pom tracers 'flaming onions'. He recalled the whole show was most spectacular and afterwards they would 'trot off to our tents feeling thoroughly entertained'.

Because of the frequency of the raids, Alexandria was, for a while, placed out of bounds except for men stationed in the city and signalmen carrying dispatches from the various camps. Ken and Blue decided to 'borrow' a signals truck, wear signals armbands and go absent without leave for a weekend in the city. They bluffed their way through the military police roadblocks, entered Alexandria then left the truck in an alley, hoping no inquisitive provost would find it, and plunged into a dive rejoicing in the glamorous name of 'Paradise'.

They had a few arracks plus peanuts, popcorn and other tit-bits which were always served in dainty dishes with each drink, when the enemy bombers came over in force. The crump of bombs, plus the air raid sirens wailing like banshees, sent all the locals, including the proprietor and staff, off in haste to the air raid shelters, wherever they were. At this point, most troops were trained to make lightning-like decisions and so the two Australians immediately emptied the bar of its complement of grog, including Scotch, gin, rum, Advokaat and the like, stacked it in their signals truck and made off for camp. But true to form they did not make it back to camp—not for a few days anyway.

On the way to Amiriya was a Polish camp of refugees who had escaped from occupied Poland to fight the Germans. Ken's mate Blue referred to the Poles as the 'Sticks' and knew a few of them. The Poles spoke very little English and the Australians' Polish was confined to *Gin dobra*, 'good day', *Dobra vetchen*, 'good evening', and *Skule* which, when drinking, is 'good luck'. But they were friends and allies, so magnanimously the renegade signallers decided to shout their friends a drink at the expense of the Paradise. The party went on all night.

'We slept a few hours the next day, then the Sticks produced some powerful schnapps which ironed us out for another 24 hours or so,' Ken said. 'At last we decided that the powers-that-be back in Amiriya must be missing our company, so we drove back, but halted the truck on the outskirts of the camp and reported in.'

They were charged and penalised for being AWOL (absent without leave). The truck was found but it could never be proved that they had used it, so nothing came of the illegal use of a vehicle—a lesson Ken and Blue had learned well on a previous occasion when they 'borrowed' Captain Rusty Reeve's utility.

Preparing for action, the signals men exercised in the desert with the brigade for several days and were visited and reviewed by General Archibald Wavell—a very impressive-looking military man with a black patch over one eye. Blue remarked that Wavell reminded him of Lord Nelson: 'one h'eye, one h'arm and one h'arsehole!'

British politician Anthony Eden was also scheduled to review the signallers the next day and Blue made the mob rock with mirth at his plum-in-mouth, mock recitation of what he anticipated this upper-class Englishman would have to say to the colonials. However, Mr Eden proved a charming and inspiring visitor and Ken recalled, 'Even the roughest and toughest liked his informal and comradely manner.'

For six months Italian and British Empire forces had fenced in Egypt's Western Desert. As 1941 began, all felt that the desert war would soon rage. The artillery received the latest 25-pounder field guns, while new signals gear and kit reached the signallers. As Ken Clift put it, 'We were now ready to go.'

Chapter 6

FIGHTING IN THE DESERT

Australia's soldiers, sailors and airmen fought in North Africa and the Mediterranean intensely for almost two years—from the time Mussolini's Italy entered the war in June 1940 until late 1942. There was the fast-moving desert warfare of Australian troops in North Africa against first the Italians and then Germany, when Hitler ordered Rommel's Afrika Korps into the campaign to prop up the faltering Italians. The Australians first fought at Bardia, then Tobruk (and the lifting of the siege there), as well as the fighting and withdrawals from Greece and Crete, and the short and bloody campaigns in Lebanon and Syria.

The first major fighting that Australian troops saw in North Africa was at Bardia, an important Italian military coastal garrison. The 16th Brigade broke through Bardia's western defensive perimeter at dawn on 3 January 1941, when the 2/1st Battalion smashed through the barbed wire defences.

The Australians were allocated positions outside the wire and tried to dig slit trenches, but it was just not possible because 6 inches down they struck solid rock. They dug long trenches and lay full-length in them. It was as hot as Hades through the day, but bitingly cold during the night. They were issued with sleeveless leather jerkins to be worn under their greatcoats. They were appreciated, as were the balaclavas from the Comforts Fund.

Gunner Bob 'Hooker' Holt of the 2/3rd Infantry Battalion was with them in the thick of the action:

> In the early hours of 3 January sappers lined up outside the Italian wire. If donkeys had been loaded up as we were, the RSPCA would have prosecuted their keepers. We were dressed and equipped in underclothes, sweaters, woollen uniforms, overcoats, leather jerkins, tin hats, extra ammunition, grenades, web equipment, gas masks and a pick or shovel. On our backs, we had sewn a patch of white cloth so that our own troops following in the dark would recognize us. (I understand this device was first used by Australians at Lone Pine on Gallipoli in 1915.)
>
> The engineers blew a hole in the wire with their Bangalore torpedoes and we followed the 2/1st Battalion through the gap. We passed a huddle of Libyan prisoners who were shivering and shaking, as if they had St Vitus Dance—the result of the Allied artillery bombardment. To this day, I do not know if the sappers filling in the anti-tank ditch were drunk, but they certainly sounded and looked like it. The fellows from the 2/1st Engineers were supermen that day. They were toiling like beavers, covered in dirt and dust from the Italian shelling and lathered in sweat. During the brief lulls in the noise you could hear them singing, 'Ho ho, ho ho, we dig, dig, dig' and roaring and shouting. Our own artillery barrage was still going on, the Italian guns were firing at the gap in the wire and it was bedlam.

> You could not hear yourself shout. I was more than pleased to get away from the wire. We came onto the first position the 2/1st Battalion had taken and our artillery had given the Italians the business. There were dead strewn around as Charlie Johnson and I came through. Charlie said, 'Jesus don't look over there.' Of course I immediately did and saw one of Musso's men cut in halves and sliced down the chest like meat in a butcher shop. I came very close to heaving, but in the next few days we saw a lot more shocking sights and it's remarkable how blase a man can become in a short space of time.

Holt's 2/3rd Battalion saw a lot of fighting in the next three days but they found they were more highly trained than they realised, and out of the 700 men in the battalion at Bardia they lost five officers and 56 men. The division and the British troops alongside them put 40,000 of Mussolini's men into the cage and 'I suppose we did them a good turn, for most finished up eating their heads off in Australia.'

The Italian artillery was at its strongest that first day and they shelled the Australians as they came on in extended order. The dust was so thick that on occasions Holt found it impossible to see the man on either side of him, as the troops marched along shouting and singing. 'There must've been something wrong with the Ities ammunition, for I've seen men knocked head over tip, but get to their feet, staggering and silly in the head, but unhurt.'

At one point C Company put in an attack on a stone wall while B Company gave covering fire. The Italians fired their weapons until the Australians got to within 40 yards. C Company had been coming forward with their rifles at the high port and when they lowered their bayonets and charged forward, bellowing and shouting and cheering, Holt said, 'it was a sight to see'.

> There was an old and excitable Polish officer who had previously served in the French Foreign Legion—Count de Telega. The Count

> balloted himself out of the charge and was standing on a small mound all by himself roaring in Polish French and English, 'Neffer haf I seen nodding like it', and 'Tres magnifique'. Here was C Company charging, B Company firing flat out and the Count in a world apart.
>
> C Company got to the wall and the white flags came out shortly afterwards all along the line. In no time at all, about a battalion lined up in marching order, ready to go to the prisoner of war cage—the officers in their flash uniforms leading a horde of undersized, shambling Dagoes in their drab ill-fitting uniforms. The Italians fought hard on occasions from behind their sangars [improvised barriers] and stone walls, but in the main when we got close enough to charge, out would come the white flags and they would emerge with their cardboard suitcases already packed.

C Company spent a good deal of time on the third day of combat in sections and platoons wandering round positions in the *wadis* and gullies near the coast, rooting out the Italians still positioned there. Holt recalled that they meandered around shouting 'Hands up—throw down your arms' in pidgin Italian, and 'it wasn't very long before nearly every section had a dozen or so prisoners in tow. It was hoped they would reveal where more of their troops were holed up.'

During this mopping up operation, Holt saw an Italian sitting just inside the entrance to a dugout and, as he took no notice of him, he fired a shot close to him to bring him out. 'He just kept looking at me which was strange, so I rushed at him to kick him. He didn't move or even blink. He was as dead as a doornail, with not a wound or mark on him. He might've had a heart attack. Or perhaps he died of fright at my handling of the Italian language.'

The battalion attacked the last Italian position on a hill against the coast. It was strongly held by Blackshirts with machine guns and artillery. Holt looked along their line at the battalion advancing with bayonets at the high port. 'The silent men of the battalion appeared giants in their leather jerkins with their bayonets glistening in the sunlight.' Not a shot was fired and it might well have been a scene from a World War I movie. It must have been unnerving to the Italians. Holt looked back over his shoulder to see the supporting lines following, but there weren't any.

They got to about 45 yards from the Blackshirts, who were milling around excitedly arguing the point with one another. Someone must have made the decision to fight, for a machine gun opened up in front. It fired only a burst or two, when battalion mortars put a 3-inch bomb into the position, which blew gun and gunners high into the air. This knocked the fight out of the Blackshirts and the white flags went up.

Signaller Ken Clift, 2/3rd Battalion, was also in the thick of the action.

> While deployed outside Bardia, we had a grandstand view from our slit trenches of a bombing attack on our brigade by our old mates the lumbering Italian biplanes. They dropped their eggs, circled in formation to return to their base when out of the blue came our first sight of a Hurricane. It swooped on a trailing bomber with two or three solid bursts and down it came crashing in massive flame and smoke, hitting the ground near our slit trenches. Three parachutes blossomed from another plane—but failed to open as the silk had burned and so the airmen plummeted into the desert within 100 yards or so of our position. The third parachute did operate and the navigator was taken prisoner a mile or so away. The plane hit the ground with terrific force. We walked over to inspect it and found it a charred mass, the pilot and co-pilot still sitting strapped in their cockpit, burnt to a cinder.

On 2 January 1941 Clift's unit was issued with extra ammunition and grenades and they checked and double-checked their weapons and equipment. The whole brigade moved up under cover of darkness to a white-taped start line running parallel with the Italian's tank ditch and barbed wire about 500 to 600 yards away.

They were in position about nine that evening, dug slit trenches and then settled down awaiting the dawn attack on the following morning. The evening provided quite a bit of entertainment. Infantry patrols were active all along the tank ditch.

The fearless sappers of the 2/1st Engineers were right to the fore with Bangalore torpedoes ready to slip under the barbed wire beyond the tank ditch and blow gaps for the infantry—allowing tanks and trucks to follow through. They had the necessary tools and gear to bridge the tank ditch by filling it in with surrounding shale to make concourses across it so that tanks, Bren gun carriers and blitz buggies would not be halted.

The night came alive with explosions, parachute flares and anti-aircraft fire aimed at RAF bombers, and shooting from the defences within the town of Bardia.

> Finally, we settled down in the bitter cold to await the dawn when we received a modest issue of rum. Just before dawn our artillery including the British—I believe we had about 300 field guns with the Italians in Bardia matching us in field artillery plus a fair wallop of emplaced heavy naval guns—opened a spectacular and rapid fire bombardment over the enemy wire, and we moved forward whistles blowing and infanteers singing.

The engineers blew the gaps in the wire and, amid the dust and noise, the enemy counter barrage was directed back at the brigade, with the 2/1st Infantry, rifles and bayonets at the high port, racing across the ditch through the gaps in the wire and veering to the left as planned, a nucleus of brigade headquarters staff among them. At the wire both enemy shelling and small arms fire were heavy. Captain Bill Stewart was killed almost instantly as he stood up about 20 yards forward of the wire. Three machine-gun bullets went through his left arm and into his heart. When Clift turned him over, he discovered a small shrapnel wound on his forehead. Sergeant Hank Findlay removed his binoculars, map case and other gear carried by an officer. Captain Bill Stewart was a fine soldier, respected and revered by his men.

> The shelling became much heavier. My mate Butta and I ran a line about 300 yards to the 2/1st Battalion where Captain Dillan (commonly known as 'Dillan the Villain') was badly wounded. His leg was later amputated. The 2/1st Battalion ran into some stiff opposition and their advance was temporarily held up.
>
> Meanwhile the 2/2nd Battalion had breached the wire away over to the right as planned, and we managed to get their communications going but they, too, were coming under a lot of small arms fire and we were battling for cable. We decided to tee into their line and get some sort of phone set-up to the 2/3rd Battalion. The 2/3rd had passed through Brigade Headquarters and gone straight down the centre between the 2/1st and 2/2nd Battalions that could be plainly seen across the desert advancing at a great speed—those 2/3rd Battalion boys were always keen!
>
> I ran into B Company who reported that his mate, Tim Dempsey, had been shot. Despite Tim's wound he was still grinning when the stretcher bearers carried him away. He died before they got him back, the bullet passing through his spine.

A stocky lieutenant from the 2/3rd, 'Slops' Calman, bounded directly in front of the leading Italian tank, armed only with a Boys anti-tank rifle. He hit the tank at point-blank range, but was killed instantly. Scrutiny after the skirmish disclosed that the bullet only caused a groove about as thick as a man's finger in the tank's armour, proving that these weapons were completely useless in these circumstances. Calman's bravery had been wasted.

Two Portees (an anti-tank gun carried on a lorry) arrived at the top of the *wadi*. One Portee was hit and destroyed by the leading enemy tank, but the other swung smartly around and gave the gunner, Sergeant 'Dead-Eye' Dick Pickett, a good traverse and a perfect view of all five enemy tanks. Although hit by a shot from one of the tanks, Pickett promptly knocked out all five with rapid fire, a 2-pound shell going into each tank, stopping them all in their tracks.

Looking down into the turrets of the destroyed tanks later was a horrifying sight even to the most hardened. The shell had gone around and around inside each tank, making mincemeat of the crew.

Clift believed if ever a soldier should have received a Victoria Cross from his actions, Dick Pickett should have. As it was he got a Distinguished Conduct Medal (DCM) and his crew Military Medals (MMs). Had those five enemy tanks broken through from battalion to brigade, they might have caused serious problems to the whole assault. 'This *wadi* became known as "Champagne Gully" because of the great quantities of grog obtained from the pillboxes after Bardia fell.'

The 2/3rd cleaned up Champagne Gully and pressed on, capturing hundreds of prisoners. Dead Italians and Australians lay everywhere. By nightfall, all British and Australian battalions had gained their objectives and settled down for the final assault on the town of Bardia the following morning.

Clift's J Section had done a good signals job. Wireless vans attached to battalions had perfect contact with the brigade. His fellow signallers Tom Brown and Blue had kept division headquarters informed of all events, as had B Section with their cables even though the advance was faster than anticipated. They improvised with a lot of Italian cable to supplement their own and the field telephone communications were satisfactory. D3 phones were a small instrument in a leather case and carried by all signallers in a forward area. They were worked by a single line of cable, as it was necessary to get a return from sender to receiver to complete a circuit. The line was connected to one terminal and the current was made by a short piece of cable to a metal earth pin driven into the ground. In the dry dusty desert it was necessary to moisten the ground around the earth pin, so the signallers improvised. 'Water was a precious commodity so every soldier near a signal point was requested to piss on the earth around the pins to keep communications running satisfactorily.'

The following day the infantry attacked with courage and determination and Bardia fell, with thousands of prisoners of war and booty of all descriptions. The town was a sorry sight after the battering by air force and navy and finally the assault by ground forces. Afterwards, Clift reported, 'The Brigade licked its wounds, buried its dead and in convoy, made for the outskirts of Tobruk where it deployed, and British armour went north to cut off an escape route on land between Tobruk and Derna.'

With resistance in Bardia crumbling, Hooker Holt was surprised at the alacrity with which the Italians surrendered—particularly their officers.

> To our amazement a host of white flags went up and out came the officers, with their batmen following, struggling along under suitcases and bedrolls. They were followed by 500 greasy unwashed soldiers with the usual cardboard cases and parcels all packed and ready to go. We lined them up, sat them down and told them that after they moved, anyone with a weapon of any kind would be shot out of hand. There was no immediate shuffling around and when we moved them off five minutes later the ground was literally covered with their bright red tin hand grenades. This happened so often that I really believe the Macaronis had been packing them in their gear for so long they didn't

realise they were carrying them. [The red Italian hand grenades were not very powerful, but they could inflict serious injuries.]

I had a haversack full of army badges and propaganda pictures, and was scratching around in a dugout. Our platoon sergeant (who was later captured in Greece and spent the rest of the war as a POW in Germany) took a dim view of my souveniring and as a punishment ordered me to take out a brigade of Italians back to the 'cage'. I, like everyone else, was tired and protested bitterly until I saw an Italian brigadier asking one of our officers where he could plant his gold fountain pen.

This was the only time during the war Holt had charge of a brigade. He lined up his men, shouted '*Avanti*', and marched them briskly over a rise in the ground until they were out of sight of the sergeant. He then gave his second order, '*Alto!*'—'Halt!'—and went through the officers' clothes and gear. 'It was like having an open go in a jewelry shop. The first article I found was a gold fountain pen on the inside pocket of the Italian brigadier and then I relieved the officers of their watches and rings.'

They marched a few miles until they came to a water point, where Holt pulled his team up for a rest. At the rear of the column were a few walking wounded, including a young Italian with a leg wound who was being pushed along in a wheelbarrow by his mate. 'I pulled the wounded man out of the column, as I knew that eventually following Transport would pull up at the water point. The Itie in the wheelbarrow whimpered and cried and the tears rolled down his cheeks. I believe he thought he was going to be shot out of hand for slowing down the column.'

While they were sitting down, Captain Calman's batman, Charlie Hughes, came along. Holt was exceedingly pleased to see him. He asked Charlie if he'd take the Italians back to the POW cage. 'My bloody oath I will. I'll march the bastards alright. Just where is the cage?' Bob didn't know where it was any more than Charlie, but said it wasn't too far away.

So Bob's Italian brigade got a new brigadier on the spot and away went Charlie with his troops. But if he thought he was going to get any loot, he was sadly mistaken as Bob had gone over the whole lot of them with a fine-tooth comb. 'He would not have found one watch. I returned to my unit and I never did tell the sergeant I'd surrendered my command to Charlie Hughes.'

One of Holt's platoon, 'Tissie' Teasdale, ratted the Italian headquarters and picked up a solid silver Sam Browne–style belt embossed with Italian insignia and with a gold scabbard for the dagger. It was such a work of art he reckoned it belong to General 'Electric Whiskers' Bergonzoli, the Italian commandant at Bardia. It must have been worth a fortune, Bob said.

With the fighting finished, B Company pulled up and was preparing to camp alongside an Italian bakery near the water. Holt heard bugles and round the bend between the hills came 'some hobo blowing Boy Scout calls on an Italian bugle he'd picked up. He was followed by a couple of characters drumming on kerosene tins. Another company in parade order was marching behind them and was really stepping it out in style.'

Holt's section was not to be outdone in the gracious living stakes, and found a sack of flour and a can of olive oil that was lying around the bakery. Charlie Johnson had liberated a bag of coffee beans and a grinder. The section lived like plutocrats for a couple of days on hot coffee and pancakes cooked in olive oil. They were delicious but the aftermath was not. All of them finished up with diarrhoea. They had been used to army rations of three men to a tin of warm bully beef that could be poured from the tin, and so they helped themselves to Italian tucker from a nearby ration dump. 'The tuna was really something, but the Italians' bully beef was even worse than ours.' They indulged themselves with porridge made from crushed army biscuits covered with lashings of Italian Nestlé condensed milk.

There was wine in abundance in the dumps around the area, and on the following day it was decided to hold a platoon drinking contest. They put a barrel on the platoon truck and drank pint for pint. Holt was one of the first to pass out, and someone threw a blanket over him.

> Seasoned drinkers weren't so lucky, as they soon ceased to take an interest in the proceedings, the good drinkers couldn't have cared less. When I woke, it was daylight and there was Clarrie Burke and the platoon sergeant still at it, drink for drink. The camp was in a mess with three parts of the platoon lying drunk in heaps of spew and vomit. There were some sick and sorry soldiers, with thick heads, and to top it all we were ordered to go out and bury dead Italians who were starting to stink. I remember one fellow we buried was really on the nose. We lassoed him by the foot and dragged him into an old trench. He was wearing a king-sized gold wristlet watch, but he was really ripe and we buried him, watch and all. It was a waste—later in the war we wouldn't have been so finicky. We'd have been arguing the point over who was going to have the watch.

After a few days, much to the troops' disgust, one of their senior officers had them out training, staging platoon and company attacks on the old Italian positions. This went against the grain, as they considered themselves 'peerless among fighting men'. Holt said the grumbling didn't get off the ground as Colonel Viv England had a sharp and rough tongue when roused. Besides, he had earned the admiration of the battalion for his courage as they saw him going around the companies during the fighting with no regard for his own safety. 'His driver had been killed alongside him and that would have cured most officers of his habit of standing up on his Bren carrier during the heaviest shell and rifle fire, but not Viv England.'

When the Italians surrendered at Bardia on 5 January 1941, two days after being attacked, the Australian and British forces took 40,000 prisoners. This success was quickly followed up by attacking the fortress and port of Tobruk to the west of Bardia, in what was then called Cyrenaica, on 21 January—capturing another 27,000 Italian prisoners.

Hooker Holt was again in the thick of the action with his 2/3rd Battalion: 'The Italians were mighty road builders and we drove 100 miles to Tobruk in captured transport in comparative comfort though we finished as dry as chips and covered in inches of dust. We immediately proceeded to dig our slit trenches and found the same set of rules as in Bardia—solid rock about a foot down.'

A little after midnight on 18 January, they marched to the assembly point for the attack on Tobruk on a bitterly cold night. Barring an occasional burst of machine-gun fire and some light Italian shelling, the night was quiet and lit up occasionally by an intermittent flare. Right on time a single artillery gun signalled for the attack to begin, and with an earth-shattering roar the British massed artillery opened up behind with a terrific bombardment. The immediate horizon was lit up with gun flashes and the noise was tremendous.

> Our company was already lined up and a platoon of C Company was settling in alongside us on the start line when there was a series of explosions as they touched tripwires on a heap of booby-traps. We could see men being thrown into the air by the explosions and the moaning and groaning was horrific until the stretcher bearers got to work and cleaned up the mess. The C Company platoon lost about 20 men killed and wounded.

Despite that setback, C Company were the first Australians into Tobruk. The men of the 2/3rd Field Company and the 2/1st Pioneers suffered casualties, and five sappers received decorations for placing the

Bangalore torpedoes under the barbed wire under fire. There was some confusion at the start, as only four of the five torpedoes exploded, but the three platoons charged through the gap in the wire closely followed by B Company. One of Holt's unit, 'Garney' Crew, was caught up in the barbed wire and tore his pants off. He spent some hours in his long-john underwear, 'until he took a replacement from a Dago officer'.

The battalion took all their immediate objectives by daylight. In the half-light some Italians came out of a strong-point that was showing the white flag. Their officer still had his pistol in his hand, whether he had forgotten it or was going to give it to Ned 'The Glut' or was just plain confused will never be known. 'Ned brought his bayonet down, stuck the officer, wiped his bayonet on the leg of his pants, picked up the Ities' pistol and left him gurgling. Ned was one of the most cold-blooded characters I've ever run into, yet he always wore a huge grin under almost any circumstances.'

The battalion marched right around the perimeter. They took numerous concrete positions and underground posts as they went. As in Bardia their colonel 'The Black Panther' (Colonel Viv England) popped up all over the place, standing up in his Bren carrier even under the heaviest fire. He was completely unafraid. 'Just to see him standing up, cool and calm, giving advice and saying "good day" occasionally, put heart into the most chicken-hearted of us. He was a man among men.'

There were plenty of spoils for the soldiers, as Holt recalled:

> We were always encumbered with heaps of prisoners and I for one had wristlet watches up both arms and a pocket full of money and rings lifted from Dago officers. We went through the dugouts looking for stragglers. Lots of these dugouts were perfumed and holy pictures and pornographic postcards were usually littered around the floor. Lots of the officers had .22, .32 and .38 calibre pistols, highly decorated with mother-of-pearl and these were much sought after. I had so many

> wristwatches that I eventually got big hearted and allowed the Macaronis to keep their pocket watches. They probably kept them until they got back to the prisoner of war cage, where the Provosts would almost certainly have helped themselves—if the Ities had managed to hide them from the support troops.
>
> There was one blond-headed six-foot Alpini officer who stood on his dignity and refused to give up a magnificent ring to Jack Kelly. He was horrified at being stood over by an unwashed digger and kept insisting he was an officer. 'Je suis officier, je suis officier.' I took over from Jack and gave him a whack in the mouth, whereupon the Alpini tore off his ring and threw it on the ground. I gave him a kick up the arse for his trouble and took his wallet as well.

Once Holt's unit was caught in the open and strafed by Italian biplanes and although his battalion had no casualties, he said, 'It was one of the few times I really had the breeze up.' After the planes made a couple of passes, Holt was more than happy to see them take off and transfer their attentions to any battalion but his.

On the last day of the fighting Holt's unit was up on the hills overlooking Tobruk harbour, which was littered with many sunken ships including the cruiser *San Giorgio*, which was still burning and belching black smoke over the harbour and foreshores.

They moved to the waterfront and made themselves temporary shelters of Italian groundsheets and blankets. Someone fixed up an Italian truck and for a few days they helped themselves to loads of Vichy water, wine and tins of tuna which were dumped alongside their makeshift humpies. The truck was eventually reclaimed, but by this time they had all the necessities for good living, including a 4-gallon aluminium water tank of arrack. This fiery, colourless liquid turned milky when mixed with water and was very potent. It was well known all over the Middle East under different names: arrack in Palestine, zibib in Egypt, ouzo in Greece, anise and anisette. The drink was treated with respect by the indigenous people, but not always by Australians.

> Our section had a couple of parties from the 4-gallon can then we gave it a miss. We had a visit from the well-educated eccentric Frankie Richardson who was in another section of 10 Platoon. In his well-modulated voice, Frankie asked us politely if we would be 'so kind as to allow him to help himself to a small concoction of this lovely drink'. We told him to help himself and with that he pulled a length of rubber tubing from his pocket and lay down alongside the can, placed one end of the tubing in his mouth and the other in the can, and proceeded to drink himself senseless.

The 16th Brigade had spearheaded the attack on Bardia and Tobruk, and mainly owing to lack of transport, they were allowed to spell while the other two brigades were battling for Derna, the next town up the coast about 100 miles further west.

The battalion received a well-publicised visit from Prime Minister Menzies. He inspected them and told them how proud he and the people of Australia were of the doings of such patriots.

Signallers were responsible for communications in battle, and they also had to fight. Signaller Ken Clift was promoted to Acting Corporal as he joined J Section in the freezing cold before the attack on Tobruk. Like Bob Holt, he was also issued with a rare official tot of rum as the artillery barrage signalling the beginning of the offensive opened up.

The engineers had cut the defensive wire so the infantry passed through the gaps and found very little immediate opposition. There was a reason for this—the Italians' infantry, except in a few pillboxes, had withdrawn pending the attack and waited until the Allied attackers were through the wire then put down an accurate 'box barrage' by their artillery to greet them.

Clift recalled, 'Everyone went to ground and for some minutes the shells probed up and down the line.' The whole front was a mass of dust and flying shale, casualties were sustained, but the brigade continued on until a suitable pillbox was captured and established a headquarters.

> At this stage, Tubby Bruce was the driver of the signals truck which had been hit in the left wheel, leaving a great hunk of shrapnel embedded in the tyre that miraculously had not punctured. Porter McKee and I were the two linesmen. I was in charge of the detail although one wouldn't think so by some of the language addressed to me by my two colleagues! We topped the rise amongst all the dust and confusion expecting to find what we fondly imagined would be the 2/3rd Battalion headquarters if its advance had been on schedule. Instead, on a salient about 150 yards away, was an enemy machine gun firing from a pillbox towards the forward troops of the company of the 2/3rd Battalion. Beyond the pillbox and 50 yards away was a battery of Italian field guns.

The enemy had obviously not sighted their truck, which Tubby smartly spun down into a gulley. The signalmen each had two rifles, plenty of grenades and a .45 pistol. Using the *wadi* as cover, they got within firing distance, keeping the enemy gun crews' heads down with rifle fire. They returned fire but the traverse of the machine gun was restricted by the concrete loopholes, so they managed to get around the back of the Italian defenders. Clift ran forward and got a grenade down the back of the pillbox and 'minced the machine gunners!'

> The enemy field guns still firing on our troops came to our attention. And we gave them some rapid fire from our rifles. They ducked down

> into a labyrinth of trenches behind the guns and waved the white flag. I advanced on them with a grenade, pin out, while Butta and Tubby covered them with rifles. Their major had been wounded in the arm and there were several badly wounded men in the gun emplacements. We got them all out, about 60 Italians, made them pile their rifles in a heap, then in came B Company.

The dawn broke and another series of Australian attacks began. They again captured a tremendous number of prisoners and war booty of all descriptions, ranging from surgical instruments to heavy transport. The captured transport was worth many millions of pounds.

Tobruk fell. Ken thought it looked bigger than Bardia, although very much like it—whitewashed buildings lurching sideways from air, sea and land attacks. The Italian flag was lowered from the mast in the main square and a Digger's slouch hat run up to replace it.

> These cheeky little Italians had the audacity to take Mussolini at his word and had built, conveniently for us, a huge compound of stakes, barbed wire gates and prisoner amenities to house any British troops who attacked the fortress of Tobruk. Because there was a delay in sending prisoners from Bardia to Alexandria and beyond, the brigade gladly took advantage of this ready-made compound and herded as many as possible of the defeated enemy and their belongings into it. Valises, banjos, guitars and such-like all went in together.

After a couple of days acclimatisation, the Italian prisoners rendered some impromptu concerts for any troops outside the compound who came to listen. One Digger, who had lost his best mate during an attack on a strong-post when they were within bayoneting distance, was annoyed to such an extent that he hurled a Mills bomb over the wire into a group of the prisoners and invited them to 'cut it up between them'. Several were killed and wounded. The perpetrator was arrested and charged accordingly.

Clift was garrisoned at Fort Pilastrino—another fort out of the pages of a Beau Geste novel, right in the heart of Tobruk. On arrival there, a signals station was established in what had been an officers' brothel complete with four-poster beds, silk drapes and other luxurious furnishings. (A similar establishment on a much larger scale existed in the port area of Tobruk.) 'We never found out just what happened to the ladies involved but imagined they must've been evacuated to Tripoli or beyond as things began to look a little too "fair dinkum" for comfort,' Clift observed.

> Our cookhouse was run by a group of rather un-military gentlemen all of whom were partial to alcoholic beverages and as Tobruk abounded in the leftovers from the Italians, such as chianti and kegs of cognac plus the addition of a splash of bottled water—if you wished to be effete—a rare old time was had by all. Next morning as we turned out for our usual morning mess of bully, biscuits and hot tea, there was no breakfast. All the cooks were blind drunk and quite incapable—a half-empty keg of cognac telling the sad story.

Senior officers were outraged. The Diggers involved were ordered to shave and smarten themselves up and all the looted grog was destroyed, causing great grief among those who had liberated it. A further report that two soldiers had died from alcoholic poisoning in Tobruk spelt the end of that particular bonanza.

But the relatively easy victory over the Italians at Tobruk was far from the end of the story. Australian soldiers were to be involved with Tobruk for far longer when the Germans entered the war.

Holt's battalion arrived in Mersa Matruh and were put into an old barracks. They had a bath, shook the dust out of their clothes and took off up the road to a British camp full of newly arrived lines-of-communication troops. 'Could you tell me where to find the canteen, mate?' Bob asked a fresh-faced young fellow.

> This creature looked us up and down as if we were scarab beetles and with an accent you would have cut with a knife he replied that he wasn't my mate. He was an officer and a gentleman and would like to be addressed as such.
>
> I noticed then that he was the proud possessor of one single shiny pip on his shoulder. He suggested I restart the conversation by saluting and calling him 'Sir'. I told him to go and get himself fucked, and left him spluttering about insubordinate colonials. We eventually found the canteen without the young gentleman's help and got ourselves a gut full of beer.

Bob and friends staggered back to their barracks about midnight, full of booze and happy, singing loudly and without a worry in the world. This happy state of affairs did not last long, as Lieutenant George Gibbons from Holt's company had been annoyed for hours by returning drunks and by the time they arrived on the scene he'd had enough—more than enough. He bellowed like a bull and roared to them to shut up and get to bed.

> We had a few words and I told him to go away and also get himself fucked. But it wasn't a new chum English one-pipper I was addressing but one of our very own Australian infantry officers. He 'cooed' for about a minute and then bellowed for the guard. It would have been foolish to hang about so I took off and wandered over to D Company's lines. I borrowed a blanket from my mate Snowy Parkinson and put my head down.

Fortunately Holt and his companions found next morning that Lieutenant Gibbons had cooled off, and apart from reading the riot act to them, he didn't carry on with the list of charges he had thought up. Besides, they were to entrain for Amiriya camp. 'Our lieutenant was a good judge of a pot of beer, and had a few himself, and in the morning may have thought the paperwork was a bit much for him. We knew we were on the move and according to which "furphy" you believed, we were going to England, Cyprus, Turkey or Greece.' In the meantime they were to get a day's leave in Alexandria.

They all had three months pay in their pockets, and prepared to spend it on a day's joyous leave. 'Tich' Parker and Holt were to go in together and Holt was nominated treasurer. They put in £50 apiece (carried by Holt) and Tich planted £10 in one of his socks for cab fares back to camp if anything went wrong.

> We started the day like two gentlemen. We had a Turkish bath and then a meal before indulging ourselves in the odd measure or two of ale.
>
> The hub of the red-light district in Alexandria was the Rue de Soeurs (Sister Street) and Tich and I decided to give it a good looking at. Judging by the hordes of AIF men milling around when we got there, most of the 6th Division must've had the same idea. Sister Street was an alleyway between the long row of three or four storey tenements. Each door and window was filled with ladies of the evening of every hue and nationality. There was a large two-up game in progress on the street and it was amusing to see the ladies betting on the pennies. The going rate for nonsense was 40 ackers (four shillings) and the ladies nearly always wagered that sum. If the girl won, the soldier threw the money up to her. If the lady lost, the AIF digger usually rushed upstairs to take his wager out in kind. Tich and I played some two-up, then sampled the delights of these latter-day houris, before settling down to some steady drinking.

It was still reasonably early and they realised if they wanted to see the finish of the day's leave they would have to use their heads for thinking instead of fighting, and decided to go to a picture show. That wasn't a great success either, for they had no sooner settled down in the theatre seats than around came a drinks waiter and introduced them to John Collins and other fancy cocktails.

They left the theatre and finished up in the out-of-bounds quarter of the city in a narrow brothel. It seemed appropriate to hire the entire staff of the bordello and put on their own version of the can-can. 'The "bludger" [brothel keeper] banged out a rhythm on a drum while his offsider blew on some weird instrument, in the middle of the circle of jigging, prancing, dancing girls who were in the altogether. There were skinny ones, fat ones and all sorts of shapes and sizes in between. Their ages ranged from 15 to 50 and to be brutally honest, there was not one good sort amongst them.' The pièce de résistance was an exhibition jig-a-jig. Holt and Tich had their wicked way with some of the ladies, drank some arrack and headed back to the city.

It was just on dark and the Australian military police were touring the city with loudspeakers on trucks, advising all Sixth Division personnel to return to Amiriya immediately. Holt and Tich decided on a trip out of the city and boarded a tram. Tich had been a 'troubadour' (tram conductor) in Sydney before enlistment, and after the driver accepted a drink or two Tich gained his confidence, speaking at length of the international solidarity of tramway men, and went through the procedure of driving a tram.

> Convinced that Tich was a veteran tram driver from Sydney, the driver gave him a turn at the controls. Tich took over all right, but apparently the speed limit in Alexandria was a lot slower than in Sydney. By the time we reached the terminal the driver was tearing his hair and praying, cursing and swearing in Arabic, French and English.

> Some of the carried-over passengers had been having hysterics as the tram rattled and crashed along with Tich at the controls. There was an awful commotion when we eventually ran out of track at the terminus. The inspectors and tramway staff convinced us both it would be better for all concerned if we returned to the city by gharry [taxi]. They were very rude and spoke to us quite sharply. To make their point quite clear all hands, including the driver and passengers, threw rocks at us until we were out of sight.

It was then back to the city and into a cabaret with drink flowing freely. Most of the more regimental soldiers had returned to camp and most of the unruly elements remained. 'Everyone was to some extent under the influence of John Barleycorn.'

The 'Top of the Pops' among all troops in the Middle East at this time was a dirty song sung to the tune of the Egyptian national anthem. A drunk from the 17th Brigade got up on the rostrum and gave a spirited rendition, deeply appreciated by the music lovers among the Australians. What the indigenous people thought about it was not considered, according to Holt:

> The way the cash registers were ringing must have brought music to their ears, however, and I really believe they would have stood up en masse and blessed themselves if someone had recited the Lord's Prayer. The Aussie version of the Gyppo national anthem song was:
>
> *And we howled 'King Farouk'*
> *He's a bloody great galoot;*
> *He's the King of all the Wogs*
> *And the jackals and the dogs.*
> *CHORUS:*
> *We're all black bastards but we dearly love our King:*

Inter quios, quicketere, mungaree, bardin.
Oh we love Queen Faridah;
How the boys would love to ride her.
We'd all like a chance
To drop her pants.
CHORUS
Italian Marshal Graziani,
How we fought your Libyan army
In the Western Desert brawl
When we answered to the call.
CHORUS
Oh we're all 6th Division
And we don't give a fuck
For the Wogs or the Jews
Or Faridah or Farouk.
CHORUS
King Farouk, King Farouk,
Hang your bollocks on a hook
Staniswire, pull your wire,
Inter quios, quicketere, mungaree, bardin.

By this time the club was really jumping, and to make room for the dancing and the brawling the unconscious drunks had been laid three or four deep alongside the walls around the establishment. Eventually treasurer Holt ran out of the 'filluse' (cash), but they'd had quite a day and were more than ready to return to camp.

> Strange to say, Tich remained popular and had girls crawling all over him, fondling and kissing him and interfering with his clothing. Now Tich was a nice enough fellow and had a pleasant grin but I couldn't really understand the carry-on as the hostesses usually drink cold tea

> instead of the alcoholic beverages and received a percentage from the management. Here was Tich with no money and still ruling the roost. It was strange. Suddenly the penny dropped. 'Where the bloody hell is the cab fare back to the camp, you undersized runt?' Tich held up about 50 ackers and gave a silly grin, so I knew the worst. He had spent our return fare on the ladies, who dropped him like a hot potato as soon as they knew he was skint.

The Australian military police arrived in force and were busy throwing drunks into the back of 3-ton trucks to return them to camp. Rather than route march all on their own, Tich and Bob climbed into one of the trucks.

> The military jacks couldn't have been too particular about who they had been firing into their vehicles for they had flung in an English swaddy [soldier]. He was still in a stupor when he woke up on the desert road. He sat up and complained bitterly about being shanghaied. 'Up the Aussies, England forever,' he shouted, and Tich flattened him. A few minutes later he sat up again—'England forever', and bang went Tich again. This happened all the way to Amiriya. If the trip had been much longer the Choom would have finished up punch drunk for sure.
>
> The Provosts threw everyone out at Amiriya camp. Tich and I got lost, had a nap and eventually found our own lines at daybreak. We were informed we were to 'saddle up' as the battalion was off to Greece. Talk about being ill! Still we didn't have this all on our own and it was a very subdued platoon that climbed up on a gangway from the wharf to board HMS *Gloucester*—a cruiser.
>
> We certainly weren't sorry to see the last of Egypt. This anonymous verse sums up the feelings of that moment:

Land of flies and sweaty socks,
Sin and sand and lots of pox;
Streets of sorrow, streets of shame,
Streets to which we give no name;
Harlots, thieves and pestering Wogs,
Dust and stink and slinking dogs;
Blistering heat and aching feet,
Gyppo gripes and camel meat;
Clouds of choking dust that blinds,
Droves of flies and shattered minds.
The Arabs' heaven, the soldiers' hell,
Land of Bastards, Fare thee well.

Chapter 7

ILL-FATED GREEK ADVENTURE

The decision to commit Australian troops to fight in Greece in early 1941 turned out to be a disaster—a combination of bad strategic intelligence, British enthusiasm for Australian involvement, indecision on the part of the Australian prime minister Robert Menzies and a strangely belated warning on the likely success of the operation by General Thomas Blamey, Australia's senior military commander.

Prime Minister Menzies went to London and joined a meeting of the British War Cabinet on 24 February 1941. At this first meeting Winston Churchill said that they 'had to reach an important decision, namely whether to open a new theatre of war in Greece'. Churchill dominated this discussion, which ended with unanimous approval for 'the despatch of military assistance to Greece' providing Australia and New Zealand agreed to the use of their forces. Menzies was dubious about the plan, but did not push his doubts at the time. Winston Churchill had form for involving Commonwealth troops in risky military ventures as he had in World War I—sending British Empire troops to the Dardanelles, ending in the defeat at Gallipoli with horrendous casualties.

Menzies remained uneasy about the possibility that Britain's great wartime leader was again pushing Commonwealth troops into another military fiasco. So was Arthur Fadden, the acting prime minister. The Labor opposition was not informed that Australian troops were committed to Greece until six weeks later, and then only because of an impending press release by the British authorities. Australia had yet again already swung into line on behalf of the Commonwealth. Australian troops had started leaving Alexandria for Greece on 6 March! Earlier, on 18 February, General Sir Archibald Wavell, commander of British forces in the Middle East, had told Blamey of the impending move of Australian and New Zealand troops to Greece. Strangely, Blamey did not express his doubts and warn Canberra about the risk of the proposal until three weeks later. His cablegram was not discussed by the War Cabinet until April, by which time Australia was irrevocably committed.

At least things began well, when 58,000 Australian, New Zealand and British troops were landed in Greece without a single casualty. Elements of the Sixth Division—including Private Bob 'Hooker' Holt's 2/3rd Battalion—were among the first out of the blocks for Greece, embarking from Alexandria on 18 March. Holt sailed on HMS *Gloucester*, where troops were 'packed in like sardines' below decks.

They disembarked in Piraeus (the port of Athens) and marched through the cobblestoned streets of the working-class area, as crowds cheered them enthusiastically, to their camp at Daphne 10 miles into the countryside. Bob's unit camped in tents among trees. 'After the dust and heat of the Western Desert the green grass and clean air was doubly appreciated.'

Whenever a move was on, the army issued troops with bully beef and biscuits, and the biscuits invariably shattered. When they reached Daphne the soldiers emptied the broken biscuits from their ration pouches by the side of the road. The next morning they were amazed to see hordes of respectable-looking old women stooping and picking up the broken biscuits that had been thrown away.

This was the Australians' first realisation that food of any description was in short supply and that meat was very nearly unprocurable. To make ends meet, quite a few families living around the camp sold homemade wine, the pungent Greek white wine retsina, and a sweet red wine, mavrodaphne, from their homes. The Greeks were suffering under inflation. The drachma had once been worth 5 shillings, but by the time the Australians arrived it was worth about a half-penny. When the war ended the drachma was worthless, with millions to the pound sterling.

Holt recalled after a visit to the paymaster, they went on a day's leave to Athens with pockets full of drachma.

> There were very few men on the streets, apart from cripples and war wounded from the front in Albania. Everything was grey and the people appeared to be undernourished. This did not stop the crowds from cheering and clapping a march of boys and girls in the uniform of the National Youth Organisation. The casualty lists were read out from the street corners and it was touching to hear the women crying and screaming.
>
> We were outside a crowded brothel in Piraeus and there were quite a few harsh words spoken to a young Greek who was importuning AIF men. He came up to us and in broken English asked for something. Thinking he was a tout, we told him to piss off, but then one of us called him back and asked him to speak slowly. It turned out he knew our battalion's chocolate and green colour patches and he was asking if anyone knew the whereabouts of his brother Peter Tambakis. His family had not heard from Peter for months and he had not arrived home, where there was to be a family reunion. Peter was an ex-10 Platoon man, an officer's batman, and had been killed in action

at Bardia. The young Tambakis was very upset, and this incident left us in the same boat.

As soldiers do, they had a look at some of the cafes and houses of ill fame in Athens and realised that most of the girls were not really prostitutes (not that that stopped them), but working in the brothels to get enough to eat.

Signaller Ken Clift and his 16th Brigade also landed at Piraeus.

It was a beautiful spring day when we disembarked at Piraeus. We were smartly turned out in shirts, shorts, slouch hats, and puttees. Members of the German Legation were at the wharf, no doubt observing our numbers and armaments. We marched through the streets of Port Piraeus besieged by pretty girls who threw flowers and ran alongside the troops offering sweets and small glasses of wine. Everywhere in Greece, 'The Woodpecker Song' was very popular. Every man, woman and child knew the words which had become a parody and, when translated, was very derogatory regarding *Il Duce* (Mussolini) and cast some reflection on his looks and parentage. It wasn't long before members of the AIF improvised their own ribald ditty in similar vein to compete, and when the Sixteenth Brigade eventually drove north they sang their own version, which began:

When we meet that Musso guy,
We'll piss right in his eye.
We had rather root him
Than salute him.
Bloody old Mussolini.

Like Private Bob Holt's 2/3rd Battalion, Clift's 16th Brigade also camped at Daphne. Holt's camp was situated in a pine forest with a tiny village only a few hundred yards away. After their evening meal, Tom Brown and Bob strolled down to the village and had a couple of glasses of wine in the sunshine, sitting at tables outside a cafe with chickens chasing in and around their legs. They were still waiting for their equipment, arms and stores to be unloaded before heading north on a reconnaissance. In the meantime they hitched a ride into Athens, and briefly glimpsed the Acropolis and the Parthenon as they made their way to the main square, 'which has a name similar in pronunciation to "pneumonia"'. From then on the 'Pneumonia Square' was used to designate the centre of the city by the Australians.

> We had drawn our pay in Greek drachmas and had large rolls of currency stuffed into our pockets. The populace viewed us much as they would millionaires. We had very little time to enjoy ourselves and made the most of it as though it was to be our last hour! The keg beer served in all the cafes was very good—similar to Aussie draft but it didn't seem as strong. It was cheap, cold and inviting so we drank and ate our fill in the sunshine and enjoyed the hospitality of our Greek allies and I'm sure this memory will live with us until the end of time.

They were less complimentary about the average Greek conscript who was clearly poorly trained, equipped, fed and paid, and Holt felt that their military education was lacking. They looked forlorn and abject, 'a one sandshoe and one galoshes job'. They did not have a chance against the Germans, despite the excellence of some of their units like the Evzones who, smartly dressed in their uniforms and kilts topped with pom-pom berets, proudly did credit to Greece. But the Greek conscripts were friendly and seemed eternally grateful that the Australians had arrived to assist their nation.

They went to great lengths to show their appreciation although the AIF invariably ended up by shouting the drinks. They were not mean, in fact they were extremely generous when they could be but, let's face it, they were also extremely poor.

Later we had plenty of opportunity to observe these simple loyal peasants as we went north. They had a mixture of small arms which must've come out of the Ark, a few ancient trucks, a conglomeration of bandoliers, different sized ammunition, some mules—and Christ only knew who fed them. However, they had unbounded faith in Greece and optimism for the future in their ability to drive off the aggressors. God help them, we thought, the poor misguided bastards!

Greece at the stage was a dictatorship. Although they had no jurisdiction over the British or Australian troops, the Greek government was extremely severe on their own troops, who were suspected of any major military crimes such as desertion or cowardice in the face of the enemy. From Athens to Albania, to the borders of Yugoslavia and Bulgaria, a shooting squad operated without benefit of court martial for the miscreants. Whether they were guilty or not, they would hold a public shooting.

On 6 April, Germany invaded Greece from the north. Hooker Holt and his 2/3rd Battalion, who had only spent a few days in the comparative luxury of the Daphne camp, were put on a train to Larisa in central Greece to the north-west, inland from the Gulf of Salonica that was used as a staging area for Greek troops on their way to the Albanian front.

At Larisa, early every day the Australians would see drafts of Greek reinforcements marching off to the war. The soldiers were dressed in poor quality drab uniforms with quite a few of them wearing captured Italian helmets and assorted pieces of foreign equipment. In their ranks were boys, still dressed in their blue-and-white Youth Organisation uniform of short pants, shirt and forage cap. Holt recalled, 'It was pitiful to see these marching men and boys, usually led by Greek officers in flash uniforms riding horses.'

The Greek police in their well-cut uniforms and ankle-length grey overcoats were armed with swords and rifles, were arrogant and very unpopular. The first the newly arrived Australians knew of a curfew being in force in Larisa was when the police fired at some of them for being on the street after 10 pm. 'When their shots were returned they took a back seat and didn't bother us again.'

Holt's unit had the enviable task of guard duties at a very substantial army food dump close to their camp. Their procedure for acquiring and on-selling the tins of various goodies was simple and effective. When they emptied one of the wooden crates, they sealed it up again and replaced it in the stack.

Some remarkable elderly eccentrics had survived the Australian recruitment process as the need for more fighting soldiers became apparent. A 10 Platoon man, Corporal Stan 'Monty' Montefiore, was a veteran of the First World War and had fought in the International Brigade on the Republican side in the Spanish Civil War. He had dined too well at a roadside cafe one evening, and on leaving the premises he happened to encounter General Sir Thomas Blamey and 'his tribe of shit kickers' all riding past on horseback. Full of *joie de vivre* and Greek wine, Monty called out, 'How are you going Tom, you white-whiskered old bastard?' This was an unusual greeting to the man who headed Australia's army. Blamey reined in his horse and told one of his side-kicks 'to tear the stripes off that man and put him under close arrest'.

Signaller Ken Clift's 16th Brigade only had a few days to enjoy the delights of Daphne camp, south of Athens, before they were trucked to the far north of Greece to the Veria Pass near the Yugoslavian border, to hold it against an invading German army. Judging by what he had seen of the poor calibre of the scratch Greek army, Clift knew that if the Germans had entered the war, 'no matter how valiant the effort by the Greeks, the Huns must prevail for the following reasons':

> At this time, the Germans, after the fall of France, were not engaged in any form of land fighting and therefore could put unlimited forces in the Balkans or anywhere else in Europe. Their German equipment including armour outmatched ours pro rata by a great number. Russia had not yet come into the war—a pity! Because of the Battle of Britain, the RAF were entirely engaged in guarding its homeland and—oh brother!—the Germans had plenty of planes as we would find out later.

The few days they'd had in Daphne allowed the Australians to pick up some basic essentials of the Greek language. *Soomee* was bread, *vino* was of course wine, *aqua* as in Italian was water, and as usual the language of love between boy and girl needed no translation. As they had plenty of drachmas, their popularity was unbounded in the little hamlets and villages visited on the trek north, camping in picnic style beside the streams each evening and going to the local inn and shouting the bar in the smoky little adobe village hotels, drinking sweet mavrodaphne wine and conversing in sign language with the local peasants who 'seemed delighted with this, and of course our undoubted ability to provide cheer for them without any obvious injury to our pockets or theirs'.

They halted at Veria Pass, pitched tents and decided on some reconnaissance. They noticed seven Wellington bombers of the Royal Air Force, heading north—the first and only British planes they saw in Greece. 'Later in Crete, we sighted one only! A lone Hurricane.' This, of course, created some AIF bitterness towards the RAF, generally referred to as 'Blue Orchids' by the Aussie troops, who also claimed their initials stood for 'Rare As Fuck'.

> At Veria we camped beside a river flowing with cold mountain water. We had since discarded our smart shorts and were now garbed in service dress with greatcoats. The weather was bitterly cold but I must proudly assert that Australian troops are easily the most hygienic soldiers, as everyone would bathe in the rivers despite the intense cold. During this period AIF Headquarters, in all solemnity, sent round a rough screed reminding troops of the small wog called 'Willie Arris' that would crawl up our rectums if we persisted in bathing in the Greek rivers, but in a very short time we were much more concerned about German tracer bullets invading our scrotums than 'Willie Arris's' activities. We never did find out what these bugs were—something like hookworms, I believe.

The 16th Brigade wasn't sure whether it would be sent to Albania to assist the Greek effort there against the Italians, or against Hitler's threatened moves from the Balkans. 'Hitler—presumably after a bit of carpet chewing—decided to "bore it up us" and sent his crack troops, plus support, through Yugoslavia to show Musso how to deal with those cheeky colonials—"Churchills Cowboys" as Lord Haw Haw called us.' There was only token resistance in Yugoslavia by Marshal Tito's army.

Records show that Germany had allocated 30 divisions to this campaign, but eventually only used 23. The AIF had two brigades—approximately 1/35th of the German force used against them—plus the British, New Zealand and Greek troops.

The first real snowfall that Ken Clift and his mates ever experienced was during their deployment in the mountains above the Struma Valley, soft flakes falling on their trucks and tents.

A small inn tucked away in the mountains, barely a mile away, beckoned and Clift and his mates trudged across the snowcapped hills to quench their thirst and curiosity.

> The inn was full of smoke and villagers garbed in rough sheepskin jackets and woollen hats like people in an old biblical picture. These friendly people welcomed us like brothers and in broken English and sign language assured us that they would give the Huns and Musso's boys short shrift should they make an appearance. A rough home guard had been formed by the simple peasant folk, the accent being on defence against parachute troops! Their equipment consisted of ancient blunderbusses—a bell-mouthed type of shot gun—pitchforks, wooden clubs and so on. Most of them were illiterate or semi-illiterate so perhaps their optimism would have been shaken had they been able to read a newspaper. However, we weren't there to be wet blankets so we fished out plenty of drachmas, put them on the rough bench that served as a bar and drank our fill along with some 'soomee' [bread] and stuff that looked like popcorn, to act as blotting paper to absorb the plonk we were downing—rough wine with the taint of pine trees.

Snow had stopped falling the following morning. A white mantel covered the pine forest and surroundings. It was crisp and cold and away in the distance cooking fires could be seen as the troops waited hungrily for the tea, bread and stew that eventually arrived in insulated 'hot boxes'.

During the night, Australian patrols contacted some Germans who had crossed the border. A few shots were exchanged but no casualties reported. Later in the morning scouts reported a few small enemy parties in the valley below their position. Patrols from the battalions went out and a battery of artillery behind them decided to stir up 'Adolf's Boys' with a few well-placed shots. As Clift recalled: 'The roar of the shells sounded like express trains passing over our heads, and in the clear crisp air could be seen exploding with a "spang" below the pine forests bordering the valley below, sending up spumes of surf-like spray which echoed and re-echoed throughout the surrounding mountains.'

German recce planes started to make their appearance and hardly an hour passed during daylight without them. They were immune from air attack as there were no Allied aircraft about.

'From the air, we came to expect and got a nice old "pizzling" almost continuously from this point on. Some of the Hun aircrews must've had a sense of humour—Teuton's aren't supposed to possess such a trait—because quite often after dropping their bomb loads, they would unroll several packs of toilet paper and let them come floating down like streamers to the enraged and frustrated Diggers below.'

News of the desert fighting in Africa and the Seventh and Ninth Divisions' retreat from Benghazi came in, and added to the Australian brigade's resentment. 'Little did we know, at this time, just what we were in for.'

Since arriving in Larisa, Bob Holt's unit had advanced further north, right to the border of Yugoslavia. They rejoined their assembled battalion, climbed into trucks and moved north into the mountains. They eventually reached their positions and dug in the forward defence location overlooking a small white village in Yugoslavia. It was bitterly cold and uncomfortable. 'Fetching, carrying, digging and trying to load Bren gun magazines in the dark and freezing weather was no joke.'

It appeared that the Germans had broken through the Greek army and they were in danger of being cut off. A bundle of mules and donkeys with their wooden pack saddles had been requisitioned from the villages. They loaded company gear onto the animals and had a quick lesson on driving donkeys from a Greek. 'To make the donkeys move or go faster, you stuck a pick handle up its bum and shouted "hoosta hrrr" and away the donkey went. It worked too, but then I suppose if I had a pick handle stuck up my fundamental orifice every so often, I'd move too.'

The troops came down the mountains and across some flats and began climbing yet another mountain. Only half of the battalion could be seen, as the leading companies had vanished into the clouds.

> We came across an unloaded donkey, caught him and loaded him. We put a little of our own gear on him and then a little more, and a little more, and with that the donkey collapsed. We unloaded him and loaded ourselves up once again. With that the donkey kicked his heels in the air, haw hawed a couple of times and then proceeded to copulate with the other exhausted animals coming down the track.

They reached the top of the mountain and were coming down the other side when darkness overtook. The Germans were in the vicinity and the Greek army was in full retreat and streaming down the mountain in disorder. They were nervous and trigger-happy and would fire first and ask questions in Greek later. After being challenged and shot at several times it was judged too dangerous to continue, and the Australians made camp by the side of the track. Sleep was impossible in the cold, wet, miserable conditions. 'At first light we moved down to the Aliakmon River after thieving a Greek army mule on the way. Sergeant Snowy McBain and his battalion of Pioneers could see us coming down and he stopped the engineers from blowing up the ferry till we came across.'

That night they all slept in the schoolhouse at Velvendos and were warm enough as there were twelve of them and the mule all packed into one small room. 'We didn't get much sleep however for the foggy night air was thick and the mule farted and stamped his feet all night. We had no food next morning and we scouted round the village without success. On returning to the schoolhouse we found our luck was really out, for the thieving Greek soldiers were missing and so was our mule.'

The shepherds around the village were a picturesque lot with their 'Allah-catcher pants' and long wooden crooks, driving their long-tailed black sheep. They were terrified, as were all the villagers, not so much of the Germans but of the Bulgarians. They had good reason to be, as an SS Division—reportedly almost all Bulgarians—was in the process of crossing the border.

On the way out of Velvendos, Snowy went to a house and offered to buy food for the Australians. The Greek householder had been in the United States in his youth and spoke some broken English. He explained that many soldiers had marched through the village and there was hardly any food left. But he did give Snowy some boiled eggs and some loaves of flat black bread. Meanwhile, Jimmy Hyland and Holt 'liberated' a donkey they saw in a shed in the backyard. They loaded it up, whistled for Snowy, and took off up the mountain track with their new beast of burden.

> We had only gone 100 yards or so when we heard a great commotion behind us. It was our erstwhile friend and his wife followed by what looked like the whole village. The wife rushed to the donkey, pulled up in front of it, put her arms around its neck and started to wail like a banshee. The American-speaking Greek stood in front of the donkey alongside his wife. He tore his shirt open and bellowed—'We have no food. I give you all the food we have and this is how you repay me. You are bandits and brigands. Shoot me, kill me, but please no steal-a the donk.'
>
> While this tirade was going on the old sheila was still screaming and when the villagers started up in sympathy with her, it was just too much. Our collective conscience wasn't all that clear so we pulled our gear off the donkey. The old girl rushed around kissing us as did her husband and we were pleased to take off up the track to the cheers of the local populous.

Holt's unit rejoined their battalion just in time to see Servia being bombed and burning. Before climbing into the waiting battalion transport, they released the donkeys that had been carrying their gear. 'Then to our eternal discredit we smashed the pack saddles to save them from falling into the hands of the Germans, who probably needed pack saddles like they needed a hole in the head. Some of the saddles were works of art and for the impoverished Greek owners to have them smashed must have been a bitter pill to swallow.'

They travelled through the mountains and over the narrow winding roads. There was a lot of bombing on the roads and somehow their platoon was separated from the rest of the battalion. Lieutenant Gibbons must have known the battalion's destination, for they went straight to Pineos Gorge outside Larisa. They were told to patrol the river and moved up at dusk.

> We patrolled all night along the river and could hear the Germans talking on the other side and throwing rocks into the water. Just before daylight we moved back half a mile and stood to. At first light we saw some of our own troops a little further back so we joined them. There were some men from the 2/2nd Battalion and some from the Guard Battalion. These were older men, quite a few with service in the First AIF who were usually used to guard divisional headquarters and so on. They were affectionately known as the 'Old and Bold', 'Ruthless and Toothless' and indeed 'Rugged and Buggered'.

The German planes were over their positions from first light and continually harassed them, though they apparently didn't know the Australians' exact location. They were lined up under trees along the road, and when the German infantry tried to cross the river as they did on numerous occasions, 'we gave them some hurry up'.

The Germans came on in a very strange fashion. One moment the open area on the other side of the river would be clear, the next black with great masses of men heading to the river. The Australians opened up with rifles and light machine guns and would be joined by the Vickers guns of the 21st New Zealand Battalion, who were positioned in the hills behind. The masses of German infantry would disintegrate and then disappear back into cover, only to attempt the same procedure about an hour later.

At about 3 pm German tanks crossed over further up the river and the Australians pulled out in a hurry. They had gone only a few hundred yards when they saw a line of Bren gun carriers dispersed on both sides of the road. Lieutenant Gibbons pulled up in a truck and Holt and his companions climbed out to support the carriers. However, they had stopped only to cover the withdrawal and when the German tanks appeared and the carriers saw there were no more Australian infantry coming, they pulled out.

> The leading German tank was belting along the rough track firing both cannon and machine guns. The first cannon shot landed to the left of our truck and the second to the right. I was sure the next one would put our truck out of business and us with it, but the rough track must have put the gunner off as our truck wasn't hit, nor were any of the platoon as we clambered back on board. I received two holes in my pants leg and a burn across my thigh from bullets as I dived across the back of the truck.

They out-paced the tanks and left the gorge in a hurry, eventually sighting their battalion, which was taking up a position between two hills. As they joined them, a pot-gutted officer came waddling over, waving his pistol. Holt thought he probably didn't know where they'd been or what his platoon had been doing all day and could have thought they were avoiding combat. 'I'll shoot any man who doesn't get out of this truck immediately,' he said. This was ludicrous, but Lieutenant Gibbons was ropeable and told this overweight officer exactly what he thought of him.

Holt and his platoon learned that the battalion had been heavily bombed on the road, and a good mate of his, 'Plonky' Dean, had been one of those killed.

The battalion held two hills on the roadway that ran through the centre of the position. Holt was on top of the hill on the right, behind a stone cairn that gave him a bird's-eye view of the whole scene. About a dozen German tanks were moving forward, slowly followed by lines of infantry. There were several New Zealand guns beside the road, shooting as fast as they could load. They were firing continuously at the tanks and getting more than their share in return. Their dead and wounded lay around in profusion. Eventually they did not have enough men left to work the guns. They then loaded their casualties and got out quickly.

Holt's platoon had been under heavy machine-gun fire for quite a while and were receiving casualties, and when they saw the New Zealand gunners pulling out, 'some clown at the bottom of the hill called out to retire'. They took off down the hill till their company commander, McGregor, roared and bellowed and wanted to know what the bloody hell was going on. Holt recalled:

> They were getting quite a lot of action at the bottom of the hill. I saw Dickie Dowd get the best wound I've ever seen. A spent bullet hit him on the wrist. He caught the end of the bullet in his teeth and pulled it out. However the bullet must've hit a nerve or something, for he had a lot of bother with his wrist and was eventually discharged with a withered arm.
>
> Our battalion medical officer Captain JAF Flashman and his overworked orderlies were attending to the wounded who are lying around the Regimental Aid Post. The doc was up to his elbows in gore when he noticed Troubles Black sitting amongst the team awaiting attention. He asked Troubles, 'Where were you hit, lad?' 'I'm not wounded, Captain, but I'm having trouble with my flat feet.' The doc blew up and roared at Troubles: 'Get to buggery and don't waste my time you cowardly, yellow-gutted bastard.' (Sadly Captain Flashman was killed in the early hours of the following morning at a German roadblock.)

Holt's unit rushed back to the top of the hill and returned the heavy German fire. The tanks were coming on faster now that the New Zealand gunners had withdrawn and they and the following infantry were moving steadily forward. Again the words came through to retire, and this time it was 'fair dinkum'. The unit came down the hill and climbed into their trucks under fire.

The battalion formed single lines on either side of the road and the companies became mixed up. There were no separate units at that stage, just the AIF. Holt did not think that any of them really expected to come out of this chaos, but would not have swapped places with any man on earth.

> On this day I was proud to be part of the 2/3rd Australian Infantry Battalion. Three or four Bren gun carriers came down the road through us. It was coming on nightfall by then, and we heard a rumbling as a partly disabled carrier came up. It was making heavy going of it and every so often would burst into flame. It eventually passed through and shortly afterwards we heard another heavy engine rumbling towards us. We thought it was another disabled carrier, but out of the murk came this tank with a cross emblazoned on its side. It had its lid open and a bloody great Fritz was standing with his body halfway out of the hatch. I believe every man in the battalion let go with his weapon on this fellow, who must've disintegrated. The rifle and machine gun fire was terrific. There were streams of tracer flying about and our fellows were charging around shooting. The tank crew must have wondered what it had run into. It was firing all its weapons and spun to the right. It caused quite a few casualties and ran over several of our fellows, squashing them into the mud before taking off at high speed.

Things quietened down almost immediately and they received orders to get into their trucks and retire.

I went over to the position on the left of the road and amongst the wounded was a Gallipoli veteran, Wally Webb, who was badly wounded in the stomach. Clarrie Burke and I got Wally into the last truck. The German tanks followed us for quite a while shooting off flares, but eventually gave up.

The Germans had blocked the main road to Larisa and we took one of the side tracks. At one stage there was a long hold up and I went along to see the reason. There had been a lot of talk about Fifth Columnists [civilian spies] and the Greek civilian who said he knew the area had got himself lost, and us with him. The Greek could hardly explain himself as he knew no English and the soldiers had no Greek. The Greek was punched silly and left by the side of the track.

They stopped and started all night with trucks following different tracks. At first light the whole of the transport column that Holt was with got bogged in a swamp. He overheard Brigadier 'Tubby' Allen say that 'it was now a case of every man for himself'.

The 2/2nd and 2/3rd Battalions bore the brunt of the action around Larisa against an overwhelming German attack, in the Tempe and Pineos Gorges area in the mountains of northern Greece, ably supported by the New Zealand brigade. It is ironic that the commander of the Australian and Commonwealth forces in Greece, General Thomas Blamey, was the same man who delayed, for three weeks, giving his warnings to the Australian War Cabinet that he considered the Allied involvement in Greece in 1941 dangerous and ill-advised—by which time Australia had committed its troops to Greece. The Germans attacked Greece from Yugoslavia on 6 April, and by the end of that month Hitler's army had driven all the Commonwealth troops from Greece. On 11 April, Blamey renamed the Commonwealth troops the ANZAC Corps.

In mid-April General Blamey ordered Brigadier Arthur 'Tubby' Allen and his two available battalions of the 16th Brigade to the Pineos Gorge, where the German thrust threatened to reach the main road where it bottle-necked through Larisa and cut off practically the entire British force. There would have to be an Allied withdrawal, but the invading Germans needed to be held back to allow that.

Ken Clift was attached to the 2/2nd Battalion in the thick of the fighting which, in these desperate critical hours, even used former 1st AIF veterans, the 'Old and Bold', in combat. 'Our only ack-ack in the whole formation was a set of Vickers guns mounted on a tripod and manned by these redoubtables at an impromptu brigade headquarters with other Old and Bolds gallantly ready to fire with rifles only, at Stukas, Heinkels, Dorniers and even at Hitler himself should he appear from the sky.'

Clift was doubtful whether they could get transport out of this desperate situation and all spare vehicles other than those needed to repel the invader were put out of action by draining the sumps and letting the motors run until they seized. This was achieved while the action and counteraction continued along the front, which was now the Pineos River. The German build-up was getting stronger by the hour but at least they were denying them use of any transport and equipment they might capture 'even if we were gone coons'.

They ran signal lines to the two battalions, but the 2/2nd seemed to be in the hottest spot as both mortar and shellfire continually put the lines out of action. Clift's mates Butta and Tubby were stationed at intervals along them to do quick repairs in order to keep their commander, Brigadier Allen, in constant touch with the action. The brigadier was grim and dejected, as well he might be. For all he knew, it would only be a matter of time before the enemy brought sufficient force to bear to make their positions completely untenable—'cut off like the proverbial shag on a rock'.

Clift was stationed with Lieutenant John Dunlop at 2/2nd Battalion headquarters and, like all that battalion's positions, it was a very hot spot indeed.

> John Dunlop was a fine, cool soldier. He detailed Corporal Arthur Hiddens with a Bren gun, and me with a rifle, to crawl down behind the sangars [earth barriers] fronting the river in order to stir up the enemy if they attempted to cross. At this juncture the 2/2nd infantry companies were heavily engaged right along the river to our right and they had repulsed several assaults and, by counter-attacking, had actually driven superior forces back. Corporal Hiddens and I crawled down unobserved—we hoped—to within about fifteen yards of the river and waited for the 'sitting ducks' to start wading. At last, they started into the river, deployed in sections and in staggered formation—with Arthur licking his chops and muttering, 'Come a bit closer, you bastards.'

They were about 25 or 30 yards distant when Hiddens let go and Clift went rapid fire with his rifle. He was delighted that although Hiddens was a signals corporal, not an infantryman, 'he could play a very pretty tune on a Bren and for a few minutes, he wrought havoc with "Herr Hitler's crack Mountain Regiment"'. What troops were left of the attempted crossing retreated back to the cover of the opposite bank with bullets flying up their backsides. 'The sanger in which we were and others around us were immediately subjected to a barrage of very large fat German mortars. Oh boy! Did we keep our heads and bottoms down.'

The Germans eventually did cross the river further upstream and even got tanks across, flushing Hiddens and Clift out 'like a couple of quail'. They scurried up the hill under cover of fire from the 2/2nd Battalion headquarters. The tanks fired tracers at them as they ran away but they made it back to headquarters and comparative safety 'in a manner that would not have disgraced an Olympic sprint champion'.

But the German tanks did not have it all their own way. Some were destroyed by a couple of extremely courageous New Zealand gun crews who engaged them over open sights while deployed to the rear and left flank of the 2/2nd Battalion, and this gave everyone concerned a short but welcome break—especially as the German aircraft gave them no respite, ranging up and down the line of the river at will.

The afternoon became a shambles despite the infantry. During the afternoon Sergeant 'Sykes' Evans killed many Germans at great personal risk. To gain longer range, he used double charges. He was one of the extraordinary characters during the withdrawal. He was awarded the Military Medal, as was Arthur Hiddens. Clift remarked, 'Everyone knew they deserved greater honour but unfortunately retreats are a difficult set-up and never carry the glories of a victory.'

At dusk tracers criss-crossed the whole valley. The immediate orders were to collect all wounded, incapacitated and personnel not capable of making the grade, then leave them in the charge of volunteer regimental aid post (RAP) orderlies.

> These RAP fellows have guts and fortitude and their spirit had to be seen to be believed. The rest of us were to split into small groups and taken on a certain route by waiting trucks and shank's pony, until we reached our own lines some hundred miles away to the south at Lamia—a grim prospect even for super optimists, especially as the Germans had flares going up at intervals, and these seem to straddle the road in a huge semicircle to the south. After the flush of exultation because of our desert victory in North Africa, our rage, frustration, disappointment or just plain disgust—call it what you will—was beyond description. We had now tasted the ashes of defeat and we didn't like it. We had even sneered at the Tommies at Dunkirk, but the chickens were now coming home to roost.

The truck, with Tubby Bruce's driver, was still intact so with Lieutenant Alan Ibbotsen and other members of the section, Clift clambered aboard and went into the gloom without lights towards the east, the general withdrawal direction. Tracers came closer and closer and criss-crossed in all directions. They were all completely exhausted. The driver turned the truck over into a creek, presumably a tributary of the Pineos River, in the darkness. 'We were flung headlong into the freezing water, dunked under the truck, Harry, Tiny and I going a long way under before scrambling out with our weapons and gear onto the bank and the blackness of the night.'

They dragged a badly injured Billy Wyatt with them, his spine crushed with a belly full of water as well, and rendered what first-aid they could in the chilly darkness. Tubby remarked that they were shivering like 'a lot of dogs shitting razor blades'.

Reluctantly, they found it necessary to take Billy back to the regimental aid post to await the coming of the enemy. (He was treated well as a prisoner of war in Germany, but he died in Yaralla later of recurring pneumonia.)

They now looked around for another means of evacuation, preferably the mechanical kind, with Tubby declaring that he didn't want to spend any time in a 'fucking Hun Constipation Camp'. They caught up with a couple of Army Service Corps trucks, but agreed to split into two groups so they could accommodate them. Clift recalled their parting moments:

> I will never forget Harry's handgrip, his handsome face and the 'good luck' as he went over the tailboard of his vehicle. Tiny walked across as Blue and I settled into our truck, giving my behind a friendly push and a slap as I clambered in. 'Good luck,' he said, still with that big friendly unafraid grin in the sickly moonlight. I never saw Tiny and Harry again, and the years have never stifled my regret. In Crete we were given tragic news that they had gone west, and as soldiers do for very close friends, we grieved—experiencing the acute sense of pain, deep inside, when someone close, such as a brother, goes away forever. Death is so definite, so final. One tries to recall their gaiety, generosity

> and comradeship which we shared with them through good times and bad for what now seemed an eternity.

Heeding Brigadier 'Tubby' Allen's call for every man to look after himself, Private Bob Holt and what remained of his 16th Brigade headed for the coast. They sloshed their way through the swamp that had stopped their trucks. The Luftwaffe was out in force, bombing and strafing. 'We eventually struck a solid road and one over-enthusiastic Luftwaffe pilot immediately came in low with all his guns blazing. I dived into the trench alongside the road, which was half full of icy water. I was cold, wet and miserable and pretty near freezing by the time Fritz turned his attention elsewhere, and I stayed that way till my clothes dried out.'

Shortly afterwards a couple of truckloads of New Zealand infantry came along and gave them a lift—but they were shadowed for miles by a mysterious armoured car and they did not know if 'it was one of ours or theirs'. They passed through the rearguard of the 17th Brigade at Lamia.

There was a lot of bombing and strafing on the roads and Lamia and Volos were certainly getting their share. Going down the Thermopylae Pass, there were signs that the various 16th Brigade units were forming up. Holt's group thanked the Kiwis for the lift and the food they had shared with them and rejoined their battalion, which was sorting itself out in the hills.

> Our platoon position was on top of the hill, overlooking the long straight road leading to the pass. The scenery was breathtakingly beautiful, but any spare time we had was used watching the planes giving the vehicular traffic a pasting, the smoke from the burning trucks dotting the road. The German aircraft not only blasted the transport off the roads but also incinerated villages, towns and cities. But there were at least some flyers with a conscience.

Just back from their position, a field ambulance was tucked right among the troops and military hardware. Holt saw several planes come strafing along the valley, but as soon as they saw the Red Cross on the tents, they stopped their strafing and zoomed off. What with the long marches, the fights around Pineos Gorge, insufficient food and constant air attacks, Holt's mob had been having a rough time and 'quite a few fellows' nerves were on edge'. They received news that the Sixth Division and the New Zealand division had been formed into the ANZAC Corps.

'In another boost to our morale, we were told that the battalion was going into an attack the following evening. There had been a spate of self-inflicted wounds, and I overheard two company commanders discussing their problems. "How many men have you got John?" The reply was 48. Just then a rifle shot was heard from over the hill. "Correction, make that 47".'

Instead of attacking, Holt's unit again piled into buses. The word was that they were to retire to the coast and would be evacuated. They were bombed and strafed on the roads. They passed the Corinth Canal, where there was to be a rearguard action, and eventually finished up in some olive groves outside Kalamata.

> We started to clean ourselves at a fountain on the grounds of a girls' school. Surprisingly we were as popular in defeat as we were when we landed. The girls washed our filthy socks and boiled us eggs and couldn't do enough for us.
>
> The Luftwaffe came over and dropped bombs around us and it was horrible to see these young girls so upset. Some of us were given hammers and told to smash up our transport vehicles. We hammered the engines, smashed the lights and windscreens and left them useless.

On the nights of 26 and 27 April, they marched through Kalamata to the docks through darkened streets with all their arms and equipment.

About 10.30 pm they saw lights flashing out to sea and shortly afterwards the destroyer HMS *Hero* came in and they embarked. 'We were packed in like sardines from the bilges to the superstructure and it was just as well we weren't on the destroyer too long, or some of us would surely have smothered.'

The embarkation was carried out in a well-disciplined manner. The battalions had been arranged into groups and they marched through crowds of Cypriots and Palestinians. *Hero* sailed out into the bay and they transferred to the British troopship *Dilwarra*. As soon as the other transports were loaded, *Hero* formed up in convoy and set sail for Alexandria.

Ken Clift also acted on Brigadier Allen's orders to head south but his group, led by Lieutenant Alan Ibbotsen, decided to travel to the east coast through the mountains and pine forests, dodging as many roads as possible, which by now were crawling with German convoys, motorcyclists and armoured transport. They aimed to get to the port of Volos. Ibbotsen believed there was a British presence and a destroyer on the tiny island of Skiathos just off the coast. 'Any British naval craft would be a welcome sight to us weary bedraggled warriors,' Clift reckoned.

They covered the distance to the coast in a couple of days. Their meagre rations had long since gone but they had the cover of the pine forests practically all the way. Water was no problem, with mountain streams criss-crossing their route constantly. Tubby had a water bottle full of rum and Ken had a bottle of whisky in his haversack filched from an abandoned dump of stores near Servia, 'so prudent use of the spirits was helpful on the journey'.

They were now a little dubious of the reaction of Greek civilians to their presence, but were welcomed like brothers. The port at Piraeus had been 'blown to hell' and was no longer useable for shipping. Other towns had also suffered the same fate, including Elasson and Larisa. German parachutists had landed a long way south in the vicinity of the Gulf of Corinth. The Greek government had capitulated and had requested the Allied troops withdraw from the mainland to save further civilian suffering, so the longer they stayed the more embarrassing they became to their hosts.

> The Huns had made it quite clear to our Greek brethren where they could, with proclamations pinned on walls and announcements put over the Greek radio to the effect that immediate reprisals in the form of execution by firing squad would be smartly carried out on any person or persons reckless enough to harbour or assist Australian, New Zealand or British troops. Little imagination was necessary to see our lot was not a happy one.
>
> But it takes more than propaganda and threats to unsettle the sturdy northern Greeks who have a long history of being overrun, and they seem to take it all in their stride.

When they did get to a little village on the coast below Volos, they were welcomed and fed by the villagers and guided to a tiny isolated Greek Orthodox church out of sight of the village to get a night's rest. As well as some more Australian troops, there were a few refugees who'd come from Yugoslavia. The local mayor, speaking in halting English, showed them the grave of a British fighter pilot who had been buried near the church by the locals the day before. They took the pilot's few papers and personal belongings into safekeeping.

A barge powered by a diesel motor lay at the wharf below and it was decided to make a recce out to the island of Skiathos, which was only about 8 miles off the coast. The date was 25 April 1941, Anzac Day, and not far east of their location was Gallipoli from where Australian troops had also had to flee nearly a quarter of a century before.

> The trip out to the island was fruitless. A base had been there all right before the German planes got to work on it and now it was a deserted, wrecked mess of wharf and naval installations with not a destroyer, corvette or even a rowing boat to be seen. We went ashore and said 'hello' to a few local inhabitants, purloined and slaughtered a stinking billy goat which Tubby barbecued, stuffed some of the bones and other remains into our haversacks for further meals, then made back under cover of darkness to a church on the mainland.

The skies up and down the coast crawled with German aircraft during daylight hours, and they seemed to take delight in blowing anything out of the water which floated—especially if it contained an Allied crew. Deciding discretion was the better part of valour, Clift's group commandeered sufficient fuel for the diesel boat and travelled down the east coast between dusk and dawn in the hope of picking up a British or Australian ship. The news over the Greek radio was that the defensive positions further south at Brallos Pass had been overrun and all Commonwealth troops were evacuating the mainland.

Nearing Chalcis they pulled in at dawn and decided, because of the condition of the vessel, they would have to continue on foot.

> A continuous loud drone unlike anything I had ever heard came from the north and wave after wave of assorted German military aircraft passed in majestic formation above us. I estimated that over 1000 aircraft were involved in a show of regal pageantry and power, designed, no doubt, to intimidate the Greeks who had already capitulated, and the evacuating forces. We felt helpless with rage on hearing the bombs 'crumping' away on the people who had already surrendered and we could have cheerfully wrung the neck of every fat-arsed Hun pilot sitting aloft immune from any battle danger. It goes without comment that we the forces of the Navy were fair game but this did

not apply now to the Greeks, either civil or military. They were obviously copping a lot of belated Teutonic spleen.

Chalcis was not yet occupied but they skirted the town, as any military movement seen from the air would have brought a wave of Stukas on their erstwhile allies. Dodging all the main roads, while heading south towards the Gulf of Corinth, they had two scouts alternating well ahead, while three or four acted as a rearguard.

On the second day the scout signalled to them to halt and take cover. Into view, roaring down the track, smothered in dust, came three armoured scout vehicles. Every weapon of the group was trained on them from behind the pine trees as they came to a halt. Happily these vehicles were driven by New Zealanders who had come looking for the Australians after a civilian Greek scout car, which had been travelling from Chalcis, reported their position. They were invited to climb in smartly, as the road ahead was about to be cut.

> We clung all over those vehicles while they made it post-haste back from whence they came. We arrived at a railway siding—the rail and rolling stock further north were now in enemy hands so troops were advised to entrain. Shortly after boarding, our old steam rattletrap took off south crammed with a hodge-podge of military personnel. The smoke from its stack soon 'drew the crabs' and a burst of machine gun fire from the air along the carriages brought everything to a halt. The Greek driver took to the scrub leaving us to our own devices. Fortunately we had a 2/1st Sapper aboard. To him, driving trains was old hat, so off we puffed away leaving our original driver to whatever fate awaited him.

Their destination, the Gulf of Corinth, was a welcome sight. Some hundreds of troops were on the beach, waiting for the safe cloak of darkness and for the craft which would evacuate them. Shortly after dusk, the Australian destroyer *Stuart* was spotted in close, with the larger bulk of the RAN cruiser *Perth* standing further out in deeper water. 'We felt bitter about leaving our Greek friends and in some respect and in some inexplicable way we felt as though we had deserted them. It was very late that night when the warships took off on what was the last of their many ferry trips between Greece and Crete where our lords and masters believed we still had a chance against the invading Germans.'

How things had changed. As dawn broke and after a good night's sleep, dinner and breakfast, the rescued Australians were feeling a lot more chipper after all the attention of their navy mates. They were well on their way south towards Crete when they were spotted by seven German Stuka dive bombers, which came down in their familiar pattern, follow the leader style, ready to attack.

> The deck was full of troops, the pom-pom navy gunners were ready and every digger had 'one up the spout' and a full magazine in rifles or Bren ready to greet our unwelcome visitors. The Bren gunners rested the legs of their gun in two of their friends' tin hats, the ship's mate further assisting by grasping the legs of the gun to steady it while the gun fired and traversed. The drill for troops combating a dive bomber was to wait until a Stuka aircraft dropped its stick of bombs which occurred at the conclusion of its dive, when the belly of the bomber turned up and was exposed. It was then that it was most vulnerable to pom-pom or small arms fire. Rapid fire right into its guts, aiming 12 degrees off, was the order of the day for all hands including the cook.

The skipper of the *Stuart* was a very cool customer and he clearly had a lot of experience evading the Luftwaffe. His technique was to watch the dive bombers peel off, wait for the bombs to drop and as soon as they left the aircraft he would bark his commands, 'hard to port' or 'hard to starboard', to the helmsman who then swung the wheel with all his might, the *Stuart* keeling over, cutting through the water at full bore like a speedboat. The skipper made his ship an elusive target.

Two Stukas were hit, one coming down into the sea without any sign of smoke or flame. Clift thought it must have been small arms fire which killed the pilot. Another Stuka made for the mainland, trailing a plume of smoke as a result of *Stuart*'s ack-ack guns. 'We revengeful types hoped the bastard wouldn't make it. None of their bombs came close enough to do damage to the ship—a great tribute again to the skipper because they dropped a stick of four bombs apiece. *Stuart* was not molested further and we arrived in Suda Bay, Crete.'

Before disembarking, they arranged for navy sailors to send cables to their families when they reached Alexandria, informing them the troops had been evacuated from Greece safely. The sailors refused to take cash to cover costs, and recorded all the names and addresses of the people they were given. Clift later knew of no instances when the telegrams were not delivered.

'No wonder the AIF loved the Royal Australian Navy!'

Chapter 8

OUT OF THE FRYING PAN INTO THE FIRE

Under the circumstances, the withdrawal of Commonwealth troops from Greece was a very credible effort despite the final chaos of what had been an utter military disaster. The total number of servicemen taken aboard navy ships in a whole series of embarkations was 50,662. In the fighting for Greece, British Commonwealth forces lost 903 killed, 1250 wounded and 13,958 captured, while the Greeks suffered 13,325 killed, 62,663 wounded and 1290 missing.

Blamey and his staff planned the withdrawal with great skill. Generals Ivan Mackay and Bernard Freyberg, both sage and cool military veterans, maintained firm and inspiring control of the fighting formations holding back the Germans to enable so many troops to leave safely. The skill and competence of the British and Australian navies ensured there were almost no casualties during the entire operation. The greatest military losses were all the vehicles and heavy weapons which had to be abandoned.

Not everyone was evacuated back to Alexandria. Those who drew the short straw were landed in Crete, another Allied military disaster in the making—like Signaller Ken Clift. Private Bob Holt and his comrades from 2/3rd Infantry Battalion made it back to Alexandria after being evacuated from Greece, shortly afterwards taking part in the Allied invasion of Syria against the Vichy French in June and July 1941.

As in Greece, the fighting in Crete was brutish and short against overwhelming German forces, and was over by the end of May 1941. The Australian troops still in Egypt, Palestine and Syria were well aware of what was going on there, and summed up the whole Greek disaster with this verse, 'The Isle of Doom'. Bob Holt recalled the words:

THE ISLE OF DOOM (Anon)
Here I sit on the Isle of Crete,
Bludging on my blistered feet,
Little wonder I've got the blues,
With feet encased in great canoes.
Khaki shorts, instead of slacks,
living like a tribe of blacks –
Except that blacks don't sit in brood
And wait throughout the day for food.
It was a month ago not more,
When we sailed for Greece to win the war.
We marched and groaned beneath our load,
While bombers bombed us off the road.
They chased us here, they chased us there,
The bastards chased us everywhere,
And while they dropped their loads of death,
We cursed the bloody RAF.
Yet the RAF was there in force
(they left a few at home of course).

We saw the entire force one day,
When one Spitfire spat the other way;
And then we heard the wireless news,
When portly Winston aired his views.
The RAF he said in Greece
Are fighting hard to bring us peace,
And so we scratched our heads and thought,
This sounds distinctly like a rort.
For if in Greece the air force be,
Then where the bloody hell are we?
Then at last we met the Hun,
At odds of 133 to 1;
Though he made it pretty hot,
we gave the bastards all we got.
The little guns whizzed, the big guns roared,
We howled for ships to get aboard.
At last they came and in we got
And hurried from that cursed spot.
And then they landed us in Crete,
And marched us off our bloody feet.
The food was light, the water crook,
I got fed up and slung my hook.
Returned that night chock-full of wine,
And next day copped a two-pound fine.
My pay book was all behind to hell,
When pay was called, I said, 'Aw well',
They won't pay me now, I'm sure of that,
And when they did I smelt a rat.
Next day when the rations came,
I realised their wily game.

For sooner than sit down and die,
We spent our dibs on food supplies.
And now it looks like even betting,
A man will soon become a Creton,
And spend his days in blackest gloom,
On Adolf Hitler's 'Isle of Doom'.

From 23 April onwards, some 30,000 troops evacuated from Greece were landed in Crete. General Freyberg, who had arrived believing he was on his way to rejoin his division in Egypt, learned that most of it was in Crete and his job was to take command of all forces on the island and defend it against probable attacks by German airborne troops. During the next two weeks, the forces on the island were hurriedly reorganised. Some 7000 men were shipped to Egypt, leaving 15,000 British, 7700 New Zealanders, 6500 Australians and about 11,000 Greeks—who were largely untrained and poorly armed with only rifles.

Signaller Ken Clift disembarked in Crete in Suda Bay, from the British destroyer *Stuart* which had evacuated him from Greece.

Suda Bay was a shambles of wrecked ships, some listing and some sunk on even keel, and the wharf and shore installations had been given a very thorough pasting by constant air attacks. The British cruiser *York* had been sunk on a dead even keel and could be seen at the far end of the bay.

The story is worth telling. A boom covered the entrance to the harbour and this had to be negotiated through a pilot which guided the incoming vessel safely through a minefield by means of markers on shore known only to the navy. According to Clift:

> The Italians had devised attack craft much like a hydroplane with a draft of only a few inches to skip over a boom while travelling at high speed.

The forward portion was a warhead which detonated on impact, and the rear with a crew of two was designed to part from the craft once they were truly on target, the warhead speeding onward rather like a surface torpedo—leaving the crew floating on the raft-like structure at the rear to await whatever fate dictated. They had no provision for returning to base—who said there were no brave Italians?

We were told the two Italians appeared out of the blue, evidently dropped by a submarine, and after skipping the boom in their craft, went helter-skelter towards the British cruiser *York*. Pom-pom and all sorts of tracers were fired at them from both the *York* and shore batteries but the war-head made it to the *York*, which was well and truly hit. One of the Italians died of wounds, the other was taken prisoner. Because of his daring, he was made a fuss of and treated well although he had dealt a very nasty blow to the defendants. The loss of the *York* was a great catastrophe to the navy but only one of the many they had already encountered and there were plenty more heartaches to endure before they were finished in this neck of the woods.

The administration at Suda Bay was in a sorry state. Clift's unit were among the last of the evacuees from Greece. Food and ammunition was short on the island. Of the 16th Brigade, the only battalion fully operational was the 2/1st under the command of Lieutenant Colonel Ian Campbell, and German records show they gave the parachutists invading Crete a terrible trouncing. They were eventually taken prisoner only because of the capitulation of the rest of the forces on the island. Lack of ammunition, supplies and food forced Campbell to surrender his men intact as a unit—but only after the 2/1st inflicted very heavy casualties on the Wehrmacht.

Russell Reeve was second in command of Sixth Division Signals on the island. An excellent leader of men, Reeve set about getting the signals organised. Clift recalled: 'Even under adversity I always found him a cheerful officer imparting confidence because of his competence and understanding of the average soldier under his command.'

Clift had plenty of action to keep him occupied. The ship on which he evacuated Greece was the *Costa Rica*, a tramp steamer which was sunk by German bombing on the way to Crete. The navy came to the rescue with the destroyer *Hero* pushing alongside and bolstering her up while all troops were transferred before she sank. Only one soldier was lost when he misjudged the jump from ship to destroyer and was crushed between the two vessels. His body was recovered and buried at sea.

> Blue and I were camped alongside a low wall outside the Suda Bay Barracks. The whole waterfront was subjected constantly to air attack by bombing and strafing during the day although, unlike our time in Greece, we did have a modicum of ack-ack from Bofors guns for protection. The nights had been comparatively quiet, but on this particular evening, Jerry decided to give Suda Bay a night raid, and they did not do things by halves. The waterfront was bombed for several hours until well after midnight. Following dawn, Blue and I dubiously inspected a huge unexploded 2000 pound bomb, which came to rest within twelve or fourteen feet of our makeshift accommodation. If it had gone off, it would have been the end of us. Evidently, on the ground, the side of the bomb struck one of the many sangars [shore walls] alongside us, tilting the missile askew from the nose. They say it's better to be born lucky than rich!

The Aussie soldiers drew some pay in Crete in drachmas, as in Greece. Blue, Archie and Ken decided to sample what delights, if any, of the nearest city, Chania. It was a drab prospect, with not much to buy. Goods and food were much more valuable than Greek currency. However, they drank some retsina, the rough Greek white wine with the taste of pine resin through it, and munched away at some stuff which looked like popcorn without the sugar, talking over the pros and cons of the war with a Greek who spoke English with a pronounced Yankee accent. 'He claimed he had spent a long time in Brooklyn, New York, made some dough and then come back to Crete to retire, but "that goddammed fucking Hitler" had loused up his plans.'

Clift and his mates headed back to Suda Bay on foot in company with other troops who were in the same composite group. They were strafed along the way by a German fighter and dived for the olive trees by the roadside, but no one was hit.

While they were in Suda Bay they were plagued with body lice. 'Blue reckoned Archie was the first to get them, and passed them around. We tried everything to rid ourselves of these most annoying mites which gave us little rest, even soaking ourselves, uniforms and kits in the warm salty waters of Suda Bay, but to no avail—like poor relatives, they hung on.'

Blue, Arch, Tubby and Ken did a lot of foraging, even collecting and eating mulberries which were reasonably plentiful along the shore. The waterfront at Suda Bay was always 'interesting'. German bombers came over daily to drop their bombs. The ack-ack gunners on the hill would have a little duel with them as they came into range. It was fortunate that the cruiser *York* had sunk in the bay on a perfectly even keel, as the Germans gave it priority bombing every time, so giving the Allies some respite. Even from the air, *York* still looked serviceable and formidable, but she was well and truly on the bottom, deserted except for ack-ack crews who sent up streams of 'flaming onions' as the Stukas went into their dives.

On Crete, news of Rudolf Hess's flight to Britain, and subsequent capture in his abortive attempt to secure a peace not sanctioned by Hitler, came over the BBC. The Australians pondered the possible outcomes. 'But,' Clift said, 'the result as history shows, was sweet Fanny Adams, except Hess was spending unlimited time as a guest of his Majesty King George VI.'

The bombing raids on the island grew in intensity and there was constant heavy strafing by Stukas. The 2/1st Battalion was in Retimo under Lieutenant Colonel Ian Campbell, determined to preserve the vital airstrip nearby. The 2/8th and 2/11th Battalions were at Heraklion, and mixed groups of British soldiers and marines manned defensive points elsewhere.

The navy had repulsed sea landings, inflicting heavy losses on the enemy, but suffering themselves. An invasion seemed imminent.

Then, early one morning, they were alerted and informed that a small composite group comprising parts of the brigade, including Clift's own J Section, some of the 2/2nd and 2/3rd Battalions plus a few engineers, were to be evacuated. Why, they didn't know, but later discovered the reason. The 2/2nd and 2/3rd Battalions were so badly mauled in Greece that Sixth Division Headquarters had decided to bring them back to regroup, so retaining the nucleus of the 16th Brigade. The 2/1st Battalion was left in Crete practically intact, where they did a magnificent job under Campbell.

By the end of May 1941, it was all over. But the withdrawal of Commonwealth troops from Crete was not a repeat of the success story of the evacuation from Greece. The navy embarked about 4000 men, but when the ships sailed, practically all the 2/7th Battalion, the marines and commandos and some 3000 others had to be left behind. About 15,000 men in all had been successfully embarked from Sfakia and Heraklion. About 12,000 were taken prisoners by the Germans in Crete, including more than 3000 Australians.

In fighting units, the Australian force lost heavily—three full battalions captured. In the operations around Crete, the combined fleet lost three cruisers and six destroyers. Two battleships, an aircraft carrier, two cruisers and two destroyers were damaged so severely they were out of action for several months.

So, by the beginning of June 1941, Commonwealth forces in the Middle East were in bad shape. The decision to invade Greece had indeed been a very costly mistake.

Chapter 9

THE ALLIED INVASION OF LEBANON AND SYRIA

Australia's participation in the Allied invasion of Lebanon and Syria between 7 June and 11 July 1941 against the Vichy French is one of the least known Australian military operations of the Second World War, involving the Seventh Division and including elements of the Sixth Division.

Syria and Lebanon had been French protectorates since the Treaty of Versailles, and a pro-German Vichy French administration had taken over following the fall of France in June 1940. The Allied aim was to prevent the establishment of a German presence in Syria and Lebanon that could threaten British bases. And it was successful, despite a more robust defence by the Vichy forces than was expected. It was actually the first Allied victory in the long-running war in North Africa and the Mediterranean.

Shortly after General Blamey was impertinently farewelled by his loyal troops at Qastina after reviewing them on parade, Gunner Ivan 'Ivo' Blazely and his unit from the Ninth Division received their orders to move to Syria. The route was by way of Haifa, Sidon and up the Lebanese coast to Tripoli and then inland to a little village called Jdeideh—some 170 miles in all. With eight or ten others, Blazely made the journey on an open truck:

> The trip started off with everyone in good spirits, singing the usual bawdy songs with a few sentimental ones thrown in. Then as darkness fell and the cold began to creep into our bones, gradually everyone became silent, and started to wonder when we were going to get to wherever it was we were heading. When we arrived at daylight the next morning, we more or less rolled off the trucks stiff with cold, to be greeted by a reception committee handing out a rum issue—the first and last I ever got as a member of the AIF.
>
> It was pretty potent stuff too on an empty stomach. I had about half a pannikin which did me, but some of the more hardened drinkers went back for seconds and thirds and spent the rest of the morning very happy with the world in general.

The next morning after Reveille, Blazely heard cries of 'Washing George' from around the perimeter of the camp. These came from the Arab women from nearby villages who were doing washing for the Australians. They worked for a few ackers and as much soap as the gunners could give them. Their washing was taken away every morning and returned squeaky clean the next. None of it was ever mixed up and nothing was ever missing—their shirts and trousers were even ironed. 'Their method of washing was as old as time. They simply took it to a nearby river and bashed hell out of it against the rocks, a bit hard on the fabrics but the results were good.'

There was quite a bit of heavy drinking among the troops in Syria, so much so that Lord Haw Haw, the British traitor who nightly broadcast propaganda from Germany, said, 'We know the 9th Australian Division is in Syria but we are not worried. Leave them there six months and they will drink themselves to death.' Ivo said, 'Even our Commanding Officer was reputedly a bottle of whisky a day man so what hope for the rank and file.'

While the troops were at Jdeideh (near the modern city of Beirut) a couple of the local belles set up shop in the vicinity of the regimental headquarters.

> These girls were affectionately known to us as the Hollywood sisters. Here in the shelter of the olive trees they plied their age-old trade for cash or barter. What the cash price was is hidden in the mists of time but the barter rate was thus:
> Sex and two eggs change for a tin of bully beef.
> Sex only for a tin of goldfish (herrings and tomato sauce).

As Ivo explained, their rates were so cheap because they had no overheads in the way of rooms or cots. Their entertaining was confined to the ground under the olive groves.

Tasmanian Gunner Clarry McCulloch, from the Sixth Division 2/1st Battalion, took part in the Syrian campaign too. The Allied force was rather a mixed lot, made up roughly as follows: part of one British cavalry division, which to McCulloch's amazement contained a yeomanry regiment (equivalent to Australian Light Horse units); one Indian infantry brigade; the Free French–supplied six infantry battalions, mostly North African troops; some artillery and a handful of tanks. Australia's contribution was the Seventh Division less one brigade which was still in Tobruk; and last but not least was the 2/3rd Machine Gun Battalion, without whose assistance, Clarry believed, victory may not have been achieved.

> A and my C company were to be attached to the Indian Brigade, together with a couple of British battalions of the Free French. On 14 June C Company left camp and headed for Damascus. Yes, we too took the road to Damascus. If not in the footsteps of that biblical bloke, Paul, certainly in the footsteps of countless armies of soldiers who had marched up and down through this land over the past 5000 years or more.

On 15 June, the C Company convoy headed north, wending its way past such historical sites as Nazareth. As with all army convoys there were lots of unexplained stops along the way, probably caused by the lack of official maps. Clarry realised that the only map that his commander had was a crudely hand-drawn sketch on a scrappy piece of paper.

They had expected to camp at Ar Rama overnight and leave early the next morning but, just on dusk, orders arrived to pack up and move on once more. Their destination this time was a crossing over the Jordan River between Lake Hula and the Sea of Galilee. The actual crossing was known as the Bridge of Jacob's Daughters—not the original structure, but the area had been a crossing point for thousands of years. Later they entered the Jordan Valley, which was a nightmare. As the day wore on, the temperature rose rapidly and by midday was well over the century mark. They learned that a battalion of Royal Fusiliers had gone up to the Golan Heights earlier and had occupied the town of Kuneitra. They had been attacked almost immediately by a Vichy French force supported by artillery and many tanks. Later, they were told, the Vichy French had captured the town when the Fusiliers ran out of ammunition. With 400 of their battalion dead in the town and surrounded by tanks, they had no alternative but to surrender.

All this was confirmed by a Fusiliers officer who had escaped. Colonel Arthur Blackburn ordered C Company, together with the two anti-tank guns, to proceed to the area of Kuneitra and occupy a suitable position to assist any attack which might take place when more troops arrived. They found a suitable ridge about a mile and a half from the town where they swung their trucks off the road, and in a matter of minutes the twelve Vickers guns were set up without a hitch. Peering over the ridge, they could see the town sitting out in the middle of a large, flat plain.

McCulloch recalled: 'Naturally everyone was a bit edgy, this being our first taste of action. Later, our platoon sergeant George Lush said that obviously our long hours of training had not been wasted after all! Our range-takers then got to work and in a few minutes we had accurate ranges to all the obvious target areas.'

Kuneitra was quite a substantial town with a tall minaret rising from a mosque in the middle. From their position they could see no troop movements of any significance. During the afternoon, in an effort to get some response from the enemy, Colonel Blackburn took a truck out onto the plain and 'did a few wheelies' to see what would happen. The Vichy French were not to be drawn, so he returned to the ridge and they waited for the other troops to arrive.

A battery of artillery arrived and set up their 25-pounder guns, and finally at 5 pm they were told that a British battalion had joined them and the attack would commence as soon as they were all in position.

At 7 pm a smoke shell fired by the artillery started the ball rolling on the first of three waves of the British soldiers as they emerged onto the plain to the right of C Company and began their steady advance. The artillery with C Company's Vickers guns immediately went into action and gave covering fire on the selected targets.

> Because of the extra range of our Mark VIII ammunition we were able to fire on the enemy artillery positions, which must've made life rather interesting for them. Twelve Vickers guns each with a firing rate of 600 bullets per minute can put down a fairly impressive volume of fire.

> A few stray shots and the occasional anti-tank shell came our way but most of the enemy fire was concentrated on the infantry. Naturally we all had a few butterflies in the tummy at first, but were soon too busy to worry much.

In two hours it was all over, as the Vichy troops withdrew and headed for Damascus. As C Company drove into town, there was plenty of evidence to show that a war had been in progress. A tank was still burning fiercely, there were smashed and overturned vehicles of all kinds, dead horses and broken equipment everywhere, but no sign of dead soldiers. They presumed that the Vichy troops had taken them, along with their wounded and the 160 prisoners from the Royal Fusiliers.

Most of the day was spent sifting through all the abandoned Vichy army equipment to find things which could be of use. C Company had left Palestine still short of some equipment so items like camouflage nets for the trucks, entrenching tools and spare water containers were quickly snapped up. The drivers were delighted to find plenty of quality tools for maintaining their trucks, as all theirs had been stolen from their vehicles in Egypt before they had arrived at Kuneitra.

The next morning C Company loaded up their trucks once more and headed towards Damascus. A Free French force which had been advancing towards Damascus was held up about 15 miles from the city and C Company were ordered to give them support. When C Company caught up with them, they found the mainly North African Colonial troops were 'a bit reluctant to press home the attack'. According to McCulloch, 'A rather strange situation then developed.'

Contrary to the accepted usage of machine-gunners, they were ordered to dash forward about 300 yards, deploy their guns on either side of the road and lay down covering fire until the infantry caught up. The same process would then be repeated. They received a modest dosage of small arms and artillery fire, but nothing very serious. That continued until dusk, when it was decided to cease the advance, so they moved out to give cover to the right flank.

> At one stage a platoon of Senegalese troops came past us. They were all over six feet tall, but we found it very strange that nearly every man carried his boots slung around his neck. Their feet must've been like iron, because the country around us was rocky. One of them had one arm in a sling, while over his other shoulder he carried a heavy anti-tank rifle.
>
> These rifles were very accurate, but had a tremendous recoil when fired and if not handled properly could be quite dangerous to fire. It seems this chap had been careless earlier and had had his collarbone broken, so when they reached us he came over and asked if we would like to have the offending rifle. We jumped at the offer and later were able to put it to good use.

Next morning the Free French troops had moved up and were fighting in the wooded area on the southern side of Damascus. C Company gave them covering fire from a ridge overlooking the city.

> What a marvellous vision it was. Nestled in a beautiful green valley surrounded by lush orchards and vineyards, it was a sight for sore eyes after the bare, stony, desolate country we'd come through earlier.
>
> About just before noon, 11 Platoon was in position beside the road when a convoy of cars came out from Kuneitra carrying a large white flag. This was the Mayor and other city officials coming to say that the Vichy troops had declared it an open city and therefore we were welcome to enter. Colonel Blackburn and a Free French brigadier general met the delegation and our commanding officer called out to my section, which was the closest, to mount our guns on our truck and follow him. The rest of 11 Platoon and two anti-tank gun

> crews who were nearby also joined the party, and in a few minutes we were following the official party down the road leading to the city. We were not yet certain it was not a trick so we were ready for anything. Colonel Blackburn and General Casseau received the keys of the city and all was recorded for posterity by a Cinesound camera crew who happened to be in the vicinity!

The main Vichy forces in the area had taken up positions on the rocky hills to the north and west of Kuneitra. They had plenty of artillery and tanks to back them up and showed no signs of giving up the struggle. Their troops had been in Syria for years, knew the terrain perfectly and proceeded to make life very uncomfortable for the advancing Australians.

By mid-June 1941 it was apparent that the pro-German Vichy French forces were going to be no pushover. The Allied advance into Syria was not going as well as had been expected. A decision was made to bolster the ranks with some of those Australians who had returned from the rout of the ill-judged Allied push into Greece. Private Bob 'Hooker' Holt, from the 2/3rd Infantry Battalion, was one of those called again to arms.

Some of the men in the 2/3rd had fought in Crete in the 16th Brigade Composite Battalion. When Crete was evacuated these men returned to the battalion with a trickle of ex-prisoners of war who had escaped the island by barge, boat and submarine. Some doubtless had hair-raising stories to tell but had been sworn to secrecy, and some of them were given the opportunity of transferring from the battalion to a non-combatant unit.

The Seventh Division had been battling with the Vichy French in Syria since early in the campaign and judging by the newspaper reports and rumours, things were not going all their own way. There were rumours in camp about a move for the battalion. Holt recalled, 'One of our companies had already gone to Syria to act as a Town Garrison, when the news broke.'

The 2/1st Infantry Battalion had had a rough time on Crete and only a handful of men had returned to Egypt. Holt was told that 100 veterans from both the 2/2nd and the 2/3rd Battalions were to be transferred to build up the numbers of the 2/1st. This caused a great deal of heart burning as long-serving mates were split up and transferred.

On 18 June the 400 men selected from the battalion left Julis and entrained at Majdal into cattle trucks. They stopped at Haifa for a short time and managed to talk to some Afrika Korps prisoners of war. They had been captured at Tobruk, but as Holt said, 'They were still an arrogant lot.'

Travelling in atrocious heat and packed like sardines on the bottom of a cattle truck was not a good start. Halfway to Deraa, the worn-out engine would not take the train up a steep incline. It took half the carriages up the mountain and was returning for the next batch of troops when its brakes failed and it crashed into Holt's train. 'This caused a number of injuries and an awful lot of swearing as we sorted ourselves out. We eventually reached Deraa which was the scene of an Australian victory over the Turks in 1918.'

At Deraa (which had a picturesque Foreign Legion–style fort on its outskirts) Holt and his comrades were told they would be going into action the following day. They boarded civilian Palestinian buses and travelled through the night. Holt spent hours with a rock chipping the plaster off the cast on his hand, broken in a fist fight a few weeks before. At daybreak they transferred into their own battalion transport and finished up on the open plain in front of Damascus.

> It was quiet, peaceful and pleasant, looking at the cool white buildings in the distance, even though I was suffering some discomfort with my injured hand. Our undermanned sections didn't worry too much about digging in—that is until the first shell came whistling over and

then we must've looked like a company of beavers. We had very few tools but if the incentive is there it is surprising just how quickly you can get under cover, even if you only have a tin hat and bayonet to dig a hole with.

The first of the incoming shells landed slap bang amongst the men around Company Headquarters, causing a number of casualties. Instead of hitting the deck and burrowing like a rabbit, one new reinforcement panicked and ran around squealing till someone knocked him down and sat on him. The shelling continued and this character was left to his own devices. He took off into the open desert and we never heard of him again. I often wondered what became of him.

Fortunately Holt had no more trouble with his hand and completely forgot the injury until he was asked about it months later at a Medical Board.

They were shelled on and off all day until they were pleased to see planes with red, white and blue markings fly over. Pleased, that is, until they started bombing them. They were Vichy French.

After the Druze rebellion in the 1920s, the French had built stone forts (each named after French commanders) around Damascus.

We were told we were to attack Goybet [a fort named after a French officer] that evening. When we started to move from the flat ground into the hills we were held up by a French machine gun firing from a post on the high ground beside us. Someone had deepened a shell hole for cover and Andy Anderson and I hopped into it. We shared it with three or four Indians and one massive, very dead Senegalese soldier with a mouthful of gold teeth. Andy and I had a Boys anti-tank rifle with us and we placed it on top of the hole. The Vichy machine gunner had the hole right in his sights and when we raised our hands above ground to shift the rifle, he'd spray bullets all around us. We would duck back under cover, while the Punjabis sat and giggled at us. These Indians were really strange and they spent their time sitting on the body of the Senegalese smoking and giggling amongst themselves. Thinking about it years later, I feel sure this was my first experience of pot smokers.

A clean, dapper English soldier came meandering down the hill, looking as if he was going to attend a parade someplace. We called out to him to get his head down before the machine gunner opened up again and knocked it off. He came over to the hole and we saw he was an officer and a very cool customer he was too. In a cultured accent, he told us chaps 'he had a job of work to do' and was in the process of doing it, 'doncha know old boy'. With a 'cheerio chaps' and the swish or two of his swagger stick on his leg, he went about his business, whatever it was.

Shortly after the British officer had departed, the battalion mortars came up and put the Frenchmen and their machine guns out of business in short order.

The company then assembled and, after a steep climb, lined up outside Goybet at dusk. The enemy weren't aware they were so close but when they were, they scurried and bustled about as the Foreign Legionnaires tried to close the gates of the fort. The barbed wire fence surrounding them must have been under construction, but although it was wide, it was neither high nor thick and had gateways through it.

'Wee' McGregor, Holt's company commander (who later in the campaign became second in command of the 2/3rd Machine Gun Battalion), gave the word and the company began to pick its way through the wire. The French held their fire until they were in the middle of the entanglement and then they blasted all hell out of them with everything they had, including rifles, machine guns and mortars.

I had just crossed the wire when someone bashed me on the thigh with the butt of his rifle. I turned to swear at the fellow for carelessness, then took another step forward and my leg collapsed beneath me. It was then I realised I'd been wounded. I just lay and waited for the stretcher bearers. These fellows were the unsung heroes of the war. They were dedicated men who would never let their mates down when the call went up for the stretcher bearers. They carried no weapons in the Middle East campaigns and were armed with an SB armband and Red Crosses on their haversacks. They saw the agony of their mates as they did their best at patching up some fearful stomach or shrapnel wounds on the spot. They were front-line soldiers without weapons. They were due to be hit sooner or later, yet they carried on in a welter of gore, knowing full well that their own turn was coming. They have my greatest admiration.

Two of them, 'General' Potts and Keith Boyd, came up. They were leaning over bandaging me, when there was a red flash and a roar and the three of us finished up in a tangled heap. A French mortar bomb had exploded underneath us and had blown all hands head over tip. Both the stretcher bearers were shaken but unhurt. However, I was hit for the second time with shrapnel in the left of my chest, and this wound was really painful.

Darkness had fallen and owing to the heavy French fire, the Allied attack had fizzled out. Jackie Searle, Tich Parker and a newly arrived reinforcement, who had been promoted to corporal, were the only men to reach the fort. They were alongside the wall of the fort with the Foreign Legionnaires chattering above their heads. 'What will we do?' asked the corporal. 'Shut your mouth, keep quiet and don't fire that bloody Tommy gun,' he was told. 'Okay,' replied the corporal and immediately let go a burst from his Thompson sub-machine gun. The startled Legionnaires threw grenades over the wall and fired furiously, but the three Diggers scampered away and remarkably none of them was hit.

The stretcher bearers were staggering along with Holt in pitch darkness as they headed back to one of the forts already held by the battalion.

There was no blackout in Damascus and it was curious to see the brilliant city lights on the flats below while men of a dozen different nationalities battled it out in the hills.

> I could hear someone following us and told the stretcher bearers. They couldn't hear anything and said I was imagining things. We started up again but I could hear stones being dislodged behind us and said so. We started up again and I cried suddenly, 'Stop!' They did and we heard the fellow following us take a couple more steps. They put me down and General Potts threw a rock in the direction of our follower and bellowed like a bull. The Frenchman or Senegalese, or whoever he was, must've thought it was a grenade and screamed and took off down the mountain. We could hear him for quite a while, yelling in some incomprehensible language while he was scrambling amongst the rocks.

After wandering round lost for quite a while, the stretcher bearers eventually found the fort they were looking for and everyone was pleased to get some sleep. The following morning the French started to mortar the fort and everyone barring the sentries went into an underground shelter. Keith Boyd and General Potts, the stretcher bearers, had gone out at daylight to try to find their company and while the mortaring was going on Bob Holt was lying, forgotten, in an outhouse with plaster coming down from the ceiling.

> French cavalry were lined up outside to attack the fort and arrangements were made to take me into Damascus and hopefully to a French hospital. The stretcher bearers carried me out under a white flag, past the Spahis with their flash uniforms and undersized horses. We made our way down the mountain and into the city, through a fair amount of shelling and past groups of soldiers of every colour and hue in a

wide variety of uniforms. Some were Vichy French and some Free French, but just which side they were on was anybody's guess. In all probability they didn't know themselves.

The position in Damascus was very confused and until the surrender of the city parties of men were fighting bitterly, battling it out against each other without ever knowing what the overall picture was, even what was going on half a mile away.

While B Company was attacking Goybet, another company had walked unopposed into another nearby fort, Sarrail, but at daybreak the French swarmed back in, causing a number of casualties and capturing the colonel and a group of Australians. A number of men who had been taken prisoner in the hills were brought into Sarrail and among them was 'Snowy' Parkinson and Sergeant Jika McVicar. An excited Vichy French sergeant punched McVicar to the ground and proceeded to kick him savagely. The French then took the other Australians out of the fort as prisoners under guard. Shortly afterwards the party ran into an Indian Bren gun carrier which sprayed the column indiscriminately, killing and wounding a number of both French and Australians. In the confusion, the men of the battalion disarmed their captors and returned with them to the fort.

Jika McVicar was very concerned about the welfare of the French sergeant who had used him as a football. He was delighted to find the Frenchman among the prisoners, alive and well. After Jika had a discussion with him he was still alive, but not so well anymore.

French armoured cars had been having things their own way in the streets of the city until they ran into some Indian artillery. Someone brought a couple of survivors into the aid post. They were in a mess with multiple wounds and what with their moaning and groaning and the French officer still spitting at me, I was more than pleased to be loaded into an ambulance and taken to the French Hospital in Damascus.

When the door of the military ambulance opened at the front steps of the hospital, Bob Holt was met by a beautiful nurse in a starched white uniform. She seemed enthusiastic about greeting an Australian soldier, had a look at his wounds and walked alongside the stretcher into the building. He was more than pleased and looked forward to a pleasant day. Once inside the front door that scene changed dramatically. Wounded were lying three deep around the corridors as Holt was carried straight to the operating theatre. 'They say a coward dies a thousand deaths and a brave man only once. I died about 999 times, as I lay beside the door of the operating theatre, watching the doctors dig shrapnel out of a groaning Senegalese without the aid of anaesthetic. I believe the hospital was very short of anaesthetics and were only giving them to Europeans.'

Bob Holt recovered from his wounds to be fit enough to join Australian troops to sail from Egypt in January 1942, bound for Australia.

After the capture of Damascus, parts of the Australian Sixth Division played a key role in the Allied drive on Beirut, the capital of Lebanon. The final significant action of the campaign took place at Damour for two days in early July. British forces then headed north to Beirut, with the Australians capturing Damour on 9 July.

On 10 July, with the Australian troops within 6 miles of Beirut, the British 7th Cavalry Brigade closing in on Homs and the Tenth Indian Division advancing into Northern Syria from Iraq, the Vichy French commander, General Henry Denz, sought an armistice. A ceasefire was arranged to begin at one minute after midnight on 12 July 1941. Two days later the armistice was signed at Acre on the shores of the Mediterranean, now in Israel.

Australian casualties during the fighting were 416 killed and 1136 wounded. Some 1000 Vichy French troops were killed during the Allied invasion in Syria and Lebanon.

Chapter 10

THE TIDE TURNS

When Italy entered the fray in June 1940, the war quickly spread to North Africa where its colony of Libya bordered the British protectorate of Egypt. On 7 September, the Italians began a land offensive. Their commander Marshal Graziani achieved early successes because of the sheer numbers of his invading army. The Italians captured the key port of Sidi Barrani and established a chain of fortified camps. But the British and Allied counterattacks launched in December 1940, led by General Wavell, quickly routed the Italians.

As the Allied armaments built up and as the Italians' dwindled, their forces retreated in chaos with so many thousands surrendering that this human tide actually impeded the Allied advance, making the movements of tanks difficult.

Hitler, enraged by the failure of the Italians, sent in the German Afrika Korps commanded by the formidable and brilliant General Erwin

Rommel. The 'Desert Fox' quickly adapted his tactics to a desert war fought in the open, with few natural obstacles and a small civilian population. He launched his first blow against the Allies in February 1941, taking the British by surprise, and with an audacious attack on the Sollum–Halfaya line on the Egyptian border. The Germans then captured the key port of Benghazi, moving on to besiege the other major port on the coast of Cyrenaica, Tobruk. So began a protracted struggle for supremacy in North Africa. The Germans were not going to be a pushover like the Italians and this would lead to the Siege of Tobruk, and eventually to the key victory by General Montgomery at El Alamein.

The Afrika Korps arrived in Tripoli in February 1941. Hitler's orders were that Rommel was to reinforce the Italians, and block Allied attempts to force them out of Libya. However, the limited extent of the German involvement was of only one Panzer division and later no more than two Panzer and one motorised divisions, as the Italians were expected to do the bulk of the fighting. But the Allied withdrawal of the majority of its most experienced forces in Syria to Greece meant that the relatively inexperienced replacements were ill-equipped to face Rommel's German armour.

Although Rommel had been instructed to simply hold the line, an armoured reconnaissance soon became a fully fledged offensive from El Agheila, east of Tripoli, in March 1941. By April the Allied forces had been forced back to the Libyan–Egyptian border and the Ninth Division was ordered to fall back on Tobruk and hold it in order to deny its port facilities to the Germans and to delay their advance—so gaining much needed time for defences on the Egyptian frontier to be prepared.

Australia's General Leslie Morshead was given command by the senior British commander General Archibald Wavell and ordered to hold Tobruk until a relief mission could be mounted. Morshead, a tough

Great War veteran, was known by his loyal troops as 'Ming the Merciless', and later simply as 'Ming', after the villain in the Flash Gordon comics. Morshead commanded an Allied force of about 20,000 men, including 14,000 Australians, four regiments of British artillery and some Indian troops, who were besieged from 10 April until the end of November 1941.

The British traitor Lord Haw Haw did them a favour by contemptuously referring to them as the 'poor desert rats . . . in a trap' commanded by 'Ali Baba Morshead, and his 20,000 thieves' in one of his Berlin-based broadcasts. With their usual dry sense of humour, the Australians immediately claimed the name as a badge of honour—even striking unofficial medals bearing the image of a rat. The metal used to make the medals came from a German bomber that the 'Rats' had shot down with captured Italian guns!

The siege was far from passive. The Australians attacked their besiegers whenever they could, gathering weapons and equipment from the briefly occupied Axis territory, often taking back prisoners for intelligence interrogation. The Rats also dug extensive tunnel networks and shelters to supplement their trenches for use when they were being shelled or bombed, which was most of the time. These tactics were personally orchestrated by Morshead, with the Ninth Division, 18th Infantry Brigade and supporting forces from various Allied nations. In so doing, Morshead decisively defeated Rommel's powerful early assaults. His tactics for the defence of Tobruk were later studied in officer training colleges all over the world as an example of how to arrange and conduct in-depth defences against a superior armoured force. An important element of this strategy was to conduct aggressive offensive operations whenever possible. It is said that when Morshead's attention was drawn to a British propaganda article titled 'TOBRUK CAN TAKE IT', he said, 'We are not here to take it—we are here to give it.'

One of the most notable single offensive actions by the Rats was a fighting patrol led by Lieutenant William Noyes, which stalked and destroyed three German light tanks, and killed or wounded the crews of seven machine-gun and eleven anti-tank gun positions and their protective infantry. As well they damaged a German heavy tank and killed and wounded 130 as they took a whole German outpost—mostly in their initial bayonet charge. Even more remarkably, the Rats suffered not a single casualty!

By July 1941 Morshead was convinced that his troops were becoming tired and their health was deteriorating—and in spite of his efforts, their morale and discipline were slipping. His view eventually prevailed, and in October, Morshead and most of the Ninth Division were replaced by the British Fourth Division. The Ninth Division moved to Syria to serve as an occupation force, as well as resting, re-equipping and training reinforcements.

The Siege of Tobruk marked a rare defeat for German forces at this stage of the war. For his role in the battle, Morshead was made a Knight Commander of the Order of the British Empire. His success at Tobruk was followed by promotion to lieutenant general and command of the entire AIF in the Middle East. Morshead, at the risk of alienating his British superiors, argued to keep the Ninth Division together in the face of British demands to detach individual brigades. He commanded the division through the Battle of El Alamein, where the Ninth Division's contribution was considered vital to the victory. During the battles, he regularly visited both the front and the wounded behind the lines.

El Alamein is 150 miles west of Cairo. By the summer of 1942, the Allies were in trouble throughout Europe. The attack on Russia—Operation Barbarossa—had pushed the Russians back, U-boats were having a major effect in the Battle of the Atlantic and western Europe was fully under German control.

Three major battles were fought around El Alamein between July and November 1942 and were the turning point in the war in North Africa. The Australian Ninth Division, led by Leslie Morshead, played a key role in two of these battles, further bolstering its reputation earned defending Tobruk during 1941.

The battles around El Alamein were critical. If the Afrika Korps got to the Suez Canal, the ability of the Allies to supply themselves would be severely dented. Their only supply route would be via South Africa—which was not only longer but a lot more dangerous due to the vagaries of the weather. The psychological blow of losing the Suez Canal and defeat in North Africa would have been incalculable.

The Allies pinned all their hopes on their new defensive position near the tiny railway stop of El Alamein. Here, the battlefield narrowed between the coast and the impassable Quattara Depression. Rommel, wanting to keep up the pressure, made his first attack on 1 July, hoping to dislodge the Eighth Army from the Alamein position and open the way to Cairo and Suez. But Sir Claude Auchinleck, Commander in Chief of the British forces in North Africa, resisted, and managed some counterattacks of his own. In early July, the fate of the whole campaign hung in the balance. Both sides, exhausted and somewhat disorganised, missed out on opportunities for decisive victories. Both drew back to re-organise.

On 10 July, before dawn, the Ninth Division launched an attack on the northern flank and managed to capture the vital high ground around Tel el Eisa. Rommel was caught off guard, as he had massed his main forces for his planned offensive in the south.

Tasmanian Gunner Ivan 'Ivo' Blazely was about to be in the thick of the savage, protracted and pivotal battles for Allied supremacy in North Africa.

His unit, the 2/8th Field Regiment, detrained at Kantara and some of the infantry were also there, with a few New Zealanders who told them what they knew. They said things up front were a shambles, 'which turned out to be the understatement of the year', according to Blazely. They had

had to fight their way out of Mersa Matruh where the 2/8th Battalion had been for some time the previous year. 'It was supposed to be a pretty good fortress. The Germans ran over it in 24 hours!'

After a meal they once more climbed into their trucks, destination unknown, stopping somewhere in the desert about 15 miles west of Alexandria to await the arrival of the rest of the regiment. The coast road, a narrow strip of bitumen, was choked with vehicles of all descriptions, heading east.

In the late afternoon Ivo and a couple of mates wandered over to where a few British trucks had stopped for the night—they were a workshop unit. They were so pleased to see Australians their cook said, 'Go and get your dixies chooms, and have some of the rice pudding.' Which they did. Then they asked the Brits what was going on, and a sergeant said, 'Fooked if I know. We got the order to retreat up near the border and we have been retreating ever since.' The Egyptian border was about 300 miles away. As night fell, the rumours were rife. (In fact, British, Indian and South African troops held the Afrika Korps at Alamein, but Auchinleck's Fourth Army had been badly mauled and demoralised. By the time the Ninth Division arrived, the Allied retreat had ended.)

'The enemy was supposed to be 30 miles up the road, over the next ridge, or behind us—whichever you thought was a fair thing,' Blazely recalled. 'We were however prepared and heavily armed with a rifle to about every sixth man, so we settled for the 30-mile story and bedded down for the night, which happily proved uneventful.'

After a couple of days a company of the 2/43rd Battalion, with some engineers, raided the enemy. They inflicted casualties and took prisoners just to let them know the Aussies were back in business. This was acknowledged by Lord Haw Haw, who broadcast from Germany that, 'Ali Baba Morshead and his 20,000 thieves had left Syria and moved to the desert.'

In August 1942, Winston Churchill was desperate for a victory as he believed that morale was being sapped in Britain. Churchill, despite his status, faced the prospect of a vote of no confidence in the House of Commons if there was no forthcoming victory anywhere. Churchill grasped the bull by the horns. He dismissed Auchinleck unfairly, and replaced him with Bernard Montgomery—who, like Auchinleck, stubbornly prepared for a counterattack his predecessor had planned. The men in the Allied forces respected 'Monty'. He was described as being 'as quick as a ferret and about as likeable'. Montgomery put a great deal of emphasis on organisation and morale. He said he spoke to his troops and attempted to restore confidence in them. But above all else, he knew that he needed to hold El Alamein in any way possible.

Rommel planned to hit the Allies in the south. Montgomery guessed that this would be his plan, as he had done it before. However, Monty was also helped by the people who worked at the top-secret code-breaking unit at Bletchley Park in England, who had got hold of Rommel's battle plan and had deciphered it. So Monty knew not only Rommel's plan but also the route of his supply lines. By August 1942, only 33 per cent of what Rommel needed was getting through to him. The Desert Fox was also acutely aware that while he was being starved of supplies, the Allies were getting vast amounts through, as they still controlled the Suez Canal and were predominant in the Mediterranean. To resolve what could only become a more difficult situation, Rommel decided to attack quickly even if he was not as well-equipped as he would have liked.

Meanwhile, Ivo Blazely's 2/8th Field Regiment gradually moved closer to the battle zone.

> A couple of days before we finally went into action on July 10, there were a few changes made in personnel. A couple of sergeants left us

to go to officer school and a couple of bombardiers were promoted to gun sergeants.

A troop meeting was held for gun sergeants to put them in the picture. While there, Sergeant Fisheyes intimated that he could do without me. One of the newly minted sergeants, a Tasmanian, said 'Well I'll have him.' When he left the meeting he came to me and asked, 'How would you like to come on to my gun?' I said, 'Anything to get away from that bastard,' and couldn't pick up my gear quickly enough.

On 9 June 1942 they moved over to the coastal section held by the South Africans, where A Troop spent the night near a British medium regiment's gun position.

On the morning of 10 July the 26th Brigade went on the attack, taking two ridges called Points 26 and 33 on the map. A heavy barrage preceded the attack. The 2/8th Field Regiment's role was to follow up the infantry to give them close support.

Blazely's A Troop moved through the wire at first light. There were a few shells landing away to their left but not close enough to worry them. A Troop took up their first position just north of the Quattara Road, which was a track running southwards for about 30 miles to the Quattara Depression. There were a couple of Italians near the site, one wounded, with his friend taking care of him. They were later picked up and taken to the rear.

After about half an hour or so we fired our first rounds, then the gun sergeants were called to the command post to be put in the picture as it were. My new gun sergeant Freddie came back with great news. 'Don't bother to put up camouflage nets or dig gun pits, only slit trenches—we had already started these—we won't be here long. Mersa Matruh in 48 hours', and more in similar vein.

This was the stuff to give the troops—the mobile warfare that we put in all that arduous training in the Syrian desert for. We were going to roll these Dagoes up like a blanket. On the strength of this information someone lit a primus to brew a billy of tea.

Rommel, however, had different ideas for the next five months. As a result A Troop changed position sideways, frontwards and backwards, but did not advance one yard through the Allies' own forward defence line.

Stukas dive-bombed the ridge in front about half a mile away, just far enough to give A Troop a grandstand view without any real danger to them. But that proved to be only a sighter, for in about half an hour the dive bombers came for them. This was Blazely's first baptism of fire. When the noise and dust settled down, he climbed out of his hole and reached for the shovel, having decided he could do with a little more depth. Up till then they had received no artillery fire.

> About mid-morning an infantry bloke came down the ridge in front, escorting a German prisoner. I asked him where he got him and he said, 'Out of a tank.' Anyway he was a fine looking specimen, tall and blond wearing the little Afrika Korps cap. The gun on the left of ours had a brew on, so they gave the pair of them a mug of tea. Meanwhile Freddie and a couple of others wandered over to find out how things were going up front. While they're engaged in discussing the situation we got our first taste of enemy shelling. About four rounds arrived together, wounding Freddie, and a young bloke from South Australia who hadn't been with us long. The prisoner showed a bit of judgement and took off at a gallop for the rear with the infantry man right on his hammer. Almost immediately the Luftwaffe put on a Stuka parade and we also got the command 'to take post', that is, man the guns, so for a time things got very hectic.
>
> The wounded were put into slit trenches until they could be evacuated. Freddie always gives credit to an officer we called 'The Beast' for sheltering him with his body while the raid was on. My theory was

that he was shoved in a slit trench, and the officer jumped in on top of him because there was nowhere else to go, but I might be doing The Beast an injustice.

Blazely recalled that one of the first casualties in the morning was 'Hampsa', a little dog belonging to one of the battery officers. The dog took cover under a truck during an air raid, but unfortunately for him the truck was loaded with mines. 'When it went up so did Hampsa. It was rumoured that the essential parts of his reproductive system landed just outside the forward defence line, where the infantry—thinking it was an anti-personnel bomb—tried to explode it with small arms fire.'

As the day wore on, A Troop gave up the idea of mobile warfare, so camouflage nets went up in between firing at counterattacks, and they started to dig gun pits. The gun crew found the quickest way to get a bit of depth was to stack the empty ammunition and shell case boxes on top of one another and fill them with sand.

The rest of the day was spent in firing and digging in and sometimes when they weren't manning their gun and the enemy shells were too close for comfort, they were stretched out 'like lizards drinking' on the floor of the gun pit.

Blazely said that once they had a reasonable gun pit constructed, the slit trenches were never used. 'There always seemed to be a bit of comfort having someone alongside you when under fire.' Another thing they discovered was that while they could man the gun under shell fire, everyone went flat once the bombs started dropping. He couldn't help but admire the crew on the Bofors gun close behind them. 'You could always hear them popping away all through the air raids—that is, until they were all wiped out one morning.'

When night fell, things quietened down and the guns were laid on defensive lines. That is, on pre-arranged targets, to be fired in case of a night attack or if the infantry put up an SOS signal. This would be a system of coloured flares, for example, red over green over red. This order was changed periodically. 'And so ended the first day, a fairly long and hard one but only just a taste of the weeks to follow.'

The next morning they stood to at first light, gave the gun a pull through, cleaned the firing mechanism and breech block, and ate a hearty breakfast of bully beef and biscuits washed down with a mug of black tea, ready for the day's events.

The pattern of the second day was very much the same as the first. Firing on enemy counterattacks, digging in and dodging 'Stuka Parades'. By this time the German artillery seemed to have A Troop pretty well located. 'How they didn't score more hits on us I'll never know. They dropped shells so consistently on the gun on our left, they got permission to move to our right thus becoming Number One gun on the site. This had bad results as they took a direct hit, killing the Sergeant, Griff, and wounding one of their gunners, Steve, the gun layer.'

Often through the day British fighter planes would return from sorties, flying low about 300 feet up, waggling their wings so the ack-ack could see the British markings and hold their fire. On one occasion some came over not long after an air raid and were fired on, but fortunately none were hit. The reason for flying low was that they were out of ammunition, and by flying low could not be dived on from above.

> At daylight on the third morning in answer to a call of nature I grabbed a shovel and headed for the area to the rear of the gun. There hadn't been time to dig latrine pits, everybody disposed of his own waste in a hole in the sand. I went a decent distance back behind the command post and not far from the Bofors gun position.
>
> I hadn't been there long when I was joined by a command post signaller with the same idea. It was a bit misty and as we squatted there we could hear planes' engines, but didn't take all that much notice until my mate Peter sang out, 'Geez Tassie, look out!' Out of the fog and

heading straight for the gun position were about twenty plus bombers. The Bofors guns opened fire immediately while Pete and I, being literally caught with our pants down, had no time to get back to cover. So we made the best use of a couple of wheel ruts where a truck or a tank had been bogged. When the raid was over we stood up and shook a bit of loose dirt off, asked each other if they were all right and made our way back to the gun position. The Bofors gun was put out of action and towed away. I found out later all the crew of nine had been killed or wounded. What helped Peter and I was that the ground in this area was more or less a salt flat, which meant the bombs went deeper into the ground which helped nullify the effects of the blast somewhat.

Through the morning we tried the idea of dropping one of the crew in turn off for a rest for an hour or so. When my turn came, I gave it away after ten minutes or so. I found lying in a slit trench with a groundsheet over the top for a bit of shade, with the temperature above the hundred mark and sand falling in on you every time the gun went off—plus the flies found you after about two minutes—wasn't my idea of relaxation. Better to be back at the gun with something to do. The rest of the crew agreed.

On 15 July Rommel's forces made their last big effort to break through on the coastal sector—or at least push the Australians off the two ridges they held at Points 26 and 33.

They put in three major attacks that afternoon with infantry, tanks, high-level bombers, artillery and in fact everything except the kitchen sink. I reckon if they had one handy they would have used that too. They had A Troop pretty well tapped with artillery, no one stuck his head up any more than absolutely necessary. Cliff our layer used to go through the sequence of laying the gun, then get off the seat and crouch down with his hand on the trigger. I was loader and I can

> assure you I wasted no time after shoving a round and shell case up the breech, before getting down—if only for a second or two. The range gradually kept dropping, and just before dark we got the order, 'Prepare for tanks'. Down came the camouflage nets so as to give us a 360 degree field of fire and out came the armour-piercing shells. Fortunately we didn't have to use them.
>
> Some tanks got through the forward defence lines and headed our way but didn't have any infantry with them. One of the observation post Diggers told me they got to within about 400 yards, then what was left of them came in with their hands up. Besides, by this darkness had fallen, and tanks are pretty blind in the dark so they headed back whence they came minus a few of their number knocked out by our gunfire.
>
> There was hardly a smoker on the gun but we all had a cigarette going, and handing them to Cliff who was using them as a light to see the air-bubbles on the dial sight.

Their last rounds that night were fired at a range of 1200 yards. Finally things quietened down about 9.30 pm. As a parting gesture the enemy artillery dropped a salvo of shells on their position, these killing a sergeant and wounding a gunner on the gun that had shifted position to their right. The official tally for the day was ten tanks and 63 prisoners.

By now nearly everyone had a touch of the 'Gypo Guts'—five or six times a day being normal. Cliff, who was doing a bit better than that, thought he might have a touch of dysentery. He reported sick and the doctor told him he would need a specimen. How could he arrange that, Cliff wondered. 'Shit in a tobacco tin,' he was told, and he did. According to Blazely:

> The specimen lay around in the pit with temperatures exceeding 100 degrees F all day, with the lid firmly on. The next morning Cliff fronted at the Regimental Aid Post which was a fair lump of a tent dug in about four feet or so, and very hot and stuffy.

'I brought you that specimen, doc,' Cliff said, opening the tin.

'Get it out, get it out,' yelled the Medical Officer following his own advice and heading for the fresh air.

I don't think the specimen was ever tested.

As it turned out, Cliff didn't have dysentery, only an extra bad attack of the runs. He reckoned he'd never seen the regimental aid post staff move so fast.

By this time, Cliff had done a bit of scrounging and was the possessor of a Breda light machine gun and a medium one, a Fiat, and plenty of ammunition for both. He rigged the Fiat to a tripod with a bit of wire and reckoned to use it as an ack-ack anti-aircraft weapon. Every morning at daylight Cliff would fire a burst to make sure it was in working order. This was all right for a few days, until one morning in the act of firing the tripod collapsed, and he couldn't get his finger off the trigger, and put a burst dangerously close to the command post. His arsenal was immediately confiscated with dire threats of what would happen if he acquired any more non-official weapons.

On 27 July, the 2/28th Battalion made the last attack to try and take Ruin Ridge. Suffice to say, they failed. The whole battalion was either killed, wounded or taken prisoner. The only ones to return were the 2/7th Artillery gunners who, with their officer, were sent back in a Bren gun carrier to take a message to headquarters to clarify the situation. Their carrier was blown up and the officer killed. Blazely said, 'I don't think we took part in the initial barrage but I remember we fired a lot of smoke the next day to try and get them out, but to no avail.'

On the night of 31 August, Rommel made his last attempt to break through to Alexandria. This was at a spot about 30 miles south of Alamein called Alam Halfa. The Germans also raided all along the line including the Australian positions.

At this particular time A Troop was in a forward position about 600 yards behind the 2/43rd Battalion and a similar distance to the right of the 2/3rd Pioneers. They were close enough to see the infantry move for cover when the Germans put on their evening hate—a couple of salvos of shells on different sections of the line as regular as clockwork, about sundown.

> This night was a pleasant moonlit one and we managed to get a few bottles of beer from somewhere and our crew put in a very pleasant couple of hours having a sip. At about 12.30 am things got very noisy up front, with mortars, machine-gun fire, rifle fire—the lot. Up went the SOS flares and A Troop went into action firing on a pre-arranged area in front of the Forward Defence Lines. After about five minutes our gun went out of action. This was reported to the gun position officer who, with a stroke of genius that makes a born leader, ordered us to send out a 'tanks sentry'. So far no tanks had been reported up front, nor as it turned out, were there any.
>
> I was a popular choice, so I grabbed a rifle and headed out 50 or 60 yards and slightly to the right. By good luck I stumbled onto a slit trench, so I got in that and awaited events. I didn't have to wait long as Jerry opened up with artillery slap on our very own A Troop. A fair amount of this was falling in the area where I was, so much so, that a couple of times in lulls between salvos they sang out from the gun position to see if I was all right! The whole show probably lasted half an hour, though it seemed much longer to me. The Germans were beaten off and peace and quiet once more descended on the desert for a short time at least.

By the end of August 1942, Montgomery was ready himself. He knew that Rommel was very short of fuel and that the Germans could not sustain a long campaign. But when Rommel attacked, Montgomery was asleep. When he was woken from his sleep to be told the news, it is said he replied, 'Excellent, excellent,' and went back to sleep again.

The British had placed a huge number of landmines south of El Alamein at Alam Halfa. German tanks were severely hit by these and the rest were held up and became sitting targets for British fighter planes that could easily pick off tank after tank. Rommel's attack started badly and it seemed as if his Afrika Korps would be wiped out. He ordered his tanks north and he was then helped by nature. A sandstorm blew up which gave his tanks much needed cover from marauding British fighters. However, once the sandstorm cleared, Rommel's force was hit by Allied bombers that pounded the area where the Afrika Korps had their tanks. Rommel had no choice but to retreat. He fully expected Montgomery's Eighth Army to follow him. However, Monty failed to do this. He was not ready for an offensive and he ordered his men to stay put while they held a decisive defensive line.

Montgomery was actually waiting for the arrival of something that the soldiers in the desert could only guess at. In fact, they were Sherman tanks—300 of them—to assist the British Commonwealth forces. Their 75-mm gun shot a 6-pound shell that could penetrate a Panzer at 2000 yards. The 300 Shermans that Monty had were invaluable.

To face Montgomery's attack, the Germans and Italians had 110,000 men and 500 tanks. A number of the Italian tanks were of poor quality and could not match the new Shermans. The Germans were also short of fuel. The Allies had more than 200,000 men and more than 1000 tanks. They were also armed with a 6-pound anti-tank gun which was highly effective up to 1500 yards. Between the two armies was the 'Devil's Garden'. This was a minefield laid by the Germans which was 5 miles wide and littered with a huge number of anti-tank and anti-personnel mines. Going through such a defence would prove to be a nightmare for the attackers.

To throw Rommel off the scent, Montgomery launched Operation Bertram. This plan was to convince Rommel that the full might of the Eighth Army would be used in the south. Dummy tanks were erected in the region. A dummy pipeline was also built—slowly, so as to convince Rommel that the Allies were in no hurry to attack the Afrika Korps. Monty's army in the north also had to 'disappear'. Tanks were covered to appear as non-threatening lorries. 'Bertram' worked as Rommel became convinced that the attack would be in the south.

On the night of 23 October 1942, a massive artillery barrage signalled a huge Allied offensive. Although the infantry achieved most of their objectives, the tanks were unable to follow through, and Montgomery was worried that his offensive was becoming bogged down. Changing tactics from the drive to the west, he ordered the Ninth Division to switch their attack to the north. The Australians survived a veritable inferno of bombs, shells and bullets to push Rommel back, with British tanks striking a decisive blow on 2 November. His Panzer army had suffered crippling losses, and the Desert Fox was forced to order a general withdrawal or face total annihilation. Rommel knew that he was beaten.

The start of the Allied attack on Rommel was code-named 'Operation Lightfoot'. There was a reason for this. A diversionary attack in the south was meant to deceive 50 per cent of Rommel's forces. The main attack in the north was to last—according to Montgomery—just one night. The infantry had to attack first. Many of the anti-tank mines would not be tripped by soldiers running over them—they were too light (hence the code-name). As the infantry attacked, engineers had to clear a path for the tanks coming up in the rear. Each stretch of land cleared of mines was to be 24 feet—just enough to get a tank through in single file. The engineers had to clear a 5-mile section through the Devil's Garden. It was an awesome task and one that essentially failed.

Just one non-moving tank could hold up all the tanks behind it. The ensuing traffic jams made the tanks easy targets for the German gunners using the feared 88-mm anti-tank gun. The plan to get the tanks through in one night failed. The infantry had also not got as far as Montgomery had planned. They had to dig in.

The second night of the attack was also unsuccessful. Monty blamed his chief of tanks, Lumsden. He was given a simple ultimatum—move forward—or be replaced by someone more energetic. But the rate of attrition of the Allied forces was taking its toll. Operation Lightfoot was called off and Montgomery, not Lumsden, withdrew his tanks. When he received the news, Churchill was furious as he believed that Montgomery was letting a victory go by.

However, Rommel and the Afrika Korps had also been suffering. He only had 300 tanks left to the Allies' 900. Monty next planned to make a move to the Mediterranean. Australian units attacked the Germans by the Mediterranean and Rommel had to move his tanks north to cover this. The Australians took many casualties but their attack was to change the course of the battle.

Hitler ordered the Afrika Korps to fight to the last man, but Rommel refused to carry out this order. On 4 November 1942, Rommel started his retreat. Some 25,000 Germans and Italians had been killed or wounded in the battle and 13,000 Allied troops in the Eighth Army.

Ivo Blazely and his fellow gunners did have an occasional brief respite. As things quietened down, they hardly fired any rounds during the day as the lines were pretty far apart and any movement very hard to pick up. About once a week A Troop would move out at last light and take up a pre-arranged position a couple of miles from its permanent one to engage in harassing fire. This consisted of firing a few rounds at staggered intervals late at night or early in the morning. Blazely didn't know whether it harassed the enemy much, but it was not popular with A Troop as they got little sleep on those nights. At first light they would move back to their gun pits and wipe out the gun tractor tracks as best they could, to avoid giving away their position to the reconnaissance planes.

About once a week Bob the ack-ack gunner would be sent with a truck back to a big English canteen at Burg-el-Arab about 80 kilometres away. There was a collection and an order with Bob for supplementary rations, such as tinned fruit, tobacco, razor blades and even beer whenever it was available. He would hand the money over to the English staff and a chit authorising the purchase signed by such well-known officers as Lieutenant Edward Kelly or Captain R.G. Menzies. 'The Poms reckoned they must've been good types of officers to look after their troops so well.'

Each gun team sent a couple from each unit back to the engineers for a few hours when they could be spared.

> There we were taught the ins and outs of mines and booby traps. This was pretty interesting stuff. Our instructors were a pretty hard-bitten lot and knew this work pretty well. One bloke was a bit of a humorist and told a story of the party of sappers who were out in front one night laying a minefield. These were laid on a staggered grid about ten feet apart and as long and deep as are required. Sappers work as a team, some digging holes, the line of which was marked by tape on the ground. Others put the detonator in the mine and placed it in the hole and last of all came the NCO. In this case he was a sergeant who covered the mine with dirt [mines were filled in with the dirt being smoothed over by hand]. This particular night the sapper who placed the last mine in position, crapped on top of the loose dirt and then retired to a discreet distance to see what would eventuate. As the instructor put it, when the sergeant started to cover the hole there was a lot of loud swearing and much drama.

On one occasion a German plane flew over very high and dropped a lot of leaflets. The leaflets didn't land anywhere near A Troop, but they caught up with them later. One said, 'Aussies you are defending the Alamein Boxes but what about Port Darwin?' Another read, 'The Yanks are having a good time in Australia—and you?'

Blazely recalled that 'One day some of us got lucky and were taken to the beach for a swim. The Mediterranean might be a tideless sea, but there was a pretty strong undertow. I remember it knocked me down and put a graze on my back which turned into a beaut Wog sore, about the size of a shilling, which I carried for weeks.'

Water was short but not as bad as some of the previous camps and there was plenty of petrol for washing clothes, which was used on everything except socks. Singlets and underpants were definitely not in fashion in the desert.

> Some Pommy tanks came and camped near us for a few days. I went over and had a bit of a shufti. They could have their job, what with being battened down inside with temperatures over the hundred, and the gun recoiling past your ear-hole every time you fired it. You wouldn't want to be suffering from claustrophobia.
>
> When they left I found a container which I took to be water, a couple of gallons or more. A chance to have a real good wash, I thought. I poured about a gallon into a tin and reckoned to wash my hair first so I grabbed the soap and dipped my head in. I should have smelt it first as it was petrol. I must've had a pretty tough skull, for after rinsing it quickly with water, I suffered no ill effects except a bit of stinging for about an hour or so. Another time I found a tin I thought was petrol and started to wash my shirt and a pair of shorts in it. This turned out to be diesel. I hate being dumb.

To stop the troops getting fat and lazy, the officers started them digging alternative positions. One man per gun was dropped off each day, mostly in the afternoon. One day the driver of the truck that came to pick up the working party said, 'I've got some good news for you, Tassie, you've cracked it for four days leave to Cairo.' Ivo reckoned it couldn't have happened to a nicer fella. It had been a long time between drinks for him as far as overnight leave was concerned. He realised he hadn't actually had any, officially, since his final leave back in Australia.

When Ivo got back to the gun, he found that George was going too, possibly the only ones in their troop to go to Cairo. Two or three others were going to Alexandria. (As far as leave time went, Alexandria was thought to be the best deal as two days were lost travelling to Cairo and back.)

The next morning the leave party fronted at the regimental headquarters and got their leave passes and received the customary lecture from the regimental sergeant major about not going absent without leave or contacting VD and letting the side down. 'All this was duly noted and forgotten.' They boarded the leave train at Burg-el-Arab.

> There was a motley collection of troops there representing every Allied force in the desert, South Africans, New Zealanders, Indians the lot. There were even a couple of Yanks hanging around. They were members of some American technical unit, or what their actual job was I don't know. They were the only ones wearing their tin hats and someone said, 'You don't want to wear them if you go up near the front or you might get shot for a Dago.'

In Cairo the New Zealanders had a club with a good bar so that became the daily headquarters. Australians were the only others, barring their own troops, who were let in. Definitely no British, South Africans or any others were allowed past the door. 'The story went that a couple of South Africans were invited to have a drink with some Maoris, but said, "We don't drink with coloured people."' They never knew what hit them and were dragged out and dumped on the footpath.

The next day Ivo and George went to see the pyramids and the Sphinx. It was a hot day and they were both hungover, so did not go inside or risk climbing them—just looked. 'Marvellous what they could do in the days of cheap labour and no unions,' Ivo remarked.

He got another break early in October when the regiment was pulled out for a rest. But on the first morning out Ivo woke up with his right eye stuck shut and 'feeling as if half the Western Desert was in it'. He was diagnosed at the regimental aid post as having conjunctivitis and evacuated to a casualty clearing station. The tent he was in was reserved for more or less minor complaints such as eye problems and yellow jaundice.

There were quite a few infantry present so Ivo just lay back and listened to their stories. They were not exaggerating, it seemed, but just telling things as they were. One bloke told a story about a fight he was in when one of the section jumped into a hole with a badly wounded German. They both sat and eyed each other for a minute or two, then the German's pain got too much and he made a grab at the Australian, who thought he was being attacked and shot him. Afterwards remorse set in. The Australian told his mates over and over, 'I've never done anything like that before.'

The reply came: 'What do you think we were back on Civvy Street, a bunch of habitual bloody murderers?' Subject closed.

Ivo was finally transferred to the 2/7th Australian General Hospital, a few miles east of Alexandria. Here he was given a cup of Milo 'by a nice little VAD [a nursing orderly]', had a good shower and settled down to a relaxed time in the eye ward. But nothing was ever perfect as they weren't allowed to read and weren't supposed to go to the pictures.

After a couple of days when he got the run of the place, Ivo looked up an A Troop gunner who was in the ward that was reserved for those who had loved not wisely but too well. This was the happiest ward in the hospital. No sisters or VADs to disturb them with their fussing about. None of the inmates seemed too worried about their condition. As one put it, 'It's a bloody sight better than being shot at.'

On a later leave into Alexandria, Ivo and a mate thought they'd have a look at a bit of the mystic East's culture.

> After making some inquiries to a young 'wallah' boy who had tried to sell us his sister who, he assured us, was 'Very clean, very sweet, very hygienic, only fifteen, George,' he introduced us to a young man who could have been his older brother, who in turn for a negotiated price led us through some back alleys until we came to a house in the out-of-bounds area.
>
> There we entered into a small room with a fairly mature 'bint'. She immediately disrobed and biting us for two cigarettes, lit them and placed them in two of the more prominent orifices of her body. Then while they smouldered away she danced a more or less sensuous dance, accompanied by her male companion banging on a drum and wailing a Wog love song.
>
> After the cigarettes had gone out, she and her boyfriend then copulated before our very eyes. This act was known in the trade as a 'can-can exhibition'. After the act drew to a climax in more ways than one, we left, leaving the couple resting, no doubt preparing for their next audience.

By the time Ivo got back to A Troop, the big battle was just about over, and looking at his mates he could see he had missed out on 'a lot of bloody hard work'. A day or so before the end, A Troop went through the wire and took up a position near the coast road. The last of the Germans soon retreated and the battle was over, at a terrible cost to the infantry—some battalions having less than 100 men left. 'We as usual had been lucky, we had a fair amount of stuff thrown at us with very little doing any damage.'

Scrounging became the order of the day. Ivo was glad to have picked up a little knowledge about mines:

> When you got to within about 100 feet or so from a German position, you had to watch where you were putting your feet on account of S mines.

These nasty little bastards were canisters full of round lumps of metal like quarter-inch ball bearings. The S mines were buried with just three prongs protruding about an inch above the ground. When trodden on, and the foot taken off for the next step, a charge sent the canister up to about groin height, where another one exploded the container with very nasty consequences for anyone in the immediate area.

There were also some impromptu celebrations, as Ivo recalled: 'The night after Jerry pulled out, the infantry in front of us treated us to a regular regatta night display. They let go tracer bullets, Verey lights—anything that would make a light or go bang.'

This went on for quite a while until the German planes came back and dropped bombs and inflicted casualties, mainly on the unlucky 2/28th Battalion. Ivo woke up in the early hours of the morning to the sound of a hostile aircraft flying around in the moonlight, the pilot firing bursts at anything he could see. He hoped it would keep well away. 'It would be crook to cop something at this stage of the game.' But gradually the sound of the engines died away towards the coast and quiet reigned once more.

Because of Ivo Blazely's eye troubles and his leave in Cairo, he missed the climactic battles that Montgomery's Allied forces fought to clinch the victory at El Alamein.

Rommel became convinced that the main thrust of Montgomery's attack would be near the Mediterranean and he moved a large amount of his Afrika Korps there. The Australians fought with ferocity—even Rommel commented on the 'rivers of blood' in the region. However, the Australians had given Montgomery room to manoeuvre.

He launched Operation Supercharge. This was a British and New Zealand infantry attack made south of where the Australians were fighting. Rommel was taken by surprise. The 123 tanks of the 9th Armoured Brigade attacked the German lines. But a sandstorm once again saved Rommel. Many of the Allied tanks got lost and they were easy for the German anti-tank gunners to pick off. Some 75 per cent of the 9th Brigade was lost. But the overwhelming number of Allied tanks meant that more arrived to help out and it was these tanks that tipped the balance.

Events were starting to wind down for the Australians in the Middle East. The night the Afrika Korps retreated from Alamein, Ivo's gun crew was having a mild celebration, but no grog was involved. About 11 pm most were bedded down except Charlie and George, both of whom could play and sing a bit. 'After about half an hour or so, Captain Swivelneck arrived and put a halt to proceedings and returned to his doover [dugout].'

The two singers chewed over the injustice of it all, and then went over to where the captain was in bed and wondered if he would like a hand grenade to keep him company.

Swivelneck even made mention of it on the A Troop parade the next morning. To save face he treated it more or less as a joke, but Ivo could have assured him that he didn't know how lucky he was. 'Charlie was a wild man and George a good backstop.'

Charlie, Dusty and Ivo set off the next day to have a look around the area known as the Clover Leaf. This was a small mound where the Germans had had a muster of strong-points and machine-gun posts. They found among other equipment a lot of German stick bombs and hand grenades. These had about a four-second fuse. 'But Charlie had a nasty habit of tossing a stick bomb about 20 feet to the side and then saying run!' Which they did very smartly.

Charlie was also good at taking the gelignite out of landmines and making bombs to blow up fish with, not that we got many. They seem to be in pretty short supply in that area.

We found two bodies, not together, an Aussie and a German. They both looked to have been dead for some months. The Aussie was wearing sand shoes so obviously had been killed on a night patrol and most likely that Jerry had too. We had no way of burying the Aussie so we did the time-honoured thing of sticking his rifle upright on the ground and placing his steel helmet on top to make the job of finding him again easier. We cut off his meat tickets [identification discs] from around his neck and handed them in when we got back. He would be picked up later by the War Graves detail and placed in the Alamein War Cemetery.

The first day out we found a lot of flare cartridges. We found out that if you pulled the wick out of the end of these and set them up on end and lit the wick they shot up in the air and whistled just like a shell did. When we got back to the ridge just in front of the guns, A Troop was just beginning to line up for the evening meal. We lined up about half a dozen of these cartridges and lit them. Up in the air they went whistling like a salvo of incoming shells. There was much ducking and diving in the dinner queue as everyone was still a bit edgy. Later I heard that Lieutenant 'Snooky' said, 'He ought to have his ears boxed.' I've often wondered who he meant.

Some of the troops went over by truck to where the British tanks had broken through on the last couple of days of the battle. The area was 'a real shambles'. Here, in military parlance, enemy guns had 'fought to the muzzle'. British tanks could be seen knocked out half a mile away and right up to the gun positions. The Germans' 88-mm anti-tank and field guns had their pits full of corpses. Tanks were lying about on their side with their tracks damaged and turrets in some cases blown off. All the bodies had been lying about under the hot sun for a week or more and were on the nose to some order. Ivo remarked, 'I don't know who had the job of cleaning things up, but I was glad it wasn't me.'

Now and then the Australians would see an Egyptian on a camel laden with rifles and ammunition, probably on their way back to Palestine, getting ready for their own private little war with the Israelis. 'No one seemed to worry about them and just let them go on their way.'

Meanwhile, life in A Troop was about as good as Ivo ever had as a soldier—no parades, only roll call in the morning. There was plenty of beer and the odd bottle of Vat 69. The beer was mostly Canadian, fairly strong stuff with an alcohol content of around 6 per cent. 'I remember at this time none of us knew what the future held, whether we would move on with the Eighth Army, stay where we were or what.'

Early in December the regiment pulled out, heading east. The rumour mill had it that they were going home, but that was not to be just yet. The regiment moved in separate convoys. Half contained signallers and a selection of miscellaneous Diggers. The ack-ack gunners left one morning; the other half with the guns the next day. The area was left as clean as possible by using the scorched earth method.

The convoy Ivo was with pulled up that night at a place called Wade Natrun, nicknamed by the troops as 'the halfway house'. It was a staging camp with a wet canteen, so this called for another mild celebration. Next day they did a sharp left turn at Cairo, junking all the immediate rumours that they were going home.

> When the gun convoy stopped at Ismalia, a nice little town on the canal, Lofty, a tall dark gunner who had joined the Fifteenth Battery at Alamein, exclaimed, 'I know this joint.' He straight away bit the nearest sergeant who had money—Fisheyes of all people—for a quid, put as much tea and sugar as he could scrounge in a sand bag and headed in the direction of the town.

He caught up with the regiment back in Palestine three days later. When he fronted for being AWOL, the commanding officer asked him what his excuse was. Lofty replied, 'The convoy stopped and I went to answer a call of nature, Sir. By the time I'd finished the convoy had moved on.'

'It must've been a long shit,' mused the colonel.

'Fined five pounds.'

Ivo felt that made it a pretty expensive one, too.

Chapter 11

RETURN TO AUSTRALIA

Until the day he died in 1998 at the age of 91, Captain John Bowden, with the Seventh Division, believed that Australia's new Labor prime minister John Curtin had demanded that the British prime minister Winston Churchill return the Australian divisions to Australia from the Middle East when Japan looked likely to enter the war late in 1941. John Bowden, who was my father, said:

> If it hadn't been for Prime Minister John Curtin, I don't know where we'd have finished up. But he had his row with Churchill when Singapore fell in February 1942, and pulled the 7th, 6th and 9th Divisions back from the Middle East to defend Australia against the Japanese threat from the north. Anyway, thank Christ I still had my testicles and whatever intelligence I possessed, and these were the things I hoped I'd get back to my wife Peggy with.

Word got around the Diggers that there was a big move on back to Australia. It was known as the 'Step Sister' move, and the first to go were the fighting units, the infantry and artillery. The odds and sods like the schools and training units and some artillery schools were shunted down to a place called Nusarat, further down the coast from Gaza.

Well, it is too late to tell him now, but this has been an enduring myth. John Curtin became Labor prime minister in October 1941, and took the defence portfolio in early 1942. His two main lieutenants were Ben Chifley and 'Doc' Evatt, Minister for External Affairs and attorney-general. The new government did not immediately bring any new policy changes from Menzies' Liberals—and despite the increasing threat from a bellicose Japan, made no move to recall Australia's troops from North Africa and Egypt. Indeed, as late as November the government approved Britain's request for yet more Australian troops for the Middle East.

Reputable British historians, like Arthur Bryant, have aired the notion that soon after Japan entered the war, the Australian government began to demand the return of our troops from the Middle East. This was not the case. Churchill (with the prompt agreement of the Australian government) dispatched the Sixth and Seventh Divisions from the Middle East to the Far East, not to Australia.

In mid-February, when Japanese troops were storming down the Malay Peninsula towards the 'impregnable fortress' Singapore, and when one of the Australian divisions was at sea, it was proposed by the British government that it not be landed in the Dutch East Indies as had been planned, but instead in Burma (where the defence was then collapsing), but the Australian government insisted that it be diverted to Australia.

Soon afterwards, at the suggestion of the Australian government, two brigades of the Second Division were landed in Ceylon (now Sri Lanka) to strengthen the small garrison there. The return of the Ninth Division was sought by Curtin, on the advice of his chief of the general staff, in mid-February 1942, but the division did not embark from Egypt until early 1943.

Alas, part of the Seventh Division stopped off to defend Java on behalf of the Dutch colonial empire—the 2/2nd Pioneers, the 2/3rd Machine Gun Battalion and 'Weary' Dunlop's medical unit—who were all captured there and joined the Eighth Division as prisoners of war of the Japanese for the rest of the war.

Ivan Blazely and his 2/8th Field Regiment gunner mates were aware that the decision had been made to send them home. 'Christmas came and went. Everyone was starting to get a bit edgy as it was only a matter of when I scored seven days leave at a rest camp in Nathanya.'

Nathanya was a little town near Haifa which was used as a convalescent camp and rest centre. Those who went there had the option at night of either returning to camp or, 'if you struck it lucky', could stop in Haifa. There was no roll call, and the troops had more or less a blanket leave pass.

Back in camp, life was more or less pleasant with 'a minimum of parades and army bullshit'. Now and again they got an issue of beer tickets which were useable at Blamey House, an establishment in Gaza where you could get a feed, have an Australian beer, write a letter or have a game of ping-pong and other comforts. This place was named after, and for a time run by, the wife of General Blamey, commander of all the Australian troops in the Middle East.

> Charlie and I went one night to Gaza, had a few beers at Blamey House and after using all our beer tickets, went in search of some

> more refreshment. After finding this and getting a couple of bottles of plonk for the morrow, we ended up in a wog café sipping tiny cups of black coffee each smoking a hubble-bubble [hookah].
>
> Two or three days before the big move we were given booster shots for typhoid and tetanus, and also a short-arm inspection. Now we knew for sure we were due to go.

One morning they were issued with paint and brushes to put identification marks on their kit bags. Later that night Charlie mistook some yellow paint for the liqueur advokaat, and took a good gulp. The next morning he reported sick with a badly burned throat and was immediately hospitalised. As a result, Blazely said, 'He missed travelling home with us and came back with some other hospital patients on the *City of Bermuda*.'

The beer ration at Blamey House was modest to say the least. 'Hardly a day went by when there wasn't at least one in our tent in Gaza "running the rabbit" for more grog.' They drank practically every kind of booze that was available except a wine called 'alicante'—which was curiously banned. Late one night all that was left was some arrack, which they drank mixed with cold cocoa. 'Delicious! We should have copyrighted it.' Blazely added, 'This drinking caper was by no means confined to the *hoi polloi*. I always reckoned if you wanted to hear a mob of screaming drunks, do a guard near the sergeants' or officers' mess on grog night.'

Finally the big day came, and with it the order to pull down the tents and tidy the area. After the last night the mess tents and any permanent buildings were also taken down. The 2/8th Regiment were taken by truck the next day across the Sinai Desert, this time bound for Suez.

They spent the night under canvas, sleeping on the sand, before they boarded lighters that took them out to their transport home—*New Amsterdam*, a former Dutch luxury liner and a substantial vessel of 35,000 tons. Blazely was allocated his sleeping quarters and told he would be on permanent duty for the voyage as ack-ack gunner and submarine sentry.

'This was a real good number. My station was on the docking bridge, which is a long narrow platform that runs across the ship just in front of the main bridge. At each side of the bridge was a Lewis machine gun. These were manned at all times by a couple of other blokes.'

There was a permanent squad of British gunners on board but not enough to man the various guns full-time; beside machine guns there were some ack-ack guns of fairly large calibre. In case of trouble the Australians' job was to hold the fort until the permanent crew arrived. During the voyage the only time they saw the English gunners was once, when there was a practice shoot somewhere on the Red Sea. 'One bloke used to come around and clean and check the gun every morning, that was all. So long as you turned up for your shift on time, no one worried us at all.'

After the *New Amsterdam* was fully loaded, they headed down the Red Sea to where the rest of the convoy lay waiting at Massawa on the Eritrean coast. As the sun sank slowly in the west and the ship pulled away from the shore, Ivo leaned on the docking bridge rail and thought of the regimental bard's immortal words: *Arabs' heaven, soldiers' hell—bastard country fare thee well.*

The convoy consisted of the *Queen Mary*, *Il de France*, *Aquitania*, *City of Bermuda* and *New Amsterdam*. They were escorted by a cruiser and a couple of destroyers down the Red Sea, past Aden and out into the Indian Ocean.

After about five days sailing, they pulled into Abbu Atoll on the southern end of a group of low-lying islands, the Maldives. Now they are pleasure resorts, but then they were a naval depot and refuelling station, so secret that very few of the troops knew where they were.

There was a party of military police on board from the feared Jerusalem Detention Centre and various other field punishment centres. They were treated like lepers by the other troops. As they were all sergeants and above, they ate after the other sergeants had finished their meals. All the other units' sergeants refused to sit at the same table with them and they had to wait on themselves as the mess orderlies had declared them 'black'. The number of the table was 44 and a new phrase was started, when the number came up in a bingo game, 'Forty-four—all the screws'.

Ivo said that later, back in New South Wales, any Ninth Division soldier who was absent without leave after his homecoming, and banged up in the Holsworthy Military Prison, was asked which ship he came back from the Middle East on. If he said the *New Amsterdam* he was automatically bashed!

'The screws were mainly ex-crews and coppers on city streets, who carried on their city job in the army, with the added bonus of an overseas trip thrown in. Whenever they came on deck, they wore no colour patches or any other identification. If anyone would have been a candidate for shark bait, it would have been them.'

After about another two weeks of watching the flying fish by day the troops on the *New Amsterdam* arrived at Fremantle, where the ship pulled into the wharf to let the Western Australians disembark.

The next morning *New Amsterdam* pulled out and set sail east across the Great Australian Bight, towards Port Melbourne. Here the returning troops were greeted on the wharf by the band of the First American Marines Division, playing all the latest hits, most of which they had never heard. Ivo commented, 'I will say this, the Marines had a good band more like a dance orchestra than an army band.'

The 'Crow-eaters' (South Australians), Victorians and Tasmanians disembarked. The Tasmanians were taken by train to a camp near Seymour, where they were issued with food ration coupons and their leave passes. Then next morning it was back down to Melbourne to board the Bass Strait ferry *Nairana* for the short overnight trip to Tasmania, berthing at Devonport.

A sergeant Ivo knew, Claude, had his wife waiting for him with a car. He offered Ivo a lift home. Claude lived at Rowella on the West Tamar. They went home the back way and finally dropped him on cross-roads about 100 yards from his family's home at Winkleigh. Just as Ivo got out of the car, his old man came out of the house to collect the mail. 'I thought that was you,' was all he said.

'Sentiment never ran very high in the Blazely family,' Ivo wrote.

After being wounded and nearly losing a leg in the Allied invasion of Syria against the pro-German Vichy French army from June 1941, Private Bob 'Hooker' Holt of the 2/3rd Infantry Battalion, Sixth Division, was not unhappy to hear his unit was to return to Australia.

At Port Tewfik, early in March 1942, Holt's unit embarked on the decrepit English tramp steamer, *Laconia*. They called into Aden, but there was no shore leave and the ship sailed on to Colombo. The war news was all bad and this was brought home to them when they came into the harbour, which had just been bombed by the Japanese. The dock area was in a mess and lots of ships had been sunk and damaged. A small Royal Navy aircraft carrier, *Eagle*, was in flames and was being towed out to sea.

The *Laconia* had stores to unload and the troops aboard were transferred to the Australian ship, *Duntroon*. They did have a night's leave in Colombo and were accommodated in what was probably 'the flashiest hotel in Ceylon', the Galle Face, although at this time it was 'far from its halcyon splendour'. Holt observed: 'There were iron bars across the windows and the cashiers were plying their trade behind iron grills and the drunken soldiery roistered, where once the crème de la crème of Ceylonese colonial society disported themselves.'

On the following night Holt sailed for Fremantle on the *Duntroon*. Shortly after leaving port, the ship was hit with something that made her shudder from stem to stern. It was strong enough to throw soldiers off their feet, but they never did find out what happened. Next morning they were told that instead of sailing to Fremantle, the next port of call was Bombay.

The *Duntroon* was a far different ship from the overcrowded and dirty *Laconia*. It was clean and the food was first class. Holt and a mate, Bluey, wrangled a job in the galley and shared a cabin. The work was easy and they did not have to attend any parades. The Australians got on well with the crew and in general lived the 'life of Riley'.

> On arrival in Bombay we were given leave for the day. About half the troops had gone ashore when the message was relayed over the loudspeaker that all leave was cancelled. Military Police were posted on the gangway to see the order was enforced. Bluey and I went to the stern of the ship and borrowed a ladder from one of the crew. We climbed down to the wharf and then held the bottom of the ladder while dozens of soldiers, who had seen what we were up to, clambered down. We let the ladder fall to the wharf only when some of the Provosts attempted to use it. Bluey and I didn't stop running until we had reached the city proper.

Bombay was a city of extremes. Splendour for the British and ruling class, abject and abysmal poverty for the workers. It was strange to see women building-workers, with loads in baskets on their backs, climbing around tall storage buildings over rickety bamboo scaffolding. Because of their appalling living conditions in the teeming, squalid slums, it was no surprise that at least some of the Indians were very militant about British rule, and riots and demonstrations were by no means uncommon.

'Bluey and I decided to have a drink at the palatial Taj Mahal Hotel but were quickly disillusioned on this score,' Holt wrote. 'This establishment was very British. Pukka sahibs and officers only were allowed through the hallowed portals. There were hordes of exotically dressed flunkies pandering to the whims of the patrons, while a hundred yards away the common people were sleeping four and five deep on the footpath.'

They bought some ivory carvings, had a few beers and then a few more, and had a visit to the tattooist. Then they decided to have a look at the notorious cages in Grant Road. They dodged the military police and saw the ladies of easy virtue, who they thought could do with a bath and who spent their spare time going through one another's hair for nits, plying their trade from iron cages. 'They looked for all the world like monkeys, and after a quick look, it was unanimously decided we would leave and have a few quick cognacs. I eventually lost Bluey among the hordes of servicemen thronging the streets.'

Bob didn't have much money and to fill in time he decided to give one of the many houses of ill fame a good looking at. He didn't intend to indulge himself, but when a young lady grabbed him 'by the whistle', his 'good intentions went out the window'.

> In a few minutes I found myself on the footpath, broke, except for a handful of *annas*. I hadn't a clue as to where I was or how I would get back to the ship. I'm positive the majority of Bombay gharry drivers have second sight, for I hailed at least half a dozen before I got one to take me to the wharf. When we arrived at the waterfront I gave the driver a fistful of worthless coins. He bellowed like a bull and inside seconds had a great tribe of Indians behind him. They chased me right to the gangway of the *Duntroon*. I left it to the armed guard on the gangway to argue the point with a crowd of what I reckon must have been half the population of Bombay.

The *Duntroon* left India and steamed to Mombasa in Kenya. To get to the port the ship had to sail for miles up a river. The jungle came right to the water's edge and was full of chattering monkeys.

Holt's trip ashore was a disappointment. They saw a spread-out dusty town and even though this was a port for the British colony of Kenya, the offices of the Italian and German shipping lines appeared to take pride of place. During a leisurely walk around the town, Holt was unimpressed to see several cases of elephantiasis.

> My father had been in the New South Wales Fire Brigade since his discharge from the First AIF and I had lived on fire stations for years, so I decided to have a look over the local station. The firemen were black as your hat and had tribal scarring on their faces. Not one of them could speak English but we conversed in sign language and they were pleased to show me over the station.
>
> Walking back to the *Duntroon* I got into conversation with an English matelot and he took me on board his ship the *Ark Royal* where we had a sandwich, cocoa and watched a film on deck. We were not sorry to see the last of Mombasa. We sailed down the coast to Durban. There we saw a lady on the breakwater signalling a welcome to us with flags. It was the famous 'Durban Signaller', who had made a name for herself during the 1914–18 war, welcoming Anzac troops passing through South Africa. She was a wealthy woman in her own right and a poet.
>
> We tied up and I was amazed at the size of the huge wharf labourers and of the rags they were wearing. They appeared to be even more poverty stricken than the Egyptians.

The troops were disembarked and taken about 10 miles out of Durban to camp under canvas at Clairemount Racecourse. A chauffeur-driven limousine pulled up and the 'Durban Signaller' was helped to the top of the vehicle, where she addressed the Australians. Remarkably, she said she would be pleased to arrange accommodation at her home for any man who cared to stay with her. Holt didn't know what he would be letting himself in for, 'so I didn't accept her kind offer', and he was to later regret this.

> She arranged leave and accommodated the men in beautifully appointed rooms and a manicured garden. It was luxury living with a vengeance, with the finest food and drink laid on, the servants at everyone's beck and call. I have wondered since if this open-hearted generous woman ever received any reward or acknowledgement from the Australian or New Zealand governments for her mighty efforts on behalf of Anzac troops in two world wars.

For the first few days Bob and his mates went into Durban and 'plied ourselves with strong drink'. The city was full of servicemen of all nationalities and survivors of ships recently sunk by the Japanese, and drunken rows were common. Bob went to a picture theatre one night and the ceiling was a moving galaxy of stars. It was the first time he had seen anything like this until he went back a second time with less grog on board, to find it was an open-air picture show!

He was certainly well lubricated when he set off to return to camp one night, but woke in the morning at the side of a railway line miles from anywhere to find that he had been bashed and robbed. Bob felt better disposed to 'one friendly black fellow who went miles out of his way to take me back to the racecourse and I didn't even have a stamp to give him for his trouble'.

The Australians were not popular with the white Afrikaaners and this feeling was reciprocated. Holt thought it was degrading for both parties when he saw huge Zulus with their magnificent head-dresses pulling overweight whites around the city in rickshaws.

> The ex-battalion butcher Alf Jackson and I only had a few shillings, so we decided to have a tour around the suburbs of Durban. We got onto a tram and went to the terminal at the Valley of the Thousand Hills. There was a pub handy and we called in and put two shillings on the bar for a drink. The middle-aged barmaid came over and said,

'I probably served your fathers in the first war, so you better have a beer on me.' We downed our drink, put two shillings back on the bar and called for another. The barmaid filled our glasses and said, 'The fellow over there has bought these for you.' The fellow waved and we drank. The rest of the afternoon no one came near us or spoke, but every time we emptied our glasses someone would shout us another. At closing time we poured ourselves out of the pub and returned to camp.

The next morning I asked Alf where he was going, and he replied, 'The same place as you.'

They headed back to the same pub and the same procedure took place as on the previous day.

The Japanese naval presence in the Indian Ocean must have eased off, as the troops left the racecourse and re-embarked on the *Duntroon*. As the ship moved down the harbour, they passed the convoy which was on its way to the invasion of Madagascar.

After their convoy left Durban, it turned south. 'We must've pretty near gone to the Antarctic for the weather was as cold as charity and the seas were really rough until we made land at Fremantle.'

Their return to Australia was an anticlimax as no one appeared particularly interested in them. The Australians had been associated with the British army for two years or more and, although there were problems at times, they at least respected them. When they saw their first new American allies in Perth, 'with their flash uniforms and loud mouths', they did not impress at all.

Some troops and stores were unloaded in Port Adelaide and there was some shore leave. 'Bluey, Green and I quaffed the odd measure or two of ale at a little waterfront pub and never did get to see the City of Churches.'

In Melbourne the returning troops helped unload stores and the Victorians disembarked (there was no leave for New South Welshmen). The waterside workers put Bob and Bluey on shore in a cargo net. 'I went into the city and had a yarn with my uncle. On the way back to the ship I had a walk through the city which was teeming with Yanks. Nearly every doorway had a Yank or Yanks canoodling with giggling girls. Melbourne was like Sister Street in Alexandria run riot.'

Duntroon left Melbourne and sailed along the coast to arrive outside Sydney's Port Jackson on the afternoon of 31 May. After waiting outside the harbour for some hours, they came in through the Heads in company with a Dutch naval vessel, the hospital ship *Orangie*. Apparently three Japanese midget submarines had followed *Duntroon* into Sydney Harbour, which was full of Allied shipping and warships. All hell broke loose in the harbour that Sunday night but the only damage the submarines caused was the sinking at its Garden Island moorings of the wooden ferry HMAS *Kuttabul*. There were a number of casualties among the seamen on board the tender. Two of the midget submarines were sunk and the location of the third remained unknown until it was discovered off Sydney's Newport Beach in 2006.

Meanwhile, Bob Holt had arrived home:

> The army authorities had not notified my parents of my return to Australia. They were astounded when I walked in the door about 7 pm with rifle, full pack and equipment, plus kit and sea bags. Tobacco was rationed and I was very popular with my father when I produced several pounds of it that I had bought in Durban. We talked for hours and I must've slept like a log because I knew nothing of the doings in the harbour until I woke in the morning.

Bob 'lived like a Prince' at home with his mother waiting on her returned son hand and foot. He could not forget the first lunch she prepared for him though. She said she had a treat in store, and sat him down to tinned herrings and tomato sauce. In Palestine he had lived on 'goldfish' for months on end and even the smell of the newly opened can made him feel nauseous. He knew he must have hurt his mother's feelings, but with the best will in the world, he just could not eat her special treat!

He learned that his fourteen-year-old brother Len had enlisted—and had then been discharged from the army when his age was revealed. He had joined under the name of Patrick Michael Timothy O'Shaunessy and had given his religion as 'C of E'.

> The Japanese had bombed Darwin on 19 February 1942 and the only thing I can think of was the army must've been terribly short of men and that some of the medicos were in need of psychiatric treatment. Len had just turned fourteen and did not look one day older. My father remarked he 'looked all boots and hat' when he arrived home in uniform. Neither parent was very happy at the youngster's choice of career, but they were prepared to let him stay—that is, until he informed them he was on a draft to Darwin.

At eighteen Len re-enlisted in the army. He joined the British Commonwealth Occupation Forces and was in Japan for three full years before being discharged. When the Korean War broke out, he again enlisted, serving with the 3rd Battalion Royal Australian Regiment. He then served in Malaya as an infantryman and finished his army career as a warrant officer parachute instructor. 'Few of the Holt family have been particularly enamoured of work! Len was no exception. He tried it for a while then enlisted in the RAAF, and served in Vietnam. He finished his air force career as a Warrant-Officer First Class with nearly as many ribbons on his chest as General MacArthur!'

As Signaller Ken Clift and his 16th Brigade thawed out from Lebanon's winter snow in the early months of 1942, there was a spate of 'furphies' about a move from the Middle East. (Furphies were a World War I rumour factory, based around the horse-drawn water tanks manufactured by the firm of Joseph Furphy, around which unreliable scuttlebutt used to be generated. In World War II unsourced gossip was vulgarised as 'shithouse rumours'.) According to Clift, 'The Russians were being badly beaten up by the Germans, and the rumour mill speculated that we would follow the convoys which were continually going through to Baghdad, still with "Britain Delivers the Goods" plastered all over them, while other speculation had their brigade on their way to Burma, Singapore, New Guinea or Rabaul.'

Troops can always sense a move afoot, and it was not long before the 16th Brigade were packed up and on their way south to Palestine.

Soon afterwards, a long convoy wound its way south of Port Tewfik on the Suez Canal. Ken's mate Blue was placed in charge of J Section's transport and equipment on board the freighter *Ben Rennies*, and along with several other J Section personnel, the Army Service Corps and the 2/3rd Battalion boarded the troop transport *Orontes*.

But where were they going? As Clift recalled, 'Singapore had fallen. Part of the Seventh Division which had left before them, was subsequently diverted to Java due to the fall of Singapore and were now either dead, or prisoners of war, as our scanty intelligence had failed to convey to the convoy—while it was still at sea—that Java was also occupied.'

Ken felt their destination had to be Burma, but the reality was that the Japanese had occupied the Andaman Islands, which looked like the obvious launching pad for an attack on Ceylon to meet up with a pincer movement closing in with their troops advancing through Burma.

Before boarding the troopship *Orontes*, J Section had acquired some new personnel. Ken said he couldn't call them recruits because they had been in the AIF as long as the originals. 'Some were desirable and some not so,' he remarked.

> The other-ranks additions to our ranks were more than satisfactory but we were saddled with an Officer Cadet Training Unit–bred officer

who was to become our Second in Command to our esteemed leader Captain Tribolet. We called him Lord Kitchener. So did he actually! He was objectionable in both breath and manner. With great aplomb, he announced to J Section on parade that he looked like Lord Kitchener and with great strictness, he intended to behave like Lord Kitchener. The only resemblance I could perceive was a scraggy looking moustache which he cultivated. He raved on, saying that he heard of J Section's recorded action and so on, but, nevertheless, Division had placed him there to 'see that discipline, administration and efficiency be maintained at all cost'.

'It was his bounden duty, as a permanent soldier with a career in front of him, to see that these orders were carried out to the letter.'

Lord Kitchener was accompanied by a ginger-headed, toadying batman, Signaller X, who was under the impression that, even during his master's absence, he could assume the same exalted rank as the lieutenant under whom he served. J Section noted this and decided to make corrections to his fantasies as soon as they could. It had the experience to deal with an officer like Lord Kitchener, 'who had spent so much time in the Middle East but had adroitly dodged the battle areas'. They foresaw he might find J Section a handful and time proved this to be so.

Our attitude perturbed Trib. He mediated, indicating that the good lieutenant after all hadn't been given a fair go, but, in his heart Trib must have known that this officer would be a dead loss to the section, in or out of action—I certainly did. Trib was so tremendous as a private, NCO and officer that he must have been aware that we were on the ball, but of course he had a job to do. We loved him, but we did not have to love no-hopers whom Division sent us in the guise of 2/IC officers to the section. However, loyalty was Trib's watchword, and one had to prove his utter unworthiness, before he gave you away—that is why he was so great!

When the *Orontes* berthed in Colombo, they were shuttled out to an improvised camp about 25 miles from the city. It was situated in a rubber plantation near the village of Horana and the weather was steamy and the climate like a Turkish bath. It was hot and sunny up till about 4 pm each day and then tropical rain would set in for hours at a time, adding to the steam bath effect.

Singapore had fallen. The lack of air cover plus lack of solid troop training from Generals Brooke-Popham and Percival, all the way down to the lowliest NCOs, was a major factor contributing to the surrender to a vastly outnumbered Japanese invading army. Because of the fiasco at Pearl Harbor, the loss of the British battleships *Prince of Wales* and *Repulse*—not leaving a capital ship from either Britain or the USA in the Far East or the Pacific—and the alarmist stories in the press, the Japanese were depicted as 'super soldiers'.

Brigadier 'Killer' Lloyd believed the breakthrough would occur as soon as his troops got to grips with 'the little yellow enemies'. Accordingly, really tough jungle training became the order of the day. The 16th Infantry Brigade adapted itself quickly to the new conditions and the men, looking and acting like Spartans, got leaner and tougher day by day.

Really strenuous training programs were put in place, including commando warfare with unarmed combat, handling explosives and use of pistols and Thompson light machine guns. This expanded into a tactical wing, involving ambushes, night exercises with attackers and defenders taking part. Chalk marks had to be left on any objective to prove the position had been taken. Jungle training was well and truly to the forefront, copying and improving on Japanese methods and using information from intelligence sources gained from the surrender of Singapore and other debacles.

The island of Ceylon experienced a couple of air raids from the Japanese. Ken Clift only sighted one from afar and it was directed on the Colombo waterfront. It did quite a lot of damage, and only one Japanese plane was destroyed by ack-ack fire. Twice J Section was woken in the middle of the night and told 'the balloon had gone up', that Japanese landings had been made on the island, but both were false alarms.

Because of this, their commander Captain Tribolet decided that if the Japanese made a landing where there were no roads, and there was signal gear to lump as well as weapons, he would like to experiment with the use of elephants, slinging baskets to either side to act as containers. The Singhalese whom Tribolet approached said he had an elephant which he would bring to brigade the following day, for practice. Clift's mate Tubby had rejoined the section and he was appointed by Tribolet as the potential *mahout* or rider.

> The thought of Tubby perched between the elephant's ears, using a stick to guide the monster, was hard to conceive. Tubby was a bit dubious too, but said he'd give it a go.
>
> The elephant, a female—but no lady—arrived on time near our tents and promptly dropped a heap of crap the size of the Great Pyramid for the Pioneer section to dispose of later. Working elephants in Ceylon or India are in two classes—one for rolling and picking up logs (mostly teak) with their trunks while the other class is trained to carry loads strapped across their backs. Once broken into their respective routines, neither can be used in any other way. It was a load carrying elephant which Trib had asked for, but the cunning old Singhalese trader—who had already trousered Trib's rupees—knew just what would happen once we tried to load her, because she was trained as a log elephant. As soon as we threw the rope across what looked like a mountain of horny elephant and tried to drag the baskets up her side, she squealed like a banshee and took off, baskets trailing, and lumbered through the plantation back to her master down by the river, leaving three or four of our EPIP tents in her wake. Trib got part of his money back and we forgot the elephant idea. It might have worked all right for Hannibal, but we preferred more conventional methods.

It was decided that the Japanese were not about to invade Ceylon (they never did) and Clift could see that the signs of a move from the island were evident. Heavy gear and stores were packed in trucks and all leave cancelled.

Along with brigade headquarters and the whole 2/1st Battalion and reinforcements, J Section embarked on the troopship *Devonshire* and a convoy bearing the rest of the brigade left Colombo harbour. Latrine rumours had them bound for Burma, but as a course was set south-west to avoid Japanese naval units, and then south-east, it became obvious, long before being told officially, that Australia was their destination. 'Most battalion "originals" had learned to read the stars during the Western Desert campaign and while in the northern hemisphere,' Clift said, and they 'could have readily laid the course themselves'.

The *Devonshire* was much more crowded than previous troopships. Each evening other-ranks were slung in hammocks above the mess tables. It was permissable to sleep on deck, but smoking was barred. Ken much preferred the deck to the smoky hot below-deck quarters. 'Being a non-smoker, I wasn't inconvenienced and every evening a group of recumbent figures wrapped in blankets could be seen like a bunch of "mummies" laid along the deck.'

It was early morning in September 1942 when the convoy pulled into Fremantle, the band of the 2/1st Battalion playing, 'There's a Boy Coming Home On Leave'. After sending telegrams from the ship informing their families of their safe arrival in Australia, the troops poured ashore.

> After a few days across the Great Australian Bight without incident, we landed in Port Phillip on a typical Melbourne day, soaking wet and cold. Buses were waiting to transport the brigade to Seymour Camp.

Allotted tent space, Blue, Butta, Tom, Tubby and I shared the one EPIP tent. Through a muddy paddock, we made our way to a large marquee—the other-ranks wet canteen—and drank some of Victoria's really excellent keg beer. It was exciting! It was marvellous! We just couldn't believe it! Imagine, back in Aussie intact, and drinking keg beer!

Because of the shortage of train space, some of the 2/2nd Battalion were allotted first leave, as they came from the far north coast of New South Wales and had further to travel than the 2/1st Battalion from Sydney, or the 2/3rd Battalion, who were mostly south-west types. The following day a few duties were required of them, but 'by and large everyone was excited as a bunch of kids before Christmas and preparing for home leave. This time we were crammed on a troop train bound for Central Railway Station, Sydney. It seemed absolutely incredible and we pinched ourselves to see if we were dreaming.'

Ken's mother had waited for two days on the platform at Central Station. She was sent home early on the first day because of the assurance of a 2/2nd Battalion infantryman, who told her that he knew Ken was rostered for leave the following day, so her wait that day would be futile.

When, amid great excitement, we detrained at Central, Mum was waiting with my brother, Ces, and my brother-in-law Jack. Ginger my oldest brother was in camp with the RAAF. We didn't say much. Mum, after a little period of silence, said I looked too thin and as she was on the verge of tears, I grabbed my kit, took her by the arm, hailed a cab and we were on our way back to the home I had known since a little boy, at North Bondi.

Don, my youngest brother, then at the ripe old age of thirteen, had taken the day off school and was waiting outside the front gate. My sister, Laura, and my pretty little niece, Margaret, were inside the house.

Margaret was only eleven. As I dropped my rifle and pack and bent down to bestow my welcoming kiss, she turned her pigtails towards me, put her little face into tiny hands and began to cry. I nearly did too! It was a wonderful family reunion and perhaps the most thrilling time of my life. I relaxed and my mother spoiled me.

Chapter 12

PRISONERS OF WAR OF THE JAPANESE

Gunner Clarry McCulloch of the 2/3rd Machine Gun Battalion, fresh from the Syrian campaign, was delighted to learn on the grapevine that his unit would be returning to Australia. On 1 January 1942 they cheerfully climbed into cattle trucks for the rail journey to the Suez Canal.

By the time they reached Port Tewfik the troops were all in high spirits, thinking they would soon be back in Australia again. The harbour was crowded with all manner of ships, large and small. They were delighted when told to board the SS *Orcades*, a fast tourist ship which, pre-war, had been on the England–Australia run.

Unfortunately, all their bags and spare gear was left behind on the wharf, in spite of requests from their CO Colonel Blackburn to load them. The reason given by the captain of the *Orcades* was that he wanted to get away from the harbour because of the possibility of air raids. Also left at Port Tewfik were all their machine guns and vehicles, which had been driven there by road from Palestine. The drivers and vehicles were later loaded onto several small steamers and eventually returned to Australia. Such are the fortunes of war, as they avoided becoming prisoners of war. Several of their sergeants who were away at training schools in Palestine at the time were also lucky to miss being POWs. Clarry McCulloch later reflected:

> I think the strangest stroke of fate was the case of a certain well-known character from C Company. A week before our departure he had fallen from the first floor balcony of a house of ill fame and had broken his arm. His only excuse was that he was drunk at the time, and he was still in hospital when we left. He also got back to Australia safely. Good luck comes in many guises.

It was very crowded on the *Orcades* and the battalion, being last to board, had to sleep on the open decks for the voyage. This turned out to be an advantage through the tropics, so there were no complaints. The meals were excellent and McCulloch thought it a good voyage as far as Colombo. 'One thing which I remember about the trip was our introduction to beer in cans for the first time. It was an American brand and, although the beer was quite pleasant, most of us thought it had a slight metallic taste.'

Naturally there was much discussion among the troops about where they were going. Opinions were varied. Most thought that Australia was the best bet, but one rumour had Burma as a likely alternative. Although this suggestion was howled down by most of the troops, it was revealed much later that Burma was actually the preferred option put forward by Winston Churchill and the British War Cabinet. The Sixth and Seventh Australian Divisions had already been ordered to head for Burma and it was only after a very bitter argument between Churchill and the Australian prime minister John Curtin that the convoy was turned around and finally headed to Australia.

Their stay in Colombo was very brief, with no shore leave granted, and soon the Australians were on a south-easterly course again. Some still favoured Australia as a destination, but after receiving lectures about the Dutch East Indies they began to think otherwise.

On the morning of 15 February they woke to find the ship threading its way between heavily forested islands, then dropping anchor in the harbour of Oosthaven on the south-western end of Sumatra. Apparently the plan was for them to help the Dutch troops defend the aerodrome at Palembang in the north of the island. As they had no machine guns, the Number One and Two of each gun team had to be given something with which to defend themselves, so they were hurriedly issued with old Ross 14 rifles from the ship's armoury. These were World War I vintage and probably well worn from much use. 'What a farce it was,' Clarry said, 'going into battle equipped like that!'

A small oil tanker was used to get them ashore and after several hours their much depleted battalion, plus the 2/2nd Pioneer Battalion, were crammed onto its deck and headed for the wharf. It was raining heavily, and as it was getting near evening the mosquitoes attacked in droves while they waited for the order to scramble ashore.

It soon became apparent that they would not be landing when a British brigadier from an advance party came to say they were too late. The Japanese had already captured Palembang aerodrome and were now only 11 miles from Oosthaven, so he had been ordered to evacuate all British troops. McCulloch recalled:

> By this time it was pitch dark. The captain of the tanker now had the unenviable task of trying to find the *Orcades*, which was still anchored about three miles out in the bay. This had to be accomplished without the aid of lights because of the danger of Japanese aircraft. Slowly we inched out into the harbour, which was crowded with other ships. At the last minute a lucky flash of lightning showed the *Orcades* only a

> few hundred yards away. We came alongside and then began the slow job of getting nearly 2000 men up a couple of narrow gangways in pitch dark and pouring rain.
>
> By this time tempers were getting a bit short, but a hot cup of cocoa and a few sandwiches cheered us up a bit, and we were soon dossed down on the deck once more. Shortly after this the ship got underway again.

Next morning they passed through Sunda Strait and later in the day tied up in Tanjong Priok, the port for Batavia (now Jakarta). Ships of all sizes and shapes cluttered the harbour, some of them escapees from Singapore. It was there they learned of the fall of Malaya and Singapore. 'We realised, of course, the seriousness of the situation, but strangely enough no one seemed worried.'

For two days they sat at the wharf, watching with great interest the actions of the native Javanese, the coming and going of many staff cars, and the Dutch dispatch riders on their big Harley-Davidson motorbikes with sidecars.

Behind the scenes, their fate was being decided. Prime Minister Curtin's argument with Winston Churchill over the placement of the Sixth and Seventh Australian Divisions had been settled. They were now on their way home instead of to Burma, but against the advice of Generals Wavell and Laverack their small group was to be thrown to the wolves as a political gesture to the Dutch. 'What a grim joke that was—a tiny force of two understrength battalions plus a few other groups, probably 3000 men in all, left in Java to bolster the Dutch army, who had no intention of making a real fight anyway. Their navy and air force fought bravely against vastly superior odds and suffered grievously as a consequence.'

(Fifty years later documents relevant to these events were released. The depth of ill-feeling that existed between Churchill and Curtin over the Sixth and Seventh Divisions is plain. This had a big bearing on their fate and explained why Churchill was so adamant that the Australians stayed in Java. Ironically, in the five books which he later wrote about the war and in which he described most theatres in detail, not one mention was made of this disaster.)

While they awaited their orders, the troops lined the ship's rail and bargained for fruit and trinkets with the locals, an event that caused McCulloch quite a bit of embarrassment.

> Because I did not like my name, Clarry, most of my mates just called me Mac, and this was fine with me. The Javanese words 'mac-mac' are a colloquialism for the act of copulation much the same as 'jiggy-jig' is used in the Arab countries of the Middle East. When the locals at the wharf heard my mates calling out to me, 'Mac, Mac,' they absolutely fell about laughing, much to our mystification, until someone with a knowledge of the language explained the significance. At this stage I thought it prudent to retire from the scene for a while until the merriment subsided. Naturally this did not stop my mates for making many jokes at my expense.

However, they soon had more serious things to worry about, as they prepared to disembark. As they came down one gangway, a large contingent of air force men and Australian nurses were going up the other one. They would make it safely home.

The battalion still had no machine guns, but the decision had been made that they would fight as infantry, so there were preparations to get more equipment. Several vessels carrying arms and ammunition to Singapore had been diverted to Java, so the cargoes were now available. Most of the cargo consisted of Bren guns, submachine guns and a few mortars, plus armoured cars, Bren gun carriers and ammunition, 'so after a bit of scrounging we were all reasonably equipped'.

Clarry McCulloch's small force was made up of the 2/3rd Machine Gun Battalion, the 2/2nd Pioneer Battalion, plus a contingent of the Guard Battalion. They were organised as a brigade and known as 'Blackforce', commanded by Colonel Arthur Blackburn, now promoted to brigadier. Also on the island was a company of Australian engineers, a small transport unit, a squadron of the King's Own Hussars with a few tanks, and strangest of all, a battery of Texas artillery, who had no idea how they came to be there at all. Last but not least was the Australian 2/2nd Casualty Clearing Unit, led by Colonel Edward 'Weary' Dunlop, who proved to be so vital for the future prisoners of war in the years ahead.

This motley collection of units, although led by Brigadier Blackburn, was under the overall command of General ter Poorton, the Dutch commander-in-chief, and he decided that we could best be occupied by guarding the aerodromes on the north-west of Java. To begin with our battalion was posted to the defence of the main Batavia airport, where most of our suffering was caused by the hordes of mosquitoes which inhabited this low-lying area. Slit trenches were dug in case of air raids, but because of the water table they quickly filled with water. They were actually used for shelter when the bombs fell there later. Being soaking wet is preferable to being hit with flying shrapnel!

When volunteers were requested for anyone who could drive Bren gun carriers I jumped at the chance to use the knowledge I had acquired earlier at Aleppo in Syria. Soon I was happily crashing around the 'drome teaching other blokes to drive. 'Crashing' was the operative word as the learners came to grips with the peculiar traits of the Bren gun carriers. Because of their heavy weight and the rolling resistance of the steel tracks, it was necessary to change gears very rapidly in order to maintain forward momentum. Most of the lads were quick learners and we soon had enough drivers to form a troop. A sergeant from B Company was put in charge, with myself as second-in-command, and soon our small force of six carriers was on its way up into the mountains to provide protection for a supposedly secret bomber aerodrome operated by the Dutch air force.

Although it was not realised at the time, this movement almost certainly cost McCulloch a chance for promotion. Had he stayed with 11 Platoon, he believed he would have been promoted to sergeant before being captured. 'The loss of promotion didn't worry me, but the extra few shillings per day going into my deferred pay over the next three and a half years would have been handy.'

Clarry's Tasmanian mate Blue—Lorimer Anzac von Stieglitz, with his flaming red hair—had decided to go along with Clarry as his Bren gunner. As Blue put it, 'Anything to get away from these bloody mosquitoes!' The aerodrome was hidden away among coconut and banana plantations and consisted of two grass runways, more or less at right angles, so the pilots had a choice for take-offs and landings. During the day these strips would be covered with coconut logs scattered over the surface. These would be removed before daylight each morning to allow the planes to take off. Immediately after the planes had returned from their raids on Japanese shipping, the logs would be hauled out again to give the impression that the strip was unused.

The first task was to maintain a constant patrol around the air strip each morning. It was quite an experience, with the early morning mist swirling around them as the ghostly shapes of the twin-engine bombers roared past on their way out to the Java Sea. Unfortunately, there were usually fewer planes coming back each time.

Their small force of six carriers and eighteen men was virtually autonomous while they were in that area, so for a couple of weeks they were a very happy group, with comfortable barracks and good food and access to the Dutch army canteen, where each afternoon they could sit back and enjoy a bottle of a very pleasant Dutch beer. 'Naturally it was too good to last.'

Finally the last remaining Dutch plane failed to return. These were very brave pilots, but like the Dutch navy which fought well in the Java Sea Battle, they were overwhelmed by superior forces. McCulloch wished he could say the same about the Dutch army, which he thought let them down badly.

With all the planes gone there was no reason to remain, so it was no surprise when a dispatch rider arrived with orders to return to Batavia, and next morning their small convoy set off. By each taking a turn at driving, they eventually arrived back at Batavia airport late in the afternoon, only to find their battalion had departed earlier in the day—destination unknown.

Shortly afterwards a dispatch rider arrived with fresh orders to rejoin the battalion, which was now operating from the hills near the town of Buitenzorg (now Bogor). Brigadier Blackburn had decided that his small force could be better employed guarding the roads likely to be used by the Japanese, if and when they landed.

Although it was not known at the time, a naval battle had been fought in the Java Sea on 27 January, with the Japanese winning that round very decisively. Two Dutch cruisers were sunk plus three Allied destroyers, so opening the way for the first division of Japanese to land on the north coast of Java, east of Batavia, the capital of the Dutch East Indies.

The Australian cruiser *Perth* and the American cruiser *Houston* escaped undamaged, returned to Batavia to refuel and load fresh ammunition, then headed for the Sunda Straits in an attempt to reach the Indian Ocean. During the night, however, they ran right into the second Japanese invasion force preparing to land on the north-west corner of Java and, although they were vastly outnumbered, attacked immediately and acquitted themselves magnificently before both were sunk with guns blazing right to the end. Many of those sailors who were washed ashore later became prisoners of war in Java.

> Then, we knew nothing of these momentous events and happily joined up with the battalion again near Buitenzorg. I must say that we had a few hairy moments driving around in pitch darkness trying to find our own section in totally unknown territory. On 3 March,

around midday, five Japanese light tanks arrived at the bridge which the pioneers were guarding. This bridge was about 100 miles from the north-west coast, where they had landed two days earlier. When some of the Jap tank crews got out to inspect the bridge, the pioneers opened fire with anti-tank rifles and managed to disable two tanks before the rest withdrew temporarily to reassess the situation.

The previous afternoon C Company of the machine-gunners had taken up positions on a small wooded hill a few miles to the left of the Pioneers. Meanwhile, 11 and 12 Platoons were on the hill, which had been a local cemetery, and 10 Platoon was in reserve a few hundred yards to the rear in a coconut plantation. That evening Captain John Kennedy and two other officers set off in an armoured car to reconnoitre the area in front of the hill, but when they had not returned by nightfall the worst was feared.

It was raining heavily. C Company then settled down for a miserable night. Forward scouts were put out in front. Just before daylight the next morning, the Japanese attacked and four forward scouts were killed, the others getting back to the hill safely. Shortly afterwards a determined attack was mounted by the Japanese, but this was beaten off with severe losses to the enemy. Twice more during the early morning they attacked and each time they were stopped by the volume of C Company's fire.

At one stage a Japanese machine gun was causing some concern, so two men from 11 Platoon, Dick Clark and Sam Wilson, crawled down behind some long grass and put it out of action with a couple of hand grenades.

Meanwhile, McCulloch's Bren gun carrier group was kept at battalion headquarters to give protection in case of a breakthrough. They could hear all the firing from the Pioneer area and also from C Company's position on the hill and wondered how soon they would be in action as well.

It was there that the Australians made their first contact with troops from the United States, an artillery unit from Texas, most of whom seemed slightly bewildered by the events that had resulted in them being in their current situation. The Australians found most of them very likeable, but the Americans were understandably a bit concerned about how they would perform in action for the first time. 'Naturally, we told them not to worry, there was nothing to it, really. We then proceeded to regale them with a few hair-raising tales about some of the battles in the Middle East. I'm not totally convinced that it really put their minds at rest!' And as McCulloch recalled, the mood was increasingly tense:

> While talking to these lads, a few stray bullets on the hill were coming over and zipping through the trees. The officer in charge of the US boys must've been a bit on edge as he came over to Major Hec Greiner, our 2IC, and complained loudly. 'Ah say major, mah men cain't operate while they are being sniped at.' Hec, a bluff farmer from Victoria, turned round and said, 'What the hell do you think is happening to my men up on that hill?' and walked away. As it happened they could not help our chaps on the hill as the opposing sides were too close together. Later, however, I believe they performed well with the Pioneers. To be fair, it wasn't good country for artillery.

After some heavy fighting and some casualties, the Japanese began lobbing in accurate mortar fire. The Dutch troops, supposedly on their left flank, were conspicuous by their absence, and the order was given to retire.

Finally on 8 March the convoy came to a halt about 6 miles from the coast. A Company was in an area of jungle with huge gorges beside the road and it was here that they were told that there were no ships at Tjilitjap and no way off the island. At this stage they also heard about the loss of the two Allied cruisers *Perth* and *Houston*.

There was a complete lack of knowledge of what was going to happen, and rumours abounded. Eventually on 9 March they were told that there was no possibility of evacuation and that the Australian government had ordered them to capitulate and surrender to the Japanese. It was a day that McCulloch would never forget:

> I think this was the lowest point of my army career. I just could not believe that a good fighting force which had not been disgraced in action could just be handed over like that. Extreme anger was the feeling of all the troops, and we felt badly let down.
>
> The order was to pile up our arms to be handed to the Japanese, but of course most of us proceeded to render our arms inoperable by removing the bolts from all rifles and machine guns and smashing them before hurling them down into the thick jungle in the huge gorge below us. A lot of the trucks were also pushed over the edge and allowed to crash into the river hundreds of feet below. At one point some of the boys discovered that one truck contained a good quantity of Dutch guilders but was destined for destruction. However we managed to liberate a portion of it. Some thought that it might be worthless after the Japs took over, but such was not the case and those who were optimistic put them to good use later.

Clarry McCulloch lost most of his gear when his knapsack was run over by a Bren gun carrier, so when he found an abandoned British officer's haversack beside the road he was very glad to make use of its contents. It contained a clean shirt, shorts and socks, a complete set of eating utensils, a beautiful Bengal cut-throat razor complete with strop and sharpening stone and, last of all, a six-shot Smith and Wesson .38 calibre revolver wrapped in waterproof material.

> I could not bring myself to throw it away so, knowing that I couldn't carry it, I covered it with grease, re-wrapped it and buried it between the roots of a large tree nearby. It seemed a pointless thing to do but

at the time we had no idea what would happen and I thought that, if things did turn nasty, it might come in handy. I often wonder if it's still there, slowly rusting away.

The next few days seemed unreal. The Australians were officially prisoners of war but there was not a Japanese in sight. 'I suppose they weren't worried, knowing that it was impossible for us to escape.'

A few small parties of men who couldn't accept the facts went off down the coast to try and find a boat of some kind. Most soon realised the futility and returned or were rounded up by the Japanese troops. It was unlikely that army personnel would have had the expertise to sail a boat on a journey of that distance and hope to survive. Later McCulloch discovered that even the sailors from *Perth* and *Houston* who tried had no luck either.

There was a suggestion they should form themselves into a guerrilla force, but that was soon ruled out because of logistics—no reserves of food, ammunition or medical supplies and no hope of reinforcements from Australia. In any case that would be futile as the Dutch had given up fighting.

After ten days at the tea plantation, they climbed into trucks and moved in convoy to a small village named Leles, 'a nice little town' where they were billeted in some open-air market buildings. It was two weeks before the Japanese turned up, so the troops there passed the time with improvised baseball games using a pick handle and tennis ball.

One engineer remarked, 'In all our experience through the Middle East, our venereal disease rate had been one per cent, but it jumped up sharply in Leles.' A sensuous fortnight was small compensation for men who had fought with such distinction in the Middle East and whose last battles in Java had been what one temporary Leles resident called 'The Black Farce' (Blackforce).

When Clarry McCulloch met his first Japanese soldiers, he was surprised they treated the Australians very correctly, 'considering they were the victors and we were the vanquished. Probably they were front-line troops and had a certain amount of respect for the way we had fought against them.'

'Unfortunately,' he added, 'the guards we had later were not so correct.'

When General Yamashita's troops stormed ashore on the north-east coast of Malaya on 8 December 1941, they faced a formidable task. But his soldiers were battle-hardened, skilled in jungle warfare and highly motivated—ready to die for their emperor. Yamashita was given some 30,000 troops from Japan's 25th Army to conquer Malaya and Singapore, although they were vastly outnumbered by the British commander Lieutenant General Arthur Percival's combined force of 85,000 men, 70,000 of them front-line troops. Yet seven weeks later the Japanese had surged down the peninsula (grabbing bicycles and any transport they could lay their hands on as they went) and for good measure, also invaded and took Singapore in that time frame. So much for the 'Impregnable Fortress'. Somehow 38 infantry battalions—thirteen British, six Australian, seventeen Indian and two Malayan plus three machine-gun battalions—could not stop them.

Admittedly some Allied units lacked experience and training and others were not at full strength. It also has to be said that many of the Indian battalions soldiers' hearts were unsympathetic to this war. In India at that time there was a strong national call for the end of British rule, and the Japanese, realising this, encouraged the Indians to swap sides, which many did, some later becoming the gaolers of their colonial masters after they became prisoners of war.

So rapid was this advance that even robust actions to stem the tide—particularly by the Australians—were inevitably turned into strategic retreats as the advancing Japanese immediately outflanked them.

The Japanese were the 'yellow peril' long feared by Australians. Towards the end of 1941 the threat of a sudden Japanese attack had brought close to reality the Australian nightmare of covetous Asiatic hordes pouring southward. Prejudice replaced military intelligence. 'The Japanese were all half blind of course,' Sergeant Stan Arneil remembers being told. 'And there was this brigade major who lectured us on how the Japanese set off crackers at night time, and we wouldn't be frightened of that. We said, "No, we wouldn't be frightened of crackers".'

Gunner Cliff Moss heard the comforting story that their rifles were no good. 'You could squeeze the bullets out like blackheads.' That is, if the myopic Japanese were ever able to hit anyone. The reputation of the Japanese as copiers of the tinsel and the tinny from the West precluded their being taken seriously as an enemy of the full might of the British Empire and the United States. It was only among a few of the senior officers and the more perceptive of the lower ranks that some were at all conscious of the efficiency of the Japanese—and of their own vulnerability.

The Japanese advancing down the Malaya Peninsula did not clash with the main Australian land forces until the middle of January. By then they were numerous and confident. Their cyclists, rifles slung on their backs, rode into the ambush set for them by the 2/30th Battalion at Gemas. Further east near Muar, the 2/29th Battalion and supporting gunners were soon in action. After coming under attack from probing patrols and infantry in the night, the Australians took up positions just forward of Bakri, where the road curved through a cutting.

Lieutenant Ben Hackney was first wounded on the morning of 18 January 1942. On that occasion Japanese tanks came right into the battalion position. They were met with an outstanding performance by Sergeant Clarrie Thornton of the 4th Anti-Tank Regiment—instead of firing away as the first tank came into sight, he waited until the first five tanks were in view before he opened fire. These were followed by three more very soon after, making a total of eight tanks that were destroyed.

Thornton was hit in the hip with shrapnel. 'The number two bloke took over swinging the gun and with me still hobbling around, that gave us two observers, which was essential as some tanks had gone past our position and others were still coming into sight.' The detail of the action remained vivid to Thornton:

> I was giving a lot of orders in respect of which targets to go on to. 'Can you front him Brownie? Can you pick him up?' Or I'd sing out to Ray Cooper, 'Ray, keep your eye on that bloke on the right.' He said, 'I've been watching him, he's okay at the moment.' That sort of talk was going on at the time. And there was a hell of a din. Other tanks were firing, shells exploding and we were banging them off as fast as we could.
>
> When we'd finished, Claudie Brown just sat back, he was older than us, and he said, 'Well, Thorny, I feel very proud, man. We've done our job. We knew we could do it if we got the chance, and luck was with us. And,' he said, 'we upheld the name of the old Diggers. We often wondered how we'd go. The old blokes had it on the record and we had to put it there.' As Captain Bill Bowing said later, 'My God, they've upheld the old Digger's name today, haven't they.'

They were not the only Australians in that short and brutal campaign who had the Anzacs in the back of their minds.

In danger of being overrun, the gun crew then had to make their own way through the jungle to escape. In later years Thornton recalled: 'After our battle with the tanks at Muar, we found ourselves surrounded by the 5th Imperial Guards Division and in the confusion that followed I found myself with twelve 2/29th Battalion chaps. After several skirmishes with the Japs, we finished up behind their lines.'

They cautiously threaded their way north along the fringe of the jungle reaching down to the road, keeping well out of sight, hoping to regroup with some of their other forces. After two days of wandering aimlessly through the jungle, they ran into an ambush of Japanese signallers. With hindsight it turned out to be a lucky break—because had they been confronted by the Japanese infantry, armed as the Australians were, they would have all been shot.

The signallers escorted them to a village that the Japanese had captured and they spent a miserable night under guard, sweating it out tethered together in the middle of the local *padang* (village square). In the morning, unfed, unwashed, wounded and feeling absolutely exhausted, they were ordered by a smartly uniformed officer, who spoke perfect English though with an American accent, to get on the back of a Jap army truck that had just driven onto the *padang*.

They clambered aboard as best they could and stood waiting as he looked them over quizzically. Thornton recalled what happened next:

> 'Are you Australians?'
>
> 'Yes'.
>
> 'All Australians?'
>
> 'Yes.'
>
> 'Then hop down off the truck.'
>
> No one moved. We were wounded, weak and weary. We were buggered, and had just climbed onto his bloody truck.
>
> Then he repeated sternly. 'Get down off the truck if you don't want to be shot. We thought you were British and were taking you into the jungle to shoot you.'
>
> Never before did a group of such unfit Aussies move with such agility. Never before had they all felt so lucky to be Australian.
>
> Then the Japanese officer asked, 'What battalion do you belong to?'
>
> 'The 32nd,' one of our spokesmen replied quickly.
>
> He whipped out his sword threateningly. 'Now listen to me you guys, do you want your lollies lopped?' Then with unbridled pride, he continued, 'I am the liaison officer for the Imperial Guards Division.

I lived in the United States for 16 years, I am a graduate of Washington University. Australia has six battalions in Singapore, the 18th, 19th and 20th, and the 26th, 29th and 30th. Now which one do you belong to?'

The 29th, we said in unison, with sudden new found respect for our interrogator.

As Thornton was the senior NCO in the party, the English-speaking officer led him off to a tent where he told him to kneel down, as he was to be interrogated by the general commanding the Imperial Guards Division. Clarrie shuddered to think how the general would have reacted had he known Clarrie had knocked out eight of his precious tanks. The shrapnel wound in his thigh was giving him hell and he knelt on the ground uncomfortably, listening to the constant rumble of a never-ending convoy of Japanese trucks as they lined up to be ferried across the river. Some time went by before the general arrived, wearing an impressive sword and row upon row of campaign ribbons. He abruptly asked Thornton what he did in Australia.

'I was a farmer from Berrigan in New South Wales,' I told him. Then he commanded, 'Tell me about the roads leading from Broome to Adelaide and Sydney.'

'I was a farmer in Berrigan, Sir, I've never been to Western Australia and I don't know anything about the roads there.'

He seemed to expect that sort of ignorant answer from a farmer and went on to boast, 'See those trucks outside? We will take Singapore in a few days,' he said pompously and snapped his fingers. 'Then we will bomb Darwin.'

'Right now the largest convoy ever to sail the ocean is on its way to Australia, and we will conquer Australia just like that,' he said, snapping his fingers belligerently. 'Australia has no resistance. What do you say about that?'

I couldn't think of anything to say, but my answer just blurted out. 'You may get to Australia but you won't take it.'

He didn't like it and took his sheathed sword and belted me around my head and shoulders for quite some time. When he had enough, he ordered, 'Take him away.'

Clarrie had a horrible gut feeling the general might just be right.

'I was hustled over to Kuala Lumpur and thrust into Pudu Prison. Hungry, smelly, my wound seeping with pus, I was way, way down in the dumps. But all of a sudden life seemed ridiculously funny.' Clarrie thought, 'If only Mum could see me now . . .'

It had never occurred to the Australians that they might become prisoners of war. The order by the British commander General Percival that they were to lay down their arms came as a complete surprise. Captain Ray Steele had been with the artillery at Muar: 'We were absolutely flabbergasted. All of us. I can remember the reactions from the various fellows—some of them just swore, some of them threw things about, some of them were just silent and shocked. We just didn't want it. We felt we were capable of fighting on.'

Most of the captives waiting to meet their captors were apprehensive. They were right to worry for they were ignorant of Japanese behaviour, which was to vary greatly at those first meetings. There was, however, mutual curiosity.

'It wasn't until the next day that we actually saw our first Japanese,' Sergeant Jack Sloan recalled. 'What impressed me was that we were looked on as curios, and we were somewhat interested in what they looked like. They seemed like ruffians. But the front-line Japanese soldier appeared to be a fellow who realised that, like himself, we were just doing a job.'

Japanese were soon moving among the dispirited troops looking for spoils. Corporal Tom Morris lost a cheap watch he had bought recently in Singapore for 15 shillings—'The little Jap already had about half a dozen on his wrist.'

In Sumatra, Private Frank Robinson learned a quick lesson in cultural compromise:

> We were treated reasonably well by the Japanese for a start, except for the fact that we had to bow to the Japanese when we met them. This was a little bit below our dignity. We didn't like the idea of bowing to a Jap, and much to our sorrow many of us were bashed about it. We decided in the finish to forget our dignity and bow to them. We realised later that to bow, and they'd bow back, was to salute them. It was just their way of life.

But few Australians could ever bow easily.

Other prisoners had more violent early encounters. Private Dick Ryan, from military transport, was recovering from a broken leg when the sector was overrun by the Japanese. He experienced two extremes of their behaviour:

> I was in hospital in Singapore when the Japanese came in, the day before the surrender. I was sitting up rolling a cigarette. I didn't want to take any notice of them, but a Japanese stood at the end of my bed and when I finished he said, 'gimme'. I licked the cigarette paper along and gave it to him. He got me to make three more for the three other blokes that were with him. They said how lovely they were. Of course they were made of Australian tobacco. They sent me in three packets of Japanese cigarettes. That was all right. The same day Japs came in and murdered one doctor in the ward, killed the patient on the table and wounded another doctor. Can you understand that sort of business?

It is now thought that some Indian soldiers retreating through the hospital grounds had fired on the Japanese. Assuming that the British had used the Red Cross to protect fighting troops, the Japanese took savage revenge. But there were no mitigating circumstances to excuse the behaviour of the Japanese described by Lieutenant Ben Hackney: 'Try and imagine a gorilla gone berserk, and that sums up the treatment of the Japanese. They had no care whatsoever for anything. Bayonets, rifle butts, anything used anywhere.'

The Japanese Imperial Guards, all six-footers, were fresh from China where no prisoners were taken. Captured at Parit Sulong after the battle at Muar, the wounded Hackney was among 110 Australians and 50 Indians who were bashed and bayoneted. Hackney, pretending to be dead even as his boots were dragged off him, was left, while those bodies which still had life in them were piled in a heap, machine-gunned, then doused with petrol and burnt.

Two days after the surrender on Singapore, nearly 15,000 Australians and 35,000 British prisoners were ordered to march to Changi on the eastern end of the island. The seemingly endless columns of men dramatised the enormity of the defeat, and the transformation of the white man, the *tuan*, from guardian of empire to prisoners of the Japanese.

Uncertain what their captors would provide at the other end of the march, men carried as much food, clothing and bedding as they could. Ray Steele said: 'It was a kind of amble or shambles—a bit like refugees, fellows carrying everything they possibly could. As the march got long and hot they tossed stuff aside until at the end some of them arrived with very little.'

According to Cliff Moss, there was a strong incentive to keep going. 'The story was that if we fell by the wayside we would be shot,' Moss said. 'That didn't happen, but it made a lot of people keep on walking when they would have preferred to lie down. It got pretty tough, and the Chinese along the way helped us. They'd watch out for the Japs.

They were flying Japanese flags on their houses, but they were running out with drinks for us. Without them we probably wouldn't have made it.'

With so many troops on the road, the march ended after dark. Gunner Don Moore recalled: 'As darkness came on us, the villages, the *kampongs*, were a bit more spaced. And when we were feeling a little low, our piper, Jimmy Oliver, started up. Then it was really good. We knew he must've been as exhausted and depressed as we were, and yet up he sounded.'

The march had been about 29 kilometres, not far for fit men, but the prisoners were exhausted by battle, wounded, ill-fed and depressed by defeat. At Changi they lay on ground or concrete. Gunner Frank Christie wrote in his diary: 'All rooted, slept where we could.'

Changi, with its rolling hills of lush vegetation, views of the sea and modern barracks, had been one of the best of the British garrison bases. But now Selarang Barracks had been through a battle. 'Everything was upside down and the place was blown to buggery,' said Private 'Snow' Peat. The barracks, once the home of 900 Gordon Highlanders, was crowded with Australians whose immediate concern was food. For the first few days they lived on the rapidly diminishing stores which they had carried with them.

Don Moore described the desperate situation:

> We went on to some very tight rations. There was just one biscuit with bully beef pasted over it for the midday meal. In the evening there was another meagre ration, some tinned vegetables smeared over a biscuit. Things were a bit tough. We were asking, 'Can't the cooks use a little bit of imagination? Can we get some more stuff?' 'Well look,' said the major, 'we've got quite a few bags of rice here. It's been coming in for the past few weeks. Would you eat that?' 'Oh Jesus! What do you think you're coming at? Of course, yes, yes, we'll eat the damn stuff!'

However, as Gunner Tom Dowling soon discovered, having rice and making it palatable were two separate issues:

> As far as rice went, we had every conceivable variety that existed, unpolished rice, mouldy rice, rice full of rats and weevils, sulphur rice and rice that smelt like shit. Nothing but rice. Our cooks didn't have the slightest idea of what to do with it. During the next four weeks we lived precariously on the results of their trial and error efforts. During this experimental period, we were subjected to all sorts of unpleasant concoctions—gritty half-cooked rice, rice burnt black, claggy masses of rice. However tasteless or unpleasant, we ate it.

As often as not the rice turned out to be a runny, sticky, gooey mess that swirled around unattractively in their dixies. Gunner 'Prawn' Hennebery complained he couldn't stomach the sight of it: 'It reminds me of a wet dream.'

As the days passed the cooks improved and began to understand what they had to do with 'the confounded stuff'. The Australians gradually became accustomed to it and for the first few weeks there was little else to eat. Tasteless though the rice was, they felt they were lucky just to have a feed and ate whatever they were given. They were all steadily going downhill, losing weight, condition and their spirits.

Don Moore recalled an unexpected development: 'Everyone became uncomfortably but steadfastly bound with constipation. Not just for a week, or a fortnight, but for over three weeks without a bowel motion. The doctor informed everyone that he suffered the same complaint and it was just a matter of biding their time and the problem would right itself.'

Prawn Hennebery had other ideas.

The Japanese paid more than lip service to the privileges of rank, and officers got much more pay than the other ranks. One of the 2/4th Anti-Tank Regiment's senior officers, 'Big Red', had elected to go it alone and live on his superior officer's pay rather than pool it with the other officers for the benefit of all. Very quickly he sullied his reputation and became extremely unpopular. His flesh still sat comfortably on his huge freckled pink frame.

Prawn suggested that Big Red come and talk to his men.

'What the hell could that lazy, fat bugger do to help us?' his fellow prisoners asked.

'Well, he'd give anyone the shits, wouldn't he?'

Humour became one of the essential elements of surviving as a POW, as shown by this 'drinking story' from Gunner Tom Dowling about the occasion of the emperor's birthday. The Japanese certainly revered their emperor, so it was natural to expect that come his birthday, there would be a flurry of excitement and festivity.

> The first time we encountered his birthday came shortly after the fall of Singapore, when at Changi we were called on parade and ordered to bring our drinking mugs. We wondered what on earth we were going to do with the mugs, but did as we were told.
>
> Along came a Jap officer resplendent with gold braid and campaign ribbons, sword swinging by his side, and he stepped up onto a well raised platform specially placed in front of the parade so that he could address us at eye level.
>
> 'Today is Emperor of Japan's birthday and we are to celebrate.' Having said that the guards accompanying him, armed with flagons, moved up and down the lines and half-filled everyone's mugs with *saki*.
>
> When the last of the mugs had been charged, the Japanese officer said, 'Now we drink to Emperor.'

This put the prisoners in 'a bit of a dilemma', Dowling recalled, and 'he had us by the short and curlies'. The idea of drinking his *sake* was appealing, but to drink to the emperor's health was quite a different matter.

'You will all drink to health of Emperor,' the officer repeated sternly.

There was 'no way the boys could bring themselves to drink to the emperor's health,' Dowling said, so they just stood there blankly, carefully holding on to their half-filled mugs of *sake*.

Then out stepped Vern Rae, a rugged 15th Battery intelligence officer, hailing from the tall cedar country of Tasmania, who thundered out, 'Boys, we will drink to the Emperor.' He held up his mug: 'FAAAARK the Emperor.'

A great roar went up.

'The Emperor—FAAAARK the Emperor,' and the Australians quaffed down their *sake*.

The Japanese officer then dutifully completed his toast. 'Ah so . . . FAAAARK the Emperor.'

Dowling could see the Japanese officer was exceedingly delighted that his emperor's health had such an enthusiastic response from his vanquished foes.

'The boys enjoyed their first encounter with *sake*, also feeling smugly satisfied that in the course of its enjoyment they too had paid their rightful dues to His Imperial Highness on his birthday.'

In round figures, 22,000 Australians became prisoners of war of the Japanese in camps in Timor, Java, Sumatra, New Guinea, Ambon, Hainan, Borneo, Singapore, Malaya, Thailand, Burma and Manchuria. Three and a half years later, only 14,000 were still alive.

In Singapore, the Japanese were surprised to find that they had some 50,000 British, Australian and Indian troops to cope with on the small island. The Japanese believed they should have committed suicide rather than endure the disgrace of capture, and so were men without honour. The Allied troops felt differently, and looked forward to getting home, eventually, to their families.

Faced with the task of managing this situation, and not wanting to involve their front-line troops in guarding POWs, the Japanese were quite smart in allowing the Australians and British to retain administrative control of their own men—in Selarang Barracks for the Australians and Roberts Barracks for the British. Senior officers over the rank of colonel were later shipped off to their own camp in Manchuria. Meanwhile, on the Changi peninsula, the POWs were set to work putting a barbed wire barrier around their own encampments.

At first the main problem for the Australian officers running Selarang Barracks was boredom, as the still fit (although ravenously hungry) men milled around aimlessly. So it was that the so-called 'Changi University' was created, but only for a few months, before the Japanese started hiving off the POWs into work gangs, first on the Singapore docks and on construction projects on the island, and then to build an aerodrome in Sandakan, Borneo—which would culminate in the infamous Death Marches, beginning in early 1945, in which 2000 Australians and 500 British would be slaughtered in the jungle and only six men survived. Things were also extremely tough from the beginning of 1943 when one in three Australians died while building the Thai–Burma Railway in atrocious conditions on starvation rations and virtually no medical supplies.

All this was unforeseen when Australian officers organised the brief flowering of the 'Changi University'. In an army, you can always find experts in just about anything.

Captain Adrian Curlewis recalled that within four days of the capitulation, Brigadier Herbert Taylor was appointed as the chancellor of the university and he was appointed dean of the Faculty of Law and general organiser. The response from the troops was amazing, they all wanted to learn. The Australian army could produce experts who could lecture on Tutankhamen in Egypt, on history, languages, mathematics, business principles, engineering and art. Curlewis himself took up the Malay language and motor engineering. There were plenty of war-damaged vehicles to pull to pieces, but the paper shortage was nearly a disaster. So they improvised blackboards and used clay from a nearby pit for chalk.

There were also many who did not have the basic education to benefit from most of the courses, and they were given the chance to acquire primary school skills. YMCA officer George McNeilly 'even found men who couldn't read and write, so we taught over 400'.

Russell Braddon was incredulous when he saw one of the classes in self-improvement in action:

> Alec Downer [later Sir Alec and a member of the Australian federal parliament] suddenly decided that he really couldn't bear any longer the way Australians spoke. He assembled a class of hairy, uncouth, pig-headed, very volatile Australian privates. They were thieves of the first order, and then survived because of their daring and recklessness. They used to sit on palm logs in front of Alec Downer while he conducted a litany of elocution. 'How now brown cow.' It was magnificent! Nobody sent them up. Nor did they send up Alec. But it was weird.

For those who wanted a more private path to advancement, there was a library of 20,000 books. Men who in other circumstances would never have had the chance or inclination to read made their way from classical, to romantic and travel literature. Colonel Edward 'Weary' Dunlop encouraged each man leaving Batavia to carry a book in his pack, and the so-called 'Java Rabble', travelling in the holds of ships and crowded into fetid railway cattle wagons, had their own circulating library.

Many prisoners remembered the pleasure of listening to recorded music in Changi's warm evenings, organised by George McNeilly, a professional singer. 'Men sat on the grass all around the huts. For some of the concerts, when I played jazz records for instance, I had an audience of 10,000. The music seemed to just float over the air into the night and the boys really loved it.'

On the second day in captivity, the Changi Concert Party was formed and began rehearsals, and continued performing all the way through the captivity to 1945. The Japanese attended the concerts, too.

Traditionally Australians are said to be willing to bet on two flies crawling up a wall, and there wasn't much else to wager on in the main Changi POW camp. Frog racing became popular—when the contestants could be spared from the pot.

'While the Melbourne Cup may have been thousands of miles away, it was never far from our minds,' recalled Don Moore. 'It was natural that in this setting, frog racing would emerge. It provided a spectacle that satisfied both our urge to gamble and gave us an even money chance with the professionals. So we believed!'

With typical Aussie racing know-how, the CFRC (Changi Frog Racing Club) was officially inaugurated to arrange regular race meets. Official positions were established and appointments made. These included president, committeemen with board member status, stewards, clerks and of course starters and judges, as well as the essential registered bookies.

According to Moore: 'Given the potential food value of their contestants, the frog owners took exceptional care in stabling them. They also had their own stable colours which the frogs wore during the race. So determined were the owners to make the event colourful and realistic, that the needlecraft of some of the surcingles [a girth to keep the saddle on a horse] would have put grandma's knitting to shame.'

On the advertised day of the meet, the race officials gathered together in the centre of the Changi parade ground and took up their assigned positions, surrounded by a huge crowd of excited punters. With strong convictions and hopeful expectations, they placed their bets with the bookies.

Once in the hands of the stewards, the frogs were then passed over to the starter, who took them to the starting stall in the centre of a large circle and placed them under an upturned bucket. All bets were called off and silence reigned. With an elegant flourish, the starter lifted up the bucket.

'They're off!' the crowd roared as the race began.

But not always, as Moore observed:

> Well! It did for some of the contestants. Some of them were so overcome by the excitement around them that they froze and remained motionless, palpitating as frogs do, and looking extremely bored with life. Others, having been trapped in darkness under a bucket for a few unpleasant moments, took one great leap to hopeful freedom and then having achieved it, stopped, uncertain as to what their next move should be. Others would take a couple of long healthy jumps, to the great excitement of the crowd, only to freeze just short of the finishing circle.

When at last the third frog passed the winning post, the race was declared over and the judges announced the place-getters.

One of the owners experienced an unusual run of success. His frog soon became a hot favourite. It seemed that particular frog began to understand what the race was all about, for as soon as the bucket was lifted it would take three or four mighty leaps and bound right across the finishing line before the other contestants had even realised the bucket had been lifted.

In the course of his duties, one of the stewards picked up this 'hot' frog to inspect the small brass buttons which held its colourful knitted surcingle in place. While examining it, he pricked his finger. A closer examination revealed one of the 'buttons' was in fact a small drawing pin cunningly aligned with the buttons in the surcingle.

'This was the equivalent of an electric battery—a major violation—and unpardonable offence,' Moore explained. 'Every time the frog landed it had an immediate incentive to leap into the air to relieve its discomfort. The higher it hopped, the more discomfort it had on landing and the more incentive it had to leap once again.'

On the evidence of the steward, a meeting of the executive members and committeemen was quickly convened and the race committee handed down a life suspension to the owner, who was also warned off the course.

For humanitarian reasons, the committee reviewed its decision a few weeks later and withdrew the ex-owner's life suspension, but with a special proviso that he was permitted to attend only as a spectator. The race committee reasoned that his ingenuity at least entitled him to enjoy the excitement of future meetings.

In Java, the remnants of 'Blackforce', sacrificed to the hopeless and lack-lustre efforts of the Dutch to hang on to their colonial empire, were enduring a mixed bag of experiences as prisoners of war of the Japanese. Gunner Clarry McCulloch remained in the village of Leles, where he had been captured in March 1943. Their guards were still front-line soldiers, who did not attempt to loot whatever meagre possessions the Australians had. Although sleeping on the ground under flimsy *atap* (palm frond) shelters, they were getting a reasonable amount of food.

> At first there was no fence around the market area, with just a few guards wandering around, and it was from here that the first escape attempt was made. Six West Australian chaps from D Company of our battalion decided to try their luck and managed to cover a few miles before being recaptured. They were then imprisoned in a camp which contained Royal Air Force personnel, but later escaped from this camp also. This attempt also ended in failure mainly because of the jungle and the hostile attitude of the Javanese population, most of whom at

> the stage were very pro-Japanese. This time the six Australians were not given a third chance and we heard later that they had all been executed.

On 14 April all the POWs were all moved to the nearby town of Garoet, where there was an improvement in accommodation. The Australians were billeted in a local school. Although the school grounds were surrounded by a high chain-wire fence, on the plus side they had electric lighting, sewerage and showers, 'the latter being very welcome in the hot tropical conditions'.

It was at Garoet that McCulloch had his first close shave with death as a prisoner. Several of his companions had contracted malaria; one man died from it. Somehow McCulloch had contracted a very nasty type of dysentery and his visits to the latrine increased dramatically. During his worst day, he had more than 60 bowel movements and was losing weight at an alarming rate. The medical staff had practically no medical supplies, so for six days the only medication available was tea without milk and powdered charcoal. This was no use whatsoever as the bacteria rapidly stripped the lining from his lower bowel. McCulloch lost more than 13 kilos in weight during that time.

> Fortunately for me, the chaps had decided to move all our group to a Dutch military camp near the city of Bandoeng. Most of the prisoners travelled by train, but the very sick, including me, were loaded into a truck and taken directly to the Dutch hospital in the camp. By this time I was so weak that I remember very little of the trip. Arriving at the hospital we were carried into the medical ward. Here a jovial Dutch doctor, Dr Heggie, took one look at me and said, 'Ha! You have bacillary dysentery—soon I will have you fit again,' and proceeded to give me a large hypodermic needle in the buttocks, with a parting assurance, 'in two days you will be cured'. I just hoped that he knew what he was talking about. I need not have worried. Miraculously the diarrhoea stopped almost immediately and I began to feel much better.

Dr Heggie explained later that without treatment McCulloch would not have lasted more than two days at the most. Apparently bacillary dysentery is a particularly aggressive type which, untreated, can kill quickly, but with the correct drug can easily be cured. There is another type known as amoebic dysentery, which is more of a chronic condition. This can be very debilitating, last a long time, and is much harder to treat. This was the type that most of the POWs experienced later in Thailand.

In a little over two weeks Clarry had regained most of his lost weight and was feeling quite fit again. 'I was also conscious of the good fortune which had moved this group to Bandoeng at that particular time. Once again Lady Luck had smiled on me and I was suitably grateful.'

Their new camp was a big improvement. It had been a permanent Dutch army camp and contained most of the facilities necessary for reasonable living. At first the Japanese did not interfere very much and it was left to their own officers to organise daily routines. Although not the most senior officer in the camp, Colonel 'Weary' Dunlop—a medical officer—by common consent became the camp commander of the very mixed collection of prisoners. There were British army, navy and air force personnel, Dutch colonial troops from Ambon and the Celebes, a few of the Texas gunners, and most of the Australians from Blackforce plus sailors from HMAS *Perth*—'altogether a fairly lively mixture'. McCulloch recalled some of the efforts of the officers:

> As our food supplies begin to dwindle some of the senior officers managed to organise a large loan of money from a wealthy Chinese merchant from Bandoeng, pledging their personal IOUs. In doing so they imagined that the Australian government would make good the money after the war, but received a nasty shock when it was not forthcoming. Fortunately the Red Cross came to the rescue and repaid the loan after the war had ended. In the meantime the money was put to good use purchasing extra food and medical supplies.

To cater for the intellectual life of the POWs, many activities were organised, the main one being the creation known as the 'University of Bandoeng'—a mirror image of the brief flowering of the 'Changi University' on Singapore island. This rather grandiose title covered a series of classes devoted to further education at all levels, from primary to tertiary, and included a number of educators, with some from Cambridge University. This was a great opportunity and McCulloch, with many others, was soon enrolled in quite a number of classes. 'I was particularly pleased with the ancient history class, run by an English classical scholar.'

It was during these classes that Clarry McCulloch first met with a remarkable man, Lieutenant Colonel Laurens van de Post, a South African by birth. Before the war, van de Post had spent time in Japan and spoke Japanese fluently, and so was able to interpret with the Japanese on the POWs' behalf. During the early part of the war, he had operated in Ethiopia as an intelligence officer and then had been sent out to the East Indies to organise guerrilla operations against the Japanese. Unfortunately for van de Post, the speed of events in this region overtook him and the plan was abandoned. He was one of the prime movers in the development of the education classes and a very valuable asset to the prisoners.

> The camp also contained quite an extensive library, many of the books being printed in English. Naturally, being an avid reader, I spent quite a lot of time there. One volume in particular caught my eye. It was titled, 'Why Japan Must Fight Britain', and had been written in 1936 by a Japanese ex-naval attache. It gave a very reasoned explanation why there were many economic factors which would eventually lead to a clash with Great Britain. For some reason no mention was made of the USA.
>
> I was amazed at the British hierarchy in Singapore. They had not given any consideration to some of the points raised. I spoke to many English officers in the camp about this book and not one even knew

of its existence. Many of the other books in the library were quite useful for our classes. Before we left Bandoeng each man was allowed to take a couple of books to keep if desired, this later proved very valuable indeed.

As in Changi, rice became the principal diet and the meals were mostly prepared by Dutch cooks. Clarry remembers lining up one day to receive his ration of rice and being offered a ladle of a very appetising-looking sauce to accompany it. Thinking it was cooked ripe tomatoes, he accepted it, only to discover too late it was pure red chili purée, which nearly burnt out the lining of his throat. 'Many of our chaps were caught this way as at that stage we were not familiar with the Javanese type of sambal. Later, when vegetables to go with the rice became scarce, we learned to use the sambal with discretion. At least it helped give the rice some flavour.'

As the weeks dragged by, morale slipped a bit, especially when signs of acute malnutrition started to show. One particular form of this was scrotal dermatitis, which was very painful indeed. It was usually referred to by the troops as 'Bandoeng Balls'. Another form of malnutrition from which many suffered was a terrible burning sensation affecting the feet. Although it was commonly known as 'Happy Feet', it was anything but that. Together with the low standard of food generally, it was not surprising that men were getting run down and as a result feeling depressed. There had also been a few deaths, mainly from malaria and dysentery.

McCulloch recalled that the super optimists who had maintained they would be free in six months were now starting to realise that it would be much longer than that. 'No one had the slightest idea just how long it would be or how much degradation we would suffer. Perhaps it was just as well.'

From time to time Japanese newspapers printed in English were circulated that occasionally provided a good laugh. For instance, one item described the gallant performance of a Japanese pilot who, when he ran out of ammunition while attacking an Allied destroyer, swooped over the ship and cut off the captain's head with his Samurai sword as he flew past!

Another article detailed the exploits of a Japanese soldier in Burma. This man had run 100 miles to deliver a message to headquarters, and had then collapsed at the feet of the general. He was examined by a doctor, who pronounced that the soldier had been dead for two days! It was only the spirit of Nippon that had kept him running.

But the item that really caught the Australians' attention was the one that described the exploits of the midget submarines when they invaded Sydney Harbour. The article was complete with a drawing of the Harbour Bridge with its 'central pylon' completely destroyed.

'I could never decide who these items were meant to impress,' McCulloch said. 'It certainly wasn't us, although they did provide us with a good laugh from time to time. Not in front of the guards though.'

Although Australian prisoners of war of the Japanese were scattered in many camps from Timor to Manchuria, the Imperial Japanese Army began to draw on as many POWs as they could for their slave-labour projects, including building an aerodrome in Borneo and the Thai–Burma Railway. These movements got underway in mid 1942, and almost all began by cramming POWs into the fetid holds of rust-bucket ships, quickly dubbed 'Hell Ships' by the Australians, transporting them to Burma and Borneo from the main camps in Singapore and Java. Forcing prisoners to work on military-related installations was against the Geneva Convention, but the Japanese ignored that and did what they wanted with their captive soldiers.

Clarry McCulloch's journey to Thailand, through Singapore, began in the Batavia port of Tanjong Priok, when 850 Australians crammed into the hold of a tramp steamer in early January 1943. They had no idea where they were going. They watched from the wharf as another group of Australians, who were ordered to board the *Waysui Maru* first, were sprayed with carbolic liquid by a team of Japanese wearing gowns and gloves and knapsack sprayers. McCulloch's group renamed their transport the *Byoki Maru* ('Sick Ship').

Any thought of a pleasant voyage was soon dispelled as they were herded along to the aft end of the ship and directed to climb down a vertical wooden ladder into the hold. In this large open area, wooden platforms about 12 feet deep had been built along each side, 4 feet from the floor. They were ordered to crawl either on to the platform or under it until there was no space left. It was possible to lie down but only just. Their packs and spare gear were all piled in the open space in the centre and around this pile all the remaining party had to find room to lie down.

McCulloch's group had been split into two parties of approximately 450 men each and divided into the two aft holds. 'It was not what I would call luxury quarters but at least it was all "one class", which meant that our officers suffered the same fate as the troops.'

By the time they were all crowded into the hold, everyone was in a pretty foul mood. Later in the morning the ship got underway and after clearing the harbour, turned northwards.

There were plenty of rumours doing the rounds. Someone mentioned an eight-day trip which fortunately turned out to be wrong. The movement of the ship combined with the foul conditions caused a few to feel nauseous but remarkably no one vomited. Around midday they were told they could eat any food they had brought with them. Colonel 'Weary' Dunlop made several requests for men to be allowed up on deck to visit the toilet and have a wash and eventually the Japanese agreed to let two men at a time go up. Later this was relaxed to allow twenty at a time. This presented quite a problem, as with 450 men jammed into a space approximately 25 by 15 metres, it meant crawling over prostrate bodies just to reach the bottom of the ladder.

McCulloch described their journey:

> By nightfall the ship was creeping up the coast of Sumatra and we learned that our probable destination was Singapore. The sea was calm, which was a godsend. Next, a hot meal of rice and soup with a cup of tea was supplied by the Japanese cook, but just getting it served in such crowded conditions in semi-darkness was a nightmare.
>
> After that there was nothing to do but try and get some rest. Naturally, with the heated cramped conditions, sleep was virtually impossible but we filled in the time by counting the giant cockroaches which swarmed around. Someone likened them to small tortoises and while it was a slight exaggeration, they were enormous.

The next day was very much like the first—the same meal for breakfast: tea, rice and soup—but at least it was refreshing to get up on deck for a wash, though it made going back to the hold even more unbearable.

On the evening of 6 January they anchored offshore and spent one last horrible night in the holds. 'In the morning we landed and after being counted many times were loaded onto army lorries. The Japs always seemed to have trouble getting the numbers correct. The lorries were not covered, so as we drove through Singapore we were able to have a good look at the city.'

After a trip of some 24 kilometres, they saw the forbidding walls of Changi Gaol appear and many thought this was their destination. But they drove on and soon reached a very pleasant-looking area with many white, two-storey barracks scattered around, surrounded by well-kept green lawns. They were greeted by a group of British officers who looked at them with very disdainful expressions as they directed the new arrivals to their billets. Well-dressed Australian soldiers were walking around looking very fit and it was impossible not to compare their condition to their own.

'Admittedly we were not looking our best after being stuck in the filthy hold of the *Byoki Maru* for two days,' McCulloch said. 'We must've looked a scruffy lot as we climbed out of the trucks.'

Because of the loss of their kitbags in Port Tewfik, in Egypt, their one change of uniform was starting to look the worse for wear. Many had been issued with various items of Dutch uniform while at Bandoeng. Also the sailors who had escaped the sinking of HMS *Perth* and USS *Houston* had got ashore practically naked, covered in oil, and had been similarly equipped. Added to this was the fact that everyone's hair had been cut close to their scalps, so they should not have been surprised when they were referred to by the Australian commander Colonel 'Blackjack' Galleghan's well-dressed officers as the 'Java Rabble'. It was a badge they wore with pride.

If the Australians had been surprised by the British reaction, worse was to come. Colonel Galleghan tried to have Weary Dunlop removed as their commanding officer on the grounds that he was a non-combatant. Weary said that was all right with him, but that no one else wanted the job in Java. Next day Brigadier Blackburn arrived and after writing a rather terse note to Colonel Galleghan (whom he outranked), it was decided that Weary would retain his position, much to the general delight of the troops.

McCulloch recalled the gaol's heirachical conditions:

> We were moved into one of the lovely, airy barracks in an area set aside for troops in transit and were at last able to get a good night's sleep. Next morning, after a lecture by the camp authorities, we were told the rules which applied here. It was possible to obtain passes to visit other areas, but we were told that every officer who we met with, a British or Australian, had to be saluted and strict protocol observed at all times. I suppose the authorities were trying to keep up the morale of the troops by insisting on a high standard of behaviour, but I think their attitude towards our group left a bit to be desired, especially regarding the issuing of new equipment to us. Galleghan's Q Store

had adequate supplies of uniforms and boots but requests by Weary Dunlop for them to be issued to us met a very negative attitude and the amount we received was niggardly indeed.

To be fair to 'Blackjack', I got the impression that he was fairly highly regarded by his own troops and he intended to see to their welfare all he could. What I could not admire was his 'bugger you Jack we're all right' attitude.

Japanese guards seemed to be non-existent most of the time and only appeared at the 5 pm roll call each day. The Java POWs only stayed twelve days in Changi, which was disappointing, as during that time many of the 'Java Rabble' were able to renew friendships with troops from the Eighth Division. Conditions were quite pleasant for the troops in this area, with a view out over the Johore Strait. Vegetable gardens had been established by the prisoners to supplement the meagre rations supplied by the Japanese, and McCulloch felt they would have been quite happy to have stayed there longer.

Naturally it was too good to last. On 20 January 1943 they were taken by trucks to Singapore railway station and crammed into steel box wagons for the trip to Thailand. Before leaving, Colonel Dunlop wrote a parting note to Colonel Galleghan: *Two weeks ago my men arrived in pitiful condition in this camp from Java. You have done nothing to alleviate their needs. Tomorrow they leave in the same pitiable condition—bootless and in rags. You have done nothing!*

'I think that summed up our feelings also,' McCulloch wrote.

Private Russell Braddon, who went on to become a highly regarded author, later wrote critically about Colonel 'Blackjack' Galleghan and the way he ran the Changi Gaol:

In the fancy-dress days of Changi when it was a holiday camp with university courses and everything else, Galleghan went so far as to issue an order that other ranks who had walking shoes would surrender them to officers—they were suitable garb for officers only. Officers must have two pairs of short pants, two pairs of long pants—I can't remember the exact numbers—but it was a handsome wardrobe. Ostensibly it was so that they would appear to be properly dressed as officers and gentlemen. Those clothes had to come from other ranks who had carried them 17 miles into Changi. They were confiscated—there was no question of being able to hide them.

Galleghan was as sincere as he was conceited and vain. He was like the monarch at the trooping of the colour. He became quite hysterical if he were denied by anyone, even officers, the military courtesies. He was in many ways egomaniacal, and although brave and conscientious, destructive.

But there were other perspectives on Galleghan's command style. Some officers notorious for their parade ground aggression were timid when confronted by the Japanese. But Galleghan was as belligerent with the Japanese as he was with everyone else. To the discomfort of his fellow officers who feared a beheading, Galleghan would thump the table and even chased one bewildered Japanese with his cane. Whatever privileges the Australian commander took, not many were in the form of food. Galleghan's weight dropped from 15 stone on his entry to Changi to just over 9 stone on his release.

Chapter 13

THE RAILWAY OF DEATH

By mid 1942, the Japanese forces in South-east Asia were losing control of the sea-ways, as the Allied naval build-up, especially American submarines, began to take control of the western side of the Indian Ocean and the South China Sea. Restricted to land corridors, the Japanese needed to supply their forces in Burma from their stronghold in Singapore and Malaya. They decided to build a railway from southern Thailand from Kanchanaburi, through to Thanbyuzayat in Burma—a distance of 416 kilometres through jungles and mountains in country so rough that such a project had never been considered by the colonial powers, let alone attempted.

The Imperial Japanese Army decided to make use of the pool of Allied prisoners of war from the main camps on Singapore and Java, and began to move men north by ship and rail. Strangely, the prisoners were not reluctant to leave Changi. Although ignorant of where they were going or what they would be doing, they thought at worst they might work harder, and eat better. The first group to go were the 3000 Australians of A Force. Optimistic latrine rumours had it that these men were to be exchanged by the Japanese for bales of Australian wool. This was embellished by the suggestion that the exchange would take place in the neutral port of Lourenco Marques in Mozambique!

But these fantasies faded away when the men sighted the ships that were to take them away. The *Toyohashu Maru* and *Celebes Maru* waiting in Keppel Harbour were small, rusty and dirty.

The Japanese guards seemed indifferent not only to human comfort but to the laws of physics as they forced more and more men into the crowded holds. Men were still being bullied on board while those clinging to the bottom of the ladders had nowhere to go. On the shelving installed between the decks, Ray Myors crouched in a space less than two feet wide, a yard long and a yard of headroom. The men could neither stand or lie—they were stowed like sitting sardines.

Jim Richardson recalled:

> When we were stationary it was hot, the perspiration just welled out of your body and face, and it even ran into your ears. I never thought it was possible to have anything like it. Diarrhoea was pretty rife, and if you wanted to relieve yourself you had to go up a vertical ladder and get out over the side, of course a lot of the time you didn't make it above the tenth rung in the hold, and down she'd come. You kept going and left the lot behind. Shocking it was.

The men were given only a quarter of an hour on deck each day. At night sleep was almost impossible. Any man who moved buffeted and jolted everyone near him, and rats 'the size of cats were running all over you'.

Some prisoners were unloaded at Victoria Point in the extreme south of Burma—the rest went further north at Mergui and Tavoy. The men taken by lighters to Tavoy had spent twelve days of cramped inactivity, and their decline in physical fitness was evident as they struggled to complete the 25-mile walk to their camp. All of A Force was instructed to level the ground for airfields. One of the most memorable characteristics of the new surroundings was the drenching monsoonal rain. It fell with such an intensity that a man seen in the distance at the end of the aerodrome would be bent at 45 degrees and literally leaning against the deluge trying to push his way through the driving rain.

With British forces on the northern border of Burma and the apparent slackness of the guards, the prisoners began talking about escape. Eight men gave it a try, and simply walked out of the camp. But local Burmese gave them away and the Japanese rounded them all up the next day. The men who had attempted to escape were all Victorians from the 2/4th Anti-Tank Regiment. Other prisoners were forced to dig shallow graves, and made to watch while all eight escapees were shot and bundled into the inadequate graves.

By September the men of A Force had finished their work on the airfield and were moved further up the Burmese coast. At Thanbyuzayat they were organised into work gangs and each man was issued with a wooden tag on which was inscribed his prisoner of war number. More troops—Dutch, British, Australian and American—began arriving and soon there were more than 9000 prisoners in camps south of Moulmein.

Other groups had been leaving Changi Gaol. B and E Forces went to Borneo, and early in 1943 men were assembled for somewhere up country. Dunlop Force left in January, then D Force, F Force, H Force and other smaller groups followed throughout the year.

Again there were rumours of better times. Geoff O'Connor, who was on D Force, said, 'All we knew was that they wanted a work party to go to Thailand. It was going to be a land of milk and honey, plenty of food and very little to do.'

Dr Kevin Fagan followed on H Force with fantasies fostered by the Japanese. 'We were told we were going to a holiday camp, good food, bring the old pianos and musical instruments.'

At Singapore Station the men were crowded into high-sided covered steel cattle wagons. Each train took about 600 men, and more than ten successive trains were needed to move the numbers involved.

The men travelling north had no real idea where they were going, but the Japanese knew exactly what they wanted the prisoners to do. They had a large army in Burma which had to be supplied and reinforced. With the sea route now compromised, the only effective alternative was to build a railway from Bampong in Thailand, north to the border at the Three Pagodas Pass, and joining the Burmese rail system at Thanbyuzayat. The railway, all 416 kilometres of it, was to be built by Allied prisoners of war and Asian labourers—who were either tricked or compelled into offering their services.

During the day the airless steel wagons were intensely hot, but at night they cooled quickly and the fleshless men had the unusual experience of feeling cold. The food they had taken with them was rancid within a few hours of leaving Singapore and little was issued on the way. One section of F Force went 40 hours without a meal. When food appeared it was likely to be a bucket of rice swarming with flies. Excretion was as difficult as ingestion.

'There were no toilet facilities whatsoever,' said Stan Arneil. 'Now you may not believe it in these modern days, but the average Australian is a very modest person. So without toilet facilities they had to be held out from the side of the steel wagons.'

Two of the stronger men braced themselves and took an arm each while the straining operator prayed that he would not be paraded past a platform of the bewildered Thais or whipped by branches. Most prisoners waited in hope for a moment of greater comfort, as Don Moore explained:

> As soon as the train would stop, they'd come out and all you'd see were thousands of bare bottoms as they'd go down. Then there'd be a blast on the whistle and some fellows used to shout out mockingly, 'Cut it short! Cut it short!' They'd come back pulling up their trousers and attending to what hygienic arrangements they could while racing for the train. I felt sure that some would be left behind. God knows what would have happened to them.

A little later the 7000 men of F Force, made up equally of British and Australian prisoners, left Bampong on a horrific forced march. The prisoners on the last train had no chance to rest before the guards were shouting orders, and as the men milled in confusion, the shouting turned to hysterical screaming. Exhausted men were slapped and kicked into conformity. The march began at 10.30 pm. Stan Arneil recalled:

> We marched for 190 miles. The first night wasn't too bad, it was on a sealed road. The Thais were like scavengers buying things from us, and we were so exhausted we were selling everything we had, jumpers or anything like that, for a fraction of their worth. We marched all night and lay down like dogs in the morning alongside the river. We went into the river and out again. But, of course, the heat was well over 100 degrees and without shade there was very little possibility of sleeping. That went on night after night.

They marched at night, but heavy rain turned the track into slippery mud. 'It was a waning moon which meant that we finished up in pitch black most of the night,' Arneil said. 'I don't know how the guards found the way. The sandflies almost bit us to death. Men cut their hair off to keep them away, and most of us carried a piece of smoking bamboo and waved it around our heads with little effect.'

At some of the daytime camps there was no shelter and shade, and the men just lay on the open ground. At Wampo an Australian officer attempting to buy additional food approached a Thai woman, who found some sago and moistened it with her own breast milk. For F Force the march ended in May 1943 at Songkurai, close to the Burmese border.

By mid 1943, 12,000 Australian prisoners of war were scattered through camps in Thailand and Burma. They were just part of the 61,000 Allied prisoners and 250,000 Asian labourers in the workforce that built the Thai–Burma Railway. The Japanese had undertaken a massive engineering task and almost the only energy they would use to clear, dig, bridge, ballast and lay tracks was human. The only incentive for the humans was that they would suffer more if they didn't work. The first task for many of the prisoners was to build their own camps. The fortunate ones found tents and *atap* thatched huts to house some of them; the rest started with a clearing in the jungle and their camp was what they could make of it.

Men worked in gangs. On the railway embankment some prisoners would be using a *chunkel*, the large Asian hoe, or a shovel; another group would have wicker baskets or stretchers made of rice bags slung between two bamboo poles to carry the freshly dug earth; and a third gang would be levelling the soil when it was dumped on the pegged line of the railway. Creeks were bridged with tiers of sleepers laid in pairs across each other—effectively giant matchstick mazes of wood. Prisoners who prided themselves on their own capacity for hard work and ingenuity were constantly surprised at what the Japanese aimed to accomplish with little more than sweat, hand tools and materials found on the site. According to Hugh Clarke:

> The men could not believe the Japanese engineer when he told us they were going to dig and dynamite their way through the cutting which became known as Hellfire Pass. It was to be over 500 yards long and 25 yards deep. Before explosives could be used, the hammer and tap men had to drill into the rock, one man holding the drill and twisting it

after each blow and the other man swinging the heavy sledge hammer. The hammer man could rest briefly while his partner scooped shattered rock dust from the drill hole with a piece of hooked metal.

Donald Stuart, who had learned a bit about hard rock mining on his travels in Western Australia, deplored the waste of human energy but admired what could be achieved with primitive machinery.

> I've seen them when they were short of dynamite, fill the drill hole with water, drive wooden rods into it, and leave it overnight. If you've got enough of the rods and they're close enough together, the swelling of the wood will bust the rock a bit. Then you get in with blunt picks and crowbars that bend like sticks of solder, and you niggle and you gouge. And gradually we got those damn cuttings through.

In Burma the men of A Force began pushing the railway south-east from Thanbyuzayat. At some of the early camps the Japanese exhorted the men to work with signs: WORK CHEERFUL AND WORK DILIGENT. At first the daily work targets weren't excessive, Arthur Bancroft said:

> We fell for the three-card trick fairly early in the piece. The Jap said, 'You have one cubic metre of sand to dig and when you finish that you can go back to camp.' Some of the energetic ones thought, 'This is good, let's get rid of the sand and we'll be back at camp by noon.' And, of course, it was a piece of cake. Our officers were saying, 'Don't go rushing into this because they'll only give you more to do.' And that's exactly what they did. They just added and added and added. Eventually they got to the stage of keeping us out all night!

Basically the Japanese didn't care how many workers died, providing the railway was built. This was not efficient. To this day, no one knows how many Asian workers died, because unlike the prisoners of war, they had no organisation. The figure is generally thought to be in excess of 350,000, but with no marked graves it could be more. The prisoners of war were starved not only of food, but of basic medicines. Had they been better fed and given simple vitamins, not only fewer would have died, but the railway would have been built more efficiently and quickly. They did at least have competent doctors who did marvels with very little, even amputating gangrenous limbs, and handy POWs even managed to make some primitive artificial limbs. The Australian doctors also improvised tubing for saline drips to treat cholera patients, and saved many lives. The Asian workers had no chance.

Just when the POWs thought that life on the Thai–Burma Railway could not get any worse, they were due for a shock.

Early in 1943 the Japanese were becoming increasingly worried about the vulnerability of their army in Burma. After a review of the Burma area army's position, Imperial General Headquarters decided that their troops could not survive if they waited to be attacked—the Japanese in Burma must go on the offensive against the British poised on the northern border. In 1943 the Burma front was one of the few places where the Japanese could still hope to advance. But the success of the Japanese offensive depended on the Burma area army being reinforced and better equipped in time to campaign in the coming dry season. The overland supply route, the Thai–Burma Railway, would have to be completed ahead of time. The tactical decisions taken by the Japanese had profound effects on the Allied prisoners of war and the Asian labourers who were the tools of Japanese policy. If the railway were to be built more quickly, then the prisoners and labourers would have to work harder and longer, wet or dry, sick or well, fed or starved. It was true that the Japanese had some elephants but, as one prisoner observed, the elephants were better than men in demonstrating that if they didn't eat, they didn't work.

The difficulties of the prisoners had already increased when the wet season set in. The sky was a massive cloud sitting at bamboo top. The rain came as a waterfall. Kevin Fagan remembered it as continuous, penetrating everything, squelching underfoot and rattling down the back of his neck. Hugh Clarke recollected:

> The ground turned to mud, your clothes rotted away, your boots, if you had any boots at that stage, rotted off. The six-foot latrine pits which we had dug filled up with water and in no time the whole camp area was crawling with maggots. In the cemetery the graves filled up with water and the bodies came to the top. But none of this affected the progress of the railway. You were just living in a watery world, and after a while it didn't occur to you that there was anything unusual about it being wet all time.

The wet further disrupted the ration supplies—trucks bogged, the barge traffic was disrupted by floods, and even the carts were down to their axles in the mud.

One hope had persisted among the prisoners—the monsoon would eventually force the Japanese to suspend work. In fact, with the rain came the demand that the railway be built with greater urgency.

Ray Parkin recalled that a Japanese officer transmitted the instructions of the Imperial General Headquarters in stark terms:

> He gave a long speech and said we were doing a good job and the railway was progressing, but the railway must be completed—'Nippon very sorry, many men must die.' Well, that began at least 150 days without a day off. These days of feverish haste were known as the 'speedo'—it came to be called that because the Japanese were always calling 'speedo, speedo' when they were hurrying us up.

Ray was in both Hintok and Kinsayok camps on the railway:

> A split bamboo has an edge like a razor blade, and when it gets in the mud and you walk and you slip, you get slices in your feet. There's nothing you can do about it, you just get absolutely fed up. This is when you're at your most vulnerable, both physically and mentally, and you wince at everything. Then you just go on and on, 150 days without a let up. During that period was just a matter of getting out of the job and getting back, and getting out and getting back, that was all. You went, and then you flopped on your bunk at night. I was in a tent at one stage with 22 others, and I couldn't have told you the names of three other people living there. We were like zombies, although on the job we were conversing and all the rest of it, but we were single-minded in just getting backwards and forwards. We were wrapped up in sheer survival.

The Japanese engineers and guards, under great pressure themselves, tolerated no excuses for being absent from work, even if their workers' bodies were grotesquely swollen with 'wet' beriberi. Stan Arneil said:

> If they wanted 200 men they had to have 200 men. The guards would deliver 200 men even if perhaps 30 of them might be on the backs of their mates. In the rain. So when we got there, if the beriberi was excessive, you might have to leave some of them on their backs with their feet up against the side of the embankment to keep the fluid flowing down through their legs into their bodies so their legs wouldn't burst. They couldn't work at all. We'd feed them at lunchtime when we had a break. They were looked after, hats placed over their faces to keep the rain out, and they were talked and joked to. They understood the position. We would carry them back at night. Usually one would die during the day.
>
> I remember a chap called 'Butcher' Smith. He was lying there like a hippopotamus. His testicles were so large they were just a little bigger

> than a normal soccer ball. My mate Doug Blanchard used to hold them in his hands and lift them up so we could turn Butcher Smith to wash and wipe him. He had no neck, just a head sitting on shoulders. He died—they all died with that type of thing.

Prisoners no longer hoped for a 'smoko' and a man who asked to go to the toilet might be bashed. It was nothing, Hugh Clarke remembered, to be hit on the head with a drill-bit or whatever the guard had handy. Major Reg Newton calculated that 68 men were battered to death in the cutting of Hellfire Pass alone.

Life was cheap in the cutting. Clarry McCulloch, who had become a prisoner of war after being off-loaded in Java with 'Blackforce' instead of returning to Australia on the liner *Orcades*, had survived combat in the desert war in Lebanon. But he came closest to death in Hellfire Pass:

> We had formed a human chain, passing the rocks hand-to-hand up the side of the cutting, but just above me was a man who had developed malaria and was really sick. Suddenly, from sheer weakness, he dropped a rock which rolled down and nearly injured the bloke further down. Our Korean guard at the time, a particularly noxious type we called 'The Crow' because of his constant harsh shouts, came rushing over and started to belabour the unfortunate sick prisoner, who by now was lying on the ground.
>
> I had heard the expression about someone seeing red, but up to that time had never experienced it. Suddenly what looked like a red mist came over my eyes and I raised the rock which I was holding with the full intention of killing the guard. Fortunately my mates saw what was happening and grabbed me and held me until the mist cleared. I was absolutely shaking with anger. It was very lucky for me that the guard was so intent on bashing the sick boy that he did not see me. Killing a guard would have earned me certain execution.

The prisoners, although numbed and exhausted, were still able to later recall a vivid picture of digging the cutting. Hugh Clarke wrote this description:

> It looked like a scene out of Dante's Inferno. The Japs decided we would work 24 hours a day, two shifts. One was the day shift and one was the night shift. Lighting became a problem but they are pretty resourceful people, and there was plenty of bamboo, so they formed a light party. Its job was to keep the fires burning all night. In addition to the bamboo fires which threw a fair bit of light, there were some bamboo containers with hessian wicks and a bit of dieseline and there were a few carbide lights. If you stood on top of the cutting you could see the burning fires at intervals of about 20 feet, you'd see the shadows of the Japanese with their Foreign Legion–style peaked caps moving around with their sticks belting men. We still had our slouch hats so you could distinguish the prisoners by being naked under the slouch hats, moving rocks around, hammering and clearing. There was shouting and bellowing. This went on all night.

In its way, Adrian Curlewis said, it was a magnificent sight. 'The flaring fires, the movement and the noise combining in an intensely dramatic scene confined by the blackness of the surrounding jungle.'

Donald Stuart claimed, 'Dante knew less about Infernos than we did. We could have given him lessons.'

The reason why most men died is simple—they starved. The greatest atrocity committed by the Japanese against the prisoners was that they did not feed them. The Australian army ration of 1941 had given the men a daily intake of 4220 calories each—they could survive and do some work on 3000. In Changi they were getting just over 2000 calories and at that level they had been losing weight and suffering from deficiency diseases. In the railway camps, the few grams of rice, watery vegetable stew and infrequent flavouring instead of meat and fish was often giving them less nourishment than they got in Changi. This diet could not sustain men who were being forced to work at maximum effort. They were vulnerable to diseases that would not have killed, and perhaps not have afflicted, the prisoners had they been better fed.

F Force, at the Three Pagodas Pass on the Burmese border, for some strange administrative reason, had their food supplied from Singapore. You can imagine the condition of cartons of unrefrigerated prawns after three weeks in the tropical heat. The medicos recommended that the men eat the boiled 'prawn soup' anyway with their rice, reasoning that the maggots would at least provide extra protein.

Nearly all the men had amoebic or bacillary dysentery, or both. Some had contracted it before they left Changi, and they were to have it in varying degrees of intensity throughout their imprisonment—some all their lives! Dysentery was enervating and demoralising. Men were attempting to stumble to muddy pit latrines twenty times in one night. Nearly all prisoners had malaria. One of the medical officers, Dr Albert Coates, was later to say at the Tokyo War Crimes Trial that 95 per cent of the men in Burma suffered from malaria. Dr Rowley Richards, who was with A Force, observed the lethal effect of diseases in combination. A prisoner with malaria would go through the cycle of high temperature, sweating and shivering, and then while his resistance was lowered the dysentery would intensify.

At times the doctors only had crushed charcoal in water to offer patients dying of dysentery when they knew that a little emetine would have saved them. The doctors were always searching at the margins of their professional experience, recalling lectures on the history of surgery so they could resurrect the techniques used before the equipment and drugs of the 1940s became became available, and pooling what they knew of the afflictions of poverty stricken and congested populations in the tropics.

One form of insidious malnutrition worried the doctors. It was caused by a lack of niacin, one of the vitamin B group. Dr Rowley Richards said:

> We remembered from our textbooks that pellagra was something which occurred in some deprived areas where they had famine on a yearly basis. The first year was characterised by skin rashes on the face, legs, and on the scrotum. Next year the condition would manifest itself as diarrhoea. The third year as dementia, proceeding death. When we had a few cases of dementia we were facing the incredible prospect of half the men going mad. In addition to the pellagra problem we also had cerebral malaria which gave people hallucinations. It was a frightening concept.

Cholera was a fearful and frightful scourge, and 40 per cent of Australian POWs who caught it died. The medical officers worked miracles to save the other 60 per cent. F Force, high on the Three Pagodas Pass, lost 600 men from cholera alone. Cholera is dramatic in its onset. There are intense cramps, the voice fades and fluid flows from every orifice. The eyes sink and the cheeks fall in, as the dehydrated body 'shrivels up like a walnut', remembered Stan Arneil.

Stan Arneil knew within five minutes whether a prisoner had cholera. 'We would place a bamboo identification disc around their wrists with his regimental number and name on it, because in four hours it was not possible to recognise a man who had contracted cholera.'

One of the symptoms of cholera is a white stool. Ray Parkin remembered sitting out on the line, having a bit of rice up on the top side, 'when this fellow came along and he squatted down just on the other side of the railway line to me'. Parkin explained, 'There was no false modesty out there, it was quite natural, in fact we were all very clinical. This fellow, an Englishman, looked down and saw a milk-white motion, and he saw that I saw it. He just gave me a look and it went right through me—it was the look of a condemned man. He knew he had it. He was dead the next morning.'

Faced with the unrelenting awfulness of their situation, some prisoners—not many—just gave up, handed their meagre bowls of rice to others, turned their faces to the wall and died, usually within 24 hours, deaf to the pleadings of their mates. The survivors were the ones who never gave up, never doubted for a moment that they would win through and get home to their loved ones and families. But diseases like cholera were unforgiving to even the most optimistic and tenacious prisoners of war.

Although one out of three Australians sent to the Thai–Burma Railway died, it is remarkable that so many survived. Indeed, Australians survived better than any other nationalities working on the line: British, Dutch, Americans and of course the hapless Asians who, without any organisation, had no chance at all. The British, who were the second biggest group, were undernourished young men recently recruited from the slums of cities like Liverpool and Glasgow, and who had only six weeks military training before being shipped off to safeguard the British Empire. Then there was the unbridgeable gulf between the officers and the men, unlike the Australians, who were not so imbued with the rigid class distinction of the English.

The Australians of the 2nd AIF had many bush boys in their ranks who could rig up temporary shelters in the jungle, get a fire going in the rain, and improvise all kinds of essential equipment. Two such men actually started a business in Thailand, somehow manufacturing billy cans out of used food tins which were then used for boiling water and cooking any food that could be scrounged.

Sometimes a scraggy yak—brought in as food for the Japanese—would wander into the jungle and fall into the hands of a skilled butcher like the redoubtable 'Ringer' Edwards, who would slit its throat, expertly cut up the meat and have the carcass buried in a matter of minutes, while the Korean guards ran around shouting impotently, having smelled the aroma of cooking meat drifting over the camp from individual Australian fires.

The fierce determination to get through any situation thrown at them by the Japanese was an essential element of survival. Equally important was good old-fashioned mateship. Men would group together in lots of three to five, and support each other. If one POW could not eat his rice because of a bout of malaria, the others in his group would share it—making sure that the favour was returned when one of them was in a similar plight.

Another key factor in survival was a shared sense of humour. Australians seemed to be able to take the mickey out of the Japanese and Korean guards—a high risk activity, of course, under the most extreme conditions, but a great boost to morale. Clarry McCulloch wrote of an incident which momentarily cheered the prisoners:

> The Japanese commander at Tarso camp had a real obsession with parades and we seemed to spend an inordinate amount of time standing on the parade ground each morning being counted, again and again and again. On one side of the parade ground a wooden stage had been constructed and each morning the Japanese officer would mount the steps, resplendent in his best uniform with knee-high leather boots shone to perfection, ready to accept our obeisances after being assured that the count was correct.
>
> Now this officer was the owner of a pet monkey which was the bane of our existence. It would often go through our huts while we were at work and purloin anything which it fancied, mostly hands of bananas

or packets of palm sugar which some unlucky prisoner had hung up in the hut over his bed. One morning during the parade this monkey, after going through the huts, was making its way home and, while taking a shortcut across one of the open latrines, had the misfortune to slip off one of the logs and become covered in excrement.

Unknown to the commander the monkey had managed to climb out and raced round behind the rostrum, jumped up on the stage and sprang onto his master's shoulder, where it sat, dripping crap all over his spotless uniform.

It was one of those moments when time seemed to stand still while we waited for the explosion. Hurling the animal to the ground he took the salute before storming off to his quarters. Naturally the prisoners thought this was Christmas and New Year rolled into one and were not really upset when we heard that the monkey had been formally executed. At least our few small luxuries were now safer again.

Even in the depths of the 'speedo' wet season cholera epidemic, morale could be raised by misfortune, as Don Moore observed:

Toilet hygiene was the single most effective way to prevent cholera. Our doctor, Captain Millard, pulled no punches. 'If you don't make it to the latrine, you will infect some of your mates and they will surely die as a result of your carelessness and stupidity. If you get caught short on your mission, you are the same as a murderer!'

Following instructions we dug a new, very deep trench and placed four strong timber planks across it. We then cleared a pathway through the jungle scrub so that the latrine could be quickly reached by those in urgent need.

In the never-ending rain the trench quickly half-filled with water and to add to our lot, the area rapidly became muddy and the wooden planks precariously slippery. It was always a race against time, and

Roly Hull in his ardour to complete his dash to the new latrine like the good doctor said, had just reached it, when he slipped, overbalanced and fell into its murky depths. His cries of distress quickly brought his mates to the scene.

'What the hell are you doing down there Roly?'

'What the bloody hell do you think I'm doing? Learning to swim?'

'Weary' Dunlop (his nickname was derived from a pun on Dunlop Tyres) was a big man, and a former university boxing Blue, who was fearless in defending his patients against the Japanese guards' lunatic obsession of getting the required number of workers to work on the cutting at Hellfire Pass no matter how sick they were. Colin Finkemeyer remembered one particular red-letter day:

> The Japanese guards would only go so far with him, and they very often did. He had an uncanny knack of making the Japs feel inferior. This incensed them and they lashed out at him whenever they got a chance.
>
> On one occasion at Hintok Camp, Weary had one of his usual tussles with the guards over men unfit for work. He told three of the very sick boys to sit down on a log and wait there while the work party for the day was being determined. The guard tallied up the men now available for the day's work. 'More men work, too many men *byoki* [sick],' he barked.
>
> 'Only these men work,' Weary said calmly.
>
> 'More men. Men not *byoki*,' the guard shrieked back at him pointing to the three sick boys Weary had singled out.
>
> 'Only these men work,' Weary said, quite unruffled.
>
> 'All men jungle go.'
>
> 'Only these men jungle go.'
>
> Enraged the guard made an impulsive swipe at Weary's chin, only to miss by inches as Weary instinctively straightened up. Fuming the

guard grabbed a box from the guardhouse, thumped it down in front of Weary, jumped up on it, and threw another punch. Weary neatly rolled his head to one side and the punch went harmlessly by.

The grin never left Weary's face as his beady eyes stared steadfastly at the Jap who threw another punch. Disdainfully, Weary dodged again. Maddened, the Jap flung punches at Weary's chin, never once connecting. Blind with rage, he overbalanced and tumbled off his box. It was all too much for him. He quit. Weary sent the three sick boys back to their bunks.

It had been a total humiliation of the guard, and Colin said that was one day the prisoners marched to work with something of a spring in their step.

Food, and the fair sharing of it, remained a preoccupation with the constantly starving POWs. The cooks became skilled at making sure each man got a standard measure. But on occasions, there was some rice left over, and the 'leggie' system was started—based on the Malay word *lagi*, again. Each man was given a number, and in turn would line up in the 'leggie' queue if there was more rice to be dished out. According to Bob Grant, the 'leggie' was like winning a prize:

> We got to the point where it was generally accepted that getting your ration was your business and jolly good luck to you. Once having received your rice, it was yours and you trusted no one with it, not even your best friend.
>
> It was Alby Broderick's lucky night, his leggie number came up and he received a generous portion of extra rice. He was ecstatic and was boasting about his good fortune when suddenly he had one of his unfortunate calls of nature. The risk of contaminating his rice by taking it with him was as great as the risk of leaving it with his 'trusted' mates.

Wearing only his G string, Alby pulled out his doodle, dipped it in his dixie of precious rice and stirred it around a couple of times. 'Look after this for me Bob. I'll be back in half a shake.' Alby could now concentrate on first things first, knowing that his dixie of bonus rice was in safe hands until he got back.

Dave Buxton, from the 4th Anti-Tank Regiment, was working on the railway on the Burma side of the border at the 150 Kilo Camp:

Conditions had become pretty rugged. Rations were close to starvation point, diseases—dysentery, dengue, malaria and ulcers—were rampant, the monsoon rains hit us and we were driven hard by the Japs. There was little to laugh about as 200 of us, without boots and clad only in our G-strings, were floundering in the thick mud struggling to build a trestle bridge. On this day the rain was pouring down.

The Jap guards supervising the work were snug and dry inside the *atap* shelter we built specially for them. And so we slogged away in the pouring rain, hauling the slippery logs into position on the bridge and setting them in place. At least we were spared the sloppy, muddy job of dragging the logs to the bridge, a job that the Japs were only too happy to assign to one of the local Thai drivers and his great lolloping elephant.

In the course of hauling the logs to the bridge, the elephant stopped in front of the Japs' shelter and unfurled its enormous organ to have a piss. Being an elephant, its piss went on and on and on, never seeming to end, much to the hilarity of our Jap guards sheltering in their shack. With bursts of laughter they threw pebbles and twigs at its massive donger.

Having finished its mammoth piss, the elephant plodded on and delivered its log to the bridge. On its way back to pick up another, dragging the empty chains behind it, the elephant stopped beside the Japs' shelter. Not in the least bit of a hurry, it stirred its trunk slowly around in the slush and elephant piss and filled it with the repulsive slops. Then slowly and indomitably turned towards the Jap guards in their shelter and, with full force, sprayed the choice mixture all over them.

Completely ignoring the howls of indignation from the enraged Japs, the elephant trudged dauntlessly on its way.

I'll swear it was chuckling. We certainly were.

Incredible as it may seem, even in the appalling conditions of the 150 Kilo Camp, amateur theatricals were turned on for the mixed group of Australian and British POWs. Buxton recalled:

One night the boys decided to have a bit of a concert and John Higgins our youthful medical officer put on an act for us. He dressed in a tutu made from a piece of grubby old mosquito net, in the guise of Shirley Temple, a popular child prodigy of our time. Imitating Shirley Temple's childish voice, he gave us a great rendition of her popular theme song but this time with an apt twist—'Animal knackers in my soup'.

We also had a very funny little Cockney sergeant, who together with Bob Skilton, father of Bobby Skilton the triple Brownlow medallist of the South Melbourne football team, put on this sketch for us.

Dick Turpin and his gang of highwaymen bailed up a stagecoach. Dick called out, 'Right gang let's go. Rob the women and rape the men.'

One of his gang piped up, 'You mean, rob the men and rape the women, don't you Dick?'

A pansy stuck his head out of the coach window and called out, 'Who's robbing this coach, you or Mr Turpin?'

Two hundred Australians leapt to their feet and shouted, 'That wasn't Dick Turpin ya Pommie mug, that was Ned Kelly.'

Uproar!

Chapter 14

SERVICE AT HOME

When the Japanese unleashed their surprise attack on Pearl Harbor, in Hawaii, on 7 December 1941, the United States of America was catapulted into the war in the Pacific, with tremendous consequences for Australia. The Australian government had been concerned well before that devastating raid that Japan would eventually enter the fray in World War II, and that in such an event it was unlikely our traditional protector, the British, would be able to help their loyal dominion very much—if at all.

As it happened, things would never be the same again for Australia in the Pacific, and from that moment on, we have looked to the United States as our principal military protector. But early in 1941, the United States had little interest in Australia as a potential ally and, in the event of a war with Japan, their preferred strategy was that the US Navy would make a westward drive from Hawaii across the central Pacific, towards Japan, well to the north of the Equator.

After Pearl Harbor those ambitions changed dramatically. On 22 February, General Dwight Eisenhower, who had returned from the Middle East to Washington to help plan the strategy towards Japan, commented: 'Circumstances are going to pull us too strongly to the Australian area.'

A month later, General Douglas MacArthur, who had been flown out of the Philippines to Darwin on the orders of US President Roosevelt, had set up his headquarters in Melbourne, arriving on 21 March. Four days before, Prime Minister John Curtin had told his Cabinet that Roosevelt had informed him that MacArthur had arrived in Australia and assumed command of all American troops there. Roosevelt added that if Australia wished, 'It would be highly acceptable to him and to the American people for the Australian Government to nominate MacArthur as Supreme Commander for all Allies in the South-West Pacific Area [SWPA].' Curtin consulted his Advisory War Council, which not surprisingly agreed with enthusiasm, and the appointment was made.

Strategically, the partnership was most advantageous to Australia, and in military terms the cooperation between the Supreme Commander Douglas MacArthur and the Australian armed forces was sensibly handled, culminating, of course, in the eventual defeat of Japanese forces that had invaded Papua New Guinea and the Pacific Islands.

Socially, there was the impact of one million American service personnel (including 100,000 African-Americans), who began arriving in Australia in December 1941. During the next four years, the effects were even more complex as the Americans became an influential presence in Australian life, opening our major cities to a new culture and making a substantial contribution to the local economy.

Australian servicemen were at a considerable financial disadvantage. The slogan coined at the time was 'Over-paid, over-sexed and over here'. The Americans were better paid and had access to more exotic consumer items in their military PX (Post Exchange), which also doubled as duty-free stores. The Americans were polite and courteous to Australian girls, had more glamorous uniforms, and had the chocolates, ice cream, hams, turkeys, silk stockings, alcohol (which Australian military canteens were not permitted to sell)—and the dollars. All this led to the GIs' considerable success in the pursuit of Australian women. In mid 1942, a reporter walking in Brisbane's Queen Street counted 152 local women in the company of 112 uniformed Americans, while only 31 women accompanied 60 Australian soldiers. Some 12,000 Australian women married US soldiers during the next four years!

Naturally, the Sixth, Seventh and Ninth Division AIF soldiers, returning from the Middle East to Australia from early 1942, were aware of what had been going on at home.

Gunner Ivan 'Ivo' Blazely's troopship, the converted Dutch luxury liner *New Amsterdam*, berthed at Fremantle early in 1942, returning from the Middle East.

> A couple of young US Marines happened to stroll along the wharf beside the ship. Fremantle at that time was among other things an American submarine base. They were silly enough to ask, 'Where are you guys from?'
>
> If anyone told them, it was drowned in catcalls, jeers and threats of, 'What we'll do to you Yank bastards when we get ashore.' They kept on going. Yanks weren't exactly the flavour of the month among the AIF. Some of the boys had got 'Dear John letters' in the short time the Yanks had been in Australia, although a lot of us took the view that they hadn't taken our sheilas, they'd only sorted them out.

The Australian authorities had not helped matters by always seeming to supply the US troops with better food and housing in camps closer to town than the general rule for the Australian troops, and in some small towns in North Queensland, like Gordonvale and Tully, right in the main street. On leave in Melbourne two weeks later, Ivo was still unforgiving about the Yanks.

Our home leave coincided with the 1st Marine division being stationed in Melbourne. They, of course, were doing it hard being camped in such places as the Melbourne Cricket Ground and other tough spots.

Some of the 9th Division troops found time to engage in a new sport of Yank-bashing. The Marines wore a large colour patch featuring a palm tree and several stars on their shoulder and everyone had more ribbons on their chest than our divisional commander, and he had been to two wars. They had them for being a good rifle shot and it was rumoured that they were awarded the Purple Heart—for being wounded in action—even if they had only contracted VD.

Norm, our snowy-headed battery headquarters driver, approached a Marine in the City Club Hotel and asked him to explain what all the stars on his colour patch were about. The Yank, who was pleased that an Australian would condescend to speak to him, explained they represent the seven major battles the First Marines had been engaged in.

'Well,' said Norm, 'here's where you get your eighth.' And dropped him. There were many such incidents. No wonder the Yanks reckoned, 'Back home we've only got one Joe Louis. Out here every second guy thinks he's one.'

One night about 5.50 pm Ivo was drinking in Young & Jacksons. The 'six o'clock swill' was in full cry, with closing time only ten minutes away, and the total bedlam can be imagined. The bar was full of soldiers, sailors and airmen, all Australians, getting their last drinks into them before lockout time. With about five minutes to go, a half-full Marine came in and tried to push his way to the bar. 'He must've been demented or totally full, because he said, "Get out of my goddam way and let a Marine get a drink",' Ivo recalled. 'He never knew what hit him. As he was going down I made a grab for his decorations as a souvenir, and managed to get one of his ribbon bars . . . Someone propped him up in a corner and we got on with our drinking. What happened to him after that I don't know.'

The Australian troops from the Middle East arrived back in their homeland that had been traumatised by the Japanese bombing of Darwin on 19 February 1942, and continuing bombing raids on northern Australia, including Wyndham, Port Hedland and Derby in Western Australia; Darwin and Katherine in the Northern Territory; and Horn Island in the Torres Strait. The last bombing of Darwin was on 12 November 1943. Even as early as 1941, before war was actually declared, there were fears that Australian coastal cities on the east coast would be attacked, and some parents sent their children to inland towns and those adults who could do so went too. These fears were later strengthened following the brazen attack in Sydney Harbour by three midget submarines on the night of 31 May 1942, and a few days later one of the larger Japanese submarines fired ten shells, fortunately mostly duds, into the coastal Sydney suburbs of Rose Bay and Bellevue Hill.

For the first time in its short history, there seemed a real possibility that mainland Australia would be invaded by a foreign power.

When Gunner Bob 'Hooker' Holt arrived back in Australia early in 1942, his first port of call was Fremantle, then Adelaide, Melbourne and finally Sydney where his family lived. Before that, the arrival in Western Australia was something of a strange anticlimax. Holt had arrived fresh from the Lebanon campaign, where the Australians had fought beside the British. 'We had our problems with the Poms at times, but at least we respected them.' He saw his first Americans in Perth and, with their flash uniforms and loud mouths, they did not impress him at all.

Bob had a home leave pass for fourteen days and 'French Leave' (absent without leave) for another fourteen. 'I went to see the family doctor in

Lakemba and told him a pack of lies about not returning to camp owing to my wounds playing up. He gave me a certificate and we spent the next hour discussing my experiences in the Middle East while the fair dinkum patients in his waiting room sat around and chewed their fingernails.'

His unit was camped at Bonegilla in Victoria. He caught the train and belatedly reported in. He expected bother with his out-of-date leave pass but no one was particularly interested in him.

Camping in huts, with sheets on their hospital beds and first-class food, this was considered really high living. There were no nominal roll calls. Soldiers off the *Duntroon* kept trickling into camp but their numbers remained much the same, 'as just as many took off on unofficial leave'.

They 'fooled around the camp' through the days and had leave every night to Wodonga and Albury. But it was not the great holiday it was supposed to be because there appeared to be no organisation at all at Bonegilla camp and no reason for its existence. Holt presented himself to 'the powers that be' and asked to be transferred to the 2/3rd Training Battalion at Bathurst. There he was greeted by many men he knew from the battalion, including 'Slim' Huntington and Johnny Perry, who had been sent home from the Middle East after it was discovered they were under-age.

> For some reason they had been off-loaded at Bombay in India. There they had cobbered up with a leading Australian jockey, Edgar Britt, who took them into his home and gave them the occasional winner. They were both very happy with this arrangement and spent their money freely at an establishment close by.
>
> It was Johnny's boast that he was known to the 'ladies of easy virtue' as the little boy with the big Zoobrick. All good things come to an end however, they were eventually shipped out and returned to Australia. As they had both turned eighteen, they were on their way back to the battalion.

The provosts ran amok in Bathurst one evening and anyone with white gaiters and puggeri (hat bands) was fair game. The Bathurst Police Station was packed to the rafters with men on leave from the training battalion. The following day they were driven back to camp by the provosts under close arrest.

For whatever reason, the provost captain threw the book at all returned men and each had a list of charges as long as their arms. The provost 'was ably supported by his fat-gutted, cowardly, underlings, but when our Colonel questioned them closely they were proved to be liars, thugs and *agent provocateurs*. Every returned man was exonerated from the dozens of soldiers charged with every sort of offence. I believe only one was ever convicted.'

Holt recalled one occasion when the troops tried to take a stand:

> There had been complaints about the food and the amenities by newly conscripted troops and the rumblings of discontent grew until a meeting was called. There was wild talk of a walk-out from the camp and a march to Bathurst. Some of the Training Battalion went to the meeting to see what was going on. There was a large crowd of men milling around, listening to fiery speeches by agitators. Eventually the call went up to march out of camp and on to Bathurst.
>
> I suppose 1000 men started off to march the mile to the gates. Along the way men dropped off the march like fleas from a Kelpie dog and by the time the main body reached the entrance to the camp, only about 50 remained. An officer told them of the penalties of what they were doing, and about half the marchers retired. The few still left marched twenty yards along the road to Bathurst where they were confronted by the camp guards with fixed bayonets on their rifles and the 'Great Bathurst Walkout' stopped right there.

The 16th Australian Infantry Brigade, which had been defending Ceylon, returned to Australia and landed in Melbourne on 8 August 1942.

They proceeded to Seymour camp, where they were issued with clothes, money and leave passes. The brigade then marched through Sydney on 12 August to the cheers of Sydneysiders and moved to Greta camp on their way to New Guinea to take part in the Owen Stanley campaign. Bob Holt joined them:

> I was medically re-boarded A1 fit, and reported back to Bathurst just in time for a move to Cowra. After a week or so, a draft consisting of old hands left to rejoin the Battalion in New Guinea. We had a long boring uncomfortable train trip to Charters Towers where we were held up waiting for a ship. There wasn't a great deal to do.
>
> An ageing harlot, Yvonne, was the only lady of the evening in this quiet Queensland country town and business in her establishment was very brisk to say the least. The army pickets stopped claim jumping in the queue, and kept order generally. At the finish of the evening, when Yvonne had shut up shop, the big-hearted whore gave the pickets a cup of tea and a free fuck.

Their draft embarked at Townsville and went up through the Whitsunday Passage to land in Papua, at Port Moresby. From there they were taken by truck a few miles out to Donadabu, where they met the 'Left Out of Battle' (LOB) Party which was commanded by Billy 'The Pig' McDonald. The 2/1st Battalion had been nearly wiped out in Greece and had to make up its numbers from other battalions in the brigade. The LOB Party had been created in the Great War, and continued in the Second World War. In the event of the battalion's luck being out in the campaign, the LOB Party would form the nucleus of the reformed battalion.

Among the sick and wounded recently discharged from hospital were Holt's mates Tommy Graham, 'Cooee' Davidson, Andy Anderson and a host of others. He was shocked at the number of casualties and tales they told of the privations over the Owen Stanley ranges.

> The rainy season had set in, and you could set your clock on the rain pouring down for an hour every afternoon. The roads were in constant need of repair and this is where we came in, shovelling metal all day to patch them. At the first opportunity I visited old mates at the Australian General Hospital. It was enough to make strong men weep to see soldiers of the calibre of 'Tich' Parker and 'Nigger' Matthews putting on a cheerful face by making light of their fearful wounds.

The heat was horrific, the drinking water warm and the food entirely unsuitable—particularly so for gravely injured men. The medical staff and orderlies did their best, but even walking through a hot tent ward with a dirt floor made Holt sick to his stomach. He was able to yarn with dozens of old hands, including the ever-smiling 'Ned the Glut', who was assisting in the operating theatre.

> Conditions in the casualty clearing station at Koitaki were even more primitive than the Australian General Hospital, but at least the men there were recuperating. Louis Whiteman was getting over a painful wound in the 'bottle and glass' that he had received at Eora Creek. He reckoned he was the only man in the brigade to be shot in the bum whilst going into an attack. Cheerful Tubby Bruce of the J Section Signals was giving the nurses 'what for' with his antics. The spirits of the wounded were terrific.

Holt recalled that at Donadabu there were several tents full of Christmas parcels. Many of the men they had been addressed to had been killed in action. Holt and his friends occasionally collected them. 'I'm sure the men would not have minded their comrades helping themselves—nor for that matter, would the senders of the parcels.' There had been talk of the garrison troops in Papua calling themselves the 'Mice of Moresby', but this did not go down well with the Middle East veterans. It was suggested that the main occupation of the 'Mice of Moresby' was nibbling away at the Rats of Tobruks' food parcels.

Stories had been circulating of the inhumane conditions experienced in the crossing of the Owen Stanley Range, and that on occasions the Japanese had eaten the Australian dead. Regimental Sergeant Major Billy Duff and three comrades were ambushed and killed while carrying ammunition to the front lines. One of the men was never found, but the other three had great chunks of meat cut off them by the 'cannibal' Japanese.

Holt was told that even among these men the exploits of 'Tarzan' Pett stood out. As a Bren gunner at Eora Creek under Major Hutchinson, he had taken out a series of Japanese machine-gun posts, for which he was awarded the Military Medal. At Oivi Ridge, Pett also was magnificent, but received a head wound and died shortly afterwards at Kokoda. He was recommended for the Victoria Cross and would have received this highest of decorations but for a senior officer refusing to sign the recommendation. 'This gentleman remarked that in his opinion the Victoria Cross was for officers only.'

They knew the remnants of the battalion fighting at Sananandа were at the end of their tether and were exhausted. While waiting around to see what was to happen, Holt's mob went to the open-air picture theatre at night or watched the show put on by the search lights and anti-aircraft as the Japs bombed Moresby, which they did most nights.

Word eventually came through that the 16th Brigade had at last been pulled out of the firing line. They came out on 23 December—152 men out of the brigade.

> If I live to be 100 I will never forget the state the men were in when they arrived at Donadabu. They were a pitiful sight. They were as thin as rakes, haggard, sick and dead beat and we were proud of them.

The cooks put on a spread for them that the sick, wounded, LOB and reinforcement drafts had forgone their beer ration for the returning men of the battalion of at least three or four bottles per man. It was a wasted effort, however, for they were in such a state that they couldn't eat more than a mouthful or two of food. Even such enthusiastic beer drinkers as Joe Hurley and Jika McVicar would drink only half a bottle of beer and then throw up everywhere and go to sleep. The brass hats realised the state of the men of the Sixteenth Australian Infantry Brigade, for they were returned to Australia for home leave at the first opportunity.

The 'Left Out of Battle' Party, the odds and sods who had not been over the Owen Stanley ranges and some of those who had been lightly wounded earlier in the campaign, left Moresby by ship early in the New Year. They landed at Cairns and went into camp at Ravenshoe up on the Atherton Tablelands behind Cairns. To show their appreciation of the valour of Australia's soldiers in New Guinea, the people of Atherton invited Diggers to their homes to stay for a couple of days.

'When we arrived in Atherton we were introduced to the kind lady who owned the guesthouse where we were to stay,' Holt recalled. 'She was very enthusiastic about meeting some real live fighting soldiers and as we sipped tea the good lady told us that the town in general and her guesthouse in particular was ours. We were then taken around and introduced to the open-hearted Syrian Mrs Malouf, who owned the cafe where we were to eat.'

Quite a few old hands of the battalion were returning from leave, hospitals and convalescent depots. Holt's unit began to receive new drafts of young reinforcements from the Canungra Training Camp.

The Third Militia Battalion, which had done so well in the Owen Stanleys campaign, came over to us in its entirety, Captain 'Whips' McCracken, Sergeant Bede Tongs and Sergeant Major 'Nobby' Clark were among the outstanding men we gained at this time. Nobby in particular would have stood out in any company. He did spend a great deal of time with us, as his true age became known to the military authorities. He put up Boer War and First World War ribbons, stopped dying his hair, indulged in strong drink and became a grey-haired old man overnight. He was honourably discharged from the AIF and returned to civilian life.

Holt's group began to train in earnest. Route marches and training exercises became the order of the day. The 2/2nd and 2/3rd Battalions had transferred about 100 men each to the 2/1st Battalion in June 1941 to build up the numbers after they had been so badly knocked about during the fighting in Greece and Crete. Their relations with the 2/1st Infantry Battalion since that time had been really good. They knew a lot of their old hands and they provided most of the competition in the sporting events of the brigade—football, swimming and boxing.

Its commanding officer Colonel Cullen had the reputation of being as eccentric as Holt's own Colonel Hutchinson where the welfare of the men of his battalion were concerned. The 2/1st had a mascot. He was a castrated goat, Stanley NX-2 (minus two). Stanley became an identity and was let out on battalion parades, bedecked in a flash jacket of the battalion colours, black over green.

Stanley was very well known throughout the Sixteenth Brigade and his demise was very sad, particularly in so far as his batman was concerned. Stanley licked a newly painted fence and up and died. His batman, who had the job of burying him, didn't dig the grave deep enough, so Stanley's legs were sticking out of the ground. So he cut them off with a shovel. The Colonel was incensed about Stanley's undignified burial, so the ex-batman finished up Confined to Barracks for his trouble, or lack of it.

Beer nights were always keenly awaited. Every company had a keg, and for an hour before the barrel was tapped, soldiers would line up with their 'Lady Blameys'—beer bottles cut off just below the neck.

> You would make your bed and when the keg was finished you would wander off and climb straight into it. You could always tell the mornings after a night by the soldiers poking at heaps of spew, looking for their missing false teeth. One night 'Boof' Barnett put a large dead snake into Ali Oop's bed. When the beer was finished Ali climbed into bed and when he discovered the snake, he let out a fearful scream. He grabbed his bayonet and was about to run amok. Boofhead ran for cover, while the rest of the fellows in the tent took time out to pacify Ali.

In Holt's company at this time were four Norfolk Islanders: Joe Menzies, Jack Quintal, 'Lovie' and Eustace Adams. These men were descendants of the mutineers on the *Bounty* of 1789. Some of the mutineers settled on Pitcairn Island in 1790 with native women from Tahiti. The island became overpopulated and in 1856 about half of the inhabitants shifted to Norfolk Island, which remained isolated even though they were bizarrely in the electorate of East Sydney. There were three or four other islanders in the brigade and when they came over to visit 'it was a pleasure to listen to them singing in harmony'. Among themselves they spoke in a patois. On Norfolk Island they illegally brewed beer which they called 'soup'.

Beer was in short supply in the Tablelands so Holt's crew prevailed on Joe to make some 'soup' for them. 'The taste was right but there was no kick to it. However we remedied the situation with some lemon essence and a jolly good time was had by all.'

Holt's unit trained long and hard to once more became an efficient team. There was no new campaign in the offing, and rumours became rife about home leave. This was denied by the authorities and there were rumblings throughout the brigade. A notice was put on the battalion noticeboard advising all and sundry to 'go through' (desert) early and 'avoid the Christmas rush'. The colonel was not amused and told them so in no uncertain terms on a battalion parade.

It was about this time that some of the men in the other divisions reckoned they were being treated like dogs, so during the evening retreat they began to bark like dogs.

> The idea took on like wildfire amongst the units of the three divisions on the Tablelands. First you could faintly hear the yapping and barking from faraway units and then louder, until it reached our camp. We would take up the call—or the bark—and then it could be heard fading away into the distance.
>
> In 1917 on the Western Front, the French armies mutinied. The poilus went into the trenches baaing like sheep as they believed they were being led to the slaughter. I believe our army authorities must've remembered this, for they did their best to stamp out the barking. For us, however, it was all in fun and if the military hierarchy didn't like it, so much the better. The authorities didn't have a great deal of success in spite of Divisional and Brigade orders, but eventually the barking died a natural death of its own accord.

The Seventh and Ninth Divisions returned to New Guinea and attacked the Japanese at Lae and Finschhafen. There was heavy fighting in these campaigns and there were strong rumours for a while that the 2/1st Battalion were to join them. But the Japanese retreated up the coast, and the Sixth Division remained on the Atherton Tablelands.

Holt remarked, 'This was something of a let-down as we were packed and ready to move.'

Chapter 15

THE SAGA OF THE FLYING FOOTSLOGGERS

Like the British Army, Australia did not have paratroops at the outbreak of World War II. However, the effective use of paratroops in the early stages of the war in Europe sparked an interest in developing a similar capability in Australia. Efforts to raise an operational parachute capability began with 40 volunteers being selected for a Parachute Training Unit (PTU), training at the air base at Tocumwal in southern New South Wales, with the first parachute course involving four jumps. Equipment for training at this stage was sparse to say the least, involving one Wirraway training aircraft and a lone DC2 aircraft (the precursor to the soon-to-be-produced enduring DC3). There were 60 parachutes, ten wooden dummies, some motorcycle helmets and some physical training equipment including a vaulting horse. As author Norm Fuller wrote, the dropping of the dummies was clumsy. Without an exit slide, 'they tumbled out in an ungainly fashion with most of the canopies not opening'.

Civil Constructional Corps (CCC) workers clearing tree stumps to enlarge the Tocumwal runways immediately went on strike, claiming any one of them could be hit by one of the falling dummies. They were awarded an extra 10 shillings a day danger money! 'This award for the CCC workers astounded the paratroops who knew the men were scattered over more than a square kilometre from where the actual dropping zone was declared to be,' Fuller recalled. 'The paratroops themselves were unskilled in what they were doing, took many risks, but received no danger money.'

Local people watching the dummies falling thought they were real men crashing to the ground. In the bar at night they would greet the soldiers with how many men they had seen falling to their death that day. 'The paratroops looked sad and said for all they knew their turn could come tomorrow. On hearing this, the local citizens bought drinks for their heroes, never letting their glasses run dry.'

Training and dropping techniques were still under experimentation. With the parachute pack on his back, the trooper clipped a static strop trailing from the apex of his chute onto a fixed line down the centre of the fuselage above his head. On stepping out of the aircraft, the parachute opened automatically, as the strop pulled the canopy out of the pack, and the trooper floated free. His next concern was landing, and the idea was, when about 4 metres from the ground—difficult to judge under the circumstances—he was supposed to pull himself up into the parachute shrouds quickly, so cushioning his landing.

The paratroops knew they were taking part in high risk activities. Leg and ankle injuries were many—but not always through jumping from aircraft. A more frequent hazard was during training, where the recruit had to jump from a wooden tower 3 metres high, thought to duplicate the landing speed from an actual jump. This practice was soon discontinued, together with the army issue of elastic ankle supports. The casualty rate was considerably reduced! Still, physical training on the ground accounted for frequent broken limbs, sprains and concussion.

It was well known in the ranks that paratroops were expensive to keep in the army, with their special equipment, vehicles, aircraft and RAAF personnel to fly and maintain them. Qualified paratroops were paid a rate equivalent to an infantry sergeant. Medical services were also more frequently used than in other army units.

Over the head of the parachute battalion hung the constant threat of being disbanded because it cost too much. Norm Fuller believed that the only reason the unit continued was that it was tolerated by the Commander in Chief General Thomas Blamey, so it was in the unit's interest to have the injury rates during training kept low key.

During a training session at Richmond, in New South Wales, recruits were required to jump over a vaulting horse after a short run, and fall to the ground using an approved-style shoulder roll. In doing so, one soldier hit the ground awkwardly, breaking his ankle in two places, then spent several weeks recuperating at Ingleburn, before being declared fit to resume training.

On his first day back at Richmond, this soldier was approached by an NCO and asked to sign a declaration that the injury had not been sustained during his parachute training course. The soldier was surprised that he had been asked to sign an untrue statement, and said so. The NCO replied that if he wished to remain with the unit, he had better sign. The soldier signed.

After the war, Norm Fuller, who knew the soldier personally, went to search the archives, but he could find no evidence that the mishap had ever occurred.

A similar mystery surrounded the first training death, involving a Private Johnson who was undertaking a normal training jump from the unit's one and only DC2 aircraft. The apex of his parachute caught on the plane's tail and nothing Johnson or the pilot, Flight Lieutenant Beeston, could do would dislodge him. A terrifying scenario then evolved.

Tocumwal's commanding officer, Wing Commander Clarence Glasscock, took off in a Wirraway in a desperate attempt to rescue Johnson.

It appeared that his plan was to bring the smaller plane up close under Johnson and signal for the dangling parachutist to release his harness and drop into the open cockpit. But once Glasscock was in position with the Perspex canopy of the Wirraway open, a now terrified Johnson waved him away, apparently fearing he would be struck by the propeller.

Beeston then decided to drop Johnson into the waters of a nearby dam. The afternoon was lengthening, and Beeston was aware of the coming darkness. He flew low at 50 metres above the water to entice Johnson to release himself. But the aircraft was so low, it nearly stalled and Beeston had to regain height quickly for fear of a further accident.

The pilot swept back over the lake, again very low, and indicated to Johnson that he had best release himself. This he did, but not until he was about 300 metres above the surface of the lake, falling backwards. He was killed either by the impact or drowning.

Fuller wrote that four days were spent dragging the lake before Johnson's body was recovered.

Training continued, and much time was spent on parachute theory which would, of course, be the lifeline of each soldier. The trainees were taught to pack their own parachutes! However, not much time was spent on this, despite the importance of the parachute opening successfully. Fuller remarked, 'This in itself gave the volunteers the impression of how expendable they were, and whether anybody cared.'

Paratroops had to be special types of men—there were no others like them—but in those days the authorities didn't really know what to look for. It was a matter of guessing whether the applicant was self-confident, and had the ability to face up to snap decisions and to questions after the event. Strength of mind and character were obvious pluses, egotism perhaps, and a spirit of camaraderie to be developed through the hazardous nature of the work. Parachutists had to be commandos, and were later trained as such.

The first training course consisted of a solo jump from 2000 feet, two solo jumps from 1000 feet and a final 'stick' (jumping with ten men) from

5000 feet. During the initial course, one Private Kew set an unenviable record by being caught in a vicious updraft which lifted him skywards out of control, so that it took him eight minutes to drop 2000 feet. The freakish winds at Tocumwal made the dropping zone (DZ) particularly dangerous.

On 12 April 1943 the Parachute Training Unit moved from Tocumwal south to the Richmond air base near Sydney, mainly because the weather was more suitable for training. Richmond had a well-equipped gymnasium, a new DC3 aircraft was provided and smaller parachutes to take the place of the older style—and the use of the Hawkesbury agricultural fields for a dropping zone and exercise area.

The first two weeks of a four-week course were devoted to physical training and skills needed for dropping. Seven jumps had to be successfully completed to qualify, including stick jumping with groups of soldiers leaving the aircraft in quick time. The last two stick jumps were with 15 to 21 men, all carrying weapons—a .303 rifle with the butt held against the cheek or the face, or a Sten gun carried horizontally inside the front of the harness, and a Bren gun carried in a felt sheath which was lowered by a cord to the ground in the last moments before hitting the ground.

Lieutenant Max Canning was in the first stick at Richmond to jump with weapons. On this occasion, according to Norm Fuller, 'A dog, a cat and a magpie were included in the exercise. The cat fell from its master ten metres from the ground, the magpie flew off and the dog spied a rabbit when also a short distance from the ground and vanished chasing it.'

The paratroop unit was becoming something of a foreign legion. It was hard to become a member, partly because of the high physical standards set and strict rules. No one, let alone its own members, knew its purpose, and many stories circulated, varying from attachments to fighting battalions, undercover work, or becoming a brigade strength force from within itself. Volunteers came from everywhere. One, who joined at Tocumwal, was a colourful character, Sergeant Leslie Morgan, who originally enlisted in Western Australia.

Morgan was also an old soldier from past campaigns, having fought in the Spanish Civil War of 1936! He was one of the most decorated men in the paratroop ranks, wearing four Spanish decorations including the Order of the Golden Fleece. He had been in action with the 2/11th Battalion, a Western Australian unit. He fought in Greece and Crete, from which he escaped by tying himself to an oil drum and drifting out to sea. He was eventually picked up by a passing British submarine. Bored with military life back in Western Australia, he joined the paratroops. Morgan had one problem—his age. He put his age down substantially to join the paratroops. When he eventually went to the battalion in Mareeba later in the war, he was constantly afraid his advanced years would be discovered, and he would be marched out as the oldest parachutist in the battalion. This never happened. Norm Fuller wrote:

> Morgan was an unusual man in many ways, and he had many attributes, one of which was his mastery of the rifle and bayonet. Reticent to speak of his early army experiences, Morgan was known to have been a gun-runner around Spanish Morocco before becoming involved in the Civil War. He would tell his listeners he had done everything in the army except jump out of an aeroplane—which is why he joined the paratroops!
>
> A tall man, Morgan had an uncontrollable twitch about his face. On one occasion while a parade was being inspected by a visiting high-ranking officer, he noticed Morgan's twitching face and exclaimed, 'Good God, this man has been in the army too long!'

Military records now show that Morgan was born in 1910, so in 1945 he was 35 years old—a mature age for a commando-trained parachutist, it is fair to say!

Night jumping at Richmond was never very successful. Trainees were understandably nervous, and after some unfortunate incidents it was cancelled. The ending of the night jumps was more than partly due to the occasion on which the pilot, Lionel Van Praag, didn't reach the proposed dropping zone. He mistook the lights of a farmhouse for the signal to drop. The paratroops left the DC3 in sticks of five, and Van Praag returned to Richmond.

The hapless soldiers had been dropped over an area covered in tall trees. Due to the darkness they had no idea what was below them, and had no option but to hang in the trees in their harnesses till morning. When the sun rose, the men released themselves and fell to the ground. Miraculously there were only a few minor injuries. The clean-up and collection of parachutes and other equipment was expensive in time, loss and damage.

The Canungra Jungle Warfare School, inland from Southport in southern Queensland, was used by the paratroops on more than one occasion. They carried out the normal training course, arriving at the camp sometimes by parachute in small groups, at other times in larger numbers more conventionally in truck convoys. On arrival at the main gate, the troops would form up in their ranks and march in—their attention being drawn to a gravesite at the side of the road, said to contain the remains of the soldier who failed to move quickly enough during his training to avoid being hit by live ammunition. Whether this grave actually did contain the remains of an unfortunate trainee is a matter for conjecture. Norm Fuller thought it might have been an instructor's ploy to warn course members how necessary it was to obey orders quickly.

Canungra consisted of an advanced reinforcement training centre for jungle warfare, a commando training battalion and any independent company that might be reforming or refitting. The infantry training centre was handling reinforcements for all combat units. Men trained to a normal Draft Priority One Standard were received at Canungra from Australian training camps for an extra four weeks in jungle warfare before being sent forward. There were 2000 reinforcements continually within the training program—500 were received each week and 500 were sent forward each week.

The training was tough and realistic in the extreme. The concept was that the men should live and train under conditions as close as possible to active service. The reinforcements were ruthlessly disciplined, put through a hard physical fitness test, and given confidence in themselves and their weapons. With practically no amenities except for a canteen and a picture night once a week, no leave except for compassionate reasons, the men were trained rigorously for twelve hours on each of six days and six nights each week for three weeks. For the fourth week they were sent into the deep and rough bush country, which closely resembled that of New Guinea, on a six-day exercise in which they carried their own food. If the men qualified on the final test, they were passed as fit for jungle warfare. Training for independent company reinforcements was even more strenuous and covered eight weeks of intense work.

Back at Richmond, on 23 October 1943, Captain Colin Dossetor died while attempting a parachute descent into the Cataract Dam, between Picton and Wollongong. His drop was experimental, with the aim of discovering how much weight in equipment and weapons could be carried by a parachutist when descending into water. Before the accident Dossetor was warned by his fellow officers that he was carrying too much weight. Lieutenant Des Green suggested he jump into a swimming pool to pre-test the weight. Dossetor was so sure of his load and his own prowess he ignored this suggestion to his great cost.

Lieutenant Max Canning, who took part in the same exercise, saw Dossetor jump and vanish into the waters of Cataract Dam, never to surface. His deflated 'Mae West' must have filled with water and taken him straight to the bottom. Realising what had happened, Canning jettisoned his own heavy equipment and jumped without it. When the plane landed, Canning hastily re-donned his overloaded equipment so no one knew he hadn't worn it when he jumped. Other heavily laden troops crashed into the shallows, bent their rifles and damaged other weapons they carried, knocking themselves about badly.

Parachute jumping into water was discontinued after the death of Captain Dossetor.

Meanwhile, the parachute training unit at Richmond continued its courses with enthusiastic trainees and equally eager staff. One phase of this training enjoyed by all ranks was jumping off a moving vehicle and hitting the ground using the prescribed left or right shoulder roll.

The paratroops would spend night and weekend leave in Sydney and their maroon berets would draw much attention from the public. They caused traffic congestion when a group would jump off moving trams, using their shoulder roll technique when they hit the street!

There were always those who missed the last train back to Richmond, and having spent all their money they had nothing to look forward to but wandering the streets till morning. Luckily the police would gather up soldiers and take them to the nearest police station, where they would sleep in the cells till morning and the first train. This practice was unofficial, of course, and there were many occasions when lost paratroops in Sydney were grateful to the police.

Several WAAAF personal were attached to the RAAF 224 group, as it was designated. These young women were fabric workers and their job was to repair and fold parachutes. They also learned the theory of parachute operations. They were examined for this work, after which they were able to fold and pack chutes without supervision. After packing a chute, the women were required to sign their names against the record book of that particular parachute. Damaged chutes that were washed and repaired were 'dummy-dropped' to make sure they hadn't lost any of their efficiency. This was also the procedure with new parachutes delivered straight from the manufacturer.

The number of WAAAF members at Richmond was increased in mid 1942. On one occasion the women were working patiently with sewing machines repairing damaged parachutes when Merle Whelan tried to raise their flagging spirits by singing a song during the tea break:

Dropping, dropping, dropping,
Hear the pennies fall.
Every one for Jesus –
He shall have them all!

The paratroops assembly room was immediately beneath the workroom. The troops threw coins and pebbles through the windows. After a couple of similarly themed songs were sung, an army officer appeared and bade the singing cease. Apparently it had never occurred to the WAAAF workers that their songs might prove unnerving to the paratroops.

In the early months of 1944 an almost complete battalion had been formed with A, B and C 2nd headquarter companies and battalion headquarters with a reinforcement company. All were understrength. Movement of the main part of the paratroops to Mareeba in northern Queensland took place early in 1944. There was great excitement among the troops during this time because they all thought the time had come for them to take an active part in the war. But that was not the case and frustration began to grow.

The battalion was now in three parts. Those at Mareeba, those in training at Richmond, and those held in what was known as the 'holding wing' camped at Clarendon Racecourse. The purpose of the holding wing was to maintain a reserve of fully trained parachutists which could be drawn from the battalion companies as they formed, as well as for any other special forces which might need such men.

Inter-company exercises were carried out during March and there was home leave. This caused further excitement as a move into action was expected to take place at the expiration of leave. Intensive training began when all troops returned and battalion exercises became a weekly affair. The first jump at Mareeba took place in September 1944 but was something of an anticlimax. Owing to strong winds at the time, 30 men were injured. Once again this set the battalion back, both in training and morale. Still there was no sign of going into action. The men were all anticipating it, and their nerves were a little ragged.

Commanding Officer Lieutenant Colonel John Overall visited Richmond and the holding wing at Clarendon on several occasions, both on administrative duties as well as to assure himself that the troops, who would make the battalion up to full strength in the event of a movement order, were in good spirits, and their training was being maintained at an acceptable standard.

The first battalion parade was held complete with a pipe band. Training continued at relentless pressure, with the mortar section completing a two-day endurance trek into the rainforest and B Company crossing the Barron River in full flood with troops in full battle order.

At Mareeba summer was approaching, and with the advent of warm weather various minor diseases and vexations occurred. Most of this was attributed to flies, particularly in the latrines which stank to high heaven. The danger of infection increased daily and it became necessary to act quickly to remedy this.

A method both simple and efficient was soon found. Generous quantities of low-grade aviation fuel were regularly poured into the French drains, rapidly destroying any chance that disease might become rampant within the camp. Then one day an event occurred which, according to Norm Fuller, 'had to happen sooner or later because the danger was always there'. Someone dropped a lighted match into the stone well behind the latrines in the company lines. The result was a tremendous explosion. The earth fairly shook and rocks flew about everywhere. Also the undergrowth and flames erupted at points where fuel pressures had accumulated. Stones, pieces of piping, timber and all manner of engineering flew into the air, much of it being caught in the trees shading the tent lines.

At the time of the explosion and demolition of the latrines, an NCO who had been using the convenience was blown up with it. Exposed portions of his body were seared and smoke-blackened. The indignity suffered by the luckless NCO was further increased when he was thrown into a bushy tree minus his clothing with the seat over the receptacle he was using firmly wedged about his nether regions. Fortunately he was not seriously injured. The perpetrator of the incident was never identified, despite exhaustive enquiries by platoon and company commanders.

Further visits by top brass continued on 26 September 1944 when staff officer General Murray witnessed a jump by the Royal Australian Engineers (RAE) section and D Company. Ground speed wind was in excess of 30 kilometres per hour, causing one stick of paratroops to miss the dropping zone altogether and land in nearby trees, resulting in several cases of concussion as well as two soldiers breaking their legs. General Murray was sympathetic to the conditions but unimpressed by the exercise. The general's impressions quickly became known in the company lines and the troops became sensitive to remarks passed, 'leading to some personal violence'.

The following week saw the battalion visited by the Australian army's Commander in Chief General Blamey, and the troops became excited again at the thought of possible movement for the battalion. Next day there was a full ceremonial parade reviewed by General Murray, Blamey having departed. Still no movement orders came.

Towards the end of 1944 the battalion carried on intensive training, with a number of drops by entire companies. The unit was warned of a possible movement order in the immediate future and excitement mounted.

During a training exercise Lieutenant Hec Howlett had a narrow escape when he was left swinging from the aircraft after making an exit. Officialdom blamed the accident on Howlett making a bad exit. Norm Fuller thought this was questionable, 'because he was an experienced parachutist, and the army like to blame accidents on soldiers making an incorrect exit'.

Lieutenant Howlett had been used to jumping with a rifle and hand grenades, but this time he was carrying an Owen gun. Upon exit the parachute retaining strop became caught over the gun's foresight, with the weapon firmly wedged under straps across Howlett's chest. Adding to the situation was difficulty with fumes from the port engine, which was throttled back while parachutists made their exits.

Howlett swung from the doorway as the parachute release strop caught around his Owen gun. Captain Bill Morse, on the ground, watched the event through field glasses and Howlett's batman called encouragement through a megaphone, inaudibly. Two officers, Major Travers and Lieutenant Menell, from the Atherton bulk canteen, and the pilot Lionel Van Praag pulled Howlett back into the plane. He was none the worse for wear despite his frightening experience. The Owen gun's barrel was bent at right angles and the squadron leader in charge of the aircraft group claimed it as a memento.

Later in the day Howlett noticed his batman wearing an officer's shirt he recognised by the holes in the epaulets made to receive pips denoting rank. Hec said quietly, 'You are wearing my shirt.' Whereupon his batman replied, 'Yes, and your socks too, Sir.'

Hec never reported his batman and the incident was closed.

Misfortunes were not only the lot of soldiers but also of the battalion pet. 'Paradog' was a little female fox terrier who had made several jumps inside a haversack attached to the chest of Captain Bill Morse. When Bill jumped, the pilot would always check to make sure the dog went with him as it could not be left behind in the plane when everyone had gone. As Bill's parachute opened, she would put her head out and watch the ground coming up.

The little fox terrier became an embarrassing nuisance at times when she would appear on the parade ground and bark. Her bark was quite penetrating and often sounded like a word of command. Some of the troops would obey this command and cause confusion during a parade. Officials tired of the dog's antics and ordered it be shot. However, this did not happen and she appeared about three weeks later in headquarter company lines.

Paradog, nicknamed 'Ike', met her end under the wheels of a truck reversing in the transport pool. She was buried with military honours and now lies under a small heap of stones on the Atherton Tablelands, among memories of the soldiers she loved.

The 1st Parachute Battalion, unsurprisingly, attracted some eccentric personalities. Norm Fuller wrote about Eric Ash, who besides being quite a character in the battalion was an innovative genius as well. 'On joining the unit he became a D Company member. His love of reptiles, already displayed at Richmond training days, was to become a feature of life in the battalion. He was treated with respect in the mess lines and there was always a comfortable distance between him and the man in front and behind just in case he had a snake hidden somewhere in his clothing.'

Eric was walking through bush near camp one day on the lookout for snakes when he came upon a large quantity of discarded material dumped by the American unit which had only recently left the area. Ever curious, he looked over the material with interest for some item he could perhaps put to good use. It was not long before he discovered the heap of material was, in fact, the remains of a still the Americans had used to make their own whisky. The main components of the still were in excellent shape, and only partially destroyed before dumping. He set about rectifying this discrepancy.

It was not many days before he had the still in working order. Liquor produced was of a reasonable blend. Everything went into it: raisins, wheat and any fermentable assets Ash could glean. Alcoholic content was introduced into the brew from compasses, rangefinders and gunsight fluid filched from various sources.

A specially designed label was made for attachment to the brew's containers—bottles weren't always used to hold the liquor. Colours were procured by soaking cigarette packets and draining off the brighter hues. One label sported a crocodile wearing a parachute harness, another a panther wearing the same gear. The art work on the labels was extremely well done by artistic members of the battalion. The labels were almost professional, and run off on a printer in the quartermaster's store. The liquor bearing the crocodile label was boldly printed with the words 'CROC'S PISS'.

Further research by Fuller revealed the officers brewed their own beer in a small cubicle near their lines. Although the result was quite good, brewing was abandoned for the very sound reason that not enough could be made to satisfy demand.

The tempo around Mareeba quickened in December 1944 and January 1945 when further jumps were carried out in the form of company exercises. The battalion was warned it might be required in an active capacity, and troops became again excited at the prospect. During these hectic weeks the battalion moved to Trinity Beach in North Queensland for more exercises. At the end of these, a review by Lieutenant General Sir Leslie Morshead took place on the Mareeba airstrip. Troops' clothing was sprayed with anti-mite solution to help against mosquito infestation as well as discouraging other voracious insects plaguing troops in the jungle.

During the last days of January 1945 the battalion returned to Trinity Beach and took part in amphibious beach landing exercises with units of the Australian Seventh Division. Participation in these exercises was carried out with great enthusiasm and, although they didn't contain elements of airborne soldiering, were near to the real thing and hinted at a movement of some kind in the immediate future.

It was rumoured that the Seventh Division was preparing for an amphibious landing assault on Balikpapan and the paratroops felt almost certain that they would be taking part.

Days went by and spirits begin to flag a little, especially when for some reason unit rationing fell into disorder. There was a complete lack of fresh or tinned vegetables. The battalion survived this period mainly through the unofficial efforts and resources of the catering section. Interest and excitement mounted again when the unit received cholera injections and was inspected by Major General Edward Milford, the commander of the Seventh Division.

The Australian Seventh Division took part in the amphibious landing on Balikpapan, on the south-east coast of Borneo, without paratroops. South-west Pacific area supremo, General Douglas MacArthur, ordered sixteen days of air and naval bombardment to proceed the Balikpapan attack, the longest pre-assault cannonade in the whole of World War II. Extensive mine sweeping operations were also undertaken, during which time six Allied ships were sunk by enemy fire and mines.

The preparations were so thorough and devastating that when Major General Milford's Seventh Division landed 5 kilometres south-east of Balikpapan on 1 July 1945, the losses were extremely light. Within two days the Seventh Division had seized Balikpapan and one of its airstrips.

Heavy fighting was necessary to drive the Japanese out of their position in the surrounding hills. By 9 July the second airstrip was in Allied hands and the Seventh Division had firm control of a beachhead 15 kilometres long and 9 kilometres deep. Organised resistance ceased in Balikpapan on 22 July, by which time about 230 Australians and 2000 Japanese had been killed.

Australian Commander in Chief General Blamey had been keen to use the Australian paratroops to their best advantage because they were so well-trained. The battalion was also extremely anxious to go and join the assault on Balikpapan, but when this was put to General MacArthur he vetoed the idea, declaring that if he used these troops he would need more aircraft and ships and none of these facilities were available.

The last jump was done by the battalion at Mareeba in August 1945 just before the Japanese surrender.

Norm Fuller wrote disconsolately: 'The First Parachute Battalion's last parade was notable by its absence. There wasn't one—an inglorious end for a unit which could have done much more towards the war effort if administration had willed it that way. There were no pictures known to have been taken.'

The battalion's war diary reveals that on 29 January 1946 orders were received to disband the unit.

Some members joined the permanent army, others were so disappointed they got themselves discharged immediately. Some had to wait weeks, sometimes months, before their turn came for discharge and they stepped out of uniform for the last time. Many of the demobilisation procedures took place at Puckapunyal and Ingleburn camps. Some soldiers moved back to the state from which they had enlisted and were discharged in their own state capitals.

The last word from Norm Fuller: 'The parachutes which had been used by the unit ended up in various army surplus stores and many were sold in Melbourne for $50 each.'

Chapter 16

THE KOKODA TRACK AND THE BLOODY BEACHHEADS

In early 1941, with the bulk of Australia's AIF troops fighting the Germans and Italians in the Middle East, the Australian government was becoming increasingly concerned about the threat of Japanese aggression into the South-west Pacific, including perhaps even an invasion of Australia, when we had so few of our own troops in the country.

So began a rapid expansion of Australia's volunteer Citizen Military Forces (also known as the Australian Militia) for the defence of the Australian mainland and overseas territories. As previously mentioned, soldiers in the Militia wore military uniform, but were looked down on by members of the AIF as they believed the 'Chocos'—Chocolate Soldiers, as they were dismissively labelled—had little chance of ever engaging in the pressures of real combat. This was not only unfair but wrong, as the Militia's fierce and gallant actions in Papua on the Kokoda Track and in the Owen Stanley Range would soon reveal, and later in continuing savage combat against the Japanese in New Guinea and the Pacific until the end of the war.

Between March and December 1941, the Australian government moved three Militia battalions to Port Moresby to defend this vital northern gateway. The average age of these Militia recruits was eighteen and a half years. As if to rub in the second-class status in the eyes of senior AIF commanders, the Militia recruits were denied adequate battle training and treated with cavalier disregard for their welfare and feelings.

While it had begun as a volunteer citizen army, after Malaya and Singapore fell to the Japanese in Febuary 1942, the Curtin Labor government ordered full mobilisation on 19 February, and all males aged 18–36 and all single males aged 36–45 could be conscripted into the Militia.

For the first half of 1942, the Commander of the Eighth Military District, Major General Morris, had no experienced AIF troops under his command in Port Moresby. His main force was the 30th Australian Infantry Brigade—a Militia formation comprising the 39th, 49th and 53rd Australian Infantry Battalions. With the exception of the 53rd Battalion, the Militia units were led by experienced AIF officers and NCOs, but the troops were almost all raw recruits.

The appalling treatment of these youthful Militia recruits is a damning indictment of the leadership of the Australian army in 1941–42. No Militia units had received proper military training before arriving at Port Moresby. The 49th Battalion reached Port Moresby without the most basic military equipment and were put immediately to work as wharf labourers, unloading ships and constructing roads and buildings. The 39th and 53rd Battalions arrived in Port Moresby on the liner *Aquitania* in January 1942 and could not immediately be fed and sheltered because food and camping equipment had been stowed in the bottom of the ship's hold. Many of the raw recruits of the 53rd Battalion had never even handled a rifle until they boarded their ship bound for Port Moresby!

So it is quite remarkable that, despite their lack of training, equipment and supplies and the appalling conditions under which they fought in New Guinea, the heavily outnumbered Militia soldiers of the 39th Battalion would play such a critical and frankly heroic role—in delaying the momentum of the battle-hardened Japanese advance along the Kokoda Track towards Port Moresby until the more seasoned AIF reinforcements could be brought into the battle.

One of these soldiers was Sergeant Joe Dawson, who had joined the Militia in Melbourne in 1939 when only seventeen but bumped up his age a year to get in.

On Dawson's twentieth birthday, 3 January 1942, the *Aquitania* stood offshore from Port Moresby about 1½ miles. There were 4600 on board the ex-peacetime luxury liner, including about 1200 men from his 39th Battalion. They disembarked in a variety of ways. Some went over the side, scrambling down large rope nets into lifeboats that were towed ashore, several in line, by a navy pinnace. As they went over the side they were advised to undo the belt of their equipment in case they fell off—'not a happy thought, especially on your birthday!'

Once ashore their companies regrouped as darkness fell. Dawson's group set off on a 9-mile march with full gear. Their camp was not far from the Seven Mile Aerodrome. There were no facilities, no mosquito nets, no tents, no water, nothing except a cleared site and 'millions of operatic mosquitoes'. It was impossible to sleep, Dawson recalled.

> We were all dusty, tired, sweaty and smelly. The only water was what we had in our water bottles. At this stage food was scarce—it was mostly bully beef and army biscuits anyway. Diarrhoea and dysentery started to move through the battalion. B Company didn't have many casualties from disease at this time, mainly I think, because our company commander, Captain Sam Templeton, was very conscious of food and hygiene discipline and he made sure this got through to his troops. I remember our first dysentery case was a lieutenant.

About two weeks later Dawson was in charge of a working party unloading stores—cases of tinned food in various sizes of boxed ammunition—from a ship called the *Macdhui*. The stores were loaded into large rope nets, hoisted out of the ship's cargo hold by a crane and then lowered onto a lighter. Also berthed at the small wharf was another ship even though there was really only room for one. The air raid siren sounded and the fellow in charge of the lighter told Dawson to get his troops onto the *Macdhui*. He said it would set sail as it was more difficult to hit while moving, and the Japanese Zeros would probably target the wharf not the ship. This was not good advice.

> As soon as they appeared it was obvious the bombers were after the *Macdhui*, which was by then on the move. I was on the boat's top deck, leaning on the rail, when there was a big splash. The noise was deafening and all hell broke loose! As I instinctively turned away and bent over, I was thrust forward onto my chest and felt strong pressure in my crutch due to my shorts being forced up. In a fraction of a second, my shoulder hit the ship superstructure below the bridge and the ship seemed to rise and fall. When I managed to stand up the ship had a substantial list to one side and was still underway. Eventually, after about 20 or 30 minutes, she returned to the wharf. As I tried to talk to one of the crew I noticed I'd gone partially deaf but that cleared up in a few days.

That day the 39th Battalion suffered its first war casualties. A few officers and other soldiers had gone down into the ship saloon for a drink when they boarded the *Macdhui*. One of the bombs had exploded down there and several men were killed and others wounded. Dawson said he 'wasn't a drinker in those days, but if I had been, I may not have survived to tell the tale'.

On another work detail, the ship Dawson's men were unloading pulled out from the wharf to let a small coastal trader in. It was loaded with troops who'd escaped from Rabaul. Some of them had been taken prisoner by the Japanese and were used as bayonet practice. With the help of their mates they managed to get out and were picked up by this little ship. 'It was there and then that I made up my mind that in no way would I be taken prisoner by the Japanese.'

On 24 June, General Morris created Maroubra Force, made up of the 39th Battalion plus some signals, supply and medical groups. Dawson's B Company was ordered to move to Kokoda overland. They carried a full backpack, webbing, ammunition pouches, a side haversack containing mess tin, personal gear and gas cape. Added to this was a rifle (or other weapon), bayonet, scabbard and full water bottle. The heavy Lewis machine gun was moved around the sections of a platoon to share the burden. It was a tough introduction to the horrors of the Kokoda Track—not, as Dawson noted acerbically, 'the Yankee sanitised "Trail" nonsense we hear it called now'.

The Militia men's first significant physical test was Ioribaiwa and Imita ridges in the Owen Stanley mountains. Even before this ordeal, some of the troops were suffering from chafing, bad knees, vomiting and sheer exhaustion. Some had to be helped. At one stage Dawson had to carry one of his men's rifle and all his equipment. The soldier was totally exhausted and continually vomiting. He also saw Captain Sam Templeton at times carrying three or four of his men's rifles as well as his own gear.

The Australians would take three steps, then hang on to a tree, or slide back without gaining height. Later on, this part of the mountains became known as the 'Golden Staircase'. After the 39th Battalion passed through, the engineers cut steps and used saplings to form a rough stairway in the mud, which helped the troops who came later. A few of Dawson's troops had to be sent back to base with bad knees and other problems.

> Apart from the ups and downs, there were the regular downpours of rain that mixed with your own sweat so you were never dry. Other joys we encountered were lawyer vines, nicknamed 'wait-awhile'. These had little hook-like things on their tendrils that literally grabbed your clothes, skin, whatever, and hung on. Then there were leeches that had the ability to get through your clothing into all parts of your body, including the most delicate parts, to suck your blood. If you moved off the narrow track to dodge the mud, you would inevitably walk into a large spider's web strung between the trees with an enormous spider in the middle, usually about face high.

Their dress at this stage was khaki shorts, shirt, boots and short gaiters, and a steel helmet. That was how they travelled, wet or dry, through Nauro, Menari, Efogi, Kagi, Isavura and Deniki. On 14 July 1942 they reached Kokoda.

B Company remained at Kokoda for about a week, recuperating, training and doing patrols around the area. Dawson's job was to organise the disbursal and distribution of ammunition, including the priming of boxes of hand grenades. This meant unscrewing the base plug of each grenade, inserting the J shaped fuse and replacing the base plug—a delicate operation.

Meanwhile, Captain Sam Templeton had gone down to Buna to meet a coastal trading vessel, the *Gilli Gilli*, which was carrying the troops' kitbags and stores from Port Moresby. 'These were brought to Kokoda by native carriers, who were later referred to as "Fuzzy Wuzzy Angels", as apart from carrying stores, they played a major role in carrying out the badly wounded,' Dawson said.

On 21 July 1942, a cruiser from the Japanese task force which had left Rabaul on 19 July began shelling the Sananda and Gona area in preparation for an amphibious landing. According to Dawson, 'Our military hierarchy didn't have a clue this was happening until they were advised by air-raid spotters on the day of the landing.' The next day, Allied planes bombed the beachhead, sank a landing barge, and damaged a transport ship that ran aground on Gona Beach that Dawson believes is probably still there. Apart from that, the landing went ahead unhindered and unopposed.

The initial Japanese landing force was about 2000 combat engineers, including the battle-experienced Yokohama Advance Butai, whose job was to prepare the way for an overland, large-scale attack on Port Moresby by the Nankai Shitai, the conquerors of Rabaul. They also had with them 1200 conscripted native carriers from Rabaul, pack horses and mountain artillery.

At this time there was a small patrol of the Papuan Infantry Battalion (PIB) who were observing the enemy movements in the area. They had neither the numbers nor the firepower to offer any resistance.

Sergeant Joe Dawson was soon in the thick of the action. On 24 July he and his unit arrived at Wairopi to back up 11 Platoon which, with some elements of the PIB, had fought a rearguard action back to Kumusi River. The platoon joined Dawson's unit on the west side of the fast-flowing Kumusi River, over which hung a cable suspension bridge—*wireropei* in Pidgin English.

Although the Seventh Division had returned to Australia in mid-August 1942 from the Middle East, and the Sixth Division later in August, there was no immediate effort by the Australian government to send the returning AIF men to boost the Militia fighting the Japanese advancing on Port Moresby. The War Cabinet was still fearful that there would be an invasion of mainland Australia, and were holding the returned men in reserve. However, on 26 August two battalions from the Seventh Division were sent to boost the exhausted Militia men of Maroubra Force.

By September, the Japanese had reached the village of Ioribaiwa only 20 miles from Port Moresby!

Those key battles on the Kokoda Track were the Militia's finest hour, and Sergeant Joe Dawson and his 39th Battalion were in most of them.

> Sam Templeton left the Wairopi position and headed towards Kokoda to meet the new commanding officer of the 39th Battalion, Colonel Owen. He was arriving by plane from Moresby. Major Watson—the Papuan Infantry Battalion commander—had also joined us at Wairopi and was now the senior officer in command. Our small force took up a defensive position undercover along the bank of the river and were told to hold fire. I had swapped my rifle for a Thompson machine gun with a 50-round drum magazine and taken a spot among the greenery just to the right of the bridge. Allan Collyer was nearby. He had been trying to work out a way to destroy the bridge.

The Japanese appeared on the eastern side of the Kusumi River at about 2.20 pm. Dawson could see them at the bridge entrance. First one scout, then another, walked onto the bridge, then a third one joined them. They seem to be having a conference. This seemed too good an opportunity to miss, and one of the Australian Lewis gunners 'got an itchy trigger finger and fired', so everyone else joined in.

> I saw one scout go down but I'm not sure what happened to the other two. We had no mortars but they did, and they brought them into action very quickly. With reasonable accuracy, numerous mortar bombs landed close to and behind our position. It's true to say I really didn't like being in the thick of that action. We continued to fire at any head that appeared on the opposite bank and also in the direction of their mortar smoke, but their barrage only got heavier. It became obvious they were moving along the opposite bank, searching for

another place to cross the river and flush out our position. No doubt they were assessing the firepower of our small force.

At that point a runner slithered up through the undergrowth and by way of greeting said, 'What's the state of your underpants, Sarge?' Before Dawson had a chance to reply, he went on to say that Captain Stevenson wanted the company headquarters to move back and join 12 platoon at Gorari. Both 11 Platoon and Major Watson were ordered to destroy the bridge and follow as soon as possible.

An ambush was set up at Gorari as a delaying tactic. This proved successful as quite a few Japanese soldiers were killed, which slowed down their forward movement. Dawson's group then pulled back to Oivi. Colonel Owen had returned to Kokoda to meet two more companies, who were flying from Moresby. He left Sam Templeton to set up a defensive position at Oivi. 'When I arrived there, Sam Templeton, who was talking to Stevenson, told me to get two men and go with Stevenson to Kokoda and return as quickly as possible.'

Unfortunately, the two extra companies did not arrive—the air force could not supply the planes to carry them in. However, two DC3s were provided and a platoon from A Company flew to Kokoda under the command of Lieutenant Doug McLean. He arrived at Oivi with half his platoon and only one Bren gun. The other half of his platoon followed in the second plane.

By mid-afternoon the Japanese had arrived and were fired upon, which halted their advance. Then followed a lot of firefighting as they probed the left flank. A few Japanese were calling out silly sentences in English. One, Dawson recalled, was 'Come forward, Corporal White.' That was responded to by a hail of hand grenades from the Australians in their direction.

Later in the afternoon, Captain Sam Templeton was concerned that the other half of McLean's platoon would be ambushed, so most unfortunately, as it turned out, he went back along the track towards Kokoda alone. There was a burst of gunfire from this direction and he did not return. That also indicated to them that the Japanese were gradually surrounding their position.

As the night wore on, the battle intensified. The mortars were falling regularly and it was obvious the Japanese had indeed cut off the track to Kokoda. The position was now rather desperate—ammunition nearly gone and the grenades were all but used up. At one stage Doug McLean and another soldier moved out on the flank and around the Japanese positions and pelted a few grenades down on them. They knew they hit a target because of the yells and screams. Dawson recalled their dire situation:

> It seemed to me at the time that we were on the verge of being wiped out. We were totally outnumbered and thought our only hope was to make a sudden charge along the track towards Kokoda and hope for the best. However, Major Watson, who was now in charge of the force, had with him a Papuan policeman by the name of Sinopa. He said he could lead us out through an area where the Japanese positions were the thinnest. The word was passed around to move out quietly in single file, holding the bayonet scabbard of the man in front, as it was pitch black. We went down the cliff face into a valley, following the course of a few streams. We were cold, wet, tired and hungry.

When daylight arrived they realised they had not travelled very far as the sounds of battle at Oivi could still clearly be heard. A few men had not received the message to move out and they were continuing to do battle with the Japanese. 'When it dawned on them what had happened they did a quick runner, most of them turning up a few days later.'

The intention was to move parallel to the Kokoda Track, cut back on to it and rejoin the troops left at Kokoda. But it was soon obvious that would not be possible as the jungle was impenetrable. They followed a different track instead, which brought them into Deniki. On arrival there someone gave Dawson a small tin of baked beans. 'My poor neglected stomach could not handle food and I promptly threw it all up.'

While the action at Oivi was underway, Colonel Owen had decided to tactically move the men he had at Kokoda up to Deniki, where there were stores and an ammunition dump. When Dawson's group arrived there, Owen then decided they should move back and occupy Kokoda. After an issue of rations, ammunition and grenades, they headed back to Kokoda, where they feverishly began setting up defence positions, digging weapon pits with whatever scarce tools were available.

> Our force now numbered about 70. We were spread around the three sides of the Kokoda Plateau with a few troops covering the rear towards the track up to Deniki. Most of our automatic Lewis guns and a couple of new Bren guns were located at the top of the ridge on the narrow end of the rubber plateau, where the track from Oivi came in. This was where the Japanese would most likely arrive. We could see the landing strip below the plateau to our left flank. It was strewn with 44 gallon drums and logs and nothing could be done to clear it as we had insufficient troops. We also, unfortunately, still had no mortars.

Later that afternoon the Japanese arrived from the Oivi track. After engaging the Australians, they started moving around the end of their perimeter, firing bursts from different directions and throwing in a few rounds of mortar fire.

> The mortar barrage grew heavier, some hitting the rubber trees and exploding in the air. Being on the wrong end of a mortar barrage is quite frightening. You hear the 'cough' like sound as they are fired, then for a fraction of a second there is a swish of air followed by the 'boom'. Once you hear it your mind starts to think, will the next one blow me

> to bits? Or, will I lose my legs? It's a long walk back to Moresby with no bloody legs.

The Japanese mounted their first offensive in the early hours of the following morning. They came up the slope in the partial moonlight while a mist of rain fell. And they kept coming, yelling and screaming, charging up the slope, ready to die for their emperor. The battle raged for some hours. Apart from the Japanese mortars, it was a small arms, grenade and hand-to-hand fight. The noise was deafening. Soon, with superior numbers and firepower, they broke through the Australians' thin line.

Almost all the ammunition had been fired, but most of their wounded had been moved out to Deniki. Colonel Owen had been wounded with a bullet in the head and died. Major Watson of the Papuan Infantry Battalion was now in charge and he ordered a withdrawal to Deniki. It was still dark and the situation became chaotic, with Japanese appearing all over the place. It was an extremely difficult operation getting the troops out, considering they had no two-way radios at that time.

> Upon reaching Deniki we regrouped and checked our numbers—the living, the dead, the wounded and the missing. The balance of the 39th Battalion companies were now arriving at Deniki, including a new commanding officer, Major Alan Cameron, who was now in charge of Maroubra Force. He apparently had a predetermined opinion of the company before he even knew what had occurred at Kokoda. Perhaps he thought we should have defeated the whole Japanese army on it on our own! Anyway, we were placed on reserve at Deniki. He then decided, without sending any patrols out, to check the lie of the land, so to speak, to counter-attack and retake Kokoda.

A Company was dispatched and they moved back into Kokoda without opposition. The company moved out on the right flank with the intention of cutting off the Oivi track but they ran into strong opposition and could not move forward. C Company moved out towards Kokoda on the left of the main track. However, the main Japanese forces had left Kokoda and were moving into Deniki. As a consequence, C Company could not maintain their forward movement, but they did delay the Japanese attack on Deniki for a short period as the Japanese commander had to send some of his force back to retake Kokoda. A two-day battle ensued and A Company, with little ammunition and no support, suffered the same fate as B Company had earlier and were eventually overrun, extricating themselves as best they could. Neither C nor D companies were able to fight their way through to their objective and eventually they withdrew back to Deniki.

> Cameron now decided that Isurava was the best place from a tactical point of view to hold the enemy. All that was left of the battalion moved into positions at Isurava and dug in, a difficult task without proper tools—we used bayonets, hats and hands. About this time Cameron got the boot and Colonel Ralph Honner arrived and took over command of the battalion. The company also received a new Company Commander, Lieutenant Bevan French. Captain Stevenson was sent back to Moresby and Gough Garland took his job as 2IC.

Large flocks of cockatoos were flying around screeching, no doubt stirred up by the Japanese movements and preparations for their attack. It is now known that by this time the Japanese had landed more troops at Gona and Buna, including artillery, horses and native carriers. They now had a reported 3000 troops on the move in the area, with only a depleted 39th Battalion between them and Port Moresby. The 53rd Battalion was to give support on the right flank but they were ambushed and several of their senior officers killed, so they had to make a disorganised withdrawal. 'Nevertheless,' Dawson said, 'we had been told and had high hopes that reinforcements were on the way. We knew that a big battle was imminent and we had to hang on no matter what.'

Dawson's B Company formed part of the battalion perimeter across a new track on a small ridge that ran up from the main track towards Naro Ridge. Their company headquarters was situated to the rear of the platoons, close to the main track behind a large fallen log. Dawson had to make various trips to these platoons, checking and taking some ammunition in the early stages until no more was available.

Then the mortars and shells started to fall. This was followed by the 'woodpeckers'—Japanese heavy machine guns—then a bugle call. Suddenly they came, wave after wave, screaming and yelling, bayonets flashing, light machine guns and rifles blazing. The air was full of lead. The cacophony of sound was beyond imagination and men were dying by the dozens. There was attack after attack on all fronts. B Company was bearing the brunt but their casualties went from a few to a flow. A platoon runner came in to say that some Japanese had got through the perimeter so the company runner and Dawson took off after him.

The platoon runner was well ahead and Dawson was close behind the company runner when the Australians came up over a slight rise that dropped to a narrow track. Suddenly the company runner fell down and Dawson fell on top of him. 'At first I thought he slipped, then I realised by the funny sounds he was making that he'd been shot. At that moment I saw a Japanese head and shoulders pop up through the scrub.'

Dawson fired two quick shots and lost sight of the Japanese. He dragged the wounded runner back into a small depression and threw a grenade to where he'd last seen the Japanese soldier and waited for it to go off. There was no return fire but he thought he may be lying 'doggo', so threw another grenade. There was still no reaction from the enemy. This meant that Dawson 'had to check up on him' because he was inside their perimeter at the rear of one of their depleted platoons. He circled around carefully and eventually discovered two dead Japanese soldiers. 'At least one of the grenades had been accurate and had made a horrible mess of the two of them,' Dawson said.

> I then ran back to our runner who was dead—he had taken at least one bullet in the head. I tried to lift him but he was too heavy for me to get high enough to carry. Fortunately a small patrol came from one of the other companies. They were on their way to battalion headquarters to report that their situation was precarious as they had been overrun. They quietly picked up the dead runner and carried him back. At this stage I heard Japanese bugle calls and whistles. Then followed a seeming easing of small arms fire from their direction, although the mortars and mountain guns continued their fanfare of death. The bugle call was obviously a signal to pull back and regroup for another attack, which soon came.

At company headquarters a runner from battalion headquarters had arrived with a message for the company commander. The runner was kneeling on one knee and referring to the falling mortar bombs when he said, 'Geez they're rockin' in ain't they!' Dawson thought it a rather odd remark at the time. The 2/14th Battalion had arrived, the intention being to relieve his battalion and mount a counterattack. However, they were having difficulty holding their positions but were instructed to hold on at all costs.

> The Japanese mortars were devastating. I recall, apart from the many other casualties, one chap who came out on a stretcher. A bomb, either mortar or grenade, had landed near his feet and I remember thinking that one of his feet looked like a big red flower. It was a horrible mess. Another casualty that stuck in my mind was a bloke who was badly wounded, pale and in shock. I remember thinking how young he looked. His bearers decided to move him below the track to try and dodge the

> mortars and gunfire. I gave them a hand to get the stretcher over the edge safely as there was a sharp drop off the track into the jungle.

Suddenly a Japanese soldier appeared seemingly from nowhere. Dawson barely had time to fire off one shot in his direction, but a colleague near him had a Thompson machine gun and fired a burst. The Japanese soldier was dead by the time he hit the ground.

The 2/14th Battalion couldn't hold on. They received orders to withdraw and regroup at another position, referred to as the Isurava Rest House. This movement was carried out at night. It was an extremely difficult exercise, carrying what stores and ammunition they could and ferrying out the wounded, while slipping and sliding in the mud, wet, hungry and completely exhausted.

'We continued the withdrawal to our new position,' Dawson wrote. 'The going was tough and we were quite dispirited. On arrival someone had a fire going and I managed to find a large dixie and a bag of rolled oats. I cooked up a pot of porridge, which was pretty lumpy but we enjoyed it in spite of that.'

By this time some of the 2nd AIF reinforcements had reached the fighting. The next day the most unfit were sent back to the rear at Myola. The battalion strength was now down to 250, with B Company (Joe Dawson's company) numbering only thirteen. In the meantime, the Japanese had moved around the flank of the Australian positions and were attacking the rear, which just happened to be B Company's position. There was an initial enemy breakthrough but fortunately another company came to their aid to strengthen the position, followed up by the 2/14th Battalion. The attacks continued with ferocity and by late afternoon they were again ordered to withdraw. This became a chaotic situation.

> The Japanese were pressing right in on our rear. We got to Eora Creek, where we were stationed to cover the withdrawal of the 2/14th and

> 2/16th Battalions but this was an extremely difficult situation. We were surrounded by high mountains and the Japanese had moved very quickly and had the advantage of high ground. They had outflanked and passed some elements of the 2/16th Battalion, which left those troops cut off. Those men did, however, manage to find another creek crossing and get around to their own battalion. We then had to climb up a steep slope from the creek to the village up top while being shot at from the mountain on the other side of the creek.

This happened to be the last action of the 39th Battalion in the Owen Stanley Range. On 1 September, Brigadier Arnold Potts ordered the 39th Battalion on to Kagi, one of the higher spots on the track over the ranges, to hold a position there until relieved by the 2/27th Battalion. Because of the battalion's small numbers Colonel Honner reorganised this into two composite companies. Dawson's group, No. 1 C Company, took up a position about two hours walk from Kagi, while No. 2 C Company moved up into Kagi village and were joined by the battalion headquarters, regimental aid post and some walking wounded from Myola. Dawson recalled, 'On the way to Kagi we had the doubtful pleasure of being bombed and strafed by a group of American Cobras!'

During the night Dawson's company were ordered to move to a new defensive position south of Efogi. Mid-afternoon, on 5 September, the 2/27th took over their positions including all automatic weapons, grenades and rations, and they then moved to Menari. The 39th Battalion strength was now only 85!

At Menari, Joe Dawson was able to clean up for the first time in weeks. His feet had been constantly wet and he'd been unable to remove his boots; his feet felt dead, as though they did not belong to him. When he removed his boots (which were falling to pieces) and then his stinking wet socks, all the skin on the soles of his feet came off, stuck to the socks, leaving his feet red-raw. After rummaging in his haversack Dawson found another pair of socks and a couple of khaki hankerchiefs. All he could do was to wrap a hanky over each foot and then pull his socks on over the top of the hankies followed by the old worn boots.

The next day, Colonel Honner called a battalion parade and advised his men of a message of appreciation he had received from Brigadier Potts, commenting on the splendid service the 39th Battalion had given under his command. Honner later wrote:

> When I glanced along the steady lines of pallid and emaciated men with sunken eyes and shrunken frames that testified to the hardships they had long endured, I saw no hangdog looks—only the proud bearing of tired veterans who had looked death and disaster in the face and had not failed. (Peter Brune, *Ralph Honner*)

The immediate threat of a Japanese invasion of Port Moresby was over. It was not only supply problems that ended the Japanese push over the Owen Stanley ranges. Following reverses at the hands of US forces on Guadalcanal, the Japanese Imperial Headquarters decided they could not support fronts on both New Guinea and Guadalcanal. Major General Tomitaro Horii, who commanded Japan's South Seas Force, was ordered by Imperial Headquarters to withdraw his troops from the Kokoda Track until the issue at Guadalcanal was decided.

Rebuffed on the Kokoda Track in late August 1942, the Japanese still had their eyes on the Papua New Guinean capital, Port Moresby. They believed that the key stepping stone to this goal was the sheltered harbour of Milne Bay on the south-eastern tip of Papua, only about 370 kilometres from Port Moresby. The Allies had earmarked it for a base. Not only did it have a safe deep-water harbour, but three airstrips had been constructed by 1942.

Late on the night of 25 August, a force of 2000 Japanese marines were landed to capture the airstrips. The Japanese began at a disadvantage when their troops were landed 11 kilometres east of their intended landing area, and their intelligence had severely underestimated the Allied garrison there. They believed the airstrips were guarded by only a few hundred Allied troops, but the reality was almost 9000 men including two infantry brigades—the 7th and the 18th. They also had Kittyhawk fighter bombers installed there. Although the Japanese had some initial success, reaching the eastern-most airstrip on 28 August, the Allied counterattack began to drive them back, and after nine days of fierce fighting it was all over.

Between 4 and 7 September, the Japanese were evacuated at night from their original landing areas at Waga Waga and Wandala. Of the 2000 marines landed, only 1318 re-embarked. It was estimated that 750 Japanese lay dead around Milne Bay, and the remainder were killed trying to escape overland to the Japanese base at Buna. Allied deaths were 167 Australians and fourteen Americans. It was a significant victory, and Milne Bay remained an important staging area for the remainder of 1942.

Field Marshall Sir William Slim later wrote in his memoir *Defeat into Victory*: 'Australian troops had, at Milne Bay, inflicted on the Japanese their first undoubted defeat on land. Some of us may forget that, of all the Allies, it was the Australians who first broke the invincibility of the Japanese army.'

In mid-September 1942 Sergeant Joe Dawson's 39th Battalion was marched out from the Kokoda Track for a brief rest and reorganisation. They were converted to AIF establishment status for rest and retraining, and received about 100 reinforcements from the former 53rd Battalion. A few days later about 300 troops arrived from Australia. Up till then the

39th Battalion had been a totally Victorian outfit, now they had quite a number of New South Wales and Queensland troops. Around 17 September they moved to a base area to be fully armed and equipped and placed under the Seventh Division.

But the Japanese had not given up, and Dawson's 39th Battalion would be back in action within a few weeks. The Japanese were being pushed back and the AIF's 16th and 25th Australian Infantry Brigades were approaching Gona and Sananda, as two untried American regiments were moving towards Buna. One was pushing up the coast track, the other from inland in a pincer movement, but they were cut about and stopped in their tracks by the Japanese. The Australian 16th Brigade, now battle weary and down below half strength, was stopped between Soputa and Sananda. The 25th Brigade also had their advance halted south of the Ulona River.

Recollecting these events, Dawson wrote:

> Apparently the supreme commander General Douglas MacArthur was pushing Australia's General Tom Blamey for a victory in the area. The 16th Brigade was not capable of mounting a sustained attack against Sananda, so the American 126th Regiment was brought in. On arrival I believe the Yanks told the Australians they could go home now, as they—the Yanks—would fix things up quick and lively. However, they were very sharply stopped by enemy crossfire and counter-attacks.

The Australian generals Blamey and Herring called on General MacArthur, who suggested they bring in the American Forty-First Division from Australia. Blamey bluntly said he would rather put in more Australians as he knew they could fight. Herring agreed. It seems MacArthur was not happy that both Australian generals did not think much of the fighting qualities of the US troops. In any case, he agreed to fly the Australian 21st Brigade to the battlefront, where they joined the 25th Brigade.

Dawson said his 39th Battalion suffered very heavy casualties. The Japanese were dug in, in well prepared and well concealed bunkers with plenty of light and heavy machine guns. The two American regiments covering Gona and Sanananda did not seem to be able to move. It was obvious more assault troops were needed to crack a victory. Blamey selected the 30th Brigade, comprising the 39th and 49th Battalions and the now amalgamated 55/53rd Battalion.

On Sunday 29 November the 39th Battalion received a movement warning order. They were issued with new jungle greens and American-style knee-high lace-up gaiters, and all their equipment and weapons were checked and extra demolition grenades issued. Dawson's platoon was also provided with the Boys anti-tank rifle, which he thought was a very awkward and difficult weapon to carry. The .5 ammunition with which they were also issued was armour piercing. It was intended to be used against Japanese landing barges carrying reinforcements, but the opportunity never came.

On 30 November at Port Moresby the battalion boarded DC3s (later dubbed 'biscuit bombers'), bound for Popondetta. There was no door on the side, just an opening. They flew over the Owen Stanley ranges, which they considered was much better than walking. After landing at Popondetta and getting themselves, weapons and gear organised, they set off on their long march. Rain started to fall and they struggled through thick, clinging mud. Dawson recalled: 'All the way along the main track were the little primitive wooden crosses, some with tin hats, marking the graves—solemn reminder of the high price in Australian lives that was being made to drive the Japanese out of this territory. However, there was no time for tears, it was just a case of boots—boots moving up and down through the mud.'

Because of the high casualty rate at Gona with so little success, General Vasey decided to launch a flank attack on Sanananda. The 39th Battalion was detached from the 30th Brigade and, together with the 1/14th

Battalion in the lead, followed a track along the coastline, which eventually fizzled out in dense jungle and swamp. With the 2/14th unable to move forward, the 39th Battalion became bunched up behind a clearing above the beach line. Two Allied aircraft, both fighters, were strafing a half-sunken Japanese supply ship in the bay, which was allegedly being used to supply the beach at night.

> Suddenly, one of the Beaufighters turned in a tight circle and came back along the beach and strafed our whole battalion! There was nowhere to go, no trees, no holes—just hit the ground and pray. The amazing thing was that the battalion suffered only five wounded. There were also two native carriers wounded. As one wag said, 'Typical air force! Couldn't hit a barn door.'
>
> As that track was impassable we had to change plans. On the night of the 3 December, we had to guard a captured food dump in case the Japanese tried to retake the food source during the night. About the middle of next day our battalion took over the positions of the depleted 25th Brigade and the Third Militia Battalion. This in itself was a difficult exercise as Japanese bullets were buzzing and crackling through the *kunai* grass. It was a case of run, crawl, keep as low as possible and hope for the best. The battalion we relieved moved out and we took over their shallow weapon pits. There is no doubt in my mind that the Gona campaign was the worst and most horrific battle the 39th Battalion fought. Certainly we won, but the price was terribly high. The casualties we suffered were higher I believe than in the Owen Stanleys campaign.

At Gona the Japanese were entrenched in dugouts among coconut palms on low sand dunes. These trenches were covered with layers of palm trunks and camouflage sand and leaves, leaving a narrow slit-like opening in front to permit the firing of the heavy and light machine guns.

Ahead of the Australians was flat ground, with *kunai* grass, some of which had been cut down to give the Japanese fields of fire.

Dawson said he would never forget that scene:

> The smell of death, the stench of decaying bodies, the smell of the mixture of mud, blood, cordite, and oppressive heat was all around us. There were millions of green flies about the size or slightly larger than a house fly. This sting, similar to a march fly, only worse, left a little round white mark on the skin that at a glance looked as though a piece of flesh had been taken. And there were the mosquitoes and ticks. We were eventually issued with two small bottles of oily substances—one was called Mary to keep the mozzies off and the other Betty to keep the bugs off—which may have worked to some extent. Our casualties were caused not just by being killed in action but also by malaria, dysentery and, worst of all, scrub typhus.

It was decided to launch a dawn attack on 6 December. It was still dark as the 39th Battalion troops readied themselves. Under a monster barrage and covering smoke, they moved forward, following one of the other companies. The smoke made it difficult for them to see clearly and the Japanese kept firing into the smoke. Casualties mounted. While many of the enemy were killed and a small amount of ground had been gained, the attack was not the hoped-for total success. B Company suffered some casualties, but the leading company in front was cut to ribbons.

Another attack was ordered and this was to be preceded by an aerial bombardment, so the troops were moved back to their previous positions as they were too close to the target in the hard-won new ground. The troops were unhappy about this.

The RAAF needed a white T-shaped sign on the ground, with the top of the T facing the enemy positions. Joe Dawson and a few other troops were chosen for this unenviable task to mark the spot. The first hurdle was to find some white material. Dawson thought the air force must've thought they all slept in white sheets!

> However I managed to gather up all the army towels from the troops. A lot of these had been cut in half to take up less space in the haversack. Fortunately there was some *kunai* grass hiding us from the sight of the Japanese. With dry throat and tight stomachs, we hacked at the grass to get a level spot to lay out our T. Strangely enough, despite all the noise we were making, not one single shot was fired in our direction.

The aerial bombardment was a farce. Carried out by Wirraways, some of the bombs landed behind the Allied lines. None of the bombs hit the target. All it did was let the enemy know to get ready for another attack. The commanding officer called off the attack at the last minute, and after the planes flew away he also asked that aircraft be kept away from the area.

The next attack was planned for 8 December, this time behind a mortar and artillery barrage. Before that, surrender leaflets were to be dropped on the Japanese Gona garrison. The attack started about 1 pm in the heat of the day and continued into the night. B Company followed the lead companies. During the night some of the Japanese tried to fight their way through these positions and all of them died. Early in the morning three Japanese crossed the track behind the Australian positions and ran into *kunai* grass. Someone threw a grenade and killed all three of them. On the following morning, most of the Japanese positions were taken except a few on the edge of the beach area. These were soon cleaned out and Colonel Honner was able to signal by field telephone: 'Gona's gone!'

It was time to bury the Australian dead and working parties were brought in. Dawson wrote later that the smell of that place still haunts him:

> There were dead everywhere. It was beyond all comprehension. We also had to check around the pillboxes to make sure there were no live

Japanese among all corpses. I came across the bodies of two Australians, their heads within a foot of the Japanese emplacement on the beach side. I thought of the time, 'just another yard, just another yard'.

Rear echelon brought us a hot meal—boiled rice with a dash of bully beef mixed through it and some hot black tea, which appeared to be a shade of purple. The brew had been made in a tin that had previously stored dried apples, which discoloured the tea. Even so, I enjoyed it and ate my rice, but not with a great degree of relish. The stench of death didn't help the appetite much.

Dawson was totally exhausted and had just laid back on his haversack on the wet *kunai* grass and was almost asleep when a voice shouted, 'Hey Sarge, there's couple of wounded Japs over here!' He grabbed his Owen gun, only recently taken from one of his unit's wounded men, and ran over to the spot. There, just off one of the narrow tracks through the high grass, were two Japanese soldiers, one lying full-length face down and breathing heavily, the other sitting cross-legged, his right arm supporting his left arm from which the bicep muscle had been carved out, most likely from a piece of shrapnel. The whole wound was just a seething mass of maggots.

I pulled out my first field dressing, ripped it open and bound up the wound, maggots and all, and called for a stretcher. At that point I was wondering about the Japanese lying down and struggling to breathe. The soldier that found them said to me, 'Why don't you just shoot them Sarge?'

'You found them, so I suppose I didn't for the same reason you didn't,' I replied.

'What do you mean?'

'Probably because we don't want to be like them,' I told him.

Native stretcher bearers picked up the Japanese with the arm wound and moved off when a lieutenant came dashing up waving

> his .38 pistol. I thought he looked rather thoughtfully at the stretcher moving off, but then turned and promptly put a bullet through the one on the ground who was going to die anyway. To this day I have wondered two things about that—first why I just didn't shoot them both, or secondly whether the poor blighter with the wounded arm survived. I'm sure that if they had been discovered during the heat of battle they would both have been shot.

It was later discovered that throughout the fighting in Papua, most of the Australian soldiers captured by Japanese troops were murdered. For the remainder of the war Australian troops generally did not attempt to capture Japanese soldiers and aggressively sought to kill their opponents—including some who had surrendered. Later, when short of food, the Japanese cannibalised parts of the bodies of the dead, their own as well as Australians. The Japanese themselves regarded capture as the ultimate disgrace and dishonour to their emperor, and often killed themselves if they had time to do so. Understandably, having seen their own comrades bayoneted to death, the Australians were not inclined to be merciful either.

The action continued, but Dawson had been feeling very sick for a few days.

> Every part of me seemed to be aching but I put it down to being tired. None of us had had a good sleep for God knows how long and we seemed to be for-ever wet. At this point the rain had cleared and it seemed a bit brighter. I was squatting down, loading up a few Owen gun magazines and trying to eat some emergency rations. A runner was sitting opposite and facing me as a few Japanese mortars went off on our right flank. I thought at the time they were probably trying to locate our mortars. It was almost dusk and we had not bothered to dig in as we were hoping to move forward the next morning.

> Suddenly one of the bombs went off very close behind us, in line with the runner. With that, he shot up in the air and took off like a rocket back along the track towards company and battalion headquarters. It took a second or two for anything to register with me. Looking back on it, I think my reaction time was beginning to slow down. Anyway, I went after him, found him at the Regimental Aid Post on an improvised stretcher with a bloody great hole in his back. The thought occurred to me at the time that he saved my life simply by sitting where he was, otherwise I would have copped that shrapnel somewhere above my belly button.

While at the regimental aid post, Dawson asked one of the orderlies to give him something to put on a painful sore in his groin which he thought might have been the start of a tropical ulcer. Before that could be looked at, the orderly stuck a thermometer in his mouth and took his temperature, reading it with difficulty as night was almost upon them. Then he looked at Dawson and said, 'Mate, if your temperature goes up another peg, you're dead! You be right back up here at first light. There is a stretcher party leaving at daylight and you're going with it.'

The orderly gave Dawson some tablets to take, to reduce his temperature. Dawson reported his situation to the company commander, who sent a runner to get another NCO to take over his platoon.

> Rain set in again. By then we were used to being wet most of the time, if it wasn't raining it was sweat. During the night in the early morning hours I was lying face down in a small depression in the ground, facing on a slight angle towards our front line and partly towards the track. I thought I saw a movement on the other side of the track. The rain had stopped and even though it wasn't light, it wasn't pitch dark.

To get a better look Dawson raised himself up on his left arm and eased his Owen gun forward slightly and caught a glint of light and white metal. It was a sword being held by a Japanese officer. In that fraction of a second, the officer spotted Dawson and charged towards him at a gallop.

> He was almost on top of me with his sword raised for the swing. I fired one short burst and he dropped. His boot landed in my lower back. Instinctively I humped up and rolled over expecting him to turn and have another go but he had gone on into the dark. I yelled out to the nearest section that there was an enemy soldier behind the lines, and to pass it on. I thought afterwards he was probably after our mortar.

Dawson decided then to move back to the RAP to await his evacuation. His head was throbbing and his whole body was aching. As it turned out, he was so seriously ill he was flown to Port Moresby and sent by hospital ship back to Australia to the Heidelberg Military Hospital in Victoria. One bonus was that, after convalescence, Joe used his brief home leave to get married to his long-time love, Elaine Colbran.

'The Beachhead Battles', as they were known, of Gona, Buna and Sananda that Joe Dawson's 2/39th Battalion took part in, rank among the bloodiest and most savage campaigns of the Pacific War, from November 1942 to January 1943, on a 25-kilometre stretch of the northern Papuan coast. The Japanese retreated there, following their defeat at Eora Creek and Oivi-Gorari on the Kokoda Track. Urgently needing a victory, the Supreme Allied Commander, General Douglas MacArthur, badly underestimated the Japanese forces that were there, fully armed, supplied and itching to do battle after the failure of the Kokoda push across to Port Moresby. MacArthur's intelligence reports told him there were only between 1000 and 4000 Japanese, most of whom were sick and wounded after the Kokoda withdrawal. He assigned the Australian Seventh Division to capture Gona and Sananada, leaving the American Thirty-Seventh Division to seize Buna. In reality, the beachheads were defended by some 10,000 well dug-in Japanese servicemen.

The campaign started at the beginning of the wet season, which compounded the difficulties of the 'green hell' the Allied troops found themselves trying to negotiate. Most of the terrain was dominated by tidal swamps, which could be ankle-deep or up to soldiers' necks. What wasn't swamp was dense jungle and scrub, while occasional open swathes of territory were covered in 2-metre-high *kunai* grass.

Trenches, and even fox holes, dug by both sides filled with water. General Robert Eichelberger, who took command of the American Thirty-Second Division in December, wrote:

> The psychological factors resulting from the terrain were also tremendous. After a man had lain for days in a wet slit trench or in the swamp, his physical stamina was reduced materially. This reduction served to make him extremely nervous and attribute the unfamiliar noises of the jungle to specters of Japanese activity. These reactions preyed on his mind until he was reduced to a pitiable, abject state, incapable of aggressive action. (James Brien, *The Bloody Beachheads: The battles of Gona, Buna and Sanananda, November 1942–January 1943*)

Disease had a far greater impact on all combatants in the Beachhead Battles than any planners could have foreseen. Malaria was the greatest threat, but scrub typhus, ulcers and dysentery were almost universal. By January, for every one battle casualty, 4.8 casualties were admitted to forward area hospitals. The Japanese attrition from disease was similarly shocking. One Japanese soldier recalled that between 20 and 30 servicemen died each day in December. Much of the Allied communications technology failed in the wet conditions and the Australians' 25-pound artillery shells were ineffective against the enemy's formidable network of trenches and bunkers protected by fallen palm logs (as described by the 39th Battalion's Sergeant Joe Dawson). Furthermore the Japanese held these positions with great tenacity and took a heavy toll on attacking infantry.

General MacArthur never visited this front during the campaign from his headquarters in Port Moresby. On 20 November MacArthur told the Australian commander General Thomas Blamey that 'all columns will be driven through to the objectives regardless of losses'. He told General Robert Eichelberger, when he replaced his predecessor:

> I want you to remove all officers who won't fight. Relieve regimental and battalion commanders if necessary, put sergeants in charge of battalions, and corporals in charge of companies—anyone who will fight. Time is of the essence . . . I want you to take Buna or not come back alive. (James Brien, *The Bloody Beachheads*)

Although victory on the three beachheads was achieved through frontal assaults, the use of light tanks and aerial bombardment, casualties on both sides were heavy. The Allies came up against the fanatical determination of the Japanese to die rather than surrender. At Buna, Lance Corporal Seiichi Uchiyama wrote in his diary: 'No thoughts of returning home alive. Want to die like a soldier and go to the Yasukuni Shrine.' (James Brien, *The Bloody Beachheads*)

Few prisoners were taken by the Allies. Even the sick and wounded in hospitals resisted capture by fighting or taking their own lives.

But despite their tenacity in defence, the Japanese could not hold out when faced with dire shortages of food and medical supplies. The last defenders at Sananada did not receive any rice rations after 8 January, and ate only what they could scavenge from their comrades or corpses. It is not surprising that many Japanese soldiers resorted to cannibalism, although with reluctance. Soldiers would carve off portions of soft flesh or liver from the bodies of friends or foes alike, which greatly angered Allied soldiers when they discovered this practice at Sananandа.

It was all over by 22 January, and MacArthur finally had 'his great victory'. The Japanese presence in Papua had been almost completely eliminated.

Important lessons had been learned by the Allies about jungle warfare, small unit tactics, the role of aircraft and artillery in the jungle, and infantry–tank cooperation. But the victory had come at a terrible cost. Australian War Memorial Scholar James Brien later wrote in 2013:

> Australian battle casualties numbered 240 officers and 3230 other ranks. The veteran Australian units which had entered the campaign returned from it a shell of their former selves. The untried American troops had also suffered heavily in their limited fighting role, with 687 men killed in action and 1918 wounded. Japanese losses were even greater. While exact estimates are difficult, it is reasonable to assume that somewhere around 7600 Japanese soldiers did not return from the beachheads. (James Brien, *The Bloody Beachheads*)

The Beachhead Battles, concluded Brien, 'deserve to be recognised in Australian military history as some of the hardest and bloodiest fighting the Australian army was involved in during the war'.

After only two weeks convalescence (and an all-too-brief week's honeymoon in Victoria), Joe Dawson was transferred to a convalescent depot in Ballarat, one of the coldest places in the state. 'Whoever decided to put it there must have been a nut case. It was a farce. We were housed in tents and issued with only two blankets and a groundsheet, with a straw palliasse for a bed. The wind blew off Lake Wendouree as if it came from the North Pole.'

Route marches around the area were the only training activity. At that time it was possible to catch a tram to Ballarat, where Dawson for the first time began to drink beer. That was not easy with beer rationed and scarce. 'But there were 80 hotels in Ballarat at that time, so with a bit of luck you could find one where the beer was "on".'

Dawson also came down with another dose of malaria—a legacy from his Kokoda Track experiences—but was eventually discharged to return to his unit which was then in the Atherton Tablelands for more combat training. (It was not his beloved 39th Battalion, which had by then been disbanded.) Later in 1943, a thoroughly bored Sergeant Joe Dawson was delighted when routine orders came out asking for volunteers for the 1st Papuan Infantry Battalion (PIB).

He applied, even though he realised it meant not coming back to Australia for a long time. He thought anything would be less boring than training and exercises around the Atherton Tablelands and he also had some knowledge of the activities of the PIB from the Owen Stanley campaign. He was accepted after an interview, and then with a few others from the area boarded the *Katoomba* on his way back to Port Moresby in October 1943.

Dawson was moved to the PIB training depot at Bisiatabu, before Owens Corner on the way to the Kokoda Track. They lived in large grass-roofed huts. Fortunately, they were issued with green mosquito nets. He was posted to Depot Company and given a squad of raw recruits, including his assistant Sergeant Samai. According to Dawson:

> He was a rather colourful fellow. He was in the first Papuan Infantry Brigade and had transferred from the Papuan Constabulary. He was very helpful in teaching me *Motuan*, the lingua franca of Papua in those days. It was sometimes referred to as Police Motu.
>
> The recruits were a motley looking lot, various shades of black and some almost white. Many of them had a skin complaint—their skin was flaking which looked like scales. They were given regular doses of

> peanut oil, which worked as their skin was soon healthy and shiny. They were all very keen to learn. The uniform was either a green or khaki *rami*—wrap-around lap-lap—with a web belt. Everything else was bare, including their feet. They were paid two sticks of trade tobacco and ten shillings a month—the NCOs got more. After a few weeks they were beginning to shape up like top parade soldiers and I was proud of them. This was followed by the all-important weapons training.

On 23 December 1943 Dawson was hit with another dose of malaria and went to the casualty clearing station. On Christmas Day he was transferred to the 2/1st Australian General Hospital. It was to be his second Christmas in hospital.

> By now, it was nearly February 1944. I was worried because I knew it was about time for Elaine to go to hospital to have our first baby and I had not heard anything. Finally, to my relief and great joy, I received a telegram about a week after the event saying they were both well. So I was now a daddy with a grin a yard wide and a relaxed feeling knowing all was well on the home front.

Dawson was returned to the unit depot at Bisiatabu, feeling fit and well, and then back to the parade ground and weapon training, turning young men into combat soldiers.

Before long, he was given more movement orders and prepared to go with his troops into battle areas. They flew out of Port Moresby in a DC3 with an open doorway on the side, ready for a quick exit. All their weapons had been cleaned and checked and ammunition issued. Dawson was given an Owen gun, by now his favourite weapon. On board were a group of reinforcements soldiers, both Papuan and New Guinean.

The PIB had become very proficient in the art of moving quietly through the jungle. They carried maximum ammunition and minimum rations. Their patrols varied in size, sometimes being a couple of platoons or more and sometimes as small as a section—about eight or ten men. Occasionally they were caught in a Japanese ambush and had to get out in a hurry with their wounded. Although a number of patrols proved uneventful, at all times the fear of death was their constant companion.

Memories of all these patrol activities blurred over time. On one small patrol the objective was to follow a track, check if it was being used by the enemy, note any enemy installations and return before dark. The Australians had been moving along the track for about three hours without incident when the forward scout signalled enemy movement. They automatically moved off the track to the left, into ambush mode. Soon a Japanese scout appeared, followed at a short distance by about four or five soldiers. They drew level and the Australians fired, and after a minute or so moved in to check. Three Japanese were dead. One of the men thought he saw a couple of them run into the jungle on the other side of the track so Dawson said to his corporal, 'Okay, move the men in line for about 20 yards, check for any wounded and return. I will watch the track.' It was a bad mistake.

> I had changed the magazine and re-cocked the Owen and was looking back and forth along the track—when suddenly a Japanese soldier burst out of the scrub. He had remained hidden just a few yards away from us all the time. He was charging straight at me, bayonet fixed. I had no time to dodge and as I reacted, his face full of hate, seemed only inches away. I swung the Owen and pressed the trigger. He started to fall. As he fell, his bayonet grazed my thigh, putting a small cut in my trousers and skin but it was deflected by the scabbard of my jungle knife. The patrol heard the shot and ran back.

During those few seconds, Dawson recalled that his body had doubled its sweat output. The practice was to look through dead enemies' pockets in case they carried maps or other vital information. 'I was never one to collect souvenirs during this task, but I decided to take that bayonet from the Japanese rifle and stuck it in my belt. I'd already had my share of near misses with bullets, bombs, grenades and mortars but somehow this seemed more personal.'

Dawson's PIB group moved with the Australian infantry units, sometimes being attached to different brigades or divisions, usually on foot. 'It was all boots again—boots, boots moving up and down—pursuing and killing Japanese and trying to avoid being killed. The Japanese camps generally had a peculiar stink, their attitude to hygiene under the circumstances left a lot to be desired.'

During July, the company was ordered to return to Bisiatabu for a rest. Then, in August, Dawson came down with another dose of fever and landed in Finschafen Hospital. Early in September 1944 he was granted home leave. He thought this splendid news—28 days off plus travelling time. On 11 September 1944 he boarded a Sunderland flying boat to Port Moresby and landed at Townsville before taking various troop trains to Melbourne.

> Then I experienced a magical moment—the reunion with my sweet Elaine and my first meeting with our darling new daughter Leigh. Leigh seemed quite dubious about me at first, probably little wonder as I suppose my complexion was a combination of suntan and jaundice—yellow due to the Atabrine tablets, a substitute for quinine, which at the time was scarce.
>
> How wonderful it was to be in the peace and tranquility of Melbourne. The war seemed far away.

But Joe Dawson's combat experience in the Pacific Islands was not yet over.

Chapter 17

THE BATTLE FOR NEW GUINEA

After the Japanese initial effort to capture Port Moresby was thwarted by the Australians, first on the Kododa Track, and second when they were ousted from the important strategic port and airstrips at Milne Bay by 22 January 1943, by 29 January the Japanese turned their attention from Papua to the north coast of New Guinea. Forces of the Empire of Japan sailed from Rabaul, crossed the Solomon Sea, and successfully reached the coastal town of Lae at the head of the Markham River in the Huon Gulf. The strategic jewels in the crown, for both the Japanese and the Allies, were the inland goldmining towns of Wau and Bulolo. But they were situated in a high mountain valley, a five-day march from the coast for fit men through horrendous steep and tangled terrain, climbing up to 1300 metres from the valley floor, which was surrounded by peaks up to 2500 metres.

It was not gold that was the objective of both sides, but the strategic airfield at Wau that held the key to the control of the Lae–Salamaua coast.

But as Captain Henry 'Jo' Gullet of the 2/6th Battalion later wrote, the airstrip was a nail-biting experience to land and take off from:

> The little airstrip was situated on a fairly steep slope, just long enough for a DC3 Dakota to land uphill, aided by the gradient. Taking off, they raced down the hill, hurtled over the edge and hoped for the best. Going out, they could only carry very light loads, which posed a considerable problem when we had to evacuate our sick and wounded. (Henry 'Jo' Gullet, *Not as a Duty Only*, p. 97)

The mountain at the end of the runway prevented a second chance at landing. Pilots had to navigate their DC3 aircraft under clouds and through dangerous passes, 'dodging a peak here and cloud there', and landing up the slope at high speeds, swinging the aircraft around at the last minute sideways to the strip for unloading. This required good visibility, but the Owen Stanley Range was beset with frequent storms, unpredictable vertical updrafts and mists that rose up from the jungle floor.

The Japanese 102nd Infantry Regiment under the command of Major General Toru Okabe was ordered to occupy Lae and Salamaua and capture the airfields at Wau and Bulolo. The Australians did not know which way the Japanese would approach Wau. The most used route from the coast was known as the Bulldog Track, a tough trek even in fine weather.

By mid-January the Australians began to reinforce Wau, but this was a slow process. A DC3 Dakota could carry 27 passengers of 4500 kilos of weight. Moving an infantry battalion required 50 plane loads; a brigade 361 flights. Poor flying weather hampered the flights from Port Moresby, aircraft often having to return because of continuing bad weather, and there had been three crashes.

What was known as the Okabe Detachment did not use the Bulldog Track, but surprised the Australians by cutting their way through the jungle parallel to a little used route called the Black Cat Track, avoiding detection by Allied aircraft.

Standing in the way of Okabe's advance was A Company of the 2/6th Infantry Battalion commanded by Captain William 'Bill' Sherlock. Okabe was running out of food for his troops and, hoping for a quick victory, ordered an all-out attack on Sherlock's position guarding Wau. On 28 January and outnumbered by human waves of Japanese, A Company was attacked but the enemy efforts to overrun their positions were defeated by a bayonet charge, led by Sherlock himself. The captain was then forced from his positions to occupy a nearby spur, from which he continued to repel frontal attacks with mortar and machine-gun fire. By 6 pm, he was almost out of ammunition and raked by Japanese machine guns, but Sherlock held his position through the night and was killed the next day trying to break through Japanese lines. (For his actions Bill Sherlock was posthumously Mentioned in Dispatches.)

The following day 57 planeloads arrived bringing most of the 2/7th Infantry Battalion, while the Japanese positions were being attacked by Beaufighters from the RAAF's No. 30 Squadron. On 31 January and 1 February, a total of 124 landings were made on the uphill Wau strip, adding 3000 men to the Allied defence. Outnumbered and outgunned, Okabe had to retreat to the coast with what was left of his 102nd Infantry Regiment. Wau was now secure.

The Australians, with assistance from US forces, began a series of actions in late January to recapture the coastal towns of Lae and Salamaua, which had become major Japanese bases. Over the next few months the Australian Third Division advanced north-east towards Salamaua. After an amphibious landing at Nassau Bay, the Australians were reinforced by a US regimental combat team which then advanced up the coast.

As the Allies kept up the pressure on the Japanese around Salamaua, in early September they launched an airborne assault on Nadzab, up the Markham River, and a seaborne landing near Lae at the river's mouth, subsequently taking the town with simultaneous drives from the east and north-west. As the situation around Lae grew more desperate, the Japanese garrison withdrew from Salamaua and it was captured on 11 September 1943. Lae fell shortly afterwards on 16 September, when troops from the Seventh Division entered it ahead of the Ninth Division, and the remaining Japanese force escaped to the north.

Less than a week later the Huon Peninsula campaign was opened as the Australians undertook another amphibious landing further east, aimed at capturing Finschhafen—which was achieved. This was a vital development which allowed the construction of an air base and naval facilities to assist Allied forces to conduct operations against Japanese bases, not only in New Guinea but New Britain, too.

In mid-October the Japanese launched a counterattack against the Australian beachhead around Scarlet Beach, about 10 kilometres north of Finschhafen. It lasted a week, and the Japanese forced a small contraction of the Australian lines and a splitting of their force before it was defeated. After this the Australians regained the initiative and began to pursue the Japanese, who withdrew inland towards the high ground around Sattelberg. Heavy fighting took place there, and a second Japanese counterattack failed. Sattelberg was secured in late November 1943 and the Australians began an advance to the north to secure a line between Wareo and Gusika, which was completed by early December. This was followed by an advance by Australian forces along the coast from Lakona to Fortification Point after overcoming strong Japanese forces fighting delaying actions.

The final stage of the Huon campaign saw the Japanese resistance finally break. A quick advance by the Australians along the northern coast of the peninsula was next, and in January 1944 they captured Sio. Mopping up operations there took until March, and then Madang was captured in April. A lull followed in northern New Guinea until July, when US forces clashed with the Japanese around the Drinuimor River.

Further fighting followed in November 1944 when the Australians opened a fresh campaign in Aitape–Wewak.

Roy Sibson was born in Bowen, Queensland, on 5 August 1920. His parents were subsistence farmers, and Roy had a knockabout childhood and minimal schooling. He left school to work on the land at fourteen. At fifteen he boosted his age to sixteen, to enlist part-time in the Australian Militia, and was called up when war broke out in 1939. Based near Townsville, he was not paid for the first two years of his service until he turned eighteen.

In mid 1942 Sibson was seconded from the army to cut cane in North Queensland because of wartime labour shortages. One bonus was that it enabled him to get married at Home Hill, though he did not see his wife again—and baby daughter for the first time—until his discharge in 1945.

Back in the army in October 1943, he was based in a big staging camp, but his unit, the 31st Infantry Battalion, was at Jacky Jacky at the tip of Cape York Peninsula at that time. Roy was bored with drill and route marching when, on parade one day, an officer asked if there were any blacksmiths in the ranks. On impulse Roy pushed the bloke beside him out and followed him. 'Cripes, I know nothing about blacksmithing,' the bloke said.

'That makes two of us,' Roy replied, 'but we'll get a trip to Brisbane out of this dump.'

The officer explained that they would be going to the Brisbane Technical College for sixteen weeks. 'When we got there they said we had to do some tests. That was when my cog started to turn. I had never seen a forge lit in my life, let alone any blacksmithing. Anyway luck was with us,' Roy later recalled.

> The two teachers we had there did their time on the Clyde in Scotland. They were 70 years old and they sure knew their job. They were

> brought back from retirement when the war started, to teach at the college. The first day I went to the teacher and had to tell him the truth that I knew nothing about blacksmithing. I told him that if he would teach me I would learn, as it would be handy for me and my farming job after the war. I told him I was bored stiff where I came from and had to get out of the joint. He was an old soldier and knew what I was talking about.

The teacher obligingly gave Roy extra tutoring and during smoko breaks he would take him into his office and teach him about tempering different kinds of steel and other metals.

In the first five days Roy made a seven-link chain with a hook and eye, fire-welding the links together, and at the end of sixteen weeks there were only five out of the 32 who got a second-class pass and he was one of them. 'I was lucky again as I was posted to a unit which had another blacksmith there, and if I got a job and I had trouble doing it, he would show me.'

So that is how Roy Sibson went to war in New Guinea as a craftsman in the 2/127th Brigade Workshop AEME, and not as an infantryman. However, he might well have been a soldier for the amount of action he survived and helped fight over the next two or so years.

Sibson's first move was to Charters Towers, then Townsville, on the way to New Guinea. At the wharf in Townsville a freighter called the *Gorgon* was waiting for them, ready to carry 800 troops. *Gorgon* had been a cattle transporter and their stalls were still in place, and it was where the troops had to sleep. As the boat pulled out from Townsville, every soldier looked back at Australia. 'I know I was wondering if I would ever see Australia and my wife and baby again. You could hear a pin drop on the deck because everybody was so quiet. We kept looking back until the boat was well past Magnetic Island and out to sea.'

They joined up with five more transport ships and two corvettes to escort them to New Guinea. The first port of call was Milne Bay—a natural harbour with water so deep that two big cruisers were in there, *Australia* and *Shropshire*. Sibson also saw a 10,000-ton ship so close to shore that she was tied up to the coconut trees.

Next day they set sail in convoy, as the battle for Lae was on. 'It was quite a sight to see for us bush lads—six ships in convoy in line, with the corvettes out wide to protect us from submarines. The ocean swells were so high in the open sea that the corvettes would disappear from sight in the troughs.'

Passing through the Pacific, the passage through the coral reefs was marked by buoys with bells on. Every ship had a dull red light at its stern, so the ones behind could follow. Day was breaking as they arrived off the coast of New Guinea and the rising sun illuminated the tops of the mountains.

The *Gorgon* passed a Liberty ship that would be sunk by a Japanese submarine that night. Liberty ships were cargo carriers, described as a big hull with an engine. They were 10,000 tons capacity and the Americans churned them out with prefabricated sections, making one every seven days!

Sibson's convoy reached Buna and an Allied aircraft came out to warn them that a Japanese submarine was in their vicinity. 'It wobbled its wings as a warning and all the foghorns started to sound as the convoy turned around as one and went hell for leather to get behind the submarine net at Buna.'

Next morning the *Gorgon* broke from the convoy as, with her top speed, she could notionally outrun a submarine. She went flat out for Lae with her 800 reinforcements on board needed to help in the battle.

The troops were ferried ashore in amphibious DUKWs. Getting into them was not easy.

> We went over the side of the ship on rope nets and some went down the gangplank. The swell was about twelve feet and as the DUKWs came up you had to judge the right time to let go the net and drop

> into them. The DUKWs ran the troops right up into the jungle which was all mud to get us out of sight of the Japanese fighters and bombers. We slept in the mud that night and many more to follow.

Most of the soldiers were from cities, and Sibson said it was funny seeing them looking for dry ground when there was none. 'I cut big armfuls of ginger plants, like lilies, and made a corduroy bed out of them. At least it kept me out of the mud. There were about 1000 different kinds of insects at Lae, and 999 crawled over us that night. The Jap bombers came looking for us, but their bombs fell short and they missed their targets.'

For Sibson and most of his mates, this was their first taste of real war. 'Every gun and the place opened up on the Japs from revolvers to 3.7 ack-ack guns. There were blokes running like hell for the slit trenches. One bloke dropped his hurricane lamp and it did not go out, so his mate who was following him gave it a drop-kick to put it out. It would have done a footballer proud.'

The engineers' first job was to cut tracks into the jungle and lay timber on the ground as corduroy so that lorries would not bog. Then they would back up and spread gravel over it and make a road. That way, they could drive in and stack ammunition in the jungle out of sight of the enemy planes. Meanwhile, Sibson said, a camp was established and the soldiers settled in.

> When I was in Sydney I tried to see a picture call 'Random Harvest', but I couldn't get anywhere near it. After about six weeks in Lae when things settled down a bit, the army put a screen up between two trees and showed 'Random Harvest'. We were sitting on logs for seats in the rain and some Japs in the jungle looking at it also. Apparently they had been cut off from their main mob. Our cook was putting on a billy of tea, and a Jap across the river shot it out of his hand!

There were two rivers not far from Lae—the Busu, and the Butibum. One had a suspension bridge over it made out of lawyer cane in the shape of a V. It had a sapling on the bottom to walk on and lawyer cane handrails on each side to hang on to. Rivers in New Guinea run very fast. 'When you looked down you got the illusion you were shooting up the river at 30 miles an hour.'

The Japanese had a hospital dug in under Lae Hill, and mounted a 6-inch gun on top.

> When our fellows took the hill, two Japanese came out holding their dresses up to their chins—they had no pants on—to let our blokes know they were females. As it turned out our fellows shot them and then found out they had a grenade in each hand. Two soldiers were sent into the hospital to get the Japs to surrender. If they didn't come out within a certain time our troops would blow up and seal off the entrances. They didn't come out so the entrances were sealed off.

From there Sibson and his fellow troops walked their way up the Markham Valley to an area called Nadzab. It was big open *kunai* grass country with a small hill in the middle. They walked all the way in muddy and steamy weather. Sibson took his recently issued tin hat and respirator, spun them three times around his head and let them go into the jungle. 'I thought a gas attack couldn't be worse than that bloody heat,' he said. 'You can imagine what a tin hat felt like. You might as well put your head in an oven. The best thing to wear was a cotton khaki beret, as it acted as a sweat rag and hat. You could dip it in the creek and wash yourself with it and also have a drink out of it.' Sibson sold his army slouch hat to some bush natives for six New Guinea shillings.

When they reached Nadzab they waited in the *kunai* grass, and a DC3 landed nearby and taxied over to where they were. A black American soldier opened the door and told them to 'hop in'. Sibson thought the plane was going to taxi on some sort of an airstrip, but it wasn't so. 'He just took off from where he was in the *kunai* grass. It wasn't until many years after that I read in the paper that the Yanks flew over the day before, grass high, to find a place where there were no logs or stones!'

(Three months later Sibson and his fellow engineers flew back from Port Moresby and landed at Nadzab and there were so many bitumen strips and bomb bays that the driver they sent to take them back to town took an hour to find the road to Lae. By then there were four-engine bombers taking off. 'The most bombers I saw at any one time was 100. Our DC3 was the first to take off and land from Nadzab.')

On that first flight from the makeshift *kunai* grass airstrip, they flew over the Owen Stanley ranges back to Port Moresby. During the flight Sibson saw many places where planes had crashed and burned. At Port Moresby they landed at the Seven Mile Aerodrome, which was more than 1.6 kilometres long and covered with interlocking steel mesh.

Sibson was then sent to Napa Napa to work on small ships in the watercraft workshops.

> It was a terrible place, very isolated and there was at least one soldier a week taken away troppo and put in Ward 15 for the insane. I nearly went mad myself there, as I tried to split a New Guinea native's head open with a tomahawk, but two mates held me down and took the axe off me. After I cooled down I thought I was qualified to be sent to the funny farm as well.

Sibson thought he was lucky to get perforated eardrums and thus spend more than a week in the Port Moresby Hospital. While there, he was transferred to another unit on the Loloki River.

> At that stage I hadn't been in New Guinea very long, but this new unit on the Loloki had been there for over 12 months. I thought they were

very strange, as they would get up in the morning and start calling their imaginary dogs—Bluey, Snip, Carlo and so on. They would make out the dogs weren't obeying them and that the dogs were lifting their legs on every tent, and would shout at them. They would make it sound so real. Some would also walk down to the ablution block in the morning in the nude, with an erection and hang their towel over it like a bathroom peg. The more boastful would tie their boots together by the laces and have bets to see who could balance the boots nearest the end of their stiffies before they slipped off the end! Cripes, I thought they should all have been in Ward 15. But after being there a couple of months I thought they were perfectly normal. I must've caught up with them.

The beer ration for the men was only two bottles of beer a week—with luck. Jungle juice made out of coconut milk and hard liquor made in illegal stills filled the gap, although, according to Sibson, it nearly sent them mad.

One bloke in my tent who was about 45 years old showed me the photo of his wife. She was a woman of the same age and had her hair done up in a bun. To me, she looked like the motherly type and was old enough to be my mother. This fellow also got a Dear John letter, saying she was leaving him for a Yank. He'd been with her for over 20 years. I would have thought he'd be hard pushed to give her away, even if he threw in a Christmas hamper and a bottle of rum. But he was devastated and took it hard.

Another of the blokes in our company met his wife through a lonely hearts club. He went home on leave to see her and he wanted her to go to Western Australia to live where he came from. She wouldn't leave her mother.

The unfortunate Western Australian got a Dear John letter to say his wife was divorcing him. He had tears in his eyes as he went around the camp, showing his mates the letter. He said to Sibson, 'I would like to kill that mother-in-law bitch and bury her so her backside stuck out of the ground so every time I went past I could kick it.'

From Loloki, Sibson went to a place called Koitaki, where there was a spectacular waterfall. From there they were flown back to the Markham Valley. 'It was very rough on the plane, as we were getting pelted with hail. The plane was bucking and diving all over the sky and the troops were very quiet. When we landed in the Markham Valley, some of the soldiers got out and started to skite how good the trip was. I was just bloody pleased to get back on the ground.'

They were driven to Lae in lorries. The lorry driver that came to pick them up got lost on the aerodrome as there were so many runways for the four-engine bombers that were landing by now—all built in three months. 'That's how quickly the Yanks got things done. Things were quite safe there by then.'

Sibson's next job was driving a steam plant for the armoury, repairing rifles. He had time on his hands so he took in washing, using the steam from the plant to steam clothes. He charged threepence an item, and had a good business going, making up to 8 shillings a day. 'Like everywhere else, when I started to make money I got shifted and had to start another racket.'

He then made bracelets out of New Guinea shillings in his spare time. What silver was left he would melt down with other silver coins and make rings of different sizes to sell to the troops so they could add bits of coloured toothbrush handles in lieu of diamonds. One weekend he melted up to £37 worth of silver coins—pure silver in those days. He also made knives with fancy handles out of brass and Perspex, with the blades made of old files sharpened on both sides. He got £2.10 shillings for each of them.

Craftsman Roy Sibson's next move was to New Britain, where the Australian Fifth Division replaced the US Fourtieth Infantry Division in October and November 1944 and continued the New Britain campaign with the aim of confining the large Japanese forces on the island to the area around Rabaul.

They were loaded onto a Liberty ship called the *Francis Parkman* for a landing in New Britain. The swells were around 3.5 metres high, and they had to climb over the side and down the net provided into a barge as it came up to wave height—then clamber up again very quickly because on the next swell the barge would crush the descending soldiers against the ship. The ship had a Malaccan crew and Sibson said, 'They cooked on an open fire on deck, mostly curry so strong it used to burn your eyes as you walked past.' All fires and lights had to be out by sundown, and not even cigarette smoking was allowed.

The Australians were landed at a place called Waterfall Bay on the south coast of New Britain, and went over the side on nets again, into barges onto the beach. They dug themselves in, and would sneak down to the beach at night to have a bath. The troops were there for seven days before supplies arrived.

> They got the first barges into us with supplies on Christmas Eve and it had mail and parcels. I got a parcel which was posted in July for my birthday which is in August. Some of the things it had in it were a bottle of mango chutney, a bottle of Rosella jam and a big marshmallow tart which was so hard I had to smash it with a bayonet. I put

> it out amongst my mates and it disappeared like a snowdrop in hell. This parcel took over four months to reach me. Out of this barge, I also got a letter from the Taxation Office informing me that they had taken 10 shillings out of my bank for back taxes. After they did that there couldn't have been much left!

When they were at Waterfall Bay and on guard duty, they had to watch the tides carefully. Parts of New Britain were in volatile volcanic areas. For example, if the low tides went out suspiciously far, this could mean a *tsunami* (tidal wave) was imminent due to undersea seismic activity, so they had to sound the alarm enabling the troops to get to higher ground. The mountains in New Britain were smoking all the time, and some of the springs were near boiling point. During one violent earth tremor, trees near their camp had branches broken off, and coconuts rained down from above. 'Everything on the ground seem to be moving about three feet back and forth. You never camped under trees in that area.'

One night Sibson was woken up by gunfire. 'The bullets were coming through the tents everywhere. I rolled out of my bunk and buried myself in the mud. As it turned out, the cook had gone berserk and cleared out into the jungle. They wanted us to go and look for him. I told the warrant officer, "Bugger that, leave him till morning".' But the crazed cook had time to reach the cookhouse and pick up a meat cleaver. A sergeant went in and tipped a table over him and brought him out and they all had a peaceful night.

Shortly after that Sibson and 24 other troops were pulled out for a long and arduous voyage around the island of New Britain from the south to the north, as a reinforcement to another unit. They boarded a 20-metre pearl lugger, *Miss Townsville.* They travelled close to the coast all day and anchored every night. It was difficult to avoid the many coral reefs, and they were lucky to scrape their bottom only once. They passed Gasmata and Arawe. At Cape Gloucester they went ashore and camped for a night and a day. They had run out of tea and sugar and got some from the Americans. Before the Americans had taken Cape Gloucester, it had some of the thickest jungle in the world. Sibson said when they finished bombing and shelling 'it looked like a ploughed field'.

The next stop was Talasea, where there were hot springs running into the sea from the volcanoes inland, and the troops luxuriated in hot baths. The following day they arrived at Hoskins Bay.

First impressions were it was a lovely place. The rain fell conveniently at night, and the days were always sunny. It had been a Japanese airstrip, and there were still a few stray enemy about.

> One night some got into our camp looking for food as they were starving in the jungle by that stage. I was camped in a 'sack-sack' [grass] hut where most of the food was kept. One night I woke up about 10 pm to find what I thought was a Jap looking through my net. I was sleeping in the nude with my net tucked under me and my rifle at least three yards away. I had thoughts of a big sword coming down on top of me. The sweat was standing out on top of my brow like threepenny pieces. In the dark, he disappeared and I thought I must've been dreaming.

Sibson grabbed his rifle, but could not hear or see anything. At 3 am some of the other sleeping men also heard intruders. Sibson and his mate scored the job of looking around for them. They heard a noise in the cook-house, so Sibson's mate went around one side and he went around the other. The idea was to shoot anything that came out. However, all Sibson saw was a big white dog. As the dog came out he fired one shot and missed him in the dark. Later they realised there must have been at least three or four Japanese because at daylight the marks of their sandshoes where they came up the beach were clearly visible. Their sandshoes had a cloven design—a covered shoe with the big toe separated from the other four.

'After that we had one of our mob "go off". He would sit on his own and tell people he had it all worked out. The Japs used white dogs on black nights, and black dogs on moonlit nights. It wasn't long after that he was a candidate for Ward 15.'

While he never got dysentery on the islands, Sibson said, most of the troops did. They would go to the latrines with one mate on each side of them as they were weak and passing blood. Sibson believed he avoided dysentery by not washing his dixie in the cook's washing up water, 'which was like soup' after a dozen men used it. He always went down to the beach or river and scrubbed it out with sand and clean water. He did not contract tinea either, as he wore no socks because they kept his feet wet all the time. 'I saw some of our lads come off patrols, take their socks off, and there would be skin stuck to their socks like rag off a Christmas pudding.'

At Hoskins Bay, there was even time for some fishing, soldier style:

> One day a Japanese bomb landed but didn't go off. (When one did, a whole house would have fitted in the hole.) We dug out the dud bomb and took the explosive out for blowing fish. I got about eight *meris* [native women] from the village to help me find the fish after discharging it. I gave them the little ones and was supposed to get the big ones. They got plenty of little ones and they would say *lik-lik masta* [just little ones, master], but I wasn't getting any big ones. Then I found out they were pushing all the big ones under a log with their feet. I suppose they would come back later to pick them up. After that I gave a couple of *meris* a kick up the backside and then they seemed to be able to find more big ones.

The next move up the coast was to a place called Ponda Ponda at Open Bay, all swampy and mangroves. Sibson and his party had to build places to sleep a couple of feet off the mud, using bush sticks. The barges they had arrived in were built of steel, were flat-bottomed and had big powerful motors that could drive them up onto the beach to load 4WD lorries and troops with all their gear. They would then reverse their motors and with the wash from the engines extricate themselves from the beach. Those steel barges were stiflingly hot and had no shade.

They had captured some Japanese barges which had twin hulls and were made of plywood. Before the Japanese abandoned them, they put sand in the engines then ran them until they seized up. The Australians' job was to pull the engines out and fit Thorneycroft motors in their place. They had to spread Australian flags on top of the wheelhouses so that Allied planes would not bomb them. 'One of our blokes got hold of a Jap two-inch mortar, which had a curved base. He thought it was fired from resting it on your knee, but when he tried it found it should have been fired off a log and it broke his leg.'

By now the Japanese were being pushed back towards Rabaul. Sibson had been in the jungle for eighteen months, and it was time for his group to be relieved and sent home. But they could not get in ships to pick them up, so the only way out was over 7000 feet mountain ranges to the southern side of New Britain. It promised to be a very rugged trip indeed, with no native carriers prepared to go with them.

> We had to carry everything—ammunition, rifles and stores. Our loads included a tin of canned heat, like a tin of boot polish, made of methylated spirits and fat, that could be lit for boiling the billy as it made no smoke. There were also tins of bully beef, a packet of hard biscuits and bars of compressed fruit and nuts—plus a handful of tea and sugar a day.

In total 135 of them set off to cut a track across the island. It never stopped raining, day or night, for five days.

> If I live to be 1000 I will never forget that trip. The first nine miles was through mangroves and roots and mud. We had to get through that

> day to reach higher ground to lie down away from the mosquitoes. When we left, most of the blokes, knowing we were on our way home, carried far too much to my way of thinking—but my upbringing stood me in good stead as I travelled light. Before I left I discarded my pack, shaving gear, half my dixie, all my clothes bar one set and all my socks. I also cut the sleeves out of my shirt, and the pockets out of my trousers and shirt, and all surplus buttons. Also all the islets and flaps off my groundsheet. My towel and soap went out and I put my side haversack on my back, took my bayonet off to stop it from flogging my leg and put it under the flap of my haversack. All this was to stop anything from catching water and adding to the load.

They had no help from the islanders. As frightened as they were that the inland natives would kill them, none were seen. The first day's trek sapped the troops' stamina and before marching on the next day they threw away a lot of gear, but according to Sibson, who'd already streamlined his load, that was not nearly enough. The next night they threw out even more, but by then they were much weaker.

> Then I knew some of us were in big trouble. That night on guard, you lay in the mud in groups, arms-length apart. You did an hour on guard, and when your time was up you touched your mate and made sure he was awake before you went to sleep. You didn't stand up and walk around, only sat up. If you wanted to relieve yourself, you rolled over on your side and did it over the edge of your groundsheet.

On the third day the leading scout spotted a Japanese patrol but they didn't see them, and in any case they were in no condition to fight so simply let them through. When they took up action positions in case the Japanese did see them, Sibson was behind a big fig tree. When he looked around to see who his backup was, he found he had six stretcher bearers, conscientious objectors who would not bear arms. 'I made sure I never got caught like that again and worked myself up to the front of our mob and became Number 2 Scout the rest of the journey.'

Coming over the mountains Sibson saw some of the straightest, biggest and most beautiful blue gum trees he had ever seen—50 or 60 feet to the first limb, and they were just as big at the top as they were at the bottom. The problem was that if one was growing near the ridge of a mountain, the slope was so steep that struggling men could only put their arms partly around the trunk to get past the huge gums. 'Many soldiers lost their footing—even the chaplain who swore vehemently—slipping a chain back down the mountain before they could grab anything to crawl back up.'

They came to a stream running so fast that the waves were 3 feet high. Unable to cross, they had to find a fallen tree. Crossing only one at a time, men were positioned in case of an ambush. If a man fell off the log that would be the end of him, as he would be smashed to pieces on the rocks.

At the end of the third day Sibson realised that things were getting very serious. By now their captain was delirious and was helped along by two soldiers. The others were starting to weaken, going down lying in the mud, crying and pleading with their mates to leave them. Twenty-two men had given up the will to live. 'It was the first time that I'd seen grown men cry.' The sick men were grouped together in a rough bough shed built for them, with seven fitter men to protect them so they could get some rest. What meagre food that could be spared was left with them. The reality was they would have to get out the best way they could. 'I don't know if they all got out or not, because when I got home I had 40 days leave, and we all got split up.'

Sibson stayed No. 2 Scout for the rest of that trip and his job was to get out in front to check for any Japanese. He had to keep the No. 1 Scout in sight and keep his eyes open for the enemy, so he could warn the mob behind in plenty of time.

At the end of the fifth day they reached the coast just south of Tol Plantation. 'I had worn out my boots so you can imagine what miserable condition our clothes were in. I don't think we were too far behind what the prisoners of war in Singapore looked like.'

There was a Salvation Army officer on the barge with hot coffee and biscuits and clean pairs of socks. They could hear Australian troops still fighting to take Tol Plantation near Rabaul. Sibson found out they put 1600 rounds of 25-pounder shells into the plantation.

That night they had to stand to in case the Australians at Tol Plantation needed support. They would have been little value, because they were so spent they could barely even help themselves. But Tol Plantation was secured during the night, and Sibson and his companions embarked on barges early the next morning and arrived at Jacquinot Bay at 8 pm. For rations each man was issued with a tin of bully beef and one packet of hard biscuits between two. There was one litre of water per man to last all day. There was no shade on the steel barges and it was terribly hot. 'The only shade you got was if your mate beside you stood up,' Sibson said.

> We were camped down alongside the 2/2nd Commandos who had a still going to make their own homebrew. Some of our fellas got stuck into it with them, and what a mess they made of themselves. There were sick blokes everywhere, and those who had false teeth spewed them out and lost them. During that episode, a new reinforcement arrived and he did everything right—got under his mosquito net and tucked himself in. One of our fellers on the homebrew got the horrors, dived on top of the net and was choking him. Those of us who didn't drink wrestled the beserk bloke away and saved him. Later when the drunks started to feel better, they went around trying to find their false teeth. When they found a set they had to try them on and see if they fitted. It was no wonder I never drank in my entire life.

After a few days rest they boarded the same cattle boat, the *Gorgon*, they had sailed on to reach New Guinea. A couple of days out in the open sea on their way back to Australia, the *Gorgon* broke a piston and lay dead in the water. They could not break radio silence because the Japanese submarines might get on to them. So they drifted for 24 hours before Sibson and other engineers could take the broken piston out. Then they moved on slowly with only two pistons.

A shoal of dolphins met the ship half a day out of Brisbane and escorted it up the Brisbane River. The troops arrived with only the clothes they stood up in. Sibson and his mates were sent to Southport for four weeks. There, all they had to do was answer the roll call. 'The rest of the day was ours to do what we liked, which wasn't much as we were as poor as blackfellas' dogs.'

Chapter 18

AN UNNECESSARY CAMPAIGN

On 22 October 1944, the Supreme Commander South-west Pacific Area General Douglas MacArthur famously waded ashore on the Philippines island of Leyte, keeping his promise of 'I shall return'. (He actually waded ashore three times to make sure the photographers and newsreel cine-cameramen got it absolutely right for posterity.)

By then the apparent Japanese threat to mainland Australia was long over, although there were many thousands of Japanese soldiers in garrisons on various islands in an arc over 5000 kilometres stretching from Borneo to Bougainville. In New Britain, there were 93,000 Japanese forces (including civilians) and in Bougainville some 40,000 Japanese. All the Japanese troops had been cut off from their supply lines, and were mostly starving and running short of ammunition. Instances of cannibalism were widely reported. The reality was they were not going anywhere, but General MacArthur insisted that the commander in chief of the Australian forces, General Blamey—who had wanted to use no more than seven brigades to essentially mount a holding operation—should use twelve brigades. He then, for reasons never really revealed, ordered Blamey on 2 August 1944 to allocate four brigades to the New Guinea mainland, three to New Britain, four to Bougainville, and one to its outlying islands.

The result was that Australian troops were kept fighting in the jungles from Borneo to Bougainville until the end of the war. The Japanese may have been weakened and starved of food and supplies, but they were still prepared to die fanatically for their emperor, and did. For example, in the Aitape–Wewak campaign from November 1944 until the Japanese surrender in August 1945, 442 Australians were killed and 1141 wounded in battle in that theatre alone. In addition, a further 145 died from 'other causes' and a staggering 16,203 men were listed as 'sickness casualties', mostly victims of the atabrine-resistant strain of malaria that infested the area.

It was no wonder that in the course of this campaign the strategic benefits were on the basis that the fighting in the south-west Pacific was often represented as an 'unnecessary campaign'. The Japanese, without continuing logistic support, were still a threat, but going nowhere—starving and some in such desperation as mentioned that they even resorted to cannibalism. The debate over the wisdom of using Australian troops, with the inevitable casualties that followed, to defeat these diminished Japanese soldiers still goes on.

Bob 'Hooker' Holt, 2/2nd Infantry Battalion, Sixth Division, veteran of fighting in the Middle East including actions in Bardia, Tobruk, Derna and Greece against the Italians and Germans, was in the thick of the fighting on New Guinea against the Japanese as well. He had briefly been in Port

Morseby in the 'Left Out of Battalion' (LOB) group in August 1942, but returned to the Atherton Tablelands to join the rest of the Sixth Division for further training. He did not return to the Pacific Islands until he and his 2/3rd Battalion were transported from Townsville in December 1944 in an 'unimpressive ship', the 6000-ton *Bonteko*, sleeping in the hold 'packed in like sardines', and landed in the crowded port of Aitape, in New Guinea.

The battalion took over an established camp from the American army, who were on their way to the invasion of the Philippines. The camp was in a filthy state, with open cans, food and gear strewn about. Holt thought it looked like an Italian camp after the battles around Sidi Barani. They were ordered to clean up the lines before they all went down with dysentery and the camp eventually became habitable.

At a native camp at the back of their lines, a 'sing sing' was in progress and it had been going on for days. The natives were dancing and singing continuously. This could be coped with in daylight hours. 'But after dark they really got into their stride and sleep was virtually impossible with the drums and chanting going full bore,' Holt recalled.

> We were welcome to visit them during the day and wandered over to have a look. There were hordes of loud-mouthed, gum chewing, cigar smoking Yankee base-troops, with their flash cameras photographing the celebrations. There weren't any good sorts amongst the dancers, only old girls with tits on them like razor strops. However, on a second visit, just on dark, we saw the younger women coming out of the jungle to join the festivities.

The Australians were at least camped close to the beach, and apart from raiding the food dumps left behind by the Americans, swimming was the only recreation.

Orders were received on 21 January that they were to march to an airstrip to relieve the 2/8th Battalion. The march was tough, as they had to plough through liquid mud which came over their boot tops. 'The track wound through the stinking, fetid, airless jungle and this did not help things either.'

Holt's company crossed the Danmap River without getting their gaiters wet. They walked across to a small island, where battalion machine-gunners were digging in, and splashed their way over to the dropping ground, then dug in on the bank of the river and erected their two-man tents. During the night the heavens opened and Holt woke just in time to salvage some gear that was slipping into the swollen river as the river bank collapsed.

> By the state of the river and the sounds of trees and rocks crashing and lights flashing on the island where the machine gunners were positioned, we knew they were in serious trouble, but we could do absolutely nothing about it. The lights on the island went out, but the roar of the raging waters continued unabated from the river. At first light we looked to the island but it had disappeared completely! Where there had been a trickle of water in the river the day before there was now a heaving, boiling mass of muddy water, 50 or 60 yards wide. We were isolated on the dropping ground. Several men and myself volunteered to try to swim across the river with ropes around our waists. There was no hope of this and after a number of attempts, we gave the idea away. It was just as well as it was really dangerous.

The river went down nearly as fast as it had risen and the following day it could be walked across again.

The 30 men of the machine-gun platoon were commanded by Lieutenant Tim Fearnside, who had been promoted from the ranks and transferred from the Ninth Division's 2/13th Battalion. He, with the rest of his platoon, had been thrown into the swirling water and, remarkably, under the circumstances, were lucky to lose only seven men. One of the last men to leave the island, Corporal 'Snowy' Parkinson, was the first to report back to the battalion, and Holt was not surprised that although 'naked, cold, mosquito-bitten and with a damaged foot, he was still wearing his trademark broad infectious grin'. It was quite amazing that 23 men survived and although quite a few were seriously injured, most reported back to the battalion after a short spell in hospital.

Shortly afterwards Holt's company was sent off by itself as a listening post a mile or so from the remainder of the battalion. The troops cut saplings, put up canvas stretcher tops and erected two-man tents. They sited and dug their foxholes and laid booby traps. The first night in the new position several of these went off. One Japanese came along the track and hit a trip wire. As he heard the pin of the grenade fly out, he rushed right through the camp screaming. He hit another trip wire going out of camp and screamed some more as he galloped off down the track.

Following a week of patrols coming and going from the company's position, the Japanese was sighted from time to time.

> He became a kind of mascot but became too cheeky—or careless—and someone shot him eventually. Camped on his own in a hollow tree, just off the track, he was a straggler. He had no food, apart from a haversack for fungus he had pulled off the side of trees.
>
> Then a Japanese scout appeared on the other side of the creek and inspected our positions. He was so nonchalant that our sentry, 'Weary' Wilmot, just stared at him dumbfounded. We all reckon he thumbed his nose at Weary before he took off back into the jungle. The following day I was on sentry duty when a mortar bomb went off close by. There was some rifle and machine gun fire and a lot of shouting. I came back into my hole in an awful hurry, but no attack developed. After a while we went out on a patrol and found a couple of rifles, and a cap abandoned near a mortar. It seemed the Japanese intended to launch a two-pronged attack on our position, but came

unstuck. By mistake, they started firing on each other and decided to call it a day and return to their own lines. They were supposedly crack troops from General Nagi's Raiding Force.

Patrols were sent out regularly. On one of these Holt came across half a dozen American skeletons on stretchers by the side of the track. 'They had been wounded and left behind by their comrades to the tender mercies of the Japanese. Each had been bayoneted dozens of times, as the stretchers looked like sieves they had so many punctures.'

On 31 January a fighting patrol of two platoons, under Lieutenant Gil Cory, came through on their way to Long Ridge, where the Japanese were known to be entrenched. Holt was in one of the platoons: 'On the track up the ridge the next day Johnny Perry was the forward scout. He made a name for himself when he sneaked up on a Nippon sentry and lopped his head off with a machete.'

It was a very rugged action on Long Ridge and the patrol had to retire eventually after killing 33 Japanese for the loss of two dead and seven wounded. They came back through the company's position, bringing their wounded with them. Lieutenants Gil Cory and Bill Weir were awarded Military Crosses and Sergeant Bede Gourley the Distinguished Conduct Medal for their parts in the action.

A few days later Long Ridge was attacked with battalion strength. On their way up the track, through the heavy jungle of the mountain-side, Holt saw the remains of the Japanese soldier that Johnny Perry had decapitated, 'now well and truly on the nose'.

The Long Ridge attack turned out to be an anticlimax, because the Japanese had abandoned their positions and had left their dead unburied. The Australian dead had been mutilated. Their pants were around their ankles and great lumps of meat had been carved from their thighs.

The Australians had to sleep alongside the Japanese fortifications that night, with the stench of dead bodies about them. Next morning Holt saw two arms with clean knife cuts at the elbows and wrists and no flesh on the bones of the arms. 'This was the first case of actual cannibalism that I saw personally, but it was far from the last, as the practice was widespread right through the campaign. I saw cases later where our dead had to be left behind. The tins of bully beef on their packs had been spiked and left to go rotten and still the Japanese cut lumps out of the thighs of the dead.'

When the battalion went into action towards the end of March, over the mountains from Dagua, Bob Holt went in with the machine-gunners. Before making the climb over the range, they saw jeeps that had been converted into ambulances by putting canvas stretchers on a frame above the chassis, bumping and sliding along the wide muddy track loaded with wounded from the 2/3rd Battalion, who could be heard in action on the mountain.

'We had pulled up for a meal at some huts by the side of the track and I noticed bundles of gear under canvas and blankets. Always on the lookout for something extra to eat, I went over to inspect and found it to be Australian dead laid out in rows.' Holt thought at the time that left to themselves the Japanese would have died in their thousands from disease and starvation and yet here were good men from the oldest division in the AIF being maimed and killed for no good reason.

They marched over the mountains, the forward companies killing a number of Japanese on the way. At the river on the other side of the range, the machine-gun platoon dug in while the battalion moved about a mile to their left. Each morning a patrol had to be sent to the battalion and another up the mountain, to make sure the track was clear for the native carriers with supplies.

> I had always imagined the wild New Guinea natives to be savages and it was surprising to find them human beings, with all faults and frailties of the so-called civilised white men. The carriers were the cleanest people imaginable. Every possible opportunity they would

> pull up and wash themselves in the rivers and creeks. In spite of their cleanliness—and believe me they were a sight cleaner than most soldiers—they always had a strong smell about them, reminding me of crushed ants. I can only surmise this was caused by something in their diet.

Surprisingly, the natives were not at home in the jungle at night. They detested it and were terrified if they were caught out in the dark. The Australians could hear the native carrier line coming from a long way off, showing lights and chanting in unison: 'All the boy he come, master, all the boy he come.'

Several times when Holt was in charge of a line of native carriers, one of them would ask him if they could stop and collect bananas. If there was time, he would say yes. A few of them would collect the bananas and come back and share them out among all hands, including the soldiers. Holt described them as socialists at heart.

Most of the Japanese had mouths full of gold teeth. Holt tells of one character in the battalion who made a hobby of collecting them. He had dilly bags of teeth and reckoned on making his fortune when he sold the gold in Sydney after the war.

> One of the machine gunners heard of his collection and decided to start his own. He attacked the head of a dead Japanese with a rock to loosen his teeth. He made an awful mess of the corpse's head without getting his molars. He then buried the Jap for a few days before borrowing a pair of pliers from an artilleryman.
>
> A line of native carriers came past as he dug up the Jap. The smell was fearful and the natives protested. 'Phew master, phew.' This creature managed to extract the now decomposing Jap's teeth. Both these teeth-collecting ghouls were out of luck because the so-called gold fillings were later found to be worthless.

The machine-gunners started patrolling as an infantry platoon along the Old German Road. This road was made of logs—corduroy—and ran from Aitape to Wewak. One morning Holt's section was patrolling and saw imprints of two-toed Japanese boots in the mud by the side of the road. The tracks had not filled with water, which meant they were fresh. The patrol left the road to follow a jungle track, and shortly afterwards a Japanese threw a grenade at their leading scout and vanished.

> We were told to move in extended order, and going past a clump of trees, I saw a Japanese in khaki banging a grenade against a tree trying to arm it. He was shot dead immediately. He had previously fought against the Australians and he had a watch inscribed with the Victorian soldier's name, number and battalion. Round his neck in a chamois leather pouch, he had something wrapped in layers of tissue paper. The way it was protected I thought it may have been a crown jewel, or at least a pearl beyond price. To my disgust, it turned out to be a cherry stone he'd probably brought from Japan as a good luck charm.

Holt went down with malaria and went to hospital. He had already had two strains of malaria that were resistant to the drugs available, and this time he was really ill. He recalled talking to himself and floating in and out of consciousness. Recovering eventually, he was still weak and ill when he was discharged from the hospital. 'Then we were paraded before a doctor, who asked if we thought we were fit enough to return to our battalions. I always found them to be sympathetic, but if the doctor said we were fit most infantrymen would not argue the point, as pride would not let it be thought we were malingering, or "swinging the lead".'

As the campaign went on, his admiration for the conscripted over-worked natives on the essential carrier lines increased. 'They did not appear to ask for anything, barring some betel nut and sticks of rough twist tobacco. The weed looked like sticks of liquorice and they smoked it, wrapped in newspaper. One draw of this was enough to lift a white man's head off!'

The carriers' noses were pierced, and the holes in their earlobes were used to carry small personal items such as tobacco. They fetched and carried for the soldiers, sometimes up to the front lines. The stretcher parties carried out wounded troops 'and in general looked after them like mother hens'. Most of the men had been forcibly conscripted from their villages to help in a war they knew nothing about. They suffered real hardships, wounds and sometimes death—and for this they were supplied with food and a miserable pittance. 'It's incredible but under a so-called socialist government, these unsung heroes were paid 10 shillings in Papua and 5 shillings in the Mandated Territory per month.'

Bob Holt came back from hospital and was outside Wewak, waiting to be repatriated to Australia as a 'low number man' (those who had been first to enlist), when word came through that the atomic bomb had been dropped on Hiroshima and Nagasaki and the Japanese had capitulated.

The official finish of the war meant very little to the men of the battalion, as the fighting in the mountains behind Wewak went on as the abandoned Japanese soldiers had no knowledge it was all over. Holt waited with some of his comrades on the beach at Wewak, preparing to board the Australian ship *Katoomba* which had just pulled in.

'I was heartily sick of the war and so was everyone else.'

Chapter 19

SAVAGERY IN BOUGAINVILLE

Bougainville is a big island. Some 200 kilometres long by 65 kilometres wide, it lies about 300 kilometres south of New Britain. A spine of rugged mountain ranges runs down its full length, rising to 2400 metres with two active volcanoes, while wide swampy flatlands border the western and southern coasts. From the air, the lowlands clothed in dense tropical jungle resemble a vast green sea, cut every few miles by swift rivers and creeks which flood regularly in the 100-inch annual rainfall.

In 1942 the Japanese, and their thrust south to Guadalcanal and New Zealand, had occupied Bougainville with more than 70,000 troops. A year later American forces had counterattacked and landed at Torokina, halfway up the west coast. They were seeking airstrips for their push north, and contented themselves with a 7-mile perimeter around Torokina, built their bomber and fighter strips, and sat tight. The Japanese 17th Army counterattacked once, lost nearly 3000 casualties, and retired. Both sides held their peace and, over the ensuing months, watched and waited.

Five Australian infantry brigades, more than one and a half divisions, took over from the US forces in November 1944. The Americans were departing for the Leyte landing in the Philippines and appeared very confident. Enemy strength was down to less than 20,000, they said, most were starving, ill-equipped and dispirited. The old New Guinea hands among the incoming Australian forces were not impressed. They had seen starving Japanese charge in waves around Salamaua—every last one had to be dug out and killed. Starving Japanese were still dangerous.

The US intelligence estimates were highly inaccurate. There were almost 40,000 of the Japanese 17th Army left on Bougainville, they were adequately equipped, and living well off an organised system of local crops and gardens.

Over half the battalion strength was made up of young reinforcements. Most had just turned nineteen and had completed the jungle training course at Canungra in Queensland, and then posted to veteran battalions just returned from New Guinea campaigns. They were well trained, well equipped, and slightly put out at being sent to what were largely Australian Militia units instead of the more glamorous formations of the AIF, such as the Sixth, Seventh or Ninth Divisions.

But as Lance Corporal Peter 'Slim' Medcalf wrote in *War in the Shadows*, 'The difference between militiamen and AIF lasted about two seconds after the first shots were fired in anger. The offensive opened in December 1944 and carried on until August 1945. Some 25,000 Australians opposed 40,000 Japanese, who matched us in artillery and suffered only the lack of airpower. It looked like a long campaign.'

Medcalf recalled: 'I don't think I ever met a hero. It is a word that has been vastly misused and to the men doing the actual fighting, was somewhat suspect . . . you just did your job. As my mate "Grovely" Joe used to say, "We're not real soldiers, we're just civilians having a hard trot."'

These young Australians certainly were 'real soldiers'. Most under 21, they did not think that the world owed them a living. They were cynical, 'but somewhat idealistic, bawdy, irreverent and highly critical of authority, but motivated by an unspoken patriotism and a deep conviction that you did not let your mates down'.

So in Medcalf's account, they are all here—cooks, corporals, padres and point scouts, sergeants and stretcher bearers and the men of the infantry. 'They were the cheerful, blasphemous, downtrodden, irrepressible foot-sloggers.' He described as accurately as possible the life of a combat infantryman in those days. 'Jungle warfare was not normally a war of vast numbers and major engagements. It was largely a silent and deadly game of stalking and bushcraft and a matter of survival under what were at times extremely adverse conditions. By 1944 the combat units of the Australian army had become particularly adept at this form of war.'

Loaded 'like Christmas trees' they moved inland to the Tavera River, 15 Platoon leading. Slim Medcalf was glad he was not a Bren gunner—with ammunition, food, gun, magazines, pack and equipment, they carried nearly a hundredweight. They trudged out onto the track in single file. 'Predictably, somebody said, "You'll be sorry!"'

The track ended abruptly at the edge of the swamp. The lead scout looked back questioningly and was waved on. Carefully he stepped into the ooze, knee-deep, thigh-deep, then waist-deep. He paused to rearrange his bandolier of .303 ammunition around his neck and out of the water and inched forward. One by one the company followed.

> The black slime crept coldly to our waists—we struggled forward, feeling for solid footing under the surface, tree roots, tussocks, sunken debris to support us. We grasped at tangled vines and tree limbs.

> Unseen swamp life wriggled and slid below the surface—I thought of leeches and shivered. Rain started to fall, soft, gentle drops forming myriads of spreading rings on the dark water.
>
> A splash—struggling, and a man sank out of his depth, his full pack giving a momentary support. Eyes staring in fright, he clutched at an extended rifle barrel and was slowly hauled up until he could grasp a low tree limb. Rain intensified, soon forming a drift of fine spray over the surface, roaring through the undergrowth, heavy drops dancing in a fine halo around our heads and shoulders.

Each man had to feel for a solid footing, grasp a vine, haul, slip and grab again, in chest-deep black slime, getting deeper as they moved forward. It seemed their haversacks were loaded with lead. Their guns were held high, belts heavy with grenades and magazines dragging down around each of their necks. Sweat was mixed with rain, as their lungs struggled for oxygen, breathing in dank moisture-laden air. The patrol slipped, floundered, and some occasionally lunged up to grab a low-hanging tree branch for support. Two hours passed, with no place to stop, boots sinking in the clinging mud beneath the surface. Every half hour the Bren gun was passed from one man to another to share the extra 30-pound load.

> The Scout from 15 Platoon inched past us, and clung, panting to a log by [Leader] Perce's side. He gestured forward with his rifle and called, keep moving—only a few hundred yards more. Bear inland a bit! We struggled on. Slowly the swamp shallowed, trees grew thicker deepening the gloom. We stopped in knee deep water and word was passed back, 'Smoko'. We stood, heads down, shaking from strain, tobacco tins and matches, tucked under berets to keep dry, were slowly produced. I rolled a cigarette with wrinkled trembling fingers, and a fat raindrop dissolved it into a sodden mess. Grovely Joe passed me one from his

tin, and somehow managed to light a match. Slowly, carefully, it was nurtured down the line—we sucked in the smoke greedily and relaxed, ignoring the mosquitoes.

By mid-afternoon their way was barred by a sluggishly flowing creek. The swamp shallowed slightly on the near bank, with dark water flowing towards the coast. Dense jungle towered on the far side and a 9-metre fallen tree bridged the stream. A gap in the thick growth on the other side suggested a track leading south. The lead platoon fanned out to cover the crossing and two scouts teetered across the log to disappear into the jungle. The troops waited, as insects and mosquitoes rose in clouds about them. Slim Medcalf thought that at least it looked like dry land over the river. The leading scout waved, and the three platoons filed carefully over the log. They were still in heavy dense jungle, but at least on dry ground out of the swamp as they halted and heaved off their packs.

This was to be their home and the company perimeter for many weeks—the base for constant patrols, ambushes and skirmishes for possession of a thin ribbon of muddy track weaving between and into vast swamps and marshes, and criss-crossed by innumerable creeks and streams.

The fight hammered and echoed ahead of them all morning. B Company were forcing the bottleneck. Heavy mortars and 25-pounders added to the din, the sounds rumbling and exploding through the dripping, tangled waste of swamp.

Gradually the noise diminished to a final thin crackle of fire, then silence. 'Saddle up,' ordered their leader Perce. They were to relieve B company when they cleared the bottleneck, and push on to the Tavera River.

The sections moved out one by one, heavily loaded. No one looked back at the perimeter by the log crossing, their home for weeks. Medcalf thought, 'We ought to fill in all the holes we dug, apologise to the boongs and go home.' They left nothing that would be missed.

B Company had fought a hard fight—their dead lay wrapped in groundsheets under banana frond shelters, and their wounded passed them, swaying heavily on stretchers on the way to the beach.

'Mary' McGee was led past the incoming patrol, field dressings swathing his eyes. 'His mate held an arm around his shoulders and kept saying, "She'll be right mate", as he tenderly guided McGee down the track.'

Some wanted to help, but McGee's mate Johnny McGann looked at the well-meaning helpers almost defiantly. 'He's all right, I'll look after him.' He led McGee slowly past the others, his own and McGee's rifles slung over his shoulder. 'He didn't want our help—he was looking after his mate. One of the walking wounded, arm in a sling, bent to get a light. "He was blinded by grenade fragments. Poor old Mary McGee."'

Slim Medcalf recalled that McGee and Johnny McGann used to put on a singing duet in the mess hut.

B Company was glad to be relieved, and Medcalf's mob quickly took over the shallow holes they had scratched in the dank earth. Behind this the bottleneck was a waste of smashed and splintered trees and odd bits of abandoned Japanese equipment.

'Nugget' lay propped against his pack, waiting for the order to retire. His hands shook with delayed shock. 'The Jap snipers were tied up in the trees firing down at us. The 25-pounders finally shifted them,' Medcalf wrote. 'Nugget gave a weak grin. "I tell you, Slim, this was no place for me mother's little boy!"'

As they took over from B Company and dug in, the rain started again, slowly increasing to a driving downpour. Night came and the rain kept on, hour after hour. Pickets were blind and deaf in the deluge, safety holes were quickly filled. They squatted through the long night without sleep, under groundsheets, and felt the water rise slowly ankle-deep through the perimeter. 'The Japanese could have walked through our positions if they had returned.'

Dawn brought fitful light, and a waste of water, trees and bushes standing in a black sea. All signs of dry land had disappeared. The rain eased to a fine drizzle, and on all sides creeks rushed through the underbrush. Listening posts were thrown out as they tried to make their perimeter livable. 'The rain stopped and the sun finally shone, bright golden shafts breaking through gaps in the dense canopy overhead, reflecting rainbows in the stream already rising from the surface of the water.'

A patrol splashed up the track, and returned by mid-afternoon—no contact.

The weather stayed fine. Slowly they improved their new home in the bottleneck, and patrols daily confirmed that the enemy had pulled back towards the dry country to the south. The water receded, the cooks provided hot meals of a sort, and mail caught up with them. It grew hotter, and they gradually became aware of a peculiar smell about the place. After a few days this sickening stench pervaded the whole clearing.

> Early one morning filing out on patrol towards the river, we found the answer. The company had obligingly left a dead Japanese just outside the perimeter. As the water drained away and the hot sun went to work he was making his presence felt. Finally the stench became too much to bear. We had to face the unpleasant task of burying the swollen, rotting remains. The job was made bearable by jokes and comments from several humorists in the burial party as we sweated with shovels alongside the offending corpse. Eventually this loathsome work was done and the detail walked back to the perimeter heaving sighs of relief.

But the smell persisted. It became stronger. It was in their water, food, clothes, in every breath they took. Only on patrol could they escape it. Medcalf eventually discovered the source:

> One morning I sat on my bunk, and looked at the ground between my boots. A large white maggot wriggled out of the dry ground—and another, and another. We had pitched our shelters on top of the shallow graves the Japanese had dug for their own dead during the battle the week before.
>
> As Sad Sack observed, 'You got to admit Slim, the place has atmosphere!'

Thick clouds gathered and short, sharp storms swept the swamps. The rain gradually set in. The water level in the surrounding marshes rose and slowly invaded their camp. They patched their tattered shelters with large banana fronds and jacked their bush bunks higher out of the mud. Food was short again, and several men were sent back suffering from skin diseases and unknown fevers. A patrol tried to find a shortcut to the coast, and became lost for two days in the swampy wastes of the Tavera estuary.

An urgent radio message was received—'Japanese reported at Sisiruai', a village about 6 miles inland. The platoon leader decided they should find the place and clean it out.

Early morning, the scouts led the platoon through the wire. Ten yards into the heavy growth the water was knee-deep. Slowly the line moved ahead. 'We sank to our waists in clammy brown slush as the ground fell away. Bert backed up suddenly and prodded a lump of floating bark with his rifle. A foot-long centipede, bright orange in the dim light, rode on the debris, its wide head waving gently as it bobbed by.'

The Australians were heavily loaded with spare ammunition and the weight around their necks dragged them off balance as the patrol tripped and stumbled on tangled snags below the surface.

> I clambered over a half-submerged log and a grenade slipped from my belt to be lost in the mire. An hour passed and we halted for a smoke. Sad Sack floundered up and took the Bren gun from Bomber and

word filtered back, a big creek, too deep to cross was ahead. The lead section turned inland to see if the creek narrowed or grew shallow. It showed as a 20-yard gap in the undergrowth with the water moving sluggishly coastwards.

After several hours they found a tall tree fallen across the stream. The patrol inched over, straddling the slippery trunk until they could swing down into the shallows on the far bank. The men lent against tree trunks up to their knees in the black mire and munched dry biscuits and bully beef from the tin. 'Joey from 6 Section was shivering and running a temperature—he could not eat, but would not let us carry his pack.' They swigged chlorinated water from their bottles and moved on.

Ahead thunder rumbled and the light faded. There was no sign of dry land. They struggled on in increasing darkness as lightning flared closer. Rain started, and it became bitterly cold. There was an ear-splitting crack of lightning. The line stopped.

> We turned our backs to the deluge—it hammered down upon us, harder, harder, deafening. The surface of the swamp was smashed upwards in flying spray. We were blind, disoriented, staggering in the flailing dark chaos. A faint, thin shout, lost in the din. I staggered, bumped into a sapling and clung frantically. Someone clutched my belt and hung on.
>
> Slowly the uproar died away. The downpour slackened and we lifted our heads, mouths gaping, gasping for breath. Men stood waist deep shivering as if beaten. The light dull, glaucous, thick with moisture and leaves and branches littered the surface of the swamp.
>
> 'Jesus,' a shaky voice said, 'wonder what it's like when the bloody drought breaks?'

The patrol slowly reformed, and the line moved ahead. Medcalf's equipment weighed him down, boots sinking in the slime. The day dragged to a close, the light died and the patrol weaved to a halt in front of a tangle of trees and looped and trailing vines.

Medcalf felt totally done, standing, his legs apart, hip-deep in swamp, drooping, completely and absolutely miserable. He looked at the rest of the section and they seemed no better. 'Eat something, and make yourself comfortable for the night,' their leader Perce said. 'We won't need pickets in this place.' He had a large, fat leech clinging to the back of his neck.

Slowly the exhausted men gathered and looked for somewhere to sleep. The ground was impossible—if there was any, it was under a metre of dark, muddy water. 'Fergie climbed a tree, hung his equipment on a branch, and draped his long frame along the thick limb.' Others followed suit, wedging themselves in tree forks or making rough nests of branches and vines.

It grew dark, and Medcalf was too tired to look for a decent tree. In desperation he cut a long length of thick vine, threw it over a branch and passed it under his armpits. He briefly relaxed, hanging in the loop, leaning back against the tree trunk.

> A firefly drifted by—blink, blink—his cold green light softly reflected on the black water. Quiet rustlings, a cough, a muttered curse as the platoon tried to settle. The water around my hips slowly grew chill. Rotting tree limbs and vegetation shone around us in a soft, eerie phosphorescent glow.
>
> Half asleep, I heard a scrabbling noise, and a loud splash. Someone had fallen out of bed!

The night turned pitch black. Too tired to care about the mosquitoes, Medcalf hung in his vine. The night dragged on.

Suddenly he woke, gasping and choking, almost underwater. The vine had broken! He staggered to his feet, clutched the tree trunk, and stood shivering, hugging it in the darkness. Incredibly he heard someone snoring.

With the dim morning light they choked down a few mouthfuls of cold rations, slung their loads and pushed on following a compass bearing, looking for Sisiruai village.

They never found it. For another two nights and three days they struggled through a waste of rotting swamp. At dusk one night they heard dogs barking but they saw no living thing, other than an army of leeches. And there were always the mosquitoes. 'They even stung through our shirts. Our faces swelled, and the backs of our hands and our faces became lumpy and stiff.'

On the third day the platoon staggered back to their camp. Some were sick, all completely exhausted—they resembled pale yellow-skinned corpses.

Slowly peeling off his rotting socks, the soles of Medcalf's feet came off with his socks.

In rear areas the cleanliness and good housekeeping of the company came under the care of the hygiene corporal. Every company had one. Slim recalled:

> Ours was five feet four, weighed fourteen stone and measured three axe-handles across his barrel chest. His ham-like fists brushed his knees as his slightly bowed legs carried him on his daily rounds. A bullet head, a face like a chunk of brown basalt and a voice like a gravel-crusher completed the ensemble. With complete logic, he was called 'Toddles'.

One of Toddles' many duties liked best was the daily burning-off of the company latrines. Every morning he would pour some 10 gallons of kerosene down the holes into the pit, so as to destroy all offensive organisms in the resulting inferno. But he possessed a sadistic sense of humour.

Having poured the fuel down the holes, he would hide the drum, drop his pants and ensconce himself on one of the seats, lean back and peruse an old copy of *Guinea Gold*, the army newspaper.

> Like a squat spider in the centre of his web he would patiently await his victims. Surprisingly, in spite of his reputation, he rarely missed. Sooner or later some hapless innocents would arrive, nod 'Owaryer mate', drop their tweeds and take their seats, to pass among other things the time of the day. Rumours were discussed, officers castigated and the Army freely criticised, until Toddles had a full house. He would arise, adjust his dress, roll a smoke and borrow a match from the man on the next hole. Stepping back he would light his cigarette and drop the match into the pit. The resulting explosion was always impressive. The shaft of yellow flame would belch two feet high out of the holes, and was guaranteed to singe every bit of body hair of the unfortunates left enthroned. In the subsequent confusion, Toddles would make his escape, his victims helpless with their pants round their ankles.
>
> It was better than swabbing with Lysol.

The beer available to the platoon was an evil brew with a snarling tiger's head on the label. It was scathingly referred to as Panther Piss, 'as it seemed to claw your throat all the way down'. The glasses were Lady Blameys—'and there was only an even chance of cutting off your top lip when you drank'.

That started Slim thinking. 'We swallowed, and shuddered, and someone said, "We've got to get some decent grog." Well we need a large container, yeast, raisins and dried fruit and sugar—in this heat she should brew up really well in a few days.'

A committee was formed. Sugar was found semi-legally in the cookhouse by cutting the cooks in on the action. Other ingredients were traded, lifted or souvenired from the various units near their lines. A field bakery was a good source of yeast. In two days the committee had marshalled the essential ingredients and had grown to a dozen shareholders. But the basic equipment, the all-important large brewing container, was missing.

Johnny McGann solved the problem. He convinced the battalion engineers of the worthiness of the cause, and two 44-gallon drums left over from the diesel fuel dump were welded together and delivered after dark. Shareholders now numbered nearly twenty.

A narrow track was cut into the thick jungle behind their tents, an area cleared and the plant established. Buckets of water were added, 'magic' ingredients dippered in and a full case of canned blackcurrant juice added for flavour and effect. The brew was left to ferment in the heat for a week.

> The mixture stewed, topped by a raspberry-coloured froth. The smell resembled that of the public urinal in the Great Southern Hotel at 6 o'clock on a Saturday. The engineers obligingly sealed the system and rigged twenty feet of rusty water pipe leading from the top of the drums. We lit a fire around the base, wrapped wet bags around the pipe, and waited. A subdued cheer went up as a bright red distillate began to dribble from the pipe and was eagerly collected into empty beer bottles.

As chief brewer, Slim took the first taste. The top of his tongue shrivelled and two amalgam fillings turned rough. 'She's ready!' he gasped, eyes watering.

After four dozen bottles had been coaxed from the still, the fire was dowsed and the liquid treasure lugged back to the company lines. A large hole was dug in the floor of a tent—all but a bottle for each of the shareholders was buried.

To celebrate the event, the brew was introduced into the unit's poker game. 'This had been progressing for a week or more, night and day—only the players and the luck changed.'

Sitting smugly on three queens, Slim 'backed them higher than a cat's back' against Slats, the sniper from 13 Platoon. Slats was considered slow, but he called, and was sitting on a full house. Slim watched his last five bob disappear off the table and took another sip of his bottle. He shuddered and said, 'Mother warned me not to play naughty games with strange men—you might as well take the bottle as well.'

As it turned out, Slim said, 'It was the smartest thing I had done all night. Billy the quartermaster sergeant grabbed the bottle and prepared for a long session.'

Next morning was Sunday, battalion parade. They lined up in company files, presented arms, and listened to the commanding officer's diatribe on their general lack of discipline. Slim had a splitting headache. The CO's sermon ended. 'Battalion! Slope . . . arms! By companies, by the right in column of threes . . . right . . . turn! Quick . . . march!'

Billy held his place alongside the company and stepped, arms swinging high. Then he started to drift gently to one side. 'Billy,' his mates hissed, 'straighten up! To your right!'

Oblivious, Billy began to waver. He marched impeccably in a tight circle. The CO looked stunned and screamed, 'That man! Get that man's name!'

They marched past. Billy leaned slowly and fell flat on his face. He was taken to hospital and diagnosed with temporary blindness and acute poisoning.

That night the committee assembled and decided it had to get rid of the booze because somebody, somewhere, might drink it!

The bottles were dug up, loaded into a Jeep and driven to American Marine Air Group 25. The feeling was that they would drink Fly-tox (insecticide) and thank you for the privilege. The guard on the gate was big, very dark, and suspicious. 'What you Aussies want?' he demanded.

McGann said, 'Mate, this is your lucky day. We are flogging top-grade guaranteed white lightning. We've even got a little sip for you to sample.' A bottle was passed to the customer from under the groundsheet.

The guard peered around, backed behind the guard box, pulled the cork and sniffed it. He took a long swallow. The grog syndicate waited with baited breath.

His eyes bulged, and he breathed deeply. 'Hot damn,' he said. 'How much?'

The price was two quid a bottle, or a carton of Lucky Strikes. Cash on demand, naturally.

'Aussie, you've got yourself a deal,' said the guard.

The moonshine was duly delivered, and the syndicate departed with its ill-gotten gains. The next night there was a riot in the Marine Air Group 25 lines. Shots were fired and officers assaulted. The brewers laid low and decided to abandon the liquor business.

Three men, moving a hundred yards out, silently circled the camp perimeter every hour throughout the day to avoid being caught by enemy probes. Slim had been patrolling with two mates when they squeezed through a break in the wire.

Harry, the tank sergeant, had the engine covers of his Matilda tank open and was probing around in the motor housing when Slim asked, 'What are you doing mate, fixing the rubber band?'

The tank sergeant's grease-smeared face rose from the recesses of his pet engine. He looked at Slim disdainfully. 'You dumb, ignorant footsloggers couldn't understand a precision machine like this! Shove off and dig another hole!'

Then, without warning, over the river came the unmistakable *Thud! Thud! Thud!* of the Japanese guns. The sergeant scooted up the tank like a ferret and disappeared into the turret. Slim was caught, out in the open!

> The first salvo was coming with a high-pitched buzzing scream. Frantically I dropped down behind the tank and tried to squeeze into the ten-inch clearance beneath it. The shells arrived and slammed through the perimeter. There was an earsplitting crack beside the tank treads. The steel hull jumped slightly and was pressing down on my head and shoulders, forcing me into the soft earth. I panicked, squirmed out into the open, and leapt wildly towards the nearest dugouts. A black hole appeared on the ground and I dived into it, colliding with the occupants.

A voice in the gloom asked, 'Ar there Slim, how are you goin' mate?' It was Possum, 4 Section's corporal.

Slim was not all right. 'That stinking tank! Got under it—bloody near got squashed! The last .75 shell landed right on the tracks. Jesus!' He sat on the muddy floor and held his head in his hands. He was shaking down to his boots.

The next salvo screamed in. The last two rounds struck the tree limbs above and spun thumping and clattering across the perimeter. They were duds!

'Just relax,' Possum continued, 'you can stay here if you promise not to fart.'

Crouched in the gloom, Possum lifted a finger and went through the motions of loading a .75 shell. Slitting his eyes and sticking out his front teeth, he bowed three times and said, '*Hai, hai, ah sooooo*.' He dropped his hands suddenly, and on cue the guns went *Thud! Thud!* across the river.

'*Banzai!*' cried Possum. The shells arrived and exploded around the cook's tent. Once again the last two rounds were duds, clipping the trees and spinning through the clearing.

Bowing and grovelling, Possum grabbed his bayonet and prepared to commit an overacted *hara kiri*. 'So sorry,' he wept. 'Have stuffed up honourable emperor's ammo. So sorry!'

Slim stared open-mouthed at him, and crouched in the muddy hole, started to laugh.

'Stick your head out a while and see if that last lot buggered our lunch,' Possum said, waving his bayonet. 'My word. I bet old Greasy the cook will be on the essence of lemon for the next week after that.'

Then he added, 'See, other people got lots of troubles besides us.'

On another patrol Slim Medcalf parted the leaves gently, and 'stepped into a cathedral of twisted vines'. The scene before him was unexpected:

> The dense underbrush had abruptly disappeared. For 100 yards vast tree boles soared and towered into the matted canopy far above, the ground below a brilliant carpet of pink blossom. From the roof of the jungle an acre of flowering creeper had gently dropped its blooms. We trod through a hushed, glowing carpet. A single shaft of sunlight, saffron in the gloom, lit softly drifting petals. We moved silently through, uneasy at the open space but awed by the beauty around us. It did not belong in our world, only in our dreams and memories. We turned north-east with 4 Section leading, sweating and shoving through a mass of wait-a-bit thorns laced with spiders' webs, disturbing hordes of voracious mosquitoes.

Finally they reached the river, and squatted to rest in low ferns with the narrow, fast-flowing stream rushing between high banks to their backs. Slim turned to speak quietly to a mate, Al, and saw him suddenly lift his Owen gun, aiming back along their tracks.

> I spun around and looked into a yellow, sweaty face, almost obscured by leaves hanging from a steel helmet. He was only fifteen yards away and looking straight at us. Instinctively I jerked the gun up and fired

a burst into his neck and shoulders, Al firing simultaneously. Muzzle smoke flared, and the Japanese was thrown backwards. Swift rustles in the bushes and movement behind him—the Japanese cried out, high-pitched, half screaming. He lay out of sight in foot high bracken between two big trees. I pulled the pin from a grenade, called a soft warning and lobbed it high and over him.

There was the heavy slam of the explosion as Slim changed his magazine, and caught the eye of the artillery signaller. He was still kneeling in shock—more than six feet tall and built like a wrestler. Slim slung his web belt around his neck, held the Owen high and plunged waist-deep against the current. They tried to find a place to climb out, then hauled Sad Sack and his Bren gun up the bank to cover the crossing. Slim knelt behind a clump of feathery palms and peered anxiously ahead while the rest of the patrol clambered out of the river. The rain had eased to a gentle drizzle, and the heavy growth seemed to open out slightly.

The patrol moved silently away from the river through a belt of banana trees to thick bush. A hundred yards in they found a large, newly built hut, no more than twenty yards away. Behind it were other huts with newly thatched roofs, split bamboo walls and the familiar latrine-like stink of an enemy camp.

We could see no low cover from where we crouched. Behind me our Leader Jeff said, 'We've gotta get out of here, what with the noise we just made. Check if they're occupied and move around to the left.' 'Jesus!' I thought, 'Officer's privileges.' Last week Bobby of 15 Platoon looked into a Japanese hut and caught four asleep, but any Japanese asleep in these huts would have to be stone deaf!

Slim looked at Bunny, and with Fergie beside him, stepped into the clearing. The doorway at the first hut looked dark and ominous.

He tiptoed to one side, approaching from the blind corner. He eased up to the corner with one eye on the gun muzzle around the door jamb. Empty. Only a low bench with a few rags and a battered tin dish on the floor.

Sweat pouring, mouth open and breathing shallowly, Slim covered Fergie while he checked the next hut. He stepped back from the doorway and moved silently to the next, a building with a long wall. There was a faint smell of wood smoke. They slid up to the door, a small crackling noise from inside. Slim's heart jumped.

They found a cookhouse—empty! The rain started again.

After they'd checked a few more huts, the patrol commander Jeff waved at them to skirt the camp. The rain increased and Slim walked around a large tree on the high bank above, tripped on a tree root and fell flat on his face.

> I heard Fergie shout, and the crack of a rifle shot. Desperately I struggled up, but the damned foresight on my Owen gun caught under a root. I tore it free in time to see shapes running in from the buildings. Fired more shots, and a Japanese sprinted behind the second hut. My burst followed him, striking and stitching a line the full length of the wall, wooden slats splintering. He didn't come out the other side. The rain intensified, roaring down and obscuring everything. Jeff shouted, 'Let's go!' And we turned and ran from the camp slipping and floundering into the welcome cover of the heavy jungle.

They knew it was Sunday because the padre arrived, escorted by a lone rifleman volunteer as usual. Padre Bill always made the rounds of the rifle companies each Sunday, rain, shine or shellfire, impartially administering religious services to Catholic, Protestant and atheist alike. On weekdays he read burial services over the dead, censored the outgoing mail and deplored their bad language. 'He was as Irish as Paddy's pig,' recalled Slim.

> Jive once told him straight-faced that he followed the Hindu faith. 'No problem, Private Horman,' said Bill, 'next time I come to see ye I'll be bringing me copy of the Kama Sutra and deal with ye.'
>
> Jive was impressed. 'Jeez,' he said, 'I'll bet he even knows the whole Bible backwards!'

Padre Bill arrived, cheerful as always. 'Today we'll be taking communion for the benefit of the C of E's and any other interested parties. You tykes had your turn last week.'

One of Slim's mates, Hank, had decided that the war was reasonably dangerous, and his soul could do with some reinforcing even at this late stage, so he lined up with the other penitents. Padre Bill draped his surplus over his muddy jungle greens and began the service. A nearby tank crew was working on their motor and a spanner dropped with a loud clang. The padre paused mid-sentence, glared at the offender and said severely, 'Keep it down. Ye'll be drawing the crabs!'

The service continued. The faithful knelt in the mud to take communion. The wafer was a piece of army biscuit and the wine cheap watered-down sherry in a tomato sauce bottle administered by means of a tin mug. Bill paused before the kneeling Hank, and possibly because of the distraction of keeping an ear cocked for the guns across the river, made a minor error and handed Hank the bottle. Hank's religious scruples dying momentarily with this rare, undreamed of opportunity, 'He grabbed the bottle and took a generous swig before Bill woke up.'

The onlookers regarded this heresy with a mixture of shock and envy. Snatching the bottle back, the padre snapped, 'What do you think this is—the public bar of the Great Southern Hotel?' He proceeded with the service without a break.

The troops thought Sunday with Bill was as good as Saturday night back home.

'How are you going to settle in when you get back to the parish, padre? Be a bit dull after this, won't it?' they asked.

'Me boys,' said Bill, 'ye may not be believing it, but 'tis nothing like the problems back home. In spite of your proclivity for bloody murder and a disgraceful amount of blasphemy in your speech, I find ye not to be too sinful a bunch. Mind you, 'tis probably due to lack of opportunity—but there's more genuine sinfulness in me parish to be dealt with than here.'

Slim thought that was hard to believe—he figured they were a pretty rough mob, as an outing with Adolf turned out to be.

'Adolf', so nicknamed because of his Hitler-style moustache, lay in knee-high fern and bracken. The Japanese fighting pits were clearly visible 40 yards ahead. Behind him the platoon struggled slowly and painfully to extract their wounded. Ten yards to his left a young Digger lay dead, riddled by machine-gun fire. Adolf's section leader crawled forward and called, 'Pull back!'

'Right,' he answered, turning back, very careful not to let his head show above the ferns. Fire still crackled through the trees. He knew what it would be like back there, slowly dragging the wounded out under fire. If they pulled out, the Japanese would surely follow—and there was the river to cross.

So the patrol stayed. As the fire slackened Adolf slowly lifted his head. The raw earth of the Japanese pits showed clearly: five, six, seven spread across his front.

Silence. A head showed over a parapet and slowly rose until the Japanese was exposed to the waist, another alongside him, and another. All held rifles. Adolf gently lifted the Owen, laying it on its side so that the magazine would not show above the ferns, and aimed. He squeezed the trigger.

The burst knocked the enemy backwards, and the one next to him staggered and fell over the parapet. The rest dived for cover—then the Japanese *Nambu* (machine guns) fired. Adolf flattened into the earth. But they must have thought he was behind a large tree, as two light machine guns sent burst after burst into it. Gradually the fire slackened.

A minute passed and slowly Adolf raised his head. There was no movement. Then a Japanese head carefully lifted over the parapet. As Adolf waited, he could hear low voices and see movement. Silence again, then another figure rose. The Japanese knelt on the parapet and peered at the big tree. Adolf lifted his own weapon and fired, the kneeling figure fell forward, kicking wildly. Immediately the *Nambu* replied, slashing long bursts into the tree.

Long minutes passed as Adolf duelled with the *Nambu*, killing or wounding four more Japanese, holding them while his platoon dragged itself back and across the river. They called in the 25-pounders and he heard the sighing rush of the first incoming salvo, flattening himself into the soft earth while the shells thundered around him.

The Japanese panicked. During the break in the shellfire Adolf lifted his head and saw a Japanese soldier struggling in the tangled vines, trying to run. He killed him with a short burst, and the shells came again.

When they could the platoon struggled exhausted out of the trees through the break in the wire. Possum, the artillery signaller, lay on a rough stretcher, arms and shoulders bandaged, unconscious. The walking wounded dragged themselves into the perimeter. Quickly the patrol members looked after those badly hit—the doctor was on his way and they worked fast.

But Adolf was not there.

Knowing they were mates, one patrol member, wiping his hand over his face leaving black smears, said, 'I'm sorry Slim. He didn't make it—someone said they saw him go down, but it could have been Hayley. There wasn't enough of us on our feet to go and find out.'

He stood there looking at Slim, saying again, 'I'm sorry.'

Slim turned away, an empty feeling inside. 'Bloody Adolf! He and I'd been together since basic training. Leave together in Sydney—we wrote to the same girls. I sat on my bunk, and looked down at the muddy water covering my boots. Bloody Adolf!'

Next morning, just after stand down, B Company called up to say, 'One of Slim's mob has wandered in from over the river.' They sent Adolf back with a couple of B Company men, the Hitler moustache looking slightly bedraggled.

'How are you mate?' he asked Slim, grinning.

'Bloody Adolf!'

Adolf was sent back to battalion headquarters, where the colonel heard his story and gave him a nip of gin. Two days later he was awarded the Distinguished Conduct Medal.

Cooley Brooks was something of a legend. He was a D Company scout and almost daily his exploits were eagerly recounted throughout the battalion, including the day he took a prisoner.

Brigade headquarters had decided it needed a prisoner, and Cooley's platoon leader, Cranky Sam, was called and duly briefed. Sam objected strongly, pointing out that prisoners were hard to come by and tended to damage easily if caught. He was told to stop arguing and carry on. Two sections of the platoon were summoned and the order relayed. They queried the sanity of those responsible for this particular piece of idiocy and were told, 'It's an order. Carry on!'

For two days the unfortunate fifteen roamed the tracks beyond the Mivo River. On two occasions Cooley took his boots off and scouted half a mile of well-used Japanese trails—if they saw his footprints they would think it was a native. Finally the platoon shot up an ammunition party, but no prisoners. Sam had the bodies laid by the track, piled the ammunition boxes in a heap and slipped a short-fused grenade under the stack. Then they retired to look elsewhere. 'They tried to grab two Japanese tending a native garden near the Oamai River,' Slim recalled, 'but the victims proved recalcitrant and ran, and had to be finished off. Cooley was one of the exterminators.'

Finally, Cranky Sam set a well-planned ambush on the Buin road at sundown, and picked a fight with more than 40 Japanese marines. They killed more than a dozen in the first hail of fire, but the ensuing running fight was messy, and Sam was lightly wounded in one hand. But again, there was no prisoner.

The following day two sections squatted by a narrow but well-used trail leading south-west and waited. Nothing. Cranky Sam's hand throbbed and he was in a foul mood. Then rain began to drift through the undergrowth and in the distance artillery rumble grumbled. An hour had passed when a lone Japanese loaded with net bags of taro and potatoes, with thick glasses and a shiny carbine, ambled into view. Urgently Cranky Sam checked up and down the trail—all clear! He motioned quickly to Cooley and Nick the Greek, hidden behind a thick bush. They crouched lower and got ready.

They took their victim with a flying tackle. Potatoes scattered, the Japanese squealed loudly and put up quite a fight. Cooley held him tightly in a headlock. Suddenly the Japanese stopped squealing, seized Cooley's hand and sank his teeth into his thumb.

> 'Jesus bloody Christ!' Coolly squeezed harder on the headlock he had his prisoner in. 'Stop dancing around and do something, the bastard's got me by the thumb!'
>
> Nick paused, 'Hold on mate, just get your scone out of the way for a bit so I can have a good bash at him.' He raised his rifle butt.

Cranky was appalled. 'Hold it, you stupid bastard. We've got to get him back in one piece!'

The Japanese continued to thrash about, his teeth still clenched firmly on Cooley's thumb.

'Got an idea,' said Nick. He pulled his bayonet from its scabbard, knelt on the victim's kicking legs, and slid the long blade between the Japanese's teeth behind Cooley's thumb. He twisted strongly. A couple of teeth splintered, and the Japanese let go. He relaxed, spat and blinked rapidly. He sat up. 'Americans,' he asked—'whisky?'

'The rotten bastard,' said Cooley. 'He's had one nip out of me already!'

They hauled their prize to his feet, bound his wrists behind his back and shoved him back up the track, not forgetting the potatoes.

Over time Cooley's personal score mounted into double figures, and he seemed to be obsessed with finding more victims, but he became withdrawn, bunked by himself and took off prowling alone when his patrol stopped at night. As Slim said, 'The trouble was he was too damned good to send back.' Cooley killed Japanese in an area known as the Badlands, and two more on a long patrol inland towards the 47th Battalion area. Finally he began attaching himself unofficially to other patrols when his own section was having a day off.

'Ain't he a little bottler,' marvelled Hank. 'He's knocking them over so fast he'll soon have as many as you Fergie!'

Fergie was unimpressed. 'Bullshit—he's troppo!'

Cooley did not last much longer. No one in his right mind would stick his neck out continually just to build up a personal score. One night he crawled out to the wire, and an artillery signaller on picket saw his shadow. Against all orders, he fired a burst from his Owen at it. Cooley died an hour later.

In his recollections, Slim lamented:

You could kill remotely, impersonally. The booby-trap you had set exploded in the darkness outside the wire, or away in the distance on some remote trail. You felt grim satisfaction, and almost never saw the smashed remains of your victim.

You could kill urgently, in frantic haste, your instinctive shot smashing into the suddenly appearing form a few feet away. Mouth open, panting shallowly, you watched him fall, watched in near panic for others to appear while you crouched and changed magazines without thinking. That night you woke often—if you had been a little slower, if you had missed . . .

And you could kill deliberately, almost coolly. Your breath short and shallow as you watch them coming closer, strange stomach feeling, hands wanting to shake a little. Your mind repeating, wait for it. Wait! Feel again with your thumb that the change lever is on full automatic—now! But you did not sleep at all that night. The shapes kept returning. You lay in your hole in the ground, staring into the darkness—thinking.

Each time it got a little easier—we did not regard them as human beings. They were strange, alien.

But how could Cooley get to like it?

The news of Japan's surrender reached Slim Medcalf and his unit early one afternoon.

We were amazed, uncertain. Strangely, no one laughed or cheered. All afternoon we sat quietly and speculated. We found it hard to understand fully—we were confused and bewildered.

Dusk approached, and the tank behind our section pits tuned its radio to a station in Queensland. Some trick of atmospherics brought

> Townsville, relaying from Brisbane the sounds of wildly hysterical crowds celebrating the news of peace. We sat silent listening. Then a strange feeling among us—we began to hate the cheering, singing crowds. As the light died we looked into the jungle wall in front of us, and resented the naked parading of their joy and relief. Somebody called, 'Turn that bloody thing off!'

The news was shocking, and no one knew how to deal with it at first. The troops sat together in small section groups, silent, feeling strange, seeking reassurance from their own closeness. Slowly it came to Medcalf that they were suddenly lost. This was the life they had come to accept and to know, however reluctantly. The prospect of any other had become strange and bewildering.

> We had become part of this, the dim tracks and in the wastes of rain-forest, the rushing rivers with their secretive tangled banks. Killing and death had become the norm, we accepted both as we accepted the constant rain, the smell of rotting growth, the night sounds of the jungle. Now this was gone, could we become part of a life we'd almost forgotten? Maybe it would be different for the older men—they would have the beginnings of something to return to. But for the rest of us, it would mark us for the rest of our lives. We were lost, we were not needed anymore, what we had become was not wanted . . .
>
> I do not understand why we felt this way, but that was what happened.

Then, as if to prove the reality, from battalion headquarters down the track came the sound of their bugler blowing the Retreat. For the first time in months, the song of the bugles drifted over the lowlands, asking them to remember their dead.

'That is exactly what it was like. It is hard to forget, even over the years. That is exactly what it was like.'

Chapter 20

BLOODY BORNEO—TARAKAN AND BALIKPAPAN

In 1942, the invading Japanese were very keen to acquire the oil port on the island of Tarakan in the Sesayap River delta of east Borneo, which produced about 5.1 million barrels a year from two fields near the centre of the island, that only measured about 24 kilometres across. It also had a small airstrip less than 2 kilometres from the town of Tarakan, where there were four oil-loading piers on the south-west coast. The interior of the island was heavily forested and the coast almost completely fringed by mangrove swamps.

The island fell to the Japanese on 12 January 1942. Tarakan oil was light, sour, crude. It was volatile enough to be used as fuel without any refining, but also contained enough sulphur to make the iron of ships' boilers brittle. But by 1944, the Japanese navy was so desperate for fuel that it began using raw Tarakan crude in their ships in spite of the risk of serious damage to their boilers.

There has been much criticism of the necessity for the Australian invasion of Tarakan at the beginning of April 1945, a bloody battle during which 240 Australians and some 1500 Japanese died. So fierce and uncompromising was the fighting that, despite the fact that so many more Japanese died than Australians, the appalling jungle conditions and constant deaths and casualties caused extreme stress and loss of morale. Many Australian soldiers suffered such severe psychological or psychiatric disturbances they could not continue.

A number of Australian commentators have argued that the Tarakan invasion was unnecessary and inappropriate since the damaged airstrip on Tarakan was unable to be used, and Tarakan could easily have been bypassed on the general drive northwards towards Japan.

Historian Peter Stanley puts a different perspective in *Tarakan: An Australian tragedy*, his 1997 book examining this rather neglected affair:

> Australian historians have generally looked askance on MacArthur's use of Australian troops in Borneo. The prevailing view derives from a widespread and vigorously nationalistic interpretation of Australian military history embodying a peculiarly Australian interpretation of the nature of military alliances . . . modern Australian nationalism has turned Australia's military past to its own use which does not entirely accord with the historical reality of the evidence of it.

In retrospect it may well be true that Tarakan could have been bypassed, but reasonable military objectives at the time indicated otherwise. This does not in any way detract from an appreciation of the courageous and tenacious campaign of the Australian forces in Tarakan. In appalling conditions and outnumbered, they triumphed against a desperate enemy prepared to fight to the death. Despite heavy casualties they maintained the highest military traditions.

The invasion force consisted of the Australian 26th Brigade and the

Ninth Division (reinforced to 12,000 men), which arrived on 1 May 1945. They faced 21,000 troops of the Japanese 455 Battalion and 2 Guard Force.

Lieutenant Ken Joyce DCM, MID recalled that some of his men in 2/23rd Battalion thought Tarakan was going to be a walk-over, but 'some of the older Diggers viewed this with deep suspicion'.

> 'They say it will be over in three or four days, Lofty. It hardly seems worthwhile landing for such a short time.'
>
> 'Yeah. Look mate, the only thing I've been short of in this bloody outfit is leave, cigarettes and beer. We haven't had a short campaign in the history of the battalion. They started off with eight months in Tobruk, and they have made long-distance records ever since. I bet they'll be shooting at us a couple of months after we land.'

So began two of the bloodiest months of the Pacific Islands war. As Ken Joyce recalled:

> The Nips were totally desperate and therefore more dangerous, many throwing their lives away needlessly. They would expose themselves fearlessly and be cut down to find out where our exact positions were.
>
> There were dozens of others along the track, rather than be taken prisoner, would commit *hari-kari* [disembowel themselves].

The 2/23rd Battalion did not escape unscathed. Fourteen officers and 211 other ranks were killed, and 40 officers and 620 other ranks were wounded. The battle only ended at 8 am on 15 August with the news that Japan had unconditionally surrendered.

The Australians had hoped that the capture of the oil field would ease the logistics of their Borneo campaign, but even that was a disappointment. The Japanese had so thoroughly demolished the field that it took a year to bring it back into production.

The Battle of Balikpapan, on the north-east coast of what is now Kalimantan, Indonesian Borneo, was the last stage of what was known as Operation Oboe, which took place in the closing weeks of the war against Japan in July 1945, conducted by the soldiers of Australia's much-travelled Seventh Division, who also fought in the Middle East.

The Australian plan for the capture of Balikpapan had three objectives: the destruction of the Japanese positions and oil storage by air and naval bombardment, the elimination of the enemy garrison and capture of the port and airfields and, last, the pursuit and elimination of the remaining elements of the enemy and the restoration of the government facilities.

On Tuesday 26 July the Commander in Chief of the Australian Army, General Sir Thomas Blamey, came aboard HMAS *Kanimbla* in Balikpapan harbour. He was met by the ship's captain, Brigadier Chilton, and the executive officer. It was General Blamey's first visit to the ship in an official capacity, accompanied by Lieutenant General Morshead, Major General Milford and Rear Admiral Albert G. Noble of the US Navy—'a generous sprinkle of high command indeed', wrote Sergeant Bill Spencer in his account of that action, *In the Footsteps of Ghosts.*

Blamey said: 'I don't know what will happen to a lot of you after the show is over. It will be decided by Washington and London as to what further contributions Australia will make in this war against Japan. It may well be that some of you with long term service will be given a spell—a spell which you have so justly earned. I know the 2/9th will want to be in the thick of it.'

A battalion wag interjected, 'Pig's arse!'

The commander in chief continued: 'And I'm quite sure that you will worthily uphold the fine traditions of the Seventh Division. You are in splendid physical condition and ready for all that may come your way. Good luck and God speed.'

Again, the comedian added his bit: 'Aren't you coming with us?'

Bill Spencer recalled: 'Although Blamey was unabashed at the interjections, they were spot on and part of every man's inner thoughts. At least Operation Oboe began on a humorous note.' (William B. Spencer, *In the Footsteps of Ghosts*)

At 3.30 am on 1 July 1945, Spencer and his comrades were awakened to discover they were surrounded by an enormous fleet of naval vessels. Those warships fired their broadsides in multiple rockets towards Balikpapan and the entire smoke-shrouded port area appeared to be on fire. 'A typical Kipling dawn came up like thunder, with Allied warships adding their thunderous roar of heavy guns, speeding their messages of death and destruction towards the shore.'

Obvious targets were seen to receive hits. Racks of multiple rockets were discharged. The smoke and debris rising into the air made it appear that there was a huge mountain range behind Balikpapan, as the entire coastline was being swept by naval gunfire.

The troops advancing towards the coast from their ships in landing craft were told to keep their heads down but the urge to look was too strong and 'many heads rose above the gunwales for a quick peep'. All boats from *Kanimbla* beached safely and without damage. Then the 2/9th Battalion moved up the beach unopposed towards its target—a cracking plant and refinery.

> Suddenly we were engulfed in heavy fire from above and for one moment thought that we were being attacked by the Japanese Air Force. Then we were able to see the markings of American Hellcat fighters from Admiral Halsey's aircraft carrier squadron. This was a typical American gung-ho operation, which adhered to the maxim that anything that moved was to be shot at, as it just might be Japanese.

We found shelter in ditches and unused concrete drainpipes, and I recall there was only one casualty from this misadventure.

The Riko River was home to the largest crocodiles Bill Spencer had ever seen. It was always wise to hug the banks of the river when navigating it, in case there were Japanese on the loose. During the night, however, it was prudent to stay about 20 yards out to avoid straying under one of the many 'over the water' toilets used by the villagers, who were gentle people. 'They loathed the Japanese and for good reason. Dayak people, who lived further inland and down the coast from Balikpapan, were known to have harassed the Japanese troops by using their lethal blow pipes and darts. They were proficient in this and could remain unseen.'

On 8 July Spencer's unit was involved in a patrol pushing up the Riko River, which was known to be used by the Japanese as a water transport corridor and needed investigating. Hugging the southern bank of the river, they moved upstream until the junction with the Mati-Riko River, a smaller tributary believed to lead to the Japanese-held village of Separi. The patrol decided to stay close to the bank and observe movements during the night. That bore fruit at 10 pm when they heard the noise of approaching engines on the Mati-Riko, accompanied by a babble of indigenous voices. This came from a string of *prahus* (long narrow canoes) towed by an enemy motor boat.

Next morning, with mist rising from the river, Corporal Ray Lalchere saw an ocean-going vessel of some 300 tons moored about 800 metres upstream. Closer inspection found it deserted, but with a cargo of rice, oil and coal. On the opposite bank was a smaller boat, about 12 metres long. The smaller vessel had been fitted with steel plates along its superstructure for protection. Battalion headquarters was advised of this by radio, and an ambush authorised to attack the enemy supply team using the river.

On 15 July, 11 Platoon from B Company moved out before dark, occupied the cargo vessel and took up positions on the starboard side. Its weapon was a PITA (projectile infantry tank attack), which fired a single bomb which was fused on the face and weighed about 4.5 kilos. This was a powerful weapon against armour—and a thoroughly devastating one against a fragile launch.

Private Jack Moore was the PITA operator, and was bursting to use his pride and joy for the first time after having carried it for years. At 10 pm his dream came true, as a motor launch appeared with the usual flotilla of *prahus* in tow. The ambush team waited till the enemy boat was abreast of them and the order to fire was given. Almost immediately the PITA bomb burst in the launch with a tremendous explosion, and was accompanied by Bren and rifle fire. A second bomb set it alight. According to Spencer: 'The ambush party recalled the happy chatter of the natives instantly changing to panic stricken yelling, as bodies flailed onto the bank and into the dense prickly undergrowth, struggling through the thorny growth into the adjoining swamp.'

There were estimated to be about twenty Japanese soldiers on the boat—five of them were found dead at the scene, and the others were injured or dead and probably floated down the river. The natives in the *prahus* escaped injury and the burning boat drifted slowly astern and sank.

The day after this incident, an American LCT (landing craft tank), armed to the teeth with a Bofors-style cannon and other heavy machine guns, chugged up around the headland. Ray Lalchere made contact and told them about the two vessels up river. Shortly after they departed for a look all hell broke loose, as the Americans fired everything they had and ended up sinking the small armoured vessel. Ray bailed them up as they were returning, but they were unrepentant. 'It moved,' they said, 'we had to retaliate.'

Then on 6 August 1945 the Americans dropped the atomic bomb on Hiroshima.

There was great rejoicing at 9.20 pm on 10 August 1945 when the 2/9th Battalion signal section picked up a radio signal originating from New York with the news that Japan was willing to accept unconditional surrender.

Spencer's diary of that day read:

> Today brings us to the victorious conclusion of the war in the Pacific. The situation in the Balikpapan area remains. Tonight has been one of celebration. As it happened it was a beer issue day—three bottles per man. Soon after the news reached them the men went berserk. Verey flares, parachute flares and tracers coloured the sky. The natives in the Netherlands Indies Civil Administration Camp commenced hilarious celebrations. Arrangements are being made to accommodate surrendering enemy troops. Perhaps we will now discover where they have been hiding.

Chapter 21

THE LOST YEARS AND DAMAGED LIVES

The dropping of the atomic bombs on Hiroshima and Nagasaki and the Soviet invasion of Japanese-occupied Manchuria in August 1945 brought World War II to an end, suddenly and unexpectedly. It could not come a moment too soon for the Australian Eighth Division prisoners of war of the Japanese, many of whom were close to death from starvation and the aftermath of the debilitating work on forced slave labour projects like the Thai–Burma Railway.

It is now known that a secret order from the Japanese high command had decreed that in the event of an Allied landing near POW camps in South-east Asia, all prisoners were to be killed. This had actually been carried out in Borneo, where some 2000 Australians and 500 British at Sandakan had been marched into the jungle and slaughtered in the infamous Death Marches in early 1945. Only six men escaped to tell the story.

You will not find many Australian prisoners of war of the Japanese who have anything but praise for the Americans for dropping the atomic bombs on Japan when they did. Even the POWs still in the main Changi camp in Singapore, situated in and around Changi Gaol, were forced to get out and dig long deep trenches outside the gaol perimeter in late 1944 and early 1945. The purpose of these pits was never explained, but the POWs believed—correctly as it happened—that they were digging their own graves and would have been machine-gunned into them had the Allies landed on Singapore island.

The sudden surrender after the atomic bombs were dropped was only successfully negotiated after the Japanese government received assurances from the Americans that the life of Emperor Hirohito would be spared, that he would be permitted to stay in his palace in Tokyo and not humiliated by any war crimes trials. The Allies were not keen to invade the Japanese homeland, which would have caused catastrophic casualties on both sides, and these terms were accepted quickly.

In round figures, of the 22,000 taken prisoner by the Japanese, 14,000 Australian prisoners of war had survived. Most of the 8000 had died unnecessary deaths through starvation, overwork and tropical diseases which could have been prevented by better food, and even minimal medicines to combat diseases like malaria, dysentery, pellagra and cholera, or through a random act of brutality by a Japanese, Korean or Formosan guard.

Travel by sea was a huge hazard for POWs. After the building of the Thai–Burma Railway the Japanese attempted to move some 4000 British and Australian POWs to Japan on tramp ships from Singapore to work as slave labourers in iron and coal mines. Many of these ships were unfortunately sunk by American submarines, their captains unaware that there were Allied POWs on board. Hundreds died and did not reach Japan. A fortunate few, after clinging to wreckage in the South China Sea for five nights and six days, were picked up by American submarines and returned to Australia in late 1944—bringing the first accurate news of what the Japanese were really doing with their Australian POWs.

But in August 1945, the surviving 14,000 were scattered through South-east Asia and beyond. The largest group, 5549, was congregated on Singapore island and Johore, but 4830 were distributed in several camps and in a number of working parties in Thailand and remote areas of Burma. In addition, 265 were in French Indo-China; about 750 were distributed throughout the islands of the Netherlands East Indies, with 385 in Java and 243 in Sumatra; about 100 were on Ambon; two were at Macassar; seven on Bali; and another 150 were at Kuching in British North Borneo. About 2700 were distributed between Japan, Korea and Manchuria, while about 200 remained on Hainan Island.

In Changi the prisoners had radios and knew what was happening in the outside world. But they could not predict how the Japanese would react, and there was evidence that the Japanese were going to be bad losers.

Sydney Piddington was a member of the Changi Concert Party and helped to run the 'The Changi Canary', the secret radio:

> The Australian command asked us to run the radio and get hourly reports, which we did. As it became more and more dangerous it was a rule not to tune in until right on time. However, I tuned in about five minutes early and heard the last few bars of Paul Whiteman's band playing 'Rhapsody in Blue'. Then I heard the first news of the dropping of the bomb on Hiroshima.

Allied troops in the main base camp, Changi, were soon aware that the war was over. 'There was a young fellow dropped onto the aerodrome and he looked like a pirate,' recalled Sergeant Stan Arneil. 'He must have been about six foot three. He seemed to be as wide as an ox, in great health, with a revolver and all that sort of thing—and he looked absolutely beautiful.'

Signaller Chris Neilson thought so too:

> You would have thought he was Flash Gordon. He looked the part—he'd have given Flash Gordon a hiding. He strolled in amongst us and we were all cheering like bloody hell. A Jap raced up to meet him. Evidently they had been told that he would be coming in on his own. This Jap came up, bowed and said, 'I will take you to the commandant of the Changi prison camp.' This bloke just went WHACK and lifted him under the chin. He said, 'You take me nowhere, you bring the bloody commandant to me,' and he gave him a kick in the arse as he ran away. The next minute up came the commandant at the double. Oh it was lovely! You should have heard us cheer. He rushed up and started bowing, and this bloke said, 'Never mind about that bloody crap. Look at those skeletons over there—you're responsible.' Oh did he tear into him!

Reactions of the former Japanese conquerors towards their POWs ranged from the obsequious to the bizarre. Private Charles 'Nutty' Almond was still in Thailand when the war ended, doing maintenance on the operational Thai–Burma Railway near the town of Bampong:

> We worked a couple of days after the war finished. We came home from work one night and flags were flying from all the huts. The Japs had finally announced the war was over. I wouldn't believe it. My mate said, 'The war is over, Chas.' And I said, 'Not again!' He said, 'It's fair dinkum this time.' I said, 'Yeah I'll believe it when I see it.' He said, 'Well, come out here.' One of our chaps was walking along with a Jap walking towards him. As they got close to each other the Jap stuck out his hand, offering to shake hands, and our bloke just hauled back and clocked him one under the chin. I said, 'The war is over fair enough!'

Prisoners in camps in Sumatra saw little of the war. Few Allied planes flew overhead and no land battles were fought anywhere in the area. Perhaps the Japanese soldiers were as ignorant of the implications of the surrender as the POWs. Sergeant Graham Chisholm remembered:

> When the war finished our local Japanese didn't surrender. It took them up to ten days before the Emperor's cousin came down and said, 'Hey, you had better surrender.' We were then told that the nations of the world were again at peace. But we had a pretty tough ten days before the surrender was confirmed, because they brought the regular troops in around the camp. They put down their chin straps, and when a Japanese soldier put down his chin strap you knew that something serious was going on. They had machine guns ringing us. So for ten days there was hardly a movement, even the birds were quiet. The Japanese had vast armies that had not been defeated and they wanted to go on fighting.
>
> But when Count Terauchi came down with a surrender order direct from the Emperor the senior officers in our area, 22 of them, had a little party. They drank saki all night and put on their ceremonial uniforms. I don't know whether they were short of swords, but when dawn came they went outside and bowed to the rising sun, went back and had another slug of saki. Each one then took a hand grenade, and they sat in a circle around the walls. On the word of command there were 22 pins pulled out of 22 hand grenades, and that led to many brown flecks on the bricks of that place. It was devastated. But in their minds they went on to an honourable after-life, rather than being dishonoured by being captured and having to continue living.

During their captivity many prisoners thought about the revenge they would take against the guards at the end of the war. The day will come, they would tell themselves—and they would imagine in fine and bloody detail the way they would square the account. At times, nearly all prisoners thought it would be worthwhile to sacrifice their own lives if only they could kill one or two of their most brutal and sadistic guards at the same time. The intense hatred that some prisoners felt might have helped keep them alive—hate was a good driving force. But at the end of the war many of the prisoners found that their passion for vengeance had gone. This is what some of them had to say:

> There were a number of dead Japanese found at the back of Changi Gaol down at the beach. Whether they were shot by Chinese or by our people, we don't know. We were so pleased, so elated, that the whole thing was over and we would be going back home, I don't think a lot of us were looking for revenge. (George Aspinall)

> It never occurred to me to bash a Japanese just because he was a Japanese. I knew enough about them to realise that their code of conduct was completely foreign to us, but that didn't justify bashing just any Jap because we had been bashed from time to time. If it was a particular Jap, well that was different in my book. We were aware that some of the occupation forces had made it possible for people to take action if they wished. I heard about one Australian who took the opportunity to punch a guard, but in so doing broke his wrist. It's debatable whether that was worthwhile. (Jack Sloan)

> Our old guards that ill-treated us were taken away and new guards brought in. The Japanese, when they knew it was all over, probably wanted to avoid incidents. The Australian attitude, I think, is that you can't kick a dog while it's down and they looked so beaten and so subservient that we couldn't do anything to them. But if it had been the ones that ill-treated us, we probably would have been into them. (Eddie Henderson)

Those Australians who did attempt to wreak vengeance were looked down on by their comrades. Ray Myors was still in Thailand when the news of the surrender broke:

> We were down at the bank of the river in Bangkok and this particular fellow and a couple of his mates were a little the worse for wear from drinking *lao*—that's the local brew of wine spirits, which was all that was available. When he saw this party of Japanese coming across the river in a canoe about 20 feet long, this fellow—without any assistance from anyone—just swam out in the river and tipped their boat over and then, one after another, held a Japanese underwater until he drowned the lot. He got his fair share of being sent to Coventry because we didn't agree. But there were other isolated incidents where a Japanese was a bit presumptuous with his attitude and a bloke would drop him. Of course, that is very natural, but there was no taking up arms and slaughtering people, or anything of that nature.

Gordon Maxwell, who was a prisoner in Japan at the time, recalled: 'One of our fellows did catch one of our Jap guards and put him in the guard room in the little solitary confinement cell that we used to be banged up in, for a couple of days. But the novelty wore off and he just let him go.'

The end of the war came more quickly than the Allies had expected. General Douglas MacArthur was determined that no local commanders would take the surrender of the Japanese before he accepted the formal surrender in Tokyo Bay. The prisoners in the camps waited impatiently for food, medicine, news, fellow countrymen and transport home. In Japan the Australians gradually began making excursions from their camps, foraging for food and delighting in their freedom. After a fortnight the prisoners had a new delivery service from the Allied air force. According to Hugh Clarke:

> Well the first time they dropped, it was a terrifying experience because we were in amongst big pine trees. We saw these B-29s fly over very low, they had the bomb bays open and we could see all the tucker and even the crew looking out. They circled the camp a few times and then came over again and made the drop. Each food container consisted of two 44-gallon drums welded together, and they dropped them with coloured parachutes, red, blue and green. As we looked up, the parachutes opened with a jerk, half these drums broke off and came hurtling down into the camp. I got my arms around the trunk of a tree. The medical orderly in the camp was an American. He got hit on the head with a case of Spam and was killed instantly. There were broken legs.

Former POWs of the Japanese who were interviewed for the ABC series *Prisoners of War: Australians Under Nippon* and historian Dr H.N. 'Hank' Nelson's book with the same title, have vivid recollections of those times:

> Another American was standing up with his arms folded. The lid of a drum buried into his chest, cut both his arms off and killed him. (Dave Runge)

> These two double drums came down and they described beautiful arcs very, very slowly. We rushed down, because we weren't going to have the Japs get any of this, to find that the control room of the mine we'd been working in had been tastefully decorated and completely ruined by chocolate and tomato juice. (Don Noble)

> They had boots, clothing, chocolate, flea powder, all sorts of stuff in the one drum, and when they came down they just crunched the whole lot up. Boots were permanently distorted—you couldn't get them on. Cigarettes, without being broken, were compressed to about an inch long. Anyhow, poor little Japanese kids came up and got onto

some of the chocolate. Later on they went back and started eating flea powder and chocolate and everything. The kids were nearly half dead. (Jim Richardson)

In his book, Hank Nelson wrote:

The parachute drops were both lifesaving and deadly. In Borneo, Thailand, Java and Japan prisoners were killed as excited men ran out into the open and drums broke away to become lethal. In Manchuria, a Chinese man, stunned by falling fruit cans, was lucky. He was just left 'fruit salad happy'. The 'Biscuit Bombers', as they were called, also introduced the prisoners to some of the technological changes that had taken place in the outside world. Among the diverse products of the consumer society that came tumbling down was DDT insecticide powder. The men pondered its use, then dusted their *tatami* sleeping mats. The fleas, as new to the insecticide as the prisoners, bounced in the air and were dead when they hit the floor.

With their food supply secured, the prisoners in Japan begin making forays further afield into town and country. Some prisoners shifted from indulgence to anarchy.

'It was about two months before we were evacuated from Japan,' Ray Parkin remembered. 'There were constant warnings coming over the radio to tell us to stay put and stay off bootleg grog. There were a few fellows died of that. Also a lot of fellows were hitching rides all over Japan—getting onto aircraft, and all sorts of transport. Some were killed as a result. There were a lot of aircraft accidents.'

Don Moore was one of the fellows having a good look around:

Then we started to go out for walks. We got a little more venturesome when we got fatigue uniforms and books dropped from the air.

> And cartons of cigarettes which were our currency. We walked onto a railway station one day. The train was very crowded. We travelled for two or three stations, then got off. We said, well, there's a good place to travel. Let's give a couple of packets to the driver and the fireman, and let's go into the cab of the engine. Then I had a small boy's ideal of travelling in the cab of a steam engine through tunnels and along the Japanese railway system of Kyushu. It was a wonderful experience.

Other ex-prisoners also took the opportunity to fulfil their ambitions, as Cliff Moss observed:

> A fella called Jack 'Gov' Blythe was one of our notable citizens. He was a good fellow, Jack, but he was a bloke that had been around in his time. Bloody good man as a POW. He said, 'I've done a lot of things in my time, but I've never cracked a bank.' He thought he'd have a go. He was living it up anyway. He had a Buick with a gas-producing unit on it. The thing was as long as a modern-day stretch limo. He also had an unpaid Japanese servant to carry a chair for him down the street, and another Japanese in charge of his umbrella. If he wanted to sit down, one bloke positioned the chair and the other held the umbrella over him to keep the sun off.
>
> He got a good waddy in his hand, walked up to the bank, where there was a guard outside the door. He smacked him over the head with the stick and he shot through. Jack walked through the door as all the girls inside disappeared. Jack, and two or three other blokes with him, gathered up a backpack full of yen and walked out. Well, they were walking down the street with a fair few yen fluttering about—they were falling out of the bloody pack. They came back to camp with about 80,000 yen—an immense amount of the bloody things. I think it all finished up back in the bank again, or practically all of it. Anyway, Jack had cracked his bank.

After the gross deprivation inflicted on all former Australian POWs over the previous nearly four years, not all were prepared to be forgiving when the atomic bombs on Hiroshima and Nagasaki suddenly gave them their freedom.

A POW gunner who kept a diary at Nakama wrote a month after the end of the war: 'It's a grouse life, eat and sleep and a boong does all the work.' They were recovering from three and a half years of debts in food and freedom—and almost everyone was acquiring their own ceremonial sword. With a little organisation and much bravado, they souvenired swords en masse. They made their best hauls by moving systematically through the carriages of trains, demanding the personal surrender of all the Japanese officers they saw. Perhaps they considered the former prisoners to be a new form of *ronin*—the wandering masterless *samurai* of Japanese literature.

Chapter 22

RETAIN ALL PRISONERS OF WAR INDEFINITELY

Although planning to recover Australian POWs from the dozens of locations all over South-east Asia and as far afield as Manchuria had begun in 1942, getting them all collected and sent home was a logistic nightmare. The strategy was to bring them in to reception camps in strategic areas. A special organisation was created to do this, the Recovery of Allied Prisoners of War and Internees (RAPWI). During the weeks after the surrender, Australian Royal Navy ships transported thousands of Australian POWs in the south-west Pacific area to RAPWI reception camps in Singapore, Labuan, Morotai and other locations. But all this took some time, and RAPWI became known by the POWs desperate to get home as 'Retain All Prisoners of War Indefinitely'.

Most prisoners of war were in poor health, still emaciated from three and a half years of starvation rations, and in the RAPWI centres they were first de-loused, bathed, re-clothed and, if they were well enough, interrogated about their experiences. They were put on high-fat diets, many putting on kilos within days of their rescue.

Once they had been fattened up and their bodies rid of the more obnoxious and debilitating prison camp afflictions, they were sent on to Australia by sea and air. Some were not yet out of danger. The Australian poet, broadcaster and author Clive James said recently that he was still haunted by the death of his father, Albert James, who was being flown home from his Japanese prison camp by the Americans in 1945 only to be killed when his military aircraft crashed. James, then six years old, and his mother had been eagerly awaiting Albert's return in Sydney. James said, 'I was there to watch my mother take the news. It still, now, deprives me of speech.'

The bulk of the surviving POWs arrived back in Australia during September and October. They had had priority. Only then could the Australian men and women serving in Borneo, Papua and New Guinea return to Australia in the final months of 1945 and early 1946.

Despite the euphoria of reaching Australia after what they had been through, most ex-POWs were mentally fragile. The awareness of what is now post-traumatic stress syndrome in 1945 was slight, and many needed counselling and treatment which they never had. As historian Dr H.N. 'Hank' Nelson wrote:

> Prisoners who had enlisted at twenty years of age were coming home at twenty-four or five. They had missed the years when their vigour was its greatest, when they would have played their best sport, when they would have selected a career, and when they would have married. They were all conscious of the distorted pattern in their lives. They felt a need to try and catch up, and some were uncertain they could do so.
>
> The prisoners were uncertain of their reception in Australia. There was no precedent. They were not like the Diggers returning from the First World War, nor the active service units that had recently paraded

through city streets to be honoured for their actions in the Middle East and the Pacific. Many English prisoners of war of the Japanese went home almost unnoticed because the war in Europe had been over for five months—the English were already consumed by problems of peace. But in Australia the main groups of prisoners were met by cheering crowds, and that perception boosted the prisoners' own sense of elation. Small boats escorted troop ships down the harbour, crowds met them on the docks, some holding notices such as, 'Where is private Harry Jackson?' City workers and shoppers gave them a boisterous reception as they went by on double-decker buses through the streets of Sydney. Those who travelled on to country towns were again greeted at railway stations by local dignitaries, old mates and flag-waving children given time off from lessons for the occasion.

Through their imprisonment most men and women thought constantly of home—and that home was particular. They knew its every detail. As they contrasted their home with the squalor and poverty of the camp they were likely to idealise it and all those who clattered backwards and forwards through its rooms. Now they faced the reality.

On arriving back in Australia, one of the first of his family, Don Moore set eyes on was his brother-in-law, Pat:

> I'd never kissed a guy in my life before, but I did then. And I looked around and Dad wasn't there. But I didn't say anything. And they said, 'Right, well, Jack's got some extra petrol because you're a POW, so we will be able to drive you back home. We live in Murrumbeena now.' 'Where's Dad?' And my sister said, 'Dad died in 1944.'

Not all the POWs returned to joyous family reunions, as the following accounts reveal:

> Some men went back happily to the arms of their wives and children, some did to their mothers, fathers and sisters, but I didn't. I was not unhappy with my mother and my brother. My wife met me too—and then cleared out. (Patrick Levy)

> I got a Dear John letter. She got word that I was missing in action, believed killed. And well, you can't blame her, can you? So then I got a divorce and that was that. (George Williamson)

> Before we were sent back to Australia we thought were going to get letters from home, acquainting us of what was going on. If that had happened there would have been less heartbreak. Lots of fellows came back to broken homes. One fellow shot his wife. Another fellow burned himself to death after he too shot his wife. (Rusty O'Brien)

Homecoming for some others was more idyllic. Captain Curlewis (later Sir Adrian Curlewis) remembered that wives and families had all been warned not to give prisoners too rich meals. 'They were to treat them very, very carefully because their stomachs wouldn't be able to take it. But somehow I got quite a good feed when I got home. And champagne. My wife had put a bottle away for three years and kept it for me.'

Lady Curlewis responded by saying, 'And it didn't seem to affect him at all. Then he just looked around and he said with a sigh, "Isn't it clean!"'

In the camps the prisoners had helped hide doubts about their virility with the line, 'And the second thing I'll do when I get home is to take my pack off!' Bob Yates recalled they had been warned: 'As far as the opposite sex was concerned we were told that after our experiences we wouldn't be much good. But that's been proved wrong fortunately.'

Daisy Sloan, like many other prisoners, was concerned about infertility due to malnutrition and disease: 'We'd been told we probably wouldn't be able to have a family for a while.' But after he and his wife had only been married for nine months, 'we had a baby boy, and a couple of years later twin girls. So that wasn't too bad on the rice diet!'

However, many ex-POWs found that there were soon immediate consequences of returning to a life of normality:

> I know this, I couldn't go into a bloody cafe. Even if I was as hungry as buggery, do you think I could go in there and order a meal? Had to find some bugger who looked like he was hungry and asked him to have a feed with me. I couldn't do it on my own. (Chris Neilson)

> You always seemed to be frightened of something. In my case, I couldn't bear to be on my own. I had to have someone with me, someone around me, even if they were strangers. To be in a room by myself was just impossible. I'd have to get out or make an excuse to go and see somebody. (Herb Trackson)

> I have an absolute horror of being shut in anywhere. I know it's silly, as long as I control the entrance to a thing I'm right. But if anyone else shut the door, my claustrophobia is up. (Sylvia Muir)

> There was this recurrent thing my husband Dick [one of the six survivors of the Sandakan Death Marches] had about lice on the bed. We would get up fairly regularly, strip everything off and examine the mattress minutely. He said to me, 'I know you don't ever think there is vermin in the bed, but look at my arms.' And he literally had bite marks on his arms and raised psychosomatic lumps on his back. One was filled with great sadness that this should have happened and I wondered how long this would have to last for him. (Joyce Braithwaite)

> I am over-fastidious with cleanliness. I'll shower in the morning and use up most of the hot water in the house. Very silly when I think of

it, because I know I've already washed and rinsed myself once, but I'll soap up and scrub a second time just to make sure. (Rod Wells)

I gave my wife a start one night. She came in and I dreamt there was a Jap outside the window and I thought, 'Oh, I'll throw a hand grenade, that'll fix him.' So I grabbed the light beside the bed, and let fly and nearly knocked her bloody head off. She wasn't real happy about that. (Geoff O'Connor)

Some years ago I was having a drink with three or four chaps and one of them came round to me and whispered, 'Whitey, do you have nightmares? About, you know, the old days?' And I said, 'Of course I do.' He said, 'How often?' I said, 'Oh, a really bad one once every couple of months but you know, might be one nightmare a week or just every now and then.' 'Oh,' he said, 'thank Christ for that. I have them too.' And I said, 'Yeah, and you thought you were going round the bend?' He said, 'Yeah, yeah, I did. It's been worrying me for a long time.' So I said to all the others, 'Righto, how many of you blokes don't have nightmares?' And they all looked at me as if I was crazy. And each one said, 'Yes of course we do.' (Roy Whitecross)

To survive, the prisoners of war had to endure and endure. The prisoners have their own heroes, and they are the men and women who again and again demonstrated that they would lead and help others through persistent horror. The prisoners do not measure themselves against national history, but they are the ones best able to express what being a prisoner did to particular lives.

Some were grateful for the experience:

Yes, it was the greatest privilege I ever had. I was so lucky to have been a prisoner of war and come to an understanding about things that are important—to my life with those POWs with whom I lived, and to make in my own tiny way, a token gesture for Australia. (Stan Arneil)

It gave me a great understanding of men. And a great appreciation of the ordinary things of life—bread and butter, a bit of jam on your toast in the mornings, a glass of beer when you're thirsty. And, the value of human relations. You know when it comes to the end, the only thing that really matters are the people whom you love and the people who love you. (Dr Kevin Fagan)

The 14,000 surviving POWs at the end of the war were scattered widely through Asia, including Japan. Some of them who were working in Japanese coal and iron ore mines actually saw the atomic bomb dropped on Nagasaki, so pivotal in abruptly ending the war. In the immediate aftermath, while waiting to be rescued, POW medico Dr Ian Duncan decided he would use this time to interview every Australian and British soldier in his camp—he was the only medical officer there.

I thought it was my duty to record their disabilities. And you'd say to them, 'What diseases have you had as a prisoner of war?' 'Oh, nothing much, Doc, nothing much at all.' 'Did you have malaria?' 'Oh yes, I had malaria.' 'Did you have dysentery?' 'Oh yes, I had dysentery.' 'Did you have beriberi?' 'Yes.' 'Did you have pellagra?' 'Yes, I had pellagra but nothing very much.' All these are lethal diseases but that was the norm, you see, everyone had them. Therefore they accepted them as normal.

Duncan remained concerned even when treating ex-POWs in post-war civilian life:

A lot of them had stomach trouble, a lot of gastric duodenal ulcers, a lot had chronic diarrhoea. But everyone who worked—certainly on the railway and in the mines of Japan—has some form of arthritic degeneration caused by the conditions of their work. I've seen X-rays of the spines of some of these men and they are really shocking—how they got around I don't know. But they did and made very light of it. The men almost invariably came in and said, 'Well I don't want to seem to be a bludger, but I've got this trouble,' or, 'I thought I'd come along and see you. I don't think I deserve any pension, we didn't do much fighting.' And this was their attitude. They actually believed that they were not entitled to a lot of the benefits of ex-servicemen. But they were. They fought a pretty hard war—as POWs.

And the last word on the POW experience is from Ambon survivor, Jack Panaotie:

When we get talking together, we say—couldn't go through it again, but we wouldn't have missed it. An experience that we know, that nobody else knows. Not that you don't want anyone else to know about it, but you cannot explain it to anybody else. Because we are unique.

Chapter 23

FINAL THOUGHTS

It is odd, that although most of us were aware last century that we would not have the World War I veterans for very long, somehow—even historians—we believed that we would have the World War II men and women forever!

Suddenly, in the 21st century, we have belatedly realised that not many are left at all. Even the teenagers who upped their ages from as young as fifteen to join the Australian Militia and the AIF are now in their 90s. My father, Major John Bowden, who enlisted in the AIF from Tasmania at the age of 33 to serve in Palestine and later in Central and Northern Australia, would be 111 if he were alive today.

In reading the mostly self-published books written by ex–World War II soldiers, I am astonished at their bravery, and self-deprecating accounts of their role in savage actions in the Middle East, Japanese prison camps in South-east Asia, and in the South Pacific area—particularly their honesty and larrikin humour in writing about what *really* happened to them on the battlefield and off.

I have been particularly privileged to get to know and enjoy the confidences of many ex–prisoners of war of the Japanese, when historian Hank Nelson and I (on his instigation) began our oral history project in the early 1980s that resulted in the ABC Radio series, and Hank's book, *Prisoners of War: Australians Under Nippon*. The men and women interviewed were then in their mid-60s, and, as mentioned earlier in this book, had strangely never spoken about their experiences, in many cases not even to their own families. Hank believed that the time had come for them to finally tell their stories, and he was absolutely right. Even after so many years, some wept as they recalled what had happened to them under the brutal Japanese POW regime. Curiously, some even felt ashamed that they had been prisoners of war, rather than 'proper soldiers'.

This, even though most of them had fought brief but gallant actions in Timor, Ambon, Java and most effectively in the brief Malayan campaign leading to the fall of Singapore in February 1942. Continued army service was unlikely to have provided the challenges, dangers and privations they endured for the following three and a half years. Yet it took a while for them to realise the quiet heroism of their captivity. Perhaps the radio series, *Australians Under Nippon*, first broadcast in 1984, helped not only to let fellow Australians know what they had been through, but triggered more books and memoirs from veterans in following years. And in 1998, the Australian prime minister celebrated Anzac Day at Hellfire Pass on the Thai–Burma Railway.

When I interviewed Sir Edward 'Weary' Dunlop in the early 1980s, one of the legendary doctors on the Thai–Burma Railway, he had this to say:

> It's quite surprising, the achievement of prisoners of war all over the country—they've done well in all sorts of occupations and activities.

> And unhappily of course there are men who were damaged psychologically, who went on the booze or smoked themselves to death. I think my major worry has been that the years have found out a lot of them that started off pretty well. They bounded back into civilian life, they didn't want pensions, they didn't want to be cushioned, but they were very tired men and they came home exhausted in the evenings. They didn't go back to tennis, bowls and golf, they put on weight and got a bit flabby. So I think that heart disease and the diseases which overtake the middle-aged and the elderly have taken a lot of them off before their time.

There are certainly parallels with the tropical experiences of the Australian prisoners of war of the Japanese with the Militia and AIF soldiers who fought in the jungles of Papua New Guinea and the Pacific Islands. Certainly the scourge of malaria, dysentery and sometimes an inadequate diet of tinned bully beef and hard tack biscuits would have been understood by the POWs, even if they would have welcomed bully beef and biscuits as manna from heaven.

I regret not knowing the authors featured in *Straight Shooters* as well as I got to know so many of the ex–prisoners of war of the Japanese in the early 1980s. I have met one, Joe Dawson, a veteran of the Kokoda Track who lived near me on the Mid North Coast of New South Wales, author of *Kokoda Survivor*, and corresponded with another, Clarry McCulloch, a fellow Tasmanian, who sent me a copy of his memoir, *Some Call It Luck*, in 2005. He wrote in the flyleaf, '*To Tim, thanks for your sense of humour—from one Taswegian to another*'.

Of course I wrote to thank him, but at that stage had not thought of writing a book which would feature his colourful account among others. Had we met, we could have swapped some shared experiences. He began his training at Brighton camp, north of Hobart, in June 1940 in the same army huts that I slept in as a fourteen-year-old member of my school's army cadet corps (nearly freezing off my developing testicles in a Tasmanian winter in 1951), and again in 1957 as a national serviceman (at least that basic training session was in the short Tasmanian summer). On both occasions we drilled with World War I–vintage .303 Lee Enfield rifles that Clarry doubtless trained with in Brighton camp also and later used as a fighting soldier in the Middle East.

Clarry McCulloch did the full tour. After fighting in the Syrian Campaign, he was to return to Australia with his battalion on the troopship (and former cruise liner) *Orcades,* after which he would have doubtless fought in Papa New Guinea or the South Pacific Islands against the invading Japanese. Instead he drew the short straw, and was off-loaded in Java to help the Dutch prop up their fading colonial empire, and after a short action spent the rest of the war as a POW of the Japanese in Java, and later on the Thai–Burma Railway.

I still have the letter Clarry McCulloch wrote to me in 2005, which began:

> Dear Tim,
> Although I had to sign the 'Dangerous Goods' declaration on the front of this package, I think the contents are unlikely to damage your health. They may promote a quiet chuckle here and there, if so I will be well satisfied as I think that your view of life is much akin to mine.

He finished his letter: 'Anyway, at my age, I have realised that perhaps we should look at life as it really is. One gigantic joke!'

I think you would have enjoyed Donald Trump's election as president of the United States, Clarry. Sorry you didn't live to see it.

As I said in the introduction to *Larrrikins in Khaki*, this book is not in any sense a conventional military history and not intended to be. But in delving into the memoirs of the blythe spirits who published their own books, I hope I have at least illustrated the sterling qualities of the Australian fighting soldier—hard to discipline, generous to their comrades, irreverent and, above all, telling it as they saw it, warts and all.

It has been a privilege to share their stories.

Tim Bowden, 2019

ACKNOWLEDGEMENTS

First, profound thanks to the eleven authors of the books quoted in *Larrikins in Khaki* who sadly cannot know of the republishing of key parts of their memoirs because they are all dead. They are: Ivan Blazely, Joe Dawson, Ken Clift, Colin Finkemeyer, Norm Fuller, Bob Holt, Clarry McCulloch, Peter Medcalf, Roy Sibson, Ken Joyce and Bill Spencer. The remarkable books written by these men were collected by both my friend Professor Hank Nelson and me over the years, when we worked on aspects of the experiences of Australian prisoners of war of the Japanese in World War II.

I regret it has not been possible, in all cases, to contact the families or descendants of the authors due to the passing of time. As I have quoted extensively from their work, I only hope that relatives of the above authors will be forbearing under the circumstances, and pleased that the stories of these remarkable soldiers will now be read by a wider and younger audience. Identification of many soldiers referred to was made further hazardous by the nicknames used by those who wished to hide the identity of particularly hated NCOs and incompetent officers. In many cases nicknames were conferred on much-loved comrades in arms.

I thank my publisher at Allen & Unwin, Rebecca Kaiser, for supporting this project, and military historian Professor Peter Stanley for agreeing to run his experienced eye over the manuscript. Historian Dr Mark Johnston gave invaluable insights and guidance of the role of Australians in the Pacific War. Also Rebecca Kaiser for her careful and painstaking work in honing my prose and picking up the instances where I have used the same adjective either in the same sentence, or in the following one, which is one of my besetting sins.

John Holmes, author of *Smiles of Fortune—A memoir of the war against Japan*, sent me a signed copy of his book when it was published by Kangaroo Press in 2001. The cover photo, also used in *Larrikins in Khaki*, is reproduced courtesy of the Australian War Memorial, negative number 013857. It depicts three cheerful wounded Australians serving with 55/53rd Battalion, making their way out of the front line to a first-aid station in Papua.

My wife Ros has once again been tolerant of losing me to my computer and study for a large percentage of our shared life, and I am grateful.

NOTES

Chapter 1 Joining up

Bob Holt, all quotes from *From Ingleburn to Aitape: The trials and tribulations of a four figure man.*

Ken Clift, all quotes from *The Saga of a Sig: The wartime memories of six years' service in the Second AIF.*

Joe Dawson, all quotes from *Kokoda Survivor, Sergeant Joe Dawson.*

Bill Young, all quotes from *Return to a Dark Age.*

Chapter 2 Very basic training

Colin Finkemeyer, all quotes from *It Happened to Us: Mark II*

Clarry McCulloch, all quotes from *Some Call It Luck: The war story of Clarry McCulloch.*

Ivan Blazely, all quotes from *Boots and All.*

Bob Holt, all quotes from *From Ingleburn to Aitape.*

Roy Sibson, all quotes from *My Life as I Saw It Boots 'n' All.*

Joe Dawson, all quotes from *Kokoda Survivor.*

Chapter 3 Sailing to war

Bob Holt, all quotes from *From Ingleburn to Aitape.*

Ken Clift, all quotes from *The Saga of a Sig.*

Clarry McCulloch, all quotes from *Some Call It Luck.*

Ivan Blazely, all quotes from *Boots and All.*

Chapter 4 Desert Diggers prepare for war

Ivan Blazely, all quotes from *Boots and All.*

Bob Holt, all quotes from *From Ingleburn to Aitape.*

Clarry McCulloch, all quotes from *Some Call It Luck.*

Ken Clift, all quotes from *The Saga of a Sig.*

Chapter 5 High jinks in Egypt

Bob Holt, all quotes from *From Ingleburn to Aitape.*

Ken Clift, all quotes from *The Saga of a Sig.*

Chapter 6 Fighting in the desert

Bob Holt, all quotes from *From Ingleburn to Aitape.*

Ken Clift, all quotes from *The Saga of a Sig.*

Chapter 7 Ill-fated Greek adventure

Bob Holt, all quotes from *From Ingleburn to Aitape.*

Ken Clift, all quotes from *The Saga of a Sig.*

Chapter 8 Out of the frying pan into the fire

Bob Holt, all quotes from *From Ingleburn to Aitape.*

Ken Clift, all quotes from *The Saga of a Sig.*

Chapter 9 The Allied invasion of Lebanon and Syria

Ivan Blazely, all quotes from *Boots and All.*

Clarry McCulloch, all quotes from *Some Call It Luck.*

Bob Holt, all quotes from *From Ingleburn to Aitape.*

Chapter 10 The tide turns

Ivan Blazely, all quotes from *Boots and All.*

Chapter 11 Return to Australia

John Bowden, all quotes from Tim Bowden, *The Way My Father Tells It: The story of an Australian life.*

Ivan Blazely, all quotes from *Boots and All.*

Bob Holt, all quotes from *From Ingleburn to Aitape.*

Ken Clift, all quotes from *The Saga of a Sig.*

Chapter 12 Prisoners of war of the Japanese

Clarry McCullough, all quotes from *Some Call It Luck.*

Stan Arneil, all quotes from Tim Bowden and Hank Nelson, *Prisoners of War: Australians Under Nippon,* ABC Radio documentary series.

Cliff Moss, all quotes from *Prisoners of War.*

Clarrie Thornton, all quotes from *Prisoners of War.*

Ray Steele, all quotes from *Prisoners of War.*

Jack Sloan, all quotes from *Prisoners of War.*

Tom Morris, all quotes from *Prisoners of War.*

Frank Robinson, all quotes from *Prisoners of War.*

Dick Ryan, all quotes from *Prisoners of War.*

Ben Hackney, all quotes from *Prisoners of War.*

Don Moore, all quotes from *Prisoners of War.*

Frank Christie, all quotes from *Prisoners of War.*

'Snow' Peat, all quotes from *Prisoners of War.*

Tom Dowling, all quotes from *Prisoners of War.*

'Prawn' Hennebery, all quotes from Colin Finkemeyer, *It Happened to Us.*
Adrian Curlewis, all quotes from *Prisoners of War.*
George McNeilly, all quotes from *Prisoners of War.*
Russell Braddon, all quotes from *Prisoners of War.*

Chapter 13 The railway of death

Jim Richardson, all quotes from *Prisoners of War.*
Geoff O'Connor, all quotes from *Prisoners of War.*
Dr Kevin Fagan, all quotes from *Prisoners of War.*
Stan Arneil, all quotes from *Prisoners of War.*
Don Moore, all quotes from *Prisoners of War.*
Hugh Clarke, all quotes from *Prisoners of War.*
Donald Stuart, all quotes from *Prisoners of War.*
Arthur Bancroft, all quotes from *Prisoners of War.*
Ray Parkin, all quotes from *Prisoners of War.*
Adrian Curlewis, all quotes from *Prisoners of War.*
Dr Rowley Richards, all quotes from *Prisoners of War.*
Clarry McCulloch, all quotes from *Some Call It Luck.*
Colin Finkemeyer, all quotes from *It Happened to Us.*
Bob Grant, all quotes from *Prisoners of War.*
Dave Buxton, all quotes from *Prisoners of War.*

Chapter 14 Service at home

Ivan Blazely, all quotes from *Boots and All.*
Bob Holt, all quotes from *From Ingleburn to Aitape.*

Chapter 15 The saga of the flying footsloggers

Norm Fuller, all quotes from *The Flying Footsloggers: Unofficial history of Australia's World War paratroopers.*

Chapter 16 The Kokoda Track and the bloody beachheads

Joe Dawson, all quotes from *Kokoda Survivor.*

Ralph Honner, in Peter Brune, *Ralph Honner: Kokoda hero.*

William Slim, *Defeat into Victory.*

Robert Eichelberger, in James Brien, *The Bloody Beachheads: The battles of Gona, Buna and Sanananda, November 1942–January 1943.*

Seiichi Uchiyama, in Brien, *The Bloody Beachheads.*

James Brien, *The Bloody Beachheads.*

Chapter 17 The battle for New Guinea

Henry 'Jo' Gullet, all quotes from *Not as a Duty Only: An infantryman's war.*

Roy Sibson, all quotes from *My Life as I Saw It Boots 'n' All.*

Chapter 18 An unnecessary campaign

Bob Holt, all quotes from *From Ingleburn to Aitape.*

Chapter 19 Savagery in Bougainville

Peter Medcalf, *War in the Shadows: Bougainville 1944–45.*

Chapter 20 Bloody Borneo—Tarakan and Balikpapan

Peter Stanley, *Tarakan: An Australian Tragedy.*

Ken Joyce, *As I Saw It . . . from Tobruk to Tarakan 1940–1945.*

William B. Spencer, *In the Footsteps of Ghosts: With the 2/9th Battalion in the African desert and jungles of the Pacific.*

Chapter 21 The lost years and damaged lives

Sydney Piddington, all quotes from *Prisoners of War.*

Stan Arneil, all quotes from *Prisoners of War.*

Chris Neilson, all quotes from *Prisoners of War.*

Charles 'Nutty' Almond, all quotes from *Prisoners of War.*

Graham Chisholm, all quotes from *Prisoners of War.*

George Aspinall, all quotes from *Changi Photographer: George Aspinall's record of captivity.*

Jack Sloan, all quotes from *Prisoners of War.*

Eddie Henderson, all quotes from *Prisoners of War.*

Ray Myors, all text from *Prisoners of War.*

Gordon Maxwell, all quotes from *Prisoners of War.*

Hugh Clarke, all quotes from *Prisoners of War.*

Hank Nelson, *Prisoners of War: Australians Under Nippon* (book).

Dave Runge, all quotes from *Prisoners of War.*

Don Noble, all quotes from *Prisoners of War.*

Jim Richardson, all quotes from *Prisoners of War.*

Ray Parkin, all quotes from *Prisoners of War.*

Don Moore, all quotes from *Prisoner of War.*

Cliff Moss, all quotes from *Prisoners of War.*

Chapter 22 Retain all prisoners of war indefinitely

Hank Nelson, all quotes from *Prisoners of War* (book).

Don Moore, all quotes from *Prisoners of War.*

Patrick Levy, all quotes from *Prisoners of War.*

George Williamson, all quotes from *Prisoners of War.*

Rusty O'Brien, all quotes from *Prisoners of War.*

Adrian Curlewis, all quotes from *Prisoners of War.*

Bob Yates, all quotes from *Prisoners of War.*

Daisy Sloan, all quotes from *Prisoners of War.*

Chris Neilson, all quotes from *Prisoner of War.*

Herb Trackson, all quotes from *Prisoners of War.*

Sylvia Muir, all quotes from *Prisoners of War.*

Joyce Braithwaite, all text from *Prisoners of War.*

Rod Wells, all quotes from *Prisoners of War.*

Geoff O'Connor, all quotes from *Prisoners of War.*

Roy Whitecross, all quotes from *Prisoners of War*.
Stan Arneil, all quotes from *Prisoners of War*.
Dr Kevin Fagan, all quotes from *Prisoners of War*.
Dr Ian Duncan, all quotes from *Prisoners of War*.
Jack Panaotie, all quotes from *Prisoners of War*.

Chapter 23 Final thoughts

Edward 'Weary' Dunlop, all quotes from *Prisoners of War*.
Clarry McCulloch, *Some Call It Luck*.

BIBLIOGRAPHY

Unpublished and self-published memoirs

Ivan Blazely, *Boots and All*, no publishing details, 1990

Ken Clift, *The Saga of a Sig: The wartime memories of six years service in the Second AIF*, KCD Publications, 1972

Sergeant Joseph Dawson, *Kokoda Survivor*, printed and bound by WHO Presentation Services, 2006

Colin E. Finkemeyer, *It Happened to Us: Mark II*, no publishing details, 1998

Norm Fuller, *The Flying Footsloggers: Unofficial history of Australia's World War paratroopers*, self-published, no date

Bob 'Hooker' Holt, *From Ingleburn to Aitape: The trials and tribulations of a four figure man*, printed by Streamlined Press, 1981

Ken Joyce, *As I Saw It . . . from Tobruk to Tarakan 1940–1945*, self-published, 1995

Clarry McCulloch, *Some Call It Luck: The war story of Clarry McCulloch*, no publishing details, 2004

Roy P. Sibson, *My Life as I Saw It Boots 'n' All*, printed by Capricorn Printing & Publishing, 1997

Bill Young, *Return to a Dark Age*, self-published, 1991

Books and papers

George Aspinall, *Changi Photographer: George Aspinall's record of captivity*, ABC Books, Sydney, 2004

Tim Bowden, *The Way My Father Tells It: The story of an Australian life*, Allen & Unwin, North Sydney, 1989

Tim Bowden, *Stubborn Buggers: The survivors of the infamous POW gaol that made Changi look like heaven*, Allen & Unwin, Crows Nest, 2014

James Brien, *The Bloody Beachheads: The battles of Gona, Buna and Sananda, November 1942–January 1943*, AWM Summer Scholar, Australian War Memorial, Canberra, 2013

Peter Brune, *Ralph Honner: Kokoda hero*, Allen & Unwin, Crows Nest, 2000

Henry (Jo) Gullett, *Not as a Duty Only: An infantryman's war*, Melbourne University Press, Carlton, 1984

Gavin Long, *The Six Years War: Australia in the 1939–45 war*, Australian War Memorial and the Australian Government Publishing Service, 1973

Peter Medcalf, *War in the Shadows: Bougainville 1944–45*, Australian War Memorial, Canberra, 1986

Hank Nelson, *Prisoners of War: Australians Under Nippon*, ABC Enterprises, Crows Nest, 1985

John Robertson, *Australia at War 1939–45*, William Heinemann Australia, 1961

William Slim, *Defeat into Victory*, Cassell & Company, UK, 1956

William B. Spencer, *In the Footsteps of Ghosts: With the 2/9th Battalion in the African desert and the jungles of the Pacific*, Allen & Unwin, St Leonards, 1999

Peter Stanley, *Tarakan: An Australian tragedy*, Allen & Unwin, St Leonards, 1997

Lionel Wigmore, *Australia in the War of 1939–45 (Army): The Japanese Thrust*, Australian War Memorial, Canberra 1957

Radio

Tim Bowden and Hank Nelson, *Prisoners of War: Australians Under Nippon*, 16-part series, ABC Radio, originally broadcast in 1984

INDEX